Blooming Spaces

The Collected Poetry,
Prose, Critical Writing,
and Letters of
Debora Vogel

Jews of Poland

Series Editor
Antony Polonsky (Brandeis University, Waltham, Massachusetts)

Blooming Spaces

The Collected Poetry,
Prose, Critical Writing,
and Letters of
Debora Vogel

Translated, edited,
and with an introduction
by ANASTASIYA LYUBAS

BOSTON
2020

Library of Congress Cataloging-in-Publication Data

Names: Fogel, Devorah, author. | Lyubas, Anastasiya, 1989- editor.
Title: Blooming spaces : the collected poetry, prose, critical writing, and letters of Debora Vogel / [Debora Vogel]; edited by Anastasiya Lyubas.
Description: Boston : Academic Studies Press, 2020. | Series: Jews of Poland | Includes
    bibliographical references and index.
Identifiers: LCCN 2020024090 (print) | LCCN 2020024091 (ebook) | ISBN 9781644693902 (hardback) | ISBN 9781644693919 (paperback) | ISBN 9781644693926 (adobe pdf) | ISBN 9781644693933 (epub)
Subjects: LCSH: Fogel, Devorah--Criticism and interpretation.
Classification: LCC PJ5129.F57 A6 2020 (print) | LCC PJ5129.F57 (ebook) | DDC 839.18/309--dc23
LC record available at https://lccn.loc.gov/2020024090
LC ebook record available at https://lccn.loc.gov/2020024091

Copyright © 2020 Academic Studies Press. All rights reserved

Book design by PHi Business Solutions.
Cover design by Ivan Grave.
On the cover: Marek Włodarski [Henryk Streng], *Kompozycja surrealistyczna / Surrealistic composition*, 1930, Muzeum Sztuki, Łódź. reproduced by permission.

Published by Academic Studies Press
1577 Beacon St., Brookline, MA 02446
press@academicstudiespress.com
www.academicstudiespress.com

This publication has been supported by the ©POLAND Translation Program
Cover image: Marek Włodarski [Henryk Streng]. Kompozycja surrealistyczna/Surrealist composition, 1930. Courtesy of Muzeum Sztuki, Łódź.

Contents

Acknowledgements — viii
Debora Vogel's *Blooming Spaces:* An Introduction — xiii

PART ONE
The Transformation of Form: Essayistic Art — 1

Essays on Literature and Poetics — 2
1. White Words in Poetry (1931) — 3
2. The First Yiddish Poets (1936) — 12
3. Stasis, Dynamism, and Topicality in Art (1936) — 16
4. The Romance of Dialectics (1935) — 22
5. Montage as a Literary Genre (1937) — 29
6. Literary Montage: An Introduction (1938) — 35

Essays on Art, Artists, and the Applied Arts — 39
7. Theme and Form in Chagall's Art: An Aesthetic Critique (1929/1930) — 40
8. The Genealogy of Photomontage and Its Possibilities (1934) — 54
9. On Abstract Art (1934) — 65
10. Henryk Streng, a Constructivist Painter (1937) — 70
11. The Dwelling in Its Psychic and Social Functions (1932) — 73
12. The Legend of Contemporaneity in Children's Literature: Fragments (1934) — 83

Essays on Socio-Critical Issues	87
13. Courage in Solitude (1930)	88
14. Exoticized People (1934)	91
15. Lviv Jewry: A Précis for a Monograph about the Jewish Quarter in Lviv (1935/1937)	101
16. A Few Remarks on the Contemporary Intellectual Elite (1936)	112

PART TWO
"An Attempt at a New Style": Poetry — 121

Selections from *Day Figures* (1930)	122
17. Preface to the *Day Figures* Collection	123
18. *Rectangles* (1924)	125
19. *Houses and Streets* (1926)	136
20. *Tired Dresses* (1925–1929)	148
21. *Tin* (1929)	164
Selections from *Mannequins* (1934)	175
22. *Mannequins* (1930–1931)	176
23. *Drinking Songs* (1930–1932)	190
24. *Shoddy Ballads* (1931–1933)	200
25. Afterword to *Mannequins*	216

PART THREE
"Marching Soldiers and Blooming Acacias": Prose — 219

Selections from *Acacias Bloom: Montage* (1935/36)	221
26. *Flower Shops with Azaleas* (1933)	223
27. *Acacias Bloom* (1932)	251
28. *The Building of the Train Station* (1931)	271

PART FOUR
From Lviv to New York: Letters (1924–1940) — 283

PART FIVE
"Distilling the Figure of Thought": Reviews and Polemics around Vogel's Work — 339

Reviews of *Day Figures* (1930) and *Mannequins* (1934) — 340

29. Ber Shnaper, "Cards on the Table: On Poetry, the Market, and Stereotypes (A Few Remarks on the New Poetry Collection)" (1930) — 341
30. Itsik Shvarts, "Modernist Poetry (On Debora Vogel's *Day Figures: Poems*. Lviv: *Tsushtayer*, 1930)" — 343
31. Ber Shnaper, "The Lyric of Cool Stasis" (1935) — 348
32. Joshue Rapoport, "The Apotheosis of Monotony" (1935) — 351
33. J. A. Weisman, "Debora Vogel and Her Monotony" (1935) — 357
34. Hirsh Segal, "Debora Vogel's New Poetry Collection *Mannequins*" (Warsaw-Lviv: *Tsushtayer*, 1934) — 359

Reviews of *Acacias Bloom* — 364
Discussions of the Yiddish Edition of *Akatsyes blien* (1935) — 365

35. B. Alquit, "Modern Prose" (1935) — 366
36. Debora Vogel, "A Response to B. Alquit's review of *Acacias*" (1936) — 370
37. B. Alquit, "A Response to Debora Vogel's Letter" (1936) — 372
38. Joshue Rapoport, "Like a Squirrel On a Wheel" (1936) — 373
39. Debora Vogel, "A Couple of Remarks on My Book *Akatsyes Blien*" (1937) — 376

Reviews of the Polish Edition of *Akacje kwitną* (1936) — 379

40. Zofia Nalkowska, "*Acacias Bloom*" (1936) — 380
41. Marian Promiński, "*Acacias Bloom*" (1936) — 381
42. Emil Breiter, "Debora Vogel—*Acacias Bloom: Montages*" (1936) — 383
43. Bruno Schulz, "*Acacias Bloom*" (1936) — 385

Index — 389

Acknowledgements

This book was made possible through the generous support of multiple institutions and individuals. I am grateful for a grant from the Polish Book Institute and the Poland Translation Program in 2019. It has been a pleasure to work with Academic Studies Press, and special thanks must go to ASP's editorial director Alessandra Anzani for her enthusiasm about the project from its inception, throughout the grant application, and for shepherding this book to publication. I am thrilled to be publishing my work in the Jews of Poland Series edited by Antony Polonsky. I am thankful for the peer reviewers' enthusiastic praise and insightful feedback—they helped me make the introduction and my editorial decisions throughout the book cohere in a much better way. I am extremely fortunate to have worked with Stuart Allen, a careful copyeditor and insightful reader. Thanks also go to Jenna Colozza, ASP's marketing associate, for explaining the ins and outs of book promotion. Thanks also to Kira Nemirovsky and the production team for their hard work in bringing my work to its readers.

When I was at graduate school, I was truly lucky to have Brett Levinson as my mentor. Brett's intellectual brilliance, rigor, generosity, and humility have influenced my thought and writing, and continue to do so as my own work unfolds. While rereading the introduction to this book, I could not help but realize that many of the ideas about language, style, and the relationship between philosophy and literature are profoundly influenced by Brett. He has the wisdom and intellectual integrity of a true teacher: he challenged me to think with precision and gave me the advice I needed as I began to come into my own as a scholar.

I am also grateful to Professors Gisela Brinker-Gabler and Neil Christian Pages for believing in this project and for aiding my development as a scholar in important ways. I am deeply grateful to Marc Caplan for being another wonderful mentor and for showing me what is possible at the intersection of Comparative Literature and Jewish and Yiddish studies.

I would like to especially thank Kathryn Hellerstein and Anna Elena Torres, with whom I am currently coediting a special issue dedicated to Debora

Vogel for *In Geveb: A Journal of Yiddish Studies*. Kathryn Hellerstein served as the outside examiner on my dissertation committee and I thank her for her thoughtful and generous reading of my work, including my translations of Vogel writing. I am grateful for her ideas about my next book project. Special thanks go to Anna Elena Torres for sharing my passion for Debora Vogel and for organizing a Vogel symposium at the University of Chicago out of which the concept for the special issue grew. Thanks also to all the symposium's participants: Karen Underhill, Allison Schachter, and Sasha Lindskog for pioneering the study of Vogel's work in North America. I also thank Karolina Szymaniak and Anna Maja Misiak, the founders of Vogel studies in Poland and Germany. I am indebted to you in so many ways. Special thanks to Ariko Kato, the Japanese scholar and translator of Vogel's work, and Hiroyuki Kimura of Shoraisha Publishing Company in Kyoto, for their assistance with obtaining Henryk Streng's illustrations to Vogel's *Acacias*. I am also grateful to Jacek Włodarski and Ewa Włodarska-Fuks for their generous permission to reproduce their father's work in this volume. I also thank Museum of Art in Lodz for permissions to reproduce images by Henryk Streng (Marek Włodarski) from their collection.

My friend Andrij Bojarov, a brilliant artist based in Lviv, helped me curate the illustrations for this book, provided comments on my introduction, and offered his expertise about photography and the work of the Artes group. My friendship with him is one of the things I cherish in life.

A 2017–2018 Yiddish Book Center Translation Fellowship was key to the completion of this book. Special thanks to my translation mentor Hugh Hazelton for his expert and thorough reading of my work. I am also grateful for Hugh's enthusiasm about the project and the letter of endorsement that he wrote ASP in support of my book proposal. Thanks to Sebastian Schulman and Eitan Kensky for their encouragement during my fellowship year and advice about publication.

It was truly a privilege to work with my cohort of fellows at the Yiddish Book Center, some of whom were the first readers of this volume. Their brilliance, immense erudition, and tactful criticism made me think about Vogel in new ways. I will never forget the sketch of Vogel's *Still Life in Glass* we made to understand the image in the poem which ignited our discussion about Vogel's interplanetary diction. For that shared sense of community, I am grateful to Ze'ev Duckworth, Saul Hankin, Jordan Finkin, Rachel Field, Beata Kasiarz, Jessica Kirzane, James Nadel, Allison Schaechter, Sean Sidky, and Andrew Sunshine.

The Vladimir and Pearl Heifetz Memorial Fellowship and the Vivian Lefsky Hort Memorial Fellowship in East European Jewish Literature provided me with the privilege of being a research fellow at the YIVO Institute for Jewish Research Library and Archives and lecturing in a public forum. I am grateful to YIVO's executive director Jonathan Brent for suggestions about publishing and interest in my lecture. I thank Eddy Portnoy, the institute's academic advisor, for orienting me during the fellowship, as well as YIVO's archivists—especially Leo Greenbaum for his enthusiasm in helping me navigate the collections. I am indebted to Judith Baumel and Philip Alcabes for opening their home to me during the duration of the fellowship and on multiple other occasions, such as during my attendance at the YIVO's Uriel Weinreich Yiddish Summer Program a couple years earlier. Judy and Phil are friends I consider family. They have sustained me with their grace, brilliance, irony, and humor throughout all these years. Thank you for believing in me and for your presence in my life.

The idea for this book originated at Binghamton University, where this translation project became integral to my attempt to critically understand the work of Debora Vogel. At Binghamton, I became passionate about showing this unknown author to my colleagues, especially Diviani Chaudhuri, Rania Said, Isabella To, and others. Our conversations about this project in Levaggio, the Shop, and elsewhere during our Binghamton years, our sisterhood across borders, your razor-sharp intellect and intellectual commitments inspire me. I thank my friend Michael Airgood who helped me figure out the sticky translation parts of *Acacias Bloom* and for taking pleasure in textual quirks with me (remember "azaleas the color of lox"?). Thanks to Seth Glick and to Maia Bull for the projects around Vogel's work we share. I am grateful to Paweł Polit and the Museum of Art in Lodz for inviting me to the scholarly forum dedicated to Debora Vogel and the Polish avant-garde. I thank Katerina Kuznetsova who invited me to speak about Vogel, in yet another language (Russian), in front of Russian and Ukrainian audiences at the Sefer Center in Moscow. Among Toronto friends, I thank Miriam Borden for our conversations about the electrifying poetry and prose of Vogel, Anna Margolin, and other Yiddish writers. I also thank the participants of my advanced literature class which I teach entirely in Yiddish in Toronto.

I prepared the material while I was a research fellow at the Modern Literature and Culture Research Centre at Ryerson University. I am grateful for the support I received there, and give special thanks to Irene Gammel for her outstanding mentorship, guidance, and close reading of my work. Her insights on the introduction encouraged me to refine my arguments and strive for clarity. I thank MLCRC's coordinator Cameron MacDonald for his counsel throughout the duration of my research fellowship and for our conversations about academic book publishing. I thank Jason Wang for his friendship and for talking to me about the joys and challenges of the academic writer's life. I thank the MLCRC intellectual community, particularly Esther Berry and Cintia Cristia.

I am grateful to Oleh Lyubas for the coffee, laughter, travel, and conversations about quantum physics, philosophy, and everything in between. Thank you for schlepping with me across the globe, thinking about where to best place bookshelves wherever we found ourselves, and for building a life full of adventure, freedom, and creativity together with me. You make it all possible.

I owe a special debt of gratitude to my parents Halyna Semchuk-Krachkovska and Vasyl Krachkovsky. No words can express my thanks to you, especially for valuing my intellectual endeavors and encouraging me to pursue my own path. I am sorry for having lived so far away for so long. Thank you for letting me tell you my dreams about all the books I want to write. When I think about my readers, I always think of you.

Anastasiya Lyubas
Toronto, June 2020

Figure 1. Debora Vogel.

Debora Vogel's *Blooming Spaces*: An Introduction

1

An artwork consists of a few basic elements. Lines, colors, and surfaces are the elements of the visual arts. Notes, meter, and tone belong to music. Artists also make use of space and time. Architects, visual artists, and musicians arrange these elements into combinations and forms, creating freshness and novelty out of that which is shared and seemingly unremarkable. Words, too, are the material which we use to construct reality and represent the world.

> Modern plastic arts grasped the fact that the surface, line, and color are simply the elements of a distinct reality constructed in a composition. In poetry, the word acquires the role of line and color. ... The role of the word in poetry is simply that of an element in the construction of a specific reality.[1]

Debora Vogel (1900–1942), the author of these words, was a poet, philosopher, and art critic who lived in Poland between the two world wars. She created her own "laboratory of language" and a literary expression unlike any other. Vogel used words as if they were building blocks—similar to lines, colors, and surfaces in painting—in order to shape her sparse constructions in Yiddish. Stripped of any trace of *homeliness* or stereotypical associations of the content of literary works in this language, these constructions, as in the poem below, are unmistakably recognizable as Vogel's style.

---

1 See the English translation of the preface to *Day Figures* in this volume, p. 123.

A gray rectangle.
A second. A third.
Seven times the tin rectangle opens.

Yellow sun. Red sun.
On one side, on another:
the day-rectangle has closed.[2]

Debora Vogel lived far from the major centers of literary Modernism and the artistic avant-garde, and yet the author studied and followed these contemporary cultural trends and integrated them into her multimodal and singular poetics. Vogel was immensely erudite and intimately familiar with the works of the Anglo-American Modernists: she read and greatly admired Joyce's *Ulysses* (1922) and wrote about the American writer John Dos Passos and his experimental novel, *Manhattan Transfer* (1925), which she read in Polish translation and in which she saw parallels to her own work.

Vogel also considered herself an ambassador of Modernism in Poland. She took it upon herself to translate the works of Yiddish Modernists into Polish in order to educate her fellow Poles and Jews about this important movement in Yiddish literature with its center in New York.

2

Blooming Spaces: The Collected Poetry, Prose, Critical Writing, and Letters of Debora Vogel spans the entirety of Vogel's career and showcases the full stylistic range of this gifted yet overlooked writer. My aim in introducing this lost Modernist voice to a modern audience is to underline a profoundly contemporary experience that the twenty-first century reader of Vogel's work will enjoy. One of the sentiments that you may share with Vogel is the sense of the value of the quotidian—the banal and tedious in life—which she rehabilitates. Simply put, everything is life, everything is art, and everything matters. The author restores the everydayness often denigrated as secondary in the hierarchy of events to the flow of life. Vogel demonstrates what such recovery of seemingly unremarkable events—and the simultaneous abolition of the privilege accorded to allegedly significant happenings—might mean. The central line of her collection of philosophical prose *Acacias Bloom* (1935/1936) juxtaposes phenomena that

---

2   See the English translation of "Day Figure" from *Rectangles* (1924), in *Day Figures*, p. 125.

usually go unnoticed: spring blossoms which are part of the cycle of nature and occurrences which are typically foregrounded within consciousness and reported by the media as important world events, such as soldiers marching to the front, the unemployed roaming the streets or workers on a strike: "the unemployed pass by blooming acacias; and the acacias bloom while revolutions are in the making."[3]

The title, *Blooming Spaces*, encapsulates the multiplicity contained in Vogel's artistic method. "Blooming" suggests becoming and process, and, thus, by implication, temporality and finitude. In short, the contingency of the blooming acacias—the organic, or the biological principle of life, as Vogel calls it, might become life's necessity. Through the cyclical recurrence and seasonal change which happens every year, this contingency is also reiterated as stable. The "event" of blooming acacias is combined with those occurrences which are more topical and dynamic, even though transitory in their own way: military parades on the streets; signs of momentous political shifts, be it revolutions or wars; or the lines of those who are out of work and have nowhere to go. Thus, there is not only a *temporal synchronicity* of unfolding events, but a *simultaneity of space* in which things and bodies find themselves—as reflected in the second part of the title. *Blooming Spaces* underscores the *dialectical tension* between stasis and dynamism—the lasting and transient, the polyphonic and colorful versus the monochrome and monotonous. Finally, the title epitomizes how art folds life into itself, and how life unfolds in art.

3

Debora Vogel was born in the town of Bursztyn in Eastern Galicia (present-day Burshtyn, Western Ukraine) on January 4, 1900. Hers was a family of *maskilim*, proponents of the Jewish Enlightenment, the Haskalah, who also instilled Zionist convictions in their daughter. Debora's father, Anselm, was a teacher and a school principal. Vogel's mother, Lea, was a teacher in the school for girls in Burshtyn and belonged to the prominent Ehrenpreis family. Vogel's grandfather, Jacob, was a publisher of Kabbalistic works and translations of German classics into Hebrew, a writer of religious treatises, and an author of popular works about the political events that shaped the Jewish world, such as the

---

3 See the English translation of the essay "Montage as a Literary Genre" (1937) in the present volume, pp. 32–33.

Dreyfus affair and the Beilis case.[4] Debora's maternal uncle, Marcus Ehrenpreis, was the chief rabbi of Stockholm and a writer in Swedish, Hebrew, and Yiddish. The family spoke Polish and German. Vogel also spoke Hebrew with her father.

From Burshtyn the family moved to Lviv (Lwów at the time), a multiethnic and culturally hybrid city in interwar Poland (known also as Lemberg in German, Lviv in Ukrainian, Lvov in Russian, and Lemberik in Yiddish)—a city at the crossroads of empires, states, and identities, all of which shaped Vogel's polyglot sensibility. There, Vogel studied in a Polish-language school. Her father was the principal of the orphanage for Jewish children on 8 Zborowska street, where Vogel's family lived. Debora and her mother Lea worked in the orphanage as educators. During the First World War, the family moved to Vienna where Vogel first studied in a Polish, and then in a German high school. After her school graduation in 1918, Vogel moved back to Lviv where she was active in the Socialist-Zionist secular Jewish youth organization Hashomer Hatsair (The Young Guard).

Vogel's training and background primed her for the innovative creative and theoretical work that she would later undertake. In 1919 she began her studies in philosophy, psychology, and Polish language and literature at Jan Kazimierz University in Lviv. She was active in the Society of Jewish Students at the university, where she met Rachel Auerbach, a fellow student of philosophy and history, as well as a journalist, historian, and a writer. Auerbach convinced Vogel to write in Yiddish. This event deserves special attention and will be discussed further.

In 1924, after her studies in Lviv, Debora Vogel transferred to Jagiellonian University in Cracow, where in 1926 she received a doctorate in philosophy for her dissertation on the cognitive value of art in Hegel's thought and its modification in the work of the Polish thinker Józef Kremer. Vogel examined whether Hegel had indeed proclaimed the "death of art," and concluded that Hegel posited, in fact, that art had an epistemological relation to the world—a novel idea, since at the time only philosophy was believed to offer systematic cognition of the world. Vogel's work on the history of aesthetics was at odds with the philosophical trends in vogue in Poland—logic and empirio-criticism. Trained in the analytical philosophy of the Lviv–Warsaw School by Kazimierz Twardowski

---

4 The Beilis case—legal proceedings organized in Kyiv in 1913 against Menahem Mendel Beilis, a Jewish shop assistant in the brick plant on charges of the ritual murder of a young Ukrainian boy, Andriy Yushchinsky. Beilis was acquitted, but his trial provoked antisemitic rhetoric and violence. This case in the Russian Empire is comparable to the Dreyfus Affair.

(an influence on the German philosophers Franz Brentano and Edmund Husserl), Vogel departed from philosophy of mental phenomena while retaining an interest in the psychology central to her mentor's method.

After completing her PhD, Vogel travelled extensively in Paris, Berlin, and Stockholm which she amply documented in her work. In her poem "Shoddy Ballad Paris," Vogel contrasted the provincial landscape of Poland with the excitement offered by world's large cities:

> And one can forget the velvet
> of sidewalks and pavements
> Paris Berlin Stockholm
> and cities I haven't seen—
>
> when you live in a country
> which is covered with fields
> where cities are like fields
> of yellow boredom and purple potatoes.[5]

In the fall and winter of 1926/1927, Vogel visited Berlin which was then the center of the avant-garde movements in art and culture. Berlin Dadaists experimented with collage and photomontage; Franz Roh theorized the new artistic movement which he called Magical Realism and which later became known as New Objectivity; and Walter Ruttmann used the technique of montage in his film *Berlin: Symphony of a Great City* (1927). The time of Vogel's sojourn in Berlin also coincided with the world premiere of Fritz Lang's *Metropolis*. Vogel went to see movies in Berlin's so-called "picture palaces." Many of the films that were shown there were produced by Germany's famous UFA film company and starred world-renowned actors like Marlene Dietrich. Vogel wrote about the new medium in her poem "City Grotesque Berlin," which includes mention of Mauritz Stiller's *Hotel Imperial* (known in Germany and in Austria under the title *Hotel Stadt Lemberg*), starring Pola Negri and James Hall:

> in purple orange-red citrus-yellow letters
> entangled fates are written:
>   UFA-FILM

---

5 See the English translation of "Shoddy Ballad Paris," in the cycle *Shoddy Ballads* (1931–1932) from *Mannequins* (1934), p. 207.

Hotel Stadt Lemberg
=UFA=[6]

After her stay in Berlin from mid-October 1926 until January 1927, Vogel travelled to Stockholm to visit her uncle Marcus Ehrenpreis and his family. The budding writer penned a travelogue about her trip in 1929 in which Stockholm appears to the reader through the author's impressions of the city's architecture and through a kaleidoscope of paintings by the Swedish artists Carl Larsson, Carl Wilhelmson, Nils Edvard Kreuger, Bruno Andreas Liljefors, Gustaf Fröding, and Olof Sager-Nelson.[7] A bit later, in the 1930s, Vogel would write essays about Polish Jewish artists in German and publish them in Swedish translations in *Judisk Tidskrift*, a Stockholm journal of Jewish literature, art, news, research, and criticism.

Paris was also a special place for Debora Vogel and she visited the city multiple times. In a letter to Moshe Starkman, a writer, journalist, and editor from Galicia who lived in New York, Vogel reflected on one of her stays in Paris. She described visiting art exhibitions, mingling with artists (Marc Chagall, for example) and art critics like Chil Aronson (author of a study of the Jewish artists of Montparnasse), and giving readings:

> Paris is indeed a symbol of always-triumphant life; it allows for no stagnation, no "shrinking to one point." … For the second time—after my travels to Berlin and Stockholm—I felt how wonderful a big city can be and how it draws me to itself and how it excites me. I have already decided that I want to test New York in this respect. In a year or two, you will probably meet me on the streets of New York … if I'm able to save some money for the trip.[8]

Like Paris, New York powerfully attracted Vogel. She attempted to organize a lecture in the city in order to visit it. Her writing reached New York and circulated in reputable Yiddish Modernist periodicals, but she never made the journey herself. Writing to Aaron Glantz-Leyeles, a Yiddish Introspectivist poet in

---

6 See the English translation of "City Grotesque Berlin," from the cycle *Mannequins* (1930–1931) in (1934), pp. 188–189.
7 See Vogel's essay in Polish "Miasto bez trosk," in *Chwila*, no. 3696 (1929): 2.
8 See the English translation of Debora Vogel's letter to Moshe Starkman, January 10, 1932, pp. 292–293. See the original in the Starkman collection, RG 279, Archives of the YIVO Institute for Jewish Research in New York.

New York, Vogel remarked that New York was "the essence of all cities" for her and expressed her regret at not living there "during her longing for urbanism":

> Will I feel the wonder of the mobile city which never grows tired when I come for a visit? The wonder of a grandiose machine soul, the soul of the city? I think that I have still retained some reserves of urban longings which await realization.[9]

After returning to Lviv from her tour of European capitals, Vogel taught at Jakob Rotman's Hebrew Teacher's Seminary as a professor of literature and psychology until the outbreak of the Second World War in Poland. Chone Shmeruk, an Israeli-Polish Yiddish literary scholar, fondly remembered Debora Vogel's lectures which were special because of his professor's ability to place "Yiddish literature into a wider European literary context."[10]

Around the same time, Vogel became active in the literary and artistic communities in Lviv. In 1929 she joined the board of the Jewish Literature and Arts Society which was founded in 1925 to promote artistic expression across media—literature, music, drama, and the visual arts—and to connect Jewish artists with the public. Vogel also became a mentor and active promoter of the work of Artes, a group of Polish, Jewish, and Ukrainian painters, photographers, and architects. Influenced by Fernand Léger's work—as well the aesthetics of Braques, Marcussi, and Picasso—the group navigated the currents of Surrealism, Constructivism, and a form of Superrealism, with its emphasis on facticity and the documentation of reality, a program similar to that of the New Objectivity movement in Germany. The members of Artes were inspired by the avant-garde, especially by Primitivism, as well as the everyday—advertising posters, the neon of film theaters, and the tackiness of commercial products. Lviv's suburban squares, with their *shund*, or trash—reminiscent of Berlin's Alexanderplatz—were as intriguing as Parisian art galleries to the artists. One of the painters who incorporated these disparate elements into his visual idiom was Henryk Streng, a friend of Vogel's and an illustrator of her books.

---

9   See the English translation of Debora Vogel's letter to Aaron Glantz-Leyeles, October 30, 1936, p. 312. See the original in the Leyeles Collection, RG 556, Box 4, Folder 5, Archives of the YIVO Institute for Jewish Research in New York.

10 See the conversation with Chone Shmeruk, "Zapomniana, nieznana. … O Deborze Vogel i literaturze jidysz z profesorem Chone Shmerukiem, wykładowcą na Uniwersytecie Hebrajskim w Jerozolimie, rozmawia Agnieszka Grzybek, *Ogród* 1 (1994): 198.

In addition to her active work as an art critic, Debora Vogel also launched her literary and journalistic career in this period. From 1928–1930, she published Polish-language essays on psychology and pedagogy, with a special focus on childhood education. At the same time, she also wrote, for the Yiddish press, reviews of art exhibitions, artistic groups, individual painters, and film. From 1929 until 1931, she was the key contributor to the Yiddish literary journal *Tshushtayer*, where she published her in-depth essays about art—such as her substantive study "Theme and Form in Chagall's Art," which is included in this volume.

Vogel also began to publish her Yiddish poetry in *Tsushtayer*. Her poem "Du bist laykht un beygevdik" (You are light and supple) appeared in the inaugural issue of the journal in 1929. This poem was reprinted under the title, "Ferd I" (Horse I) as part of the diptych in the author's debut poetry collection *Tog figurn* (Day figures) published in 1930 by *Tsushtayer* publishing house in Lviv.

4

Vogel turned to Yiddish as an adult under the influence of her university friend, the writer, journalist, and historian Rachel Auerbach. Auerbach reflects upon this in her memoir "Nisht oysgeshpunene feder" (Unspun threads).[11] She discusses not only Vogel's linguistic choice, but also the agenda of the intellectual Yiddish-speaking milieu in Galicia. A strong proponent of the "turn to Yiddish," Auerbach tirelessly worked to convince her fellow Jewish intellectuals to embrace and cultivate Yiddish, the *mame-loshn*, rather than the more readily available and prestigious Polish. The latter was regarded as the language of what Auerbach called the "assimilation" of Polish Jewry, its acculturation, a negative development in Auerbach's view.

Several writers, most notably women, who chose to write in Yiddish in interwar Poland—Vogel, Auerbach, and Rokhl Korn, for example—were also fluent in other languages, and many of them simultaneously participated in non-Jewish cultural milieus. For some of them, Yiddish became their sole creative language, while others continued to work in Polish. The reasons and circumstances of these decisions varied. Rokhl Korn, for instance, wrote in Polish before she began to compose exclusively in Yiddish, which she continued to do until the end of her life. Korn discovered Yiddish culture for herself and

---

11 See Rokhl Oyerbakh, "Nisht oysgeshpunene feder," *Di goldene keyt* 50 (1964): 131–143.

decided to contribute to it. Scholars have also maintained that Rokhl Korn's decisive break with Polish came after the horrifying Polish pogroms in the wake of the First World War. When Auerbach solicited her work for *Tsushtayer* in the late 1920s—a journal of literature and culture which Auerbach envisioned as a platform in which Yiddish culture in Galicia could flourish—Korn had already been writing in Yiddish for some time and was a published author with one poetry collection to her name.[12]

For Debora Vogel, who made her poetic debut in *Tsushtayer*, Yiddish was not a mother tongue, *mame-loshn*, but a "language mother," an adopted language. In 1924, Vogel wrote a letter to her uncle Marcus Ehrenpreis soliciting advice regarding the publication of her avant-garde German-language poetry for which she could not find venues in Poland. Vogel's uncle was the chief rabbi of Stockholm at the time and an author in Hebrew, Yiddish, and Swedish—and considered "one of the finest stylists of Swedish literature," a rare case of near-absolute bilingualism in Hebrew and Yiddish, according to Shmuel Niger, an important critic of Yiddish literature.[13] Vogel could have no better adviser on linguistic and publication matters. Inspired by Nietzsche's conception of the power of the individual, on the one hand, and by Georg Brandes' ideal of Europeanism,[14] on the other, Ehrenpreis believed in a synthesis of cultural and spiritual Jewish thought with the non-Jewish world through the power of language and literature.[15] These ideas must have also influenced his niece.

While Ehrenpreis chose the European, non-Jewish language of Swedish to bring about the spiritual renewal of Jewish religion and culture, Vogel utilized the medium of one of the Jewish languages, Yiddish, for some of the most advanced writing to come out of European Modernism. 1928 marked the year in which Marcus Ehrenpreis founded *Judisk Tidskrift*, a journal of Jewish literature, art, news, and research published in Swedish in order to reach both Jewish and Gentile readers and fulfil his wish to unite Jewishness and Europeanness.

---

12 To learn more about Rokhl Korn's linguistic choices and the Galician milieu that she, Rokhl Oyerbakh, and Vogel shared, see Karen Underhill, "Bruno Schulz's Galician Diasporism: On the 1937 Essay 'E. M. Lilian' and Rokhl Korn's Review of *Cinnamon Shops*," *Jewish Social Studies* 24, no. 1 (Fall 2018): 1–33.

13 Shmuel Niger, *Tsveyshprakhikayt fun undzer literature* [Bilingualism in Jewish literature] (Detroit: Louis Lamed Foundation for the Advancement of Hebrew and Yiddish Literature, 1941), 53.

14 See more on Marcus Ehrenpreis in Stephen Fruitman's book *Creating a New Heart: Marcus Ehrenpreis on Jewry and Judaism* (Umea: Universitet Umea, 2001), 131.

15 See Göran Rosenberg, "Philo of Stockholm: The Ecumenical Heresies of Rabbi Marcus Ehrenpreis," *Nordisk judaistik* 30, no. 2 (2017): 8–20.

In the same year, Vogel started experimenting with Cubist and Constructivist influences in her Yiddish poetry.

Vogel published two poetry collections in this language—*Tog Figurn* (Day Figures) in 1930 and *Manekinen* (Mannequins) in 1934. The first collection draws upon the geometrical tendencies of Modernist art. It is an example of Cubist-Constructivist verse in Yiddish. Her second collection engages with *shund*, or "lowbrow" popular culture and its possibilities for high Modernism.

In her poetry, Vogel sought to capture the sensibility of the inhabitants of cities and provincial towns alike in the age of rapid urbanization, mechanization, and technological progress. For Vogel, to evolve the creative process—and thereby maintain contact with broader dialectical societal developments—meant proceeding with formal experiments in her first poetry collection *Day Figures* (1930), only to diverge from them later. This collection paid tribute to modern painting and philosophy by tracing the process of the formation of abstract notions in terms of geometrical shapes, lines, and colors shaped by boredom, happiness, and melancholy. Her next phase, and subsequent book *Mannequins* (1934), commented on the phenomena of mass culture and modern society by reworking tacky visual features like shop signs and advertisements, and included linguistic manifestations of *shund*—lines from potboilers, popular tango songs, and graffiti in the back alleys of the city, for example. The songs one sings in a bar somewhere in a port city, or the campy fashions one flaunts on Montmartre are reconciled with the "high art" produced in Montparnasse. People walking the streets simultaneously look like mannequins in barber shop windows, the statues of gods in antiquity, and the figures of "seers" in Giorgio de Chirico's metaphysical paintings. Moreover, these "living" paper dolls seem to be little different from furniture, houses, and objects.

Vogel's choice to write her innovative poetry in Yiddish was profoundly contrarian. Her own family and intellectual milieu was acculturated—they functioned in Polish. Yiddish was the language of the masses and was perceived derogatorily as *zhargon*, jargon, by Debora's father and many other Jews of similar social standing and intellectual background. "For whom does one write in Yiddish?" Vogel asked in a 1938 letter to Bruno Schulz, a Polish Jewish writer with whom she is often associated.[16] This question emerged out of pondering

---

16 See the translations of Vogel's surviving letters to Schulz in Jerzy Ficowski, ed., *Regions of the Great Heresy: Bruno Schulz: A Biographical Portrait*, trans. Theodosia S. Robertson

the paradoxical makeup of her audience at a literary reading: acculturated intellectuals with limited Yiddish; no Yiddishists.

5

Debora Vogel met Bruno Schulz in 1930, around the time of the publication of *Day Figures*. The meeting took place through their mutual friend Stanisław Ignacy Witkiewicz, known as Witkacy, a prominent Polish writer, artist, and literary theorist. Shortly thereafter, Vogel and Schulz began to exchange letters and a celebrated partnership—romantic and intellectual—soon followed. It is out of the postscripts to the letters he wrote to Vogel that Schulz's book *Sklepy cynamonowe* (*The Street of Crocodiles*, 1934) emerged. In 1936, Schulz wrote to one of his correspondents, Romana Halpern, "It is a pity we didn't know each other a few years ago; I was still able to write beautiful letters then. It was out of my letters that *Cinammon Shops* [the Polish title of *The Street of Crocodiles*—A. L.] gradually grew. Most of these letters were addressed to Debora Vogel."[17]

Vogel was often considered as merely Schulz's muse or Witkacy's brilliant interlocutor, and her aesthetics were described as derivative when compared to the work of these male intellectuals. Critics repeated this judgement as a refrain when Vogel's own prose *Akacje kwitną* (Acacias bloom) was published in Polish in 1936, two years after Schulz's collection came out with the same publishing house (Rój) in Warsaw. These critics completely overlooked and disregarded her role as Schulz's mentor, someone who encouraged him to publish, and a sophisticated critic of his writing. They dismissed Vogel's thought, despite the fact that she had two highly original poetry collections to her name. Schulz himself attested to the fact that her aesthetics was unique and in no way secondary to his own while reviewing *Acacias*:

> Some readers and even reviewers noted an analogy to *Cinnamon Shops* in this book. This observation does not demonstrate a great perceptiveness. In its essence, the book originates from a thoroughly different and original worldview. A singular worldview—not rationalized but intrinsic

---

(New York: W. W. Norton, 2003), 57–62. See also Jerzy Ficowski, ed., *Letters and Drawings of Bruno Schulz: With Selected Prose*, trans. W. Arnd and V. Nelson (New York: Fromm International Publishing Corporation, 1990), 23, 234.

17   See the letter to Romana Halpern in ibid., 141.

and originary, already inherent in every sensation—is, according to St. I. Witkiewicz, the dowry with which a true poet comes into this world. This absolutely organic worldview permeates and constructs this book.[18]

While Schulz's review of *Acacias Bloom* is very perceptive, it is not, however, entirely unproblematic. The reader can judge for themselves: the piece is included in the "Reviews and Polemics" section of the present edition.

Only a few of Vogel's letters to Schulz from 1938–39 have survived.[19] The letters that Schulz wrote to Vogel have vanished. Debora Vogel valued her relationship with Schulz as one of the most exquisite and, in her own words, "colorful" events in life. Her mother, though, was strongly against the romantic nature of the relationship and the possibility of marriage between her daughter and Bruno.

In 1931, Vogel married the civil engineer Shalom Barenblüth, with whom she had a son Asher Joseph in 1936. Even though Vogel's correspondence with Schulz became intermittent, it never stopped entirely. Both writers continued to maintain their intellectual friendship until the late 1930s.

6

The mid–1930s was an extremely productive period for Debora Vogel. She published her prose collection *Akatsyes blien* (Yiddish, 1935), *Akacje kwitną* (Polish, 1936) (Acacias bloom) with differences in the sequencing of parts and wording between the two versions. The author called her work a "montage novel." Like her poetry collections, which gave a nod to philosophy and painting, this work went hand in hand with developments in photography and film, in addition to increasing awareness of the importance of socially engaged art.

In *Acacias*, Vogel presents a world of impersonality and immobility: engineer's instructions and worker's movements at a construction site and the

---

18 See the English translation of Bruno Schulz's review of *Acacias Bloom* in this volume, p. 387. Jerzy Ficowski, Schulz scholar, mentions Schulz's relationship to Vogel in his biography of Schulz, *Regions of Great Heresy*. The problematic aspect of perception of Vogel as Schulz's muse was considered by Annette Werberger, the German scholar of Vogel in her essay, "Nur eine Muse? Die jiddische Schriftstellerin Debora Vogel und Bruno Schulz" [Only a muse? Yiddish writer Debora Vogel and Bruno Schulz], in *Ins Wort gesetzt, ins Bild gesetzt. Gender in Wissenschaft, Kunst und Literatur*, ed. Ingrid Hotz-Davies and Schamma Schahadat (Bielefeld: Transcript Verlag, 2007), 257–286.
19 See Ficowski, ed., *Letters and Drawings of Bruno Schulz*, 23.

"life" of materials used in the process of construction of a train station (clay, concrete, and glass) appear in a series of movie-like stills. Vogel juxtaposes several images in a virtuoso manner without overlaying them with interpretations. Instead, she invites reader to piece them together and reach their own conclusions. Her method of montage is both social critique and a sophisticated aesthetic. Coffee is being poured into a cup in a room in an affluent European household. This image is paired with a journalistic account about international trade in coffee beans, trade sabotage, and agrarian crisis. The second image is then layered with images of the bodies of black workers in Brazil and California, and white workers in European factories—neither of whom can afford coffee, a luxury drink.

A series of other images in Vogel's work comment on the multifaceted nature of reality: soldiers march in a perfect rectangle, flowers appear in the shape of perfectly round circles in a flower shop, specks of dust swirl above the pavement, and unemployed workers linger in front of shops with goods that they cannot purchase and can only admire from afar.

Vogel's subsequent work continued many of the threads that the author had sketched in her earlier pieces. Both her poetry and prose in the late 1930s—scattered in periodicals—illuminated the hypocrisy of international diplomacy, the brutal machinery of the impending war, and the ruthless mechanisms of the world economy. Just as there are links between the contents and various forms and genres of the writer's literary output, it is also useful to think of Vogel's praxis and theory as interconnected. By infusing her poetry and prose with philosophical insights and her philosophical reflections with artistic sensibility, Vogel created an equivalency between the two modes of thinking and writing.

"Every word Debora utters is lined with at least three books she has read," remarked the Yiddish writer Melekh Ravitch about Vogel's vast erudition, which shines through the diverse corpus of her essays and interests.[20] Every critical piece—on racism and antisemitism, educational psychology, interior design, fashion exhibitions, or book typography, to mention only a few subjects—contains gems of insights and opens hosts of new worlds. When reading her poignant assessment of Marc Chagall's work ("Theme and Form in Chagall's Art: An Aesthetic Critique"), one discovers her immense expertise as an art critic. For instance, when Vogel discusses animal motifs in the paintings, she compares them with similar motifs in the work of Wassily Kandinsky, Franz

---

20 See Melekh Ravitch, "Dvoyre Fogel," *Mayn Leksikon* (Montreal: A Committee in Montreal, 1945), 189.

Mark, and Emi Roeder—the latter artist's work exhibited as part of the infamous Nazi *Degenerate Art Exhibition* only seven years after the publication of the essay. While writing a review of the novel *Karl and the Twentieth Century* by the now largely forgotten Austrian novelist Rudolf Brunngraber ("The Romance of Dialectics"), Vogel invites readers to understand the book as a response to the Great Depression of the 1930s and the philosophy of Taylorism—a system of thought which reshaped the world economy by means of a scientific management and optimization of the work process, often leading to workers' alienation from their labor and unemployment. Further, Vogel encourages her audience to reflect about the motivation behind Brunngraber's decision to use a web of statistics, data, and information as part of his literary method. When one reads her incisive theory of literary montage ("Literary Montage: An Introduction" and "Montage as a Literary Genre"), one recognizes Vogel's impressive connoisseurship not only of the iconic Modernist texts by John Dos Passos, Guillaume Apollinaire, and André Breton, but also a theoretical sophistication comparable to the writings on epic and the novel by Walter Benjamin and Georg Lukács.

The questions at the core of Vogel's essays are central to the Modernist project in general. In her essay "A Few Remarks on the Contemporary Intellectual Elite," for instance, she delved into one such question—the issue of form versus commitment. In her essayistic appraisal of formalist antisubjective and antisentimental aesthetics (which she discusses against the background of the ever-present workings of the oft-sentimental politics of commitment), Vogel argues that a rejection of narratives and programs informed by ideologically naïve realism is the responsibility of intellectuals; she urges the intelligentsia to embrace an idiom which links ethics and politics instead. Even though Vogel was writing in a very different time than ours, her reflections are thought-provoking and relevant to the present.

Vogel's sophisticated division of labor between writing essays in Yiddish and in Polish merits special mention, as does her choice of publication venues. Only in Polish did Vogel launch into a defense of the Jews ("Exoticized People"), while only in Yiddish did she feel called upon to defend her "elitism" ("Courage in Solitude"). She narrated the history of Yiddish secular writing in Galicia since the sixteenth century in her essay "The First Yiddish Poets," which was written in Polish and published in the left-leaning periodical *Sygnały*. Her goal might have been to raise awareness about cultural production in Yiddish in Poland and to garner support for Yiddish cultural activity among the periodical's progressive readership.

Similarly, *Sygnały* seemed to be the perfect venue to discuss the photomontage by the Polish and Jewish artists of the Artes group and to analyze their work in a wider European context. The essay "The Genealogy of the Photomontage and Its Possibilities"—known in Poland as Vogel's signature essay—was published in the journal, which actively promoted the work not only of Polish, but also of Jewish and Ukrainian visual artists and writers.

In her essays written in Yiddish, most notably "White Words in Poetry," Vogel sought to educate her Yiddish readership about the latest trends in modern poetry in Yiddish literature (Introspectivism) and in other European literatures (Spanish and Anglophone poetry, as well as German Dadaism). In this essay, Vogel also drew striking parallels with modern art—by invoking the philosophy behind Cubism and the work of the German art critic Franz Roh. Placed in this wider context, Vogel's discussions of the innovations of the Yiddish poets Rokhl Korn, Kadya Molodowsky, A. Leyeles, and Moyshe Kulbak, interspersed throughout the essay, inevitably lead the reader to understand Yiddish literature as part of a shared European cultural space. It is also clear from this essay that Vogel sought to propel Yiddish literary expression into the European vanguard. In another essay "Stasis, Dynamism, and Topicality in Art," she attempted to place her own work in the context of larger philosophical ideas—and, importantly, she discussed the most sophisticated matters, such as notions of stasis and dynamism throughout the course of history, and mentioned ideas as diverse as those of the pre-Socratic philosophers, French Romantic artists, Modernist auteurs, and proletarian writers—and all of this in Yiddish.

7

In addition to her impressive essayistic output, Vogel maintained an ambitious correspondence with many Jewish intellectuals, writers, editors, and public figures in Europe and America—to which a wide selection of her letters in this volume attests. Among her correspondents were Dr. Shloyme Bikl, a leading essayist and critic in interwar Romania, the Bessarabian-born Ezekiel Brownstone (a writer and the editor of multiple journals based in Los Angeles), and an important Yiddish cultural figure Melekh Ravitch. Vogel also exchanged letters with Moshe Starkman, the Yiddish and Hebrew writer and YIVO's director, and Hirsch Segal, professor of mathematics and lecturer on Yiddish literature in Czernowitz.

One of Vogel's main interlocutors was Aaron Glantz-Leyeles, an American Yiddish Introspectivist poet and critic. Leyeles's correspondence with Vogel lasted from 1933 until 1939. This exchange is represented by a considerable number of letters in the present volume. Aaron Glantz-Leyeles lived and worked in the Anglophone milieu and was a refined literary critic familiar with the work of the Anglo-American Modernists who occupy a central place in the Modernist canon—Gertrude Stein, Mina Loy, Ezra Pound, T. S. Eliot, and others. He passed a favorable judgment on Vogel's writing by mentioning that the author's first collection of Cubist-Constructivist poetry *Day Figures* was the "ultimate modern book from Europe ... proving that Lviv is very close to New York."[21]

In *In zikh*, the journal of the Yiddish Introspectivists in America, Leyeles discussed what he considered inadequate examples of modern poetry—that which fell short in terms of form and in terms of conveying the sensibility of a modern person—and poems which were formally and thematically excellent. In his rubric "Dos lid fun khoydesh" (The poem of the month) in 1934, he analyzed Vogel's poem "Balade fun dem sene taykh" (Ballad of the Seine) as an example of formal and thematic excellence, which opened the door to the poet's subsequent joining of the Introspectivist circle.

Vogel started publishing her work in *In zikh* in 1935. Her first poem "Legende fun zilber" (The legend of silver) described the world economy in 1933 and addressed the question of the gold reserve and the value of silver in poetic terms. The poem is an example of documentary poetry informed by facts at a specific moment in history. Even though Vogel was never officially a member of the Introspectivist group, she was part of the cohort of poets closely affiliated with *In zikh* and was singled out by Leyeles as one of the European Yiddish Modernists from some one hundred poets and writers in his 1940 essay "Twenty years of *In zikh*."

Vogel's "belonging" to *In zikh* could be understood in this way: the author aligned with some of the Introspectivists' aesthetic views and their program for Yiddish poetics which included seeking new forms and their transformation, as well as pondering the relationship between art and life and "Jewish" and "universal" themes. Vogel's poetry—like that of the Introspectivists—lacks overtly Jewish themes. And yet it was written in a Jewish language, Yiddish. The author's poetry was also penned in a simple, focused, and precise language and presented intellectual insights characteristic of much Introspectivist verse.

Vogel's letters to A. Leyeles are of interest not only in terms of their quantity but also in terms of their quality. They shed light on Vogel's creative method, on Leyeles's work, and on her ideas about Yiddish Modernism, as well as the movement's center in New York and its "European connection." From

---

21 See Aaron Glantz-Leyeles, "Debora Vogel," *Unzer bukh* 3 (1939): 67.

the letters that Vogel wrote to A. Leyeles, the reader gleans insights into Debora Vogel's own account as to how she entered Yiddish literature, her often difficult relationships with the Yiddish literary milieu in interwar Poland, and her discussion of the challenges she faced—whether the lack of publication venues, gender-based discrimination, or the absence of financial means. What also becomes clear is the remarkable nature of what Debora Vogel was able to accomplish—a tireless commitment to great art, a poetic evolution which unfolded in sync with the latest trends in world Modernism, and a justifiably self-proclaimed role as the "ambassador of Modernism in Poland."[22]

The correspondence between A. Leyeles and Debora Vogel also makes the reader who is familiar with American Yiddish poetry see that there are profound parallels waiting to be explored between Vogel's documentary poetry, her theory of montage, and Leyeles' kaleidoscopic verse. Vogel and Leyeles were both interested in theorizing new poetics for Yiddish literature and in transforming the use of everyday words and trite expressions in the poetic idiom. In this regard, Leyeles' essay "Poetic Re-creation" (1920)[23] and Vogel's "White Words in Poetry" (1931) might suggest intriguing parallels. Similarly, both Leyeles and Vogel were also invested in examining questions of art, form, technique, and rhythm: Leyeles undertook his investigation of these topics in the essays "Rhythm—the Inner Essence of the Poem" (1923)[24] and "Form and Technique" (1923),[25] while Vogel conceptualized monotony as rhythm in her essay "Stasis, Dynamism and Topicality in Art" (1936), which she published in *In zikh*. The contribution of A. Glantz-Leyeles as an important theoretician and poet-innovator of *In zikh* before WWII is recognized, while Vogel's high-caliber essayistic oeuvre and correspondence deserve a wider readership and scholarly appraisal.

8

Vogel's mandate to serve as the ambassador of Yiddish Modernism in Poland was manifold and included a wide array of activities—from giving lectures

---

22 See the English translation of Vogel's letter to A. Leyeles, May 23, 1939, p. 337. See the original in the Leyeles Collection, RG 556, Box 4, Folder 5, Archives of the YIVO Institute for Jewish Research in New York.
23 See the English translation of A. Leyeles's essay "Poetic Re-Creation" (1920) in *The American Yiddish Poetry: A Bilingual Anthology*, ed. Benjamin Harshav and Barbara Harshav (Berkeley: University of California Press, 1986), 788.
24 Ibid., 773.
25 Ibid.

about the Introspectivists[26] to writing notes in Jewish and Polish-Jewish newspapers in order to advertise the Introspectivist journal.[27]

Most important of all in this respect was Vogel's assiduous work as a translator and mediator between Poland and the United States, Poles and Jews. She viewed her translation efforts "programmatically and systematically," as she wrote in a letter to A. Leyeles.[28] This is evident in the sheer quantity, as well as the impressive quality and range of Vogel's translations. She translated across genres and across languages: poetry and essays by the Introspectivists from Yiddish into Polish, poems by her fellow Yiddish writers in Poland into Polish, and poetic works by the French poet, writer, and Zionist activist André Spire from French into Yiddish. As is apparent from her correspondence, Vogel was enthusiastic about the value of translation for promoting Yiddish literature and reaching non-Jewish audiences. In a letter written in 1933, Vogel thanked the writer and editor Ezekiel Brownstone for the chapbooks released through his journal *Lid* (published in Los Angeles) and expressed her belief in the importance of translating Yiddish poetry into other languages:

> It would be so great if each chapbook included a page or two of translations from Yiddish poetry into all foreign languages (French, German, English), or they could even be alternated. What we lack is … advertisement: no, not noisy self-promotion, but other literatures getting to know us, promotion which is also undertaken by the better-known and established literatures. I think one can find translators and recruit them for this effort (I myself can translate from German). … If a new journal, a continuation of *Tsushtayer*, is published in Lviv, I would like to try to include a translation supplement there as well.[29]

---

26 See "Vogel, "Okres modernizmu w literaturze żydowskiej," *Chwila* 20, no. 6796 (1938): 13. This is a summary of the first talk from the series of talks dedicated to the centennial of Yiddish poetry "100 lat poezji żydowskiej" (talk, Towarystwo żydowskiego Uniwersytetu Ludowego im A. Einsteina, Lviv, 1938).

27 See Debora Vogel, "Der khoydesh zhurnal 'In Zikh,'" *Nayer Morgn* 92 (1936): 6.

28 See the English translation of Vogel's letter to Aaron Glantz-Leyeles, April 10, 1937, p. 321. See the original in the Leyeles Collection, RG 556, Box 4, Folder 5, Archives of the YIVO Institute for Jewish Research in New York.

29 See the English translation of Vogel's letter to Ezekiel Brownstone from June 12, 1933, p. 297. See the original in the Ezekiel A. M. Brownstone Collection, RG 344, Box 5, Archives of the YIVO Institute for Jewish Research in New York.

From 1931, Debora Vogel was hard at work promoting Yiddish poetry to Polish and Polish-speaking Jewish audiences. Vogel's translations of Kadya Molodowsky's poems appeared in 1931 in *Chwila*, a Jewish-Polish daily published in Lviv.[30] Vogel's translations of poetry by the writers from the *Tsushtayer* literary circle—Sh. Ashendorf, Nahum Bomse, and Ber Shnaper—were published in 1934.[31] She also translated the work of the Franco-Jewish poet, theorist of poetic language, and committed Zionist André Spire: her Yiddish translations of his "Regn" (Rain) and "Der frimorgn" (The dawn) appeared in *Literarishe Bleter* in 1934.[32]

In the mid- to late 1930s, Vogel continued to carry out her mandate of promoting Yiddish literature to her fellow Jews and Poles and focused her efforts specifically on Yiddish Modernists. Throughout 1937–38, she published Polish translations of poems by Aaron Glantz-Leyeles, H. Leyvik, Anna Margolin, Yankev Glatshteyn, I. L. Teller, Avrom Tabachnik, N. B. Minkoff, and planned to publish renditions of poems by B. Alquit, J. A. Weisman, and Sh. Shvarts. She published her translations in *Sygnały*, the leading periodical of the leftist Polish intelligentsia, and in *Nasza Opinia*, a Polish-Jewish weekly—both publications known for their high intellectual standards—as well as in other venues.

The Polish and Jewish readers of these publications were exposed to some of the best examples of urbanism in Yiddish poetry and learnt about the writers from Vogel's short notes accompanying her translations. These examples included A. Leyeles' celebration of the Manhattan Bridge in the poem with the same title, the poet's depiction of the melancholy green of Crotona Park in the Bronx in "November," and the description of a diverse crowd in the poem "In the Subway."[33] Vogel translated a large selection from Anna Margolin's poetic output—her debut poem "At the Café," "Girls in Crotona Park" (from *Sun, Asphalt, Roads*), with its impressionistic painterly images of young women, "as if in Boticelli's paintings"; and the poetry of dusk in "Broadway Evening," with its imagery of evening blossoms, shop windows, billboards, and the rustle of cars and voices,

---

30 See Vogel's Polish translation, "Kadie Molodowski. (Niekedy stopień kamienny …)," *Chwila* (1931): 10.
31 See the following translations by D. Vogel and S. Aszendorf, "Wiersz o moim chorym ojcu i jego nowych trzewikach," *Sygnały*, no. 10–11 (1934): 29; N. Bomze, "Konie w nocy," *Sygnały*, no. 10–11 (1934): 29; B. Sznaper, *Z cyklu Moje Miasto*, *Sygnały*, no. 10–11 (1934): 29.
32 See Vogel's Yiddish translations of Andre Spire's poems "Regn" and "Der frimorgn" in *Literarishe bleter* 22 (1934): 348.
33 See the following Vogel translations into Polish, which include the author's bio: A. Glantz-Leyeles, "Most Manhattan" and "Listopad," *Nasza Opinia*, no. 77 (1937): 7; A. Glantz-Leyeles, "W metro," *Nasza Opinia*, no. 81 (1937): 6.

and "Evening on Fifth Avenue," with its impressionistic images of people set like gemstones on the steps of a hotel, limousines floating like mysterious ships, and young women strolling like butterflies.[34] Even though the theme of urbanism seems to predominate in Vogel's translations, she carefully selected the works she translated. They were by no means only those with urban themes.

Vogel's other translations, for instance, include Yankev Glatshteyn's "A boy and a roll," a poem stylized as a nursery rhyme with wordplay and fresh turns of phrases from the author's virtuoso experiments in *Yidishtaytshn* (Exegyddish)—one of the most brilliant collections of Yiddish poetry and one of the most difficult to translate;[35] Y. L. Teller's "Objectivist" verse from the *Miniatures* collection;[36] and the Neo-Impressionist poetry of Avrom Tabachnik, "A tseakert feld" (A plowed field) and "Ruinen" (Ruins), from his *Van Gogh Bilder* (Van Gogh's Paintings).[37] Vogel also translated the work of one of the founders of *In zikh*, N. B. Minkoff: his sophisticated and complex verse from *Undzer Pyero* (Our Pierrot).[38]

In addition to poetry, Debora Vogel rendered in abridged form H. Leyvik's essay "Literatur in klem" (Literature in distress), which the poet delivered as a lecture on October 20, 1935, and which first appeared in *In Zikh* in 1936.[39] Vogel wished to communicate to her educated readers in Poland some of the pressing issues which Yiddish literature faced at that particular moment, as outlined by H. Leyvik in his lecture. These included Yiddish literature's dispersal across many countries and continents, the state of Soviet literature which was "cut off" from other centers of Yiddish literary production, the language wars with the Hebraists, assimilation, and the lack of organization and unity in the ranks of the intelligentsia and workers. It was no small feat for Vogel to bypass

---

34 See Vogel's translations into Polish and Anna Margolin's bio in Anna Margolin, "Piąta Avenue o zmierzchu," *Kontratak*, no. 14 (1937): 4; Anna Margolin, "W kawiarni," "Dziewczęta w parku," "Broadway o zmierzchu," *Nasza Opinia* 75 (1937): 10. See Shirley Kumove's English translations of these poems in *Drunk from the Bitter Truth: The Poems of Anna Margolin* (Albany: SUNY Series, Women Writers in Translation, 2017).

35 See Vogel's Polish translations and Glatshteyn's bio in J. Gladstein, "Noc w metro," "Chłopczyk i bułka," *Nasza Opinia*, no. 88 (1937): 10.

36 See Vogel's translations of J. L. Teller, "Ego" and "Jesień" in "W drodze," *Kontratak* 24 (1937): 3.

37 See Vogel's translations of "Ruiny" and "Pole zaorane o zachodzie" in A. Tabacznik, "Obrazy van Gogha," *Kontratak* 21 (1937): 4.

38 See Vogel's translations of N. B. Minkof's "Ja-Kid Karter" [from *Nasz Pierrot*], *Kontratak* 15 (1937): 6. See also N. B. Minkow, "Meg Bojrnet," *Nasza Opinia*, no. 144 (1938): 1.

39 H. Leyvik's lecture, "Literatur in klem," was delivered on October 20, 1935 and published in *In zikh* 20 (1935): 48–59.

censorship and publish her translation of the essay, which theorized the state of Yiddish literature in this vein. She placed the translation in *Sygnały*,[40] a left-leaning journal which was increasingly coming under the scrutiny of the nationalist Sanacja, the government body which exercised censorship under Pilsudski's government in Poland (1926–1939). Besides the examples of Vogel's active cultural "ambassadorship" which I have briefly mentioned, there are countless others which you will discover in the materials that I have gathered in this volume from multiple archives and publications.

9

Vogel is a key—yet unrecognized—figure of import not only for the beginning and mid-twentieth century when she lived, but also for the late twentieth and the twenty-first century: her poetics of montage, repetition, simultaneity, and intermingling of "high art" and *shund* paved the way for developments in the postwar Postmodernist aesthetics. Moreover, besides practices in visual arts, the writer's poetics anticipated many questions which defined language-centered writing and language-centered theory.

Among these questions is the broad one of the relationship between philosophy and literature as the intersection of the aesthetic and epistemological, or of sense and the sensuous, and how this plays out in the intermixing of philosophical and literary idioms. One of the principal ways Vogel's work does this by is by staging an encounter between affect, language, and conceptual understanding in her literary idiom; she takes affective states, like boredom or melancholy, to develop a writing based on repetition, monotony, and the iteration of linguistic signs in order to philosophize about the world.

What is most remarkable about Vogel's artistic and philosophical creations—her "constructions of reality"—is not the author's choice of a niche experimental form associated with Modernist expression. It is not even her choice of a minority language, Yiddish, even though this fact is undoubtedly important. Her gesture is more daring. "Becoming minor" for Vogel is about *forcing language itself to its limits*. By making us stumble over language, Debora Vogel renews it.

All other questions are inextricably connected to language. The question of conventional binary oppositions like form/content is not only an issue in

---

40 See Vogel's Polish translation, H. Lejwik, "Uwagi o współczesnej literaturze," *Sygnały*, no. 16 (1936): 9.

aesthetics. By taking up the life of matter, often rendered in abstract terms as feminized, Vogel works not only on the limit of the spirit/matter distinction, she also addresses the feminine/masculine dichotomy and crosses the boundary of sexual difference. The question of sexual difference—or any other difference—is for her a question of linguistic alterity. Thus, her radical gesture is not simply to write as the Other—a Jewish woman in a minority literature who realizes her own avant-garde philosophical program of static expression in contrast to Modernism's overly privileged masculine dynamism. If we were to speak in terms of particulars, that is how we might describe her "otherness."

Yet, Vogel's daring is not *to write as the Other*, but *to write the Other*—to make language Other, through a mode of writing which scratches the surface of language or creates a "burrow" in an apt metaphor for Kafka's work from Deleuze and Guattari. Much like Kafka's "burrow," Vogel's "blooming spaces"—the multiplicity of her style—unsettles language in a revolutionary way, changes language by working on its limit. Not only is Vogel's style singular in relation to Yiddish, it also changes the (English) language into which it is translated.

Just as Kafka's language might have seemed like a foreign, unfamiliar German to the literary establishment of his time, so did Vogel's critics have qualms about her language, or, rather, languages. When the author wrote in Polish, an antisemitic reviewer stated that "this language is as if Polish, yet foreign, a language which no Pole would understand."[41] This is certainly a hostile way of viewing the otherness in language, a view which lacks an awareness language is "always already" hospitable to the Other. Upon deciding to write in Yiddish—a language she did not speak at home, but which had strong associations with *homeliness*—Vogel also encountered resistance to her *unhomely* use of Yiddish:

> [Her] poems are "monotonous" because the poet forgot to take the most important weapon for her hunt—language (the poverty of language causes monotony). … I hope that Debora Vogel who conducts such an energetic experiment in order to take her place in Yiddish poetry, moves away from monotony as soon as possible, and befriends the Yiddish language.[42]

These criticisms need to be read while keeping in mind the historical and cultural context in which they were written. The contemporary reader of Vogel

---

41 See the introduction to *Montages: Debora Vogel and the New Legend of the City* (Lodz: Museum of Art, 2017), 19.
42 i. a. v. n. [J. Weisman], "Debora Vogel un ir 'monotonie,'" *In zikh* 16, no. 11 (1935): 206.

who has read Samuel Beckett or Gertrude Stein and is familiar with poststructuralism might recognize Vogel's work for all the challenges that it presents, yet nevertheless appreciate Vogel's reckoning with linguistic difference.

As part of my engagement with Vogel, I chose to give the reader a taste of what I mean by the author's elaborate style of "becoming minor." While most of the translations in this volume, which include Vogel's poetry, essays, letters, as well as and reviews of her work, are drawn from only one language and source, I introduced synoptic translations for Vogel's prose—working with two texts and languages.

My decision is also an editorial one. It allows me to attempt to account for the complexity of *Acacias Bloom* publication history and the author's writing method. Vogel originally published fragments of her montage pieces in Polish, her native tongue.[43] Yet the book itself first appeared in Yiddish, the language Vogel learned as an adult. The Yiddish version was published in 1935, and the Polish version followed a year later. The latter version of *Acacias* established Vogel's reputation in Polish literature.

Within the book itself there are three cycles. The sequence of these cycles, or mini-collections in my translation follows the reverse chronological order of the Polish original publication—from *Flower Shops with Azaleas* (1933), and *Acacias Bloom* (1932), to *The Building of the Train Station* (1931). The sequence in the Yiddish text is chronological—the mini-collection written in 1931 came first, while *Flower Shops with Azaleas* (1933) appeared last. The Polish textual version is better known and has been used as a primary source for the publication of Vogel's montage novel edited by Karolina Szymaniak.[44] The Polish text has also served as the basis for the recent translation of Vogel's *Acacias* into German by Anna Maja Misiak in 2016.[45]

By introducing parallel versions of the text in the English translation where there are discrepancies between words, expressions, sentences, and at times even the order of paragraphs in Polish and in Yiddish, I hope to show Vogel's dialectical method of oscillating between the two possibilities through which a new artistic form emerges. Neither Yiddish nor Polish texts are treated as authoritative texts or as finished works. Rather, Yiddish and Polish versions

---

43 See "Budowa stacji kolejowej," *Sygnały*, no. 10–11 (1934): 29.
44 Debora Vogel, *Akacje kwitną. Montaże*, ed., trans., and with an afterword by Karolina Szymaniak (Kraków: Wydawnictwo Austeria, 2006).
45 Debora Vogel, *Die Geometrie des Verzichts. Gedichte, Montagen, Essays, Briefe* [The geometry of renunciation. Poems, montages, essays, correspondence], trans. from Yiddish and Polish, ed. and with an introduction by Anna Maja Misiak (Wuppertal: Arco Verlag, 2016).

enter a dialogue, the work becomes processual and offers multiple possibilities for reading and interpretation. Vogel's dialogism is apparent in her unique approach to self-translation: neither textual version of the work can be classified as the "original" and the other as the "translation" in the conventional sense of these terms, where one text is the source and the other its derivative. The two versions exist simultaneously and are not renditions but rather rewritings of each other. Inasmuch as they create a semblance of similitude, the Yiddish and Polish texts differ. Linguistic difference and stylistic multiplicity further unfold in the English translation. This unfolding subverts linguistic hierarchies where "becoming minor" unsettles not only particular languages (Yiddish, Polish, and English), but, rather, language itself, forcing mere language to its limits and inviting the translator and the reader to theorize alongside Vogel.

10

At the beginning, I mentioned that Vogel believed in the interrelatedness of art and life, and was committed to exploring the relationship between the two. The author pursued her probing into the nature of reality and its representation in art in her essay on photomontage:

> A question arises in art: which facts are important? Notably, the seemingly complex "facts" which take up a large surface of life may turn out to be pointless for life itself, and also for form as a result, even if that fact is that a person has been shot.[46]

The question of a phenomenological selection of facts rather than their ontological existence raised here precedes an important conclusion for Vogel—there are no "pure" facts; they are always layered with interpretations.

We know this not only from art but also from history. Nazi propaganda footage showed the deplorable living conditions, the prevalence of disease and malnutrition, and other horrendous "facts" about Jewish ghettos all over Europe, while interpreting and presenting these "facts" as the result of "deficiencies" in the Jewish character and, thus, as a basis for the Final Solution. Vogel and her family were shot with countless others—many of them nameless and unidentified—on a street in the Lviv ghetto in August 1942 in one of many Nazi *Aktionen* which add up to the enormity of the Holocaust. Debora Vogel's

---

46 See Debora Vogel, "Genealogia fotomontazu i jego możliwości," *Sygnały*, no. 13 (1934): 9.

body, as well as those of her husband Shalom, mother Lea, and son Asher, were found by her friend, the artist and illustrator Henryk Streng.

Vogel's life has no shortage of "what ifs": *what if* she had published her second collection of poetry, which contained many Parisian themes in the avant-garde Triangl publishing house in Paris as she initially planned but did not manage to do due to monetary constraints? *What if* she had written in French or in German and not in Polish or in Yiddish? *What if* her parents had allowed her to marry Bruno Schulz, the great love of her life? *What if* she had gone to New York or to Palestine? *What if* she had escaped the Nazi occupation? All these "what ifs" seem to pale in comparison with the question: "What if she had not perished when she was only forty-two?" What would she have written? Regardless of how compelling it might be to entertain these unrealized possibilities, they divert from a potentially more productive engagement with Vogel's life and her work.

Debora Vogel's texts which you will find in the following pages do not only represent human experience—whether particular or universal—they also shape or reconfigure it. What's more, they chart new worlds by inviting you as their reader to the realm shared by narrative and practical action, the realm of *as if*. This is the place that makes political and ethical claims on us not only to rework our understanding of the existing world, but to transform it.

"Courage in Solitude," an essay which Debora Vogel composed at the beginning of her career—as if anticipating the misunderstanding, misreading, and underappreciation of her work which would accompany it during her lifetime—includes the following words attributed to the Polish critic Karol Irzykowski who reassured the artists that "there is no solitary thought which will not reach another person at some point who will then surely understand it."[47] Having had to endure solitude for much of her career and life, which was tragically cut short, this must have been both Debora Vogel's encouragement to herself and her wish for the future of her texts. This is also my hope for you: that you discover Debora Vogel's *untimely* work for yourself.

Anastasiya Lyubas

---

47 See Debora Vogel, "Der mut tsu zayn aynzam," *Morgn*, no. 1223 (1930): 7. See English translation of the essay "Courage in Solitude," p. 90.

Part One

The Transformation of Form: Essayistic Art

Essays on Literature
and Poetics

1

White Words in Poetry (1931)[1]

1. ANALOGIES

Modern painting reveals a principal tendency to reduce reality to the last layer of facticity, to the skeleton of things. Moreover, it has a tendency to reduce the principle and the law, according to which things exist, to painterly matter.

Things exist according to the principle of the limit and balance, or stasis. This principle of construction made its way into the content of painting in Cubism and Légerism.[2] It is not objects linked among themselves according to a predetermined rule that is important. Objects are important only as a means of making boundaries and balance concrete. And thus, the concrete material is often diminished to the minimum of materiality—to the geometrical figure, to contrasting geometrical and stereometric forms. In this respect, a vertical line between two objects expresses the same thing as the tree with two bodies on two sides did before.

---

1   See Debora Vogel, "Vayse verter in der dikhtung" [White words in poetry], *Tsushtayer* (April 1931): 42–48.
2   Fernand Léger was a Cubist painter whose simplified treatment of subject matter, the streamlining of forms, and attention to ordinary objects in his "mechanical" works of the 1920s–1930s, including his paintings and film, were extremely influential on the group of the avant-garde Polish group Artes. Vogel was a mentor to, and an art critic for, the groups' members, many of whom studied under Léger in Paris at the Académie Moderne. For a more in-depth discussion of Léger's artistic method in comparison to one of his Polish students, see Vogel, "Henryk Streng, a Constructivist painter," which is part of these selected works in translation.

And thus the "pure form"³ of the object world is distilled—purified of corporeality and chaotic plenitude, reduced to the minimum of life matter. In this way one "paints the categories of things" (Franz Roh).⁴

Experimentation in modern poetry and the theory of poetics has not reached this level yet. The attempt to treat words or word compounds in a sentence exclusively as material rather than as carriers of notions can be considered merely the first stage in these experiments—even if not an entirely successful due to its intellectually formulated nature. Each attempt to free poetry from literariness, to treat it as a construction from word material, contributes to the development of modern poetry (see, for instance, innovations in contemporary English and Spanish poetry, Dadaism, and in our literature, to a certain extent, Introspectivism).⁵ Like the theory of static facticity and objectivity in the plastic arts, a theory of a new poetry of stasis needs to be advanced. The starting point for this theory must be a differentiation between the lyric of dynamism and the lyric of stasis.

2. METAPHORICAL STYLE

The significations of things may lose their contours. The categories of things enter social use, and after a certain time, they become mechanic.

Once they talked about the "flowers of feelings," the "ways of the heart," and the "son of life" and similar designations which contained a range of associative content. At present these expressions are ludicrous and they signify absolutely nothing. To the extent that they enter common usage, there emerges a

---

3 "Pure form" was a notion introduced by the Polish writer, philosopher, and art critic, Stanisław Ignacy Witkiewicz (1885–1939). See his English essay, "New Forms in Painting and Misunderstandings Arising Therefrom" (1919) and "Pure Form in Theatre" (1922) in *The Witkiewicz Reader*, ed., Daniel Gerould (Evanston: Northwestern University Press, 1992), 107–116, 147–152.

4 Franz Roh (1890–1965) was a German art critic who was best known for coining the term the "Magical Realism" in his 1925 study *Nach Expressionismus: Magischer Realismus: Probleme der neuesten europäischen Malerei* [After expressionism: magical realism: problems of the newest European painting] (Leipzig: Klinkhardt & Biermann, 1925). What he termed "Magical Realism" later came to be known as New Objectivity.

5 The high Modernist movement in American Yiddish letters. It began with the Introspectivist manifesto of 1919 which outlined the relationship between art and life, writing in a Jewish language but not necessarily on Jewish themes, and encouraged the cultivation of introspection—hence the name of the group, In zikh [In itself]. The group was active until 1940, and besides a manifesto, it published an anthology of Introspectivist poetry and a journal *In zikh*. Among its members were A. Leyeles, Y. Glatshteyn, Mikhl Likht, and others.

mechanism of seeing and a certain orientation. The comic nature of the obsolete and worn-out categories originates in this mechanism.

The process of ordering and systematizing leads to a specific number of abstract concepts in which concrete events, grimaces, and gestures are condensed. Notions such as "lonely," "sad," "strange," "wonderful," and others do not designate simple, factual properties, but rather a whole complex of properties aggregated according to a specific point of view and later assigned a conventional, and thus an easily comprehensible, name.

The jargon of common and banal designations, along with their laughable mechanicalness and dullness, becomes ubiquitous. There are two ways to overcome the exhaustion of words. Metaphor is one such possibility. Adding a new representation to a previous one—specifically a representation which belongs to a supposedly foreign and distant circle of materials and objects—can intensify the content of a thing. However, adding fresh associations to previous ones is simply reminiscent of a new patch on an old dress. As a result, a baroque, naturalistic, ornamental style is a desperate and impatient bid to overcome the drabness of a signification by introducing more significations, and similar to the plastic arts' use of multiple restless and deformed objects. Such a style arises during times of formal transformation—an expression of unruly dynamism.

The fluid boundary between metaphoric style and scribbling originates in the incomprehensibility of things: in the first case, due to the difference between tensions and associations; in the second case, due to lack of content, disguised as expression and signification.

3. CONCRETE STYLE

The second way to overcome the banality of trite, abstract designations, condensations of multiple properties of things, events, and gestures, is to break them down into their component parts. This produces a picture of the world which is revealed in concrete things—objects and gestures, and their relationships and transformations—instead of concepts or their combination in metaphor. Concrete poetry will deal with concrete things and gestures.

The above become symbols for the most complex inner events, since this approach to things allows us to see their "faces." One simply needs to combine a few concrete elements which, in turn, yields a psychic event. Concrete things combined in a particular way become a metaphor for reality.

However, it is odd to consider the concrete in a thing and a gesture to be just an accessory element, or an addition which reveals itself and exists beside the essential event. In fact, these seemingly accessory, marginal, elements are the factual expression of the formless mass of life at any one moment, which merely becomes concrete in them, rather than in the abstract mass of concepts. And the concepts are additions to things; they are attached to the facticity of life.

The principal event with the multiplicity of its moments and features should be concerned with these seemingly accessory moments, rather than simply with a name which is only justified by the frequency of its use. Such use has accumulated many associations, from which seeming colorfulness and wealth—those parasites of an abstract concept—are later created. Here are some examples.

The principle of monotony may appear: 1) as an ordinary name; 2) in the form of a metaphor—"the serpent of monotony," "the lump of monotony," "the desert of monotony," and others (these are fictional examples); 3) in the form of an image where absolutely no name is used, only so-called "accessory" concrete specificities. For example, the elements of repetition and numbers are a case in point. The universal and stable ("eternal") elements are the highest in the hierarchy of concrete things.

I have attempted to express the essence of a principal fact in life with seemingly banal and self-evident (and therefore "redundant") statements of fact: "Red sun. On one side, on another";[6] "three months of blue skies and sticky sprouts"; "three months of yellow metal flowers, birds and clothes, etc.";[7] or with the counting of the fact, "one gray house, the second gray house, a third, and fourth gray house."[8]

When one wishes to express growing old or passing away, instead of using abstractions like "old age," or "loneliness" one tells a story of "lacquered shoes" that have become "simple and worn-out," or of the "brightly colored dress" which changed its color to "brown" (K. Molodowsky)—this is an example of the concrete method.[9] Also when one wishes to describe the loneliness of a particular season, one simply mentions that they have taken the "last cabbage from the cellar" (Rokhl Korn).[10] The pace of a big city can be captured

---

6 See the poem "Day Figure" in *Day Figures* (1930), p. 125.
7 Both citations from the poem "Cross-section," p. 127.
8 From the poem "Gray Houses," p. 136.
9 Kadya Molodowsky (1894–1975)—one of the most famous and prolific Yiddish writers; active in Warsaw and New York. Besides poetry, she also wrote plays, and was an educator and editor.
10 Rokhl Korn (1898–1982) was a Yiddish poet and a short story writer from Galicia who later immigrated to Canada. She was applauded for her lyrical style that celebrated nature and village life. She became involved with the Tsushtayer group circle that included Vogel and other Galician Jewish writers.

by listing things, "On Broadway, on the great white road electric lamps blazed. Red, green, yellow, and purple," or, "on the posters—chewing gum, corsets, collars and cuffs, cigarettes, car tires, oriental baths, typewriters, pens, leather, silk drapes—you should absolutely buy, buy, buy" (A. Leyeles).[11]

And since the number of stable things is limited, and their structure is very simple, poetry which utilizes them can appear "impoverished and cold." The poetry of cold stasis will eventually find its recognition, just as the lyric of colorful dynamism and metaphor did before. The poetic element in poetry is not dependent on a dynamic, metaphorical style.

In this regard it would be worthwhile considering the Polish critic Karol Irzykowski.[12] He distinguishes between the "great" and the "small" metaphor. Irzykowski writes, "When a poet wants to still his metaphorical urge, he needs not do it with metaphor on a small' scale since there are other mediums and poetic forms which contain metaphorical elements." Irzykowski stipulates further, "there is also stylistic development ... for us the advancement of content is more important." Such content comes about when the whole pieces of life receive significance and become annexed to poetry ... these are cultural achievements which could be considered as the metaphorical achievements of the "new trembling" ... a poet who works on a large marble block need not be preoccupied with the small work of chiseling which would harm the whole. ... Naturalism, the discovery of pathos of the everyday was for its inventors a metaphor, and for their followers a method. ... Every interpretation in drama can become a *pars pro toto*. ... The simplicity of style and the renunciation of the picturesque ... could also produce a new effect."

According to Irzykowski, poetry is always metaphorical, not only when it deploys metaphor in its usual meaning. To understand this point better, we may say that every concrete name is already poetic, a form of reality.

---

11 A. Leyeles (1889–1966) was a pseudonym of Aaron Glantz, the poet, journalist, translator, and formalist literary critic who was born in Lodz and lived in New York. He was one of the main Introspectivist poets and theoreticians.

12 Karol Irzykowski (1873–1944) was a Polish writer, literary critic, and one of the earliest film critics in interwar Poland. He wrote some of the first texts on metaphor in Polish. See "Zdobnictwo w poezji. Rzecz o metaforze" [Ornamentation in poetry: concerning metaphor], in *Walka o treść: studja z literackiej teorji poznania* [The struggle for content: a study of the literary theory of cognition], ed. Karol Irzykowski (Warszawa: Hoesick, 1929), 1–68. Another text about metaphor is his "Od metafory do metonimii" [From metaphor to metonymy], in *Wybor pism krytycznoliterackich*, ed. W. Glowala (Wrocław: B. N. S. I., 2006), 643–653. Polish Modernist poetry does not use traditional metaphor but rather employs metonymy, and Irzykowski reflects on this practice.

There is also a negative side to every simple and concrete style: on the one hand, the danger of rhetoric, and on the other, of banality. Differentiation into concrete facticity can bring us back to the conceptual element because of its greater simplicity, reduction, and condensation of the life matter which the concept contains. One could also utilize too many concrete names in their accepted social use, which leads to the rise of banality. However, the boundary is blurry here, and the control over these matters remains with the artist and his artistic intuition.

Amid the suggested new types of poetry (i.e. metaphorical style and concrete style), the following kind is highest in the hierarchy.

4. WHITE WORDS

The dynamic is colorful. Dynamism is the origin of abundance which arises out of the search for balance and out of the struggle with things; it arises from the boundaries between us and things.

The second principle of life is stasis. It embraces not only that which is immobile and unchanging, but the repetition of things—an illusion of the movement and event. Stasis is the principle of balance; it does not possess the abundance and colorfulness of the dynamic worldview. Like monotony, stasis has neither boundaries, nor colorfulness, or polyphony of designations. Stasis is expressionless and nameless.

And if one wanted to name it, one would come up with strange expressions. These expressions name nothing if one were to "translate" them or replace them with other words. And yet they seem to be comprehensible to all. These words are so meaningless, neutral, and formless, like monotony. And I will call these "silly," helpless, and banal designations "white words." They condense the utmost stillness, the renunciation of illusory possibilities, the sweetness of stasis.

The expression "white words" does not merely originate in the apparent lack of color and content of such words. Rather, it is a reference to an artistic theory of "white flowers" by the Polish poet, thinker, and painter K[amil] Cyprian Norwid.[13]

---

13   Cyprian Kamil Norwid (1821–1883) was one of the most celebrated Polish Romantic poets. His collection *Czarne Kwiaty. Biale Kwiaty* [Black flowers. White flowers] consists of two parts. The first is an account of meetings with famous people of his time, including Adam Mickiewicz and Frederic Chopin. The part entitled "White Flowers" takes the form of a journal which outlines Norwid's "theory of silence, absence, and tragedy deprived of pathos." See more at http://culture.pl/en/artist/cyprian-norwid.

Norwid calls stillness the essence of poetry. There are many types of stillness: dramatic stillness and the stillness of everyday events. Theater contains "still, wordless places" in action, and through them "drama becomes sculpture."

"And as there are different types of stillness, so there are different types of words which give stillness its name. … Colorless, impersonal words which seemingly describe nothing … such expressions in poetry are similar to the white color on the palette, or to basso in after music…"

To provide an example of the "white flower," Norwid cites lines from a folksong:

> A przyjechać do niej trudno
> A odjechać od niej nudno.[14]

We may find such white words in our poetry, for instance, in Kulbak's poetry: "it was as it had to be," "you live only once …" ("The Wedding"), or "how good it is to have nothing, and not to wish for anything," "when I stand, there is too much of me, and when I go, I carry the fragrance of darkness. What can I do with my hand, the unnecessary one, or with my superfluous heart …" (from *Poems of the Poor Man*).

Here are more examples: "I have reminded myself that I am in my thirties," "and nothing matters anymore, nothing at all," "what would have happened if I had met you a few years earlier" (A. Leyeles). There are also the following sentences, "and nothing ever happens," "nothing could happen anymore," "everything should be as is," "nobody needs all of that anymore."

These expressions circulate anonymously without an exclamation or name for the pressure of the events. They are like a sweet, sad sigh which completes the abundance and dynamism with a deep chord of resignation.

The banality of such words! They are universal and typical; therefore, they do not overwhelm with foreignness or the unknown qualities of a new metaphor. These words appear as gray and every day, since we have heard them too often. They are so "banal" that it seems one is ashamed of them.

Our attitude to them will change once we understand them as formulations that are rarely successful, as names for things that are in fact nameless.

---

14 From a Polish folk song. Translation is as follows: "It is difficult to come to her / it is boring to depart."

5. THE REHABILITATION OF BANALITY

Banality should be elevated to the level of poetic value. Not the banality of mechanized categories and concepts, but rather the banal of life's monumental stability within basic events—the banality of yearning and resignation. Such banality is the material for life's grotesqueness.

However, one utilizes banality in the right way when it gets introduced like a costly material, little by little, and due to its rarity, it becomes costly.

Banality can become drops of colorfulness and melodiousness in the angular atonal rhythm of cubic landscapes and hard unadorned words not made dynamic. Like in modern music—a cheap melody in the midst of an atonal rhythm of pure sounds.

The banality of shoddiness can sometimes resemble the incomprehensible tragedy of life: the sad banality of "postcards" with red sunsets; of cheap, kitschy "Sunday best" clothes which passersby wear on a stroll; of a vulgar lipstick shade, or a popular song played in a suburban bar.

We should also add to this type of banality in poetry those already banal categories to which we always return even after they have been long excluded from poetry. We experience their cheap sadness and helplessness, and in a short while they become close, radiating new possibilities and associations which make them useful for poetry again.

6. THE FANTASTIC OF SIMPLICITY

There is seemingly no place for the inexpressive element and the distance of perspectives in the construction of simple and white words, as in a cool geometrical ornament. Here all things are mass, numbers, calculation; everything is balance and stasis, finitude, fixed boundaries, without intimations about that which has not been expressed.

Thus, speaking about the fantastic in this case may sound like a paradox. One might think that the fantastic and numbers are mutually exclusive.

And yet, in cool, measured, and simple constructions there is an element of the fantastical: the gray color and the geometrical line; banal words are the condensations and ultimate stages of the dynamic colorfulness which further manifest in them. And, thus, we should note the elements of novelty in such constructions! The wonder is that space could be fit into the boundaries of construction with very little—a couple of simple elements.

The new elements in art are not yet overgrown with too many associations, even though they almost always possess naturalistic elements. Perhaps the impression of the impoverishment and dryness of the simple constructions stems from this. And yet, the frequent use of geometrical elements in art also enriches them with necessary associations, so that one day these elements will also become "colorful" and "melodious."

2

The First Yiddish Poets (1936)[1]

Yiddish poetry in the former Austrian province[2] is very young, as is all secular writing in Yiddish. The "secular" needs to be emphasized here, since ethical-religious poetry written in the language dates back to the sixteenth century. This poetic tradition was initiated, and for a long time cultivated by, women poets who, as a rule, did not have access to the Hebrew language and the philosophy of the Talmud (even though there are interesting exceptions). For the first time, poetry discussed everyday topics in the then-German dialect modified by the Hebrew lexicon and the particularity of the Jewish psyche.

The date of birth of the poet considered to be the pioneer of Yiddish secular poetry in Galicia testifies to the fact that non-anonymous secular, Jewish poetry is a relatively recent phenomenon. The poet's name is Mikhl Wirta; he was born in Lemberg in 1877 and died in Vienna in 1919. He did not leave us a single volume of poetry, only some texts scattered across diaries and "calendars." For a long time, calendars—almanacs of sorts—were the only places where Jewish writings were assembled, due to the lack of the publication venues such as conventional journals.

The lyricism of M. Wirta incorporates a line from a folk song and its ballad tone—half sad, half dramatic. One example is the poem about Mirele. Beautiful and unreachable, she "stands in the window and only laughs" at the sighs of those who court her until old age erases her beauty, bends her body, and her eyes start to cry,

> Pretty Mirele, sugar sweet,
> Mirele ... Mirele! ...
> White arms, white teeth
> O Mirele ... Mirele! ...

---

1 See Debora Vogel, "Pierwszi poeci żydowscy," *Sygnały*, no. 14 (1936): 5.
2 Galicia.

Lads under her window faint from longing
But Mirele's heart is colder than ice ...
O Mirele ... Mirele! ...
[second stanza]

The moon is bright, and the stars are shining down
On Mirele, Mirele!
She stands in the window, sorrowful and sad
O Mirele, Mirele!
As the clouds float by here and there
Mirele's eyes well up with tears ...
Cry, Mirele ... Mirele
[last stanza][3]

The founders of Galician Yiddish poetry who live in Galicia today are Sh[muel] Imber[4] and D[ovid] Kenigsberg.[5] M[elekh] Ravitch is the third founding figure;[6] yet he has not resided in his homeland for a long time. There are also famous poets of the younger generation who left for America (M[oyshe] L[eyb] Halpern,[7] R[euben] Iceland,[8] [Zisha] Weinper,[9] M[oyshe] Nadir).[10] In the work of Imber and Kenigsberg (the latter considered Imber to be his mentor), there are still elements of folk songs, but at the same time European poetic influences like Neo-Romanticism and Impressionism emerge.

---

3   The fragments of Wirta's poems which have rhyme and the rhythm are not translated with the rhyme scheme: they are free translations. [Vogel's note.]
4   Shmuel Yankev Imber (1889–1942?) was a famous poet and a pioneer of modern Yiddish poetry in Galicia.
5   David (Dovid) Kenigsberg was a pioneer of Neo-Romanticism in Galicia. The themes of his poems reflect the mentorship of Shmuel Imber who was a teacher of many Yiddish poets of this generation.
6   Melekh Ravitch (1893–1976) was a Yiddish poet, essayist, dramatist, and cultural activist. He was born in Galicia, and lived in Warsaw, Melbourne, and Montreal. He participated in avant-garde groups such as Di Khalyastre [The gang] in Warsaw, and he also supported the Yiddish journal *Tsushtayer* in Lviv.
7   Moyshe Leyb Halpern (1886–1932) was a Yiddish poet who lived and worked in New York. He was connected to the Modernist group Di Yunge.
8   Reuben Iceland (1884–1955) was a Yiddish poet, member of Di Yunge, and editor of many publications, such as *Der Inzl* where Vogel published her work.
9   Zisha Weinper (1893–1957) lived in Warsaw, emigrated to America, and travelled in the Middle East. Many of the themes of his poetic work are connected to Ukraine.
10 Moyshe Nadir (1885–1943) was a poet, novelist, theatrical critic, translator, and a member of Di Yunge.

Sh[muel] Imber made his poetic debut in 1907 with his collection *Vos ikh zing un zog* (What I sing and speak).

The foundational tonality of Neo-Romanticism is expressed in the titles of Imber's collections and poems—*Royznbleter* (Rose leaves), *The Pilgrim's Poems*, *Printsesin Toybnharts* (Princess Dove Heart). The primary themes of Imber's poetry are yearning for unknown happiness, symbolized by love, regret for things passing by, and waiting for wonderful adventures. At a later stage in his work, a philosophical quality dominates:

> There is more beauty in a blade of grass than in all the flowers
> More depth in a tear than in the bottom of the ocean
> Happiness which comes upon the blades of grass
> May yoke the legs of a giant.

The philosophical attitude and the work of making Yiddish elastic—a language which was still raw and unshaped in its diverse elements at the time—are Imber's contributions to Yiddish literature. However, the author's idiolect contained a lot of "Germanisms." In Imber's early poetry, Romantic syntax and vocabulary, adapted to express the refined and delicate experiences of longing, beauty, and love, are still present.

D[ovid] Kenigsberg made his debut in 1912. His principal poetic collection *100 Sonnets* appeared in 1917. He is the creator and master of the sonnet in Yiddish poetry.

At times, Kenigsberg's Romanticism is characterized by the heroic, for instance, in an image of a marching phalanx; at other times, the poet is sentimental, as is evident in the programmatic poem published a few years ago "Ikh benk nokh an eynfakhn poshetn lid" (I long for a very simple poem). In the poem, the poet is saddened by the fact that "Europe grew in us like a bloody mushroom" and "you (the younger generation) accepted this amid the screech of thousand lies." This positing of simplicity has nothing to do with the contemporary tendency towards simplicity—secondary and complex in its essence—which is different from the simplicity in his meaning.

Impressionism receives the greatest artistic development in Kenigsberg's writing. An alternation of gestures, events with a mood of wonder and secrecy, the themes of different seasons and times of day—all reach perfection in the poet's work. Poems about the evenings and autumn are sometimes similar to the decadent melancholy in the poetry by Li Tai Bo.

The shine of light has turned bleak
It saddens in a dull, deaf, forsaken way.
I will stay in my room the whole day
The windowpanes are covered with mist
Come, friends, and give me a cheerful song.

3

Stasis, Dynamism, and Topicality in Art (1936)[1]

1. INTRODUCTION

In this essay, I would like to turn to two critics who considered the idea of stasis in art in relation to the programmatic concerns and their realization in two of my poetry collections *Day Figures* and *Mannequins*.

I do not make these remarks on polemical grounds. Rather, they will serve as a point of departure for a more general discussion of stasis or dynamism in art.

Ber Shnaper's[2] criticism (in *Literarishe bleter*)[3] could be formulated in the following way: "Let us assume that abundance and colorfulness are simply the illusory outcomes of a couple of monotonous and stable facts in reality, and yet we yearn for the very illusion of colorfulness which is synonymous with dynamism."

And J[oshue] Rapoport[4] (in *Vokhn-Shrift*)[5] voices his criticism thus: "the superstructure becomes the essence ... what then becomes of the person next to us? He consists of a certain number of materials in certain quantities. A sure thing. And yet, a person in general, and particularly our neighbor is not just a

---

1   See Debora Vogel, "Statik, dinamik un aktualitet in der kunst," *In zikh* 17, no. 27 (1936): 74–79.
2   Ber Shnaper was born in Lviv, studied at the Hebrew Teachers' Seminary in Vienna, and lived in Warsaw where he contributed to various Yiddish publications.
3   Vogel has in mind Shnaper's review of her work "Di lirik fun kiler statik" [The lyric of cool stasis], *Literarishe bleter* 12, no. 40 (1935): 642. The translation of this review can be found in the reviews section.
4   Yehoshue (Joshue) Rapoport (1895–1971) was a well-known Yiddish literary critic and translator who lived in Berlin, Warsaw, and Melbourne. His essay "And so it begins ..." (Jewish Cultural Work in Shanghai)" (1941) was published in English in *Voices from Shanghai: Jewish Exiles in Wartime China*, ed., trans., and with an introduction by Irene Eber (Chicago: University of Chicago Press, 2008), 65–69.
5   See Joshue Rapoport, "Apoteoz fun monotonye" [The apotheosis of monotony], *Vokhnshrift far literatur, kunst un kultur*, no. 49 (1935): 4–5. The translation of this review can be found in the reviews section.

billion times more than the elements to which he is reduced, but also something completely different. What is true in life is true also of poetry. ... Poetry becomes poetry only when static becomes dynamic."

This criticism operates from the vantage point of a misunderstanding: assuming that stasis is a certain raw material in which dynamism originates as something entirely different—in the exact same way as the "person" who is different from the quantity of elements in our analogy. However, stasis in my framework is a result and ultimate stage of abundance and dynamism, the content of all dynamic colorfulness and warmth, which it simply regulates and balances.

Besides, the poetry of stasis—very much like the person and his constitutive elements—is not identical but rather quite distinct from the stasis itself, from the material where it originates, the monotony of a couple of repeated gestures in life. The product of poetry in this case is vastly different from its raw material, just as the soul is different from the chemical material of the body! Since raw material is in its literal sense the repugnant and dull material of monotony—the expressionless fact hard to bear—poetry only originates in it and works with colorfulness and rhythm, the "soul" of expressionless monotony.

However, J. Rapoport's conclusion is a classic attempt to demonstrate that only dynamism and not stasis could and should be the material for poetry. His review is an argument for dynamism in art. I would like to begin my discussion from here.

2. ARGUMENT

The arguments for either stasis or dynamism as the singular principle of life have been provided from Heraclitus to Klages (proponents of dynamism), and from Plato to Spinoza (proponents of stasis). One movement laid out its arguments, and the other suggested counterarguments which were just as convincing.

Incidentally, every proponent of stasis can argue for dynamism as a life principle in the following way: there is no leaf identical to any other leaf which it could replace; there is no spring which would be the same as any other; and neither is there similar happiness nor sadness; and yet all of these are perpetually assigned the same name.[6] The empirio-critics argue that even the cells in human body are different, and thus, the memory of the events vanishes from the body.

---

6 Compare to Friedrich Nietzsche's reflections in his essay "On Truth and Lies in an Extra-moral Sense" (1873).

Nevertheless, spring comes every year, all the leaves are called a "leaf"—a sign of their similarity. And birth, love, and death recur incessantly. Like number, such recurrence is a sign of the principle of stasis, proof that life stays the same and that change is only an illusion which only takes place on the surface, on an outer layer of the thing, and that the essence of the thing remains the same.

From this we can only draw a single conclusion: there is no logical argument for the exclusivity of one or the other principle. Stasis and dynamism belong to life like two sides of the whole which continually pass into one another.

The only available argument is an emotional one. One of the two principles may cast a spell on us and move us in such a way that we become its poets.

However, the argument based on feeling does not suffice to claim the universality of one or the other life principle. Objective rationality is always a dialectical necessity; it allows us to elaborate one of the two principles. The symbol of our time—construction—moves in the direction of the apotheosis of stasis.

3. ADDITIONAL REMARKS ON STASIS

Stasis should not be understood as deadened, petrified rigidity, although W[ładysław] Strzemiński,[7] a painter and art critic, elaborated this concept in his Unism artistic movement.[8]

Neither should stasis be considered a lifeless schema that has pushed "life" far away from itself. In stasis, the colorfulness of life is simply framed into a stable appearance and its inherent immobility, like in an amalgam of every color in the spectrum which yields gray.

Baudelaire caught sight of decay in a vision of a blossom; in the most transient life he perceived the rigidity of death. Only in lifelessness can you perceive the poetry of life for the first time, and only afterwards does a thing become an object of poetry.

---

7   Władysław Strzemiński (1893–1952) was a pioneer of the Polish Constructivist avant-garde. Together with the sculptor Katarzyna Kobro, his wife, he established the a. r. group. He was also a member of other groups like Blok and Presens. He is best known for establishing the theory of Unism and creating the first Polish museum of Modern art in Łódź.
8   In 1927 Władysław Strzemiński formulated the theory of Unism which consists of the elimination of contrasts and dynamism, the limitation of compositional elements and colors, and the foregrounding of monochrome surfaces, the homogeneity of which are differentiated only by painterly texture.

In yet another misunderstanding, stasis is equated with passivity. Passivity in life is not a prerequisite for stasis in art. It is exactly the opposite: passivity always awakens in people the longing for dynamism and illusory colorfulness. You expect from it everything you do not have in life. This leads to the apotheosis of dynamism which would grow out of proportion like every unknown thing. There is also no opposition between the will to change the conditions and forms of life and the recognition that things always return, simply framed differently.

A knowledge of dynamism is a requirement for the appreciation of stasis. Only then you may grasp the wonder and the fruitfulness of balance, of number, of mass, and of the organized monotony in the pathos of gray. And you can stubbornly gather all the examples of monotony and consider them the richest part of life content-wise.

Thus, stasis is rehabilitated not as an element in its essence foreign to life, but rather as a stable element inherent in the dynamism of life and its transformations.

Finally, there is a historical argument: there has always been the requirement that art should treat the "stable" (or so-called "eternal") elements of life. High art has always treated stable and universal moments, which is precisely the fulfillment of the principle of stasis in art. Nowadays it is only the vocabulary that has changed; previous terms are altered, the concept of "stasis" has introduced where before there was talk of the "eternal element."

Balzac depicted the pettiness and depravity of a particular social class—the French bourgeoisie—doomed to downfall. The lasting value of his novels lie in his depictions of the weaknesses and desires best expressed by the circumstances of the bourgeois life as if they were stable elements of human nature rather than isolated cases.

Céline managed to find the eternal passions, anxieties, and weaknesses of people in modern times. Even the greatest art of Romanticism (Victor Hugo or Delacroix), which in its program postulates the thesis of dynamism, is valuable only because it treats dynamism as an eternal principle and the single stable thing in life. It was widely believed that only "eternal yearning", or a "longing for infinity"—dynamic tension, as we would call it nowadays—could lead to a fulfilling life. This went as far as the promotion of a "longing for longing" itself where it was lacking. This summarizes the historical argument for stasis.

However, stasis can take on various shapes—from the notion of "stable elements" to a stage in their development when they become a theme in themselves and should be shown with the help of the life's material.

The usual relation is reversed in this form, and it is no longer the stasis of events, but rather stasis itself as content which uses the elements and events in life to find its own form. (Something similar happened in "abstract art," in which thought categories were treated like things and thus attained their own corporeality.)

4. THE SOCIAL DEMAND

The social demand—the need for a specific dialectical stage, which is manifest in the higher value assigned to one principle which is carried out in the program of art—is decisive for the choice of one or the other principle in life and poetry.

The principle of dynamism in its usual sense of abundance, transformation, emotionalism, becomes a "symbol" in times of social change, in times of the search and discovery of new relationships in the world of things.

Thus, the concepts of dynamism and relevance go hand in hand: a topical element which changes and dictates immediate tasks already contains dynamism at the level of content.

Today, dynamism in art is identified with "social and revolutionary" art, and, in turn, with "proletarian" art, which needs to align with the social demand of the day.

There is no place here for analysis of the complexity of the concept of "proletarian art," which perpetually remains unclear.

There is also no place here to analyze whether the tendency for dynamism is, in fact, an expression of current needs and not something ostensible, illusory, and superficial, behind which in fact hides a material tendency to constructive stasis.

In this context the relation between the "topical" and the "dynamic" is all that matters. First, we need to differentiate between the topical and accidental elements. Then one can even prove that the treatment of topical themes in poetry also needs a certain quantity of stasis.

The topical element remains accidental as long as one does not interpret it, combine it with other facts, and limit it by the contour of other events and considerations. This element remains accidental until the thing remains a singular fact. The singular fact is always raw expressionless material which is "incomprehensible" and "accidental"—not yet topical.

The following arguments can further illuminate the difference between the two. A human life which was cut short and now lies on the street is more important in its direct relevance—it takes up more space in life—than even the best poem about the person's death.

There is a hint of something decorative in the fact that this event is chosen as a theme—that a fact of life becomes a theme for art; it is a sad paradox of the production we call art.

There are also times of war and revolution, of universal and personal catastrophe, which expose the decorative nature of every art, even the most revolutionary one.

The notion of the decorative suggests interpretation, limitation, measure, and regularity. All of these are the elements of stasis. Thus, we conclude that every art, including dynamic revolutionary art, contains in itself a drop of stasis.

However, stasis can reach magnitude in its highest degree. At that moment, it takes on a different quality, just as the highest intensity of pain results in pleasure, and an excess of pleasure transforms into pain. This originates the art of stasis, which in its essence is different from dynamic art.

4

The Romance of Dialectics (1935)[1]

Novels about human fate have previously focused on the themes of love, pursuits, and disillusionment, since the history of human fate, as a rule, boils down to this small number of events and situations.

What we call the historical novel is quite similar in this regard. The only difference is that people's fates are transposed against the past, against an "historical" background. The protagonist and his fate have always been at the core of the novel. Every event in the novel took place from the protagonist's point of view and served as a background to his life or raw material for his actions.[2]

This method went hand in hand with the cult of the individual in Romanticism, and belief in his absolute autonomy and decisive role in history. This ideology was comprehensively formulated and perfectly rationalized in Carlyle's *On Hero Worship*.[3]

---

1 See Debora Vogel, "Romans djalektyki," *Przegląd Społeczny* 9, no. 10 (1935): 243–247.
2 The crisis of the modern novel and biographical narrative in comparison to the "social/historical" novel was widely discussed by critics at the time. For instance, in 1930 Walter Benjamin wrote about Alfred Döblin's *Berlin Alexanderplatz*, and expressed his belief that the contemporary novel comes close to the epic. The difference between the novel and the epic lies in the fact that in the latter what is represented is not the life of a unique individual but rather the "sea" of life, the world at large. Benjamin voices these remarks in his review of Döblin's book, "Krisis des Romans. Zu Döblins *Berlin Alexanderplatz*," in *Gesammelte Schriften*, vol. 3, ed. Rolf Teideman et al. (Frankfurt am Main: Suhrkamp Verlag, 1972), 236. Vogel does something similar in her essay, which is in a way a review of Brunngraber's book. The German Döblin and the Austrian Brunngraber are united in their view of reality as a document. Both novels have features of the aesthetic which in the 1920s came to replace Expressionism, namely, a new "documentary style." The human being appears in her surroundings, among things and social ties; the fictional and documentary are linked together, whether in the polyphony of heterogeneous elements, such as Berlin in Döblin's novel or in juxtapositions between the protagonist and time in Brunngraber's novel.
3 Thomas Carlyle (1795–1881) was a British author, journalist, and philosopher. See his work *On Heroes, Hero Worship, and the Heroic in History* (1841), which discusses the "cult of the hero" and the pathos of the individual in Romanticism. This book is mentioned because, for

Such an interpretation of history as a collection of heroic deeds and their consequences resulted in the following: the historical novel in the past did not depict the "lively" aspects of history, including the colorfulness of facticity and banality, the "novelistic" sides of historical processes.

Only a specific interpretation—the reduction of history to production, with capital as its principal engine—brings forth colorfulness. (The question of production emerges when an excess of commodities is dangerous in the same way as their deficit, and only war helps to restore balance. This question is likewise pressing when war is a product of the interests of the capital accumulated in that branch of industry which has no other raison d'être than war; and when these interests go beyond production, become a principal idea, and eventually become absurd, even though they were once thought to express a natural logic—as in the Taylorization of the world of labor, for instance.[4] It seems that ideas, like actions, have consequences and result in catastrophes.)

In this interpretation of history people are merely Hegel's "agents of the world-spirit,"[5] and they are of interest to the novelist only as such. Brunngraber's novel *Karl and the Twentieth Century*[6] could be considered historical in this sense. Its protagonist is impersonal time—part of the twentieth century and the end of the nineteenth century—the latter as the preparatory stage for the

---

Carlyle, history is driven by exceptional people—"heroes" who surpass ordinary people with their deeds.

4 In Brunngraber's novel there is an interesting depiction of the negative effects of Taylorist system of thought. Karl Lakner, the protagonist, is connected to Taylor via the theme of the train. Taylor "installed the rails" on which the twentieth century rode, and in the end of the novel Brunngraber's protagonist Karl throws himself under this train.

5 Hegel writes about this, most notably, in his *Philosophy of History*. The relation of one time to the next is one of development, yet no one can anticipate the unfolding of spirit. The next stage comes through the dialectical movement of the world spirit. The acts of the great people are the embodiment of this spirit, although they are not fully aware of the significance of their actions. Nevertheless, they are the agents of world history, which is the self-caused movement of a reason that takes nations in account rather than individuals. History, for Hegel, is the progress of freedom—that is, reason realizing itself in the world.

6 Rudolf Brunngraber (1901–1960) was an Austrian writer popular in the 1930s–1950s. His first social novel *Karl und das zwanzigste Jahrhundert* [Karl and the twentieth century, 1932], about the the economic crisis brought him fame in Austria and beyond. Traditionally, the socio-historical context limits narrative in Brunngraber's novel; however, the context of the twentieth century plays a significant role, as does information about economics and politics, facts and statistics. The transition from "grandiose" to "small" events in Karl's life creates a complex mosaic structure in the novel.

former.⁷ The "novel's protagonist" is no longer as important as before. He does not become the agent of history, with his fate; he does not shape the history of ideas, but, rather, he himself becomes the passive product of history. Here an old scheme is in effect: a person is represented against the background of history.

In his *Magic Mountain*, Thomas Mann presented in a fresh way the banal conception of humans as the "products of conditions and social relationships."⁸ Mann worked through the transformative potential of the strange being of "time." He determined the impact of time not only on a person's soul, but also on his body. For instance, Hans Castorp does not love his work, he "liked better to have his time free … not weighted with the leaden load of effort; lying spacious before him, not divided up by obstacles one had to grit one's teeth and conquer."⁹ Work does not agree with Castorp since it does no good for his body, it is useless. Mann expressed the idea of time devoid of ideals that places no requirements on people.

In his novel, Brunngraber chooses "ideal" time as the raw material, yet not in the sense of the struggle for ideals. This is the time of the idea's negative side—the destructive time of capital's parasitism.

Brunngraber's choice of a certain kind of protagonist surely demonstrates the dependency of the individual on "time": a person with an essentially romantic nature, full of idealistic beliefs about the unique inner possibilities of individuals which define their fates. The protagonist's personal luck and, perhaps, every aim in life fail due to outside circumstances, which are themselves a result of the economic and political transformations.

The conflict between the person and time comes to the fore in such reflections: "O, where is the love, which the thirteen-year-old Karl carried into the world, and which he rightfully expected from it in return? Love is a feedback loop … a system which has to be assumed to exist, while it is inconceivable that the world is not submerged in it as if in god's breath."

Three newspaper clippings from February 23, 1931, under the same title "The world carries on" serve as an ending to this novel of the twentieth century.¹⁰

---

7   What is meant here is the equality between the two story lines, the line of Karl Lakner from birth until death, and the line of development of the twentieth century.
8   This novel is considered the key novel about time, *Zeitroman*.
9   See Thomas Mann, *The Magic Mountain*, trans. H. Lowe-Porter and with an afterword by the author (London: Secker and Warburg, 1927), 34.
10 We may call such composition "documentary." Brunngraber was under the influence of the ideas of the Viennese sociologist Otto Neurath, namely his method of Pictorial Statistics.

The first clipping is a report about the suicide of Karl Lakner, an unemployed man.

The second is a curiosity. The value of a human being is calculated in marks (a person's value is exactly four marks if one were to consider the raw materials of which he consists to be the value of the commodities that could be produced from him—for instance, seven pieces of soap, a medium-sized iron nail, a dose of magnesia, etc.).

The third piece presents a story of storks. In Catkin Peak in Natal, government officials noticed "large white areas which they believed closely resembled snow. They were pinpointed to a hill where storks gathered to fly to Europe every year. As the officials got closer, they saw that there were, in fact, thousands of dead storks. The birds had been killed by a hail storm and smashed to the ground where they now lay piled on top of one another with their broken wings and legs. Clouds of other storks circled above. They seemed to be mourning their dead friends."

The three clippings seemed to be independent from one another and assembled as if only accidentally, and yet they belong together perfectly.

The first clipping, the suicide of an unemployed man, is linked to the second one, the calculation of the person's value in four marks, through reflection on the apparent uselessness of the human being in life. Such a juxtaposition expresses an implicit protest, despite the alleged objectivity of its factual presentation.

The third piece has a symbolic value. It clarifies and highlights the other two. The helplessness of beings is established by considering the objective constraints and logic of the "force of nature," which is more universal than the logic of yearning for life.

Thus, nothing differentiates the fate of a person being crushed by the logic of history from the fate of storks which die at the exact moment their new life was about to begin.

Therefore, we may establish the second principal tendency in life that goes hand in hand with the logic of historical dialectic. It could be designated as the

---

Neurath's most famous work *International Picture Language* was published in 1936. The purpose of this visual "language" was to present knowledge that the public could understand but that wouldn't be reductive. The representation of information through statistics was considered important for creating connections between facts and reality. The juxtaposition of the three cutouts in the novel plays a significant role. It does not give the reader any ready-made conclusions, instead allowing her to decide for herself by comparing the social (the calculation of the value of human life) and biological (the association of the tragedy of the human life with the natural world of birds). These tendencies are also important in Vogel's work.

"biological longing for life." This tendency is discussed in the novel with great sympathy.

The novel's protagonist, Karl Lakner, discovers a thesis suggested by the author that "the economical motivation for his desires is just as compelling as the biological." Karl has this experience, even though he is absolutely uninterested in economic processes and is incapable of grasping the connection between the world events and his own singular fate and everyday life.

"He was not interested in politics, he even felt aversion to politics where it was most apparent—in attacks on the established order. Everything which pertained to history and old age incited a reverent shiver in him. That is why he was against the socialists whose system entirely negated the previous order." Brunngraber outlined his protagonist's relation to the phenomena which would eventually destroy the protagonist's life.

Karl Lakner was brought up in the interwar period's culture of individualism. It existed as a psychic predisposition, even when the menacing outlines of events that would lead to catastrophe loomed in the background. This individualism encouraged a firm belief in life and the world, as well as a firm conviction that every person shapes his own destiny and is solely responsible for both his own reputation and decline. As such, individualism was imbued with optimism which was a result of belief in one's own power.

The author described the correlations between such optimism and the social conscience in Karl Lakner: "precisely this optimism isolated him from making real conclusions about the world, since he, generally speaking, knew nothing of the world at all." This isolation was a result of Karl's absolute trust in life. The war, and the bars swarming with dancers, the bars where the resistance of the populace was pacified and where soldiers stopped by on their way to the front—all of the above was a natural part of life for Karl.

"He had an acute awareness of all the things around him as a whole, but not of each individual phenomenon." This is Brunngraber's diagnosis of Karl.

The moment when Karl becomes conscious that true salvation for him would entail "being a number in a series, a link in a chain—to be a miner, or a factory worker" and "having a day job and remuneration"—is a turning point for him. Only by way of this detour, by experiencing frustration and fatigue, does the novel's protagonist realize he longs to be a member of society. This is how it looks from the perspective of a single human life.

The most intriguing part of the book is the arrangement of the story of the dialectic if history on the basis of dry numbers and dates. Life as an intricate knot of causes and consequences, the rhythm of grayness and fatalism is represented here through impersonal lists of numbers and the enumeration of facts.[11]

These matter-of-fact dates and facts constitute a different kind of the fantastic—in comparison to that of dreams and the colorfulness of human fate, which always contain the unforeseeable.

And precisely this new form—the fantastic of banal gestures and numbers—triumphs in the novel due to their brightness when compared to the colorfulness of so-called life, when compared to this intangible, incomprehensible matter we call "life" which we nevertheless seem to understand so well.

Finally, we may wish to know the definitive conclusion of the novel.

Anyone who claims that reportage as a method of composition consists only in differentiating between closely related facts, and that it should not be burdened with the superstructure of judgments is wrong. The selection of facts, and their assemblage, already passes judgement. The reflections suggested by combinations of dates and numbers are the compositional elements in the novel in question.

When logic and inevitability are established within the dialectic of life, such reflections should be understood as no different than a rehabilitation of intangible romanticism and a longing for the nebulous which we call "beauty" or "happiness," or in contemporary terms a "person's biological yearning."

Moreover, the choices of a character who "does not like politics," such as the protagonist in the novel, exemplifies such a rehabilitation as a protest against the negation of the individual by the logic of capital, which seems to be our historical stage at the moment.

At the same time political and industrial history is represented as inescapable, and "when people come close to the inevitable, then history exhibits noisy zeal and people are its fanatical agents."

Inherent in the book's method of reportage is an adherence to facts and tendencies. Despite their ideological treatment, however, this is not a propaganda book. The tendencies of life which might be better concealed for the sake of ideological clarity—for instance, the banal tendency of a "person's biological longing"—are not glossed over tacitly here.

---

11 The author enumerates facts about the war, the number of the fallen soldiers, information about the arms industry, and other economic factors. Numbers and statistics are provided without commentary and serve as a new type of imagery.

The protest against a history where humans appear as helpless, worthless toys, is followed by a demand for someone who can grasp history and take a conscious approach to his own life, methodically shaping it in the form of a dialectic of the moment, the form which is essential at present.

The effect of this book could be attributed to the nature of reportage in its fullest sense. Here facts are provided with their ideology—however, without any propaganda superstructure. The facts here should speak for themselves rather than be conveyed through directly represented, mentally simplified propaganda. The elasticity and simplicity of concepts which are sometimes bent too easily for the purpose of simplification or avoidance is renounced in favor of life itself, which is always difficult and multifaceted. Thanks to this method, it was possible to capture the relevance as an artwork, which for certain reasons is not as simple as it may seem.

5

Montage as a Literary Genre (1937)[1]

Montage is more than a formal experiment. It is an essential expression of a worldview.

1. THE NOTION

The notion of montage already contains the term's conventional use and its principle: the combination of elements—each simultaneously an autonomous totality for itself, independent from all the other elements—into a whole.

This definition forms the image of the mechanical montage. Its properties are the same in the literary montage.

Here the singular situations are linked directly, without the circular detours of the plot which we know from the traditional novel. Thus, the machinic rhythm of montage originates.

Continuity, the smooth sequencing of associations which fill the empty spaces between important, exemplary events—the situations which illustrate the thesis of the novel—is called "fabula," or "plot," in the novel[2] and "melodiousness" in poetry. Montage renounces the principle of plot or melodiousness. It allows for empty spaces between situations, in much the same way as they occur in life. It utilizes those specific tensions in life which collide with its machinic, atonal, and a-melodious rhythm.

---

1 See Debora Vogel, "Di literarishe gatung montaz," *Bodn* [New York] 4, no. 3–4 (1937): 99–105.
2 Joseph Roth claims in his "Di gesprengte Romanform" [The exploded form of the novel], *Die Literarishe Welt*, no. 3 (1930): 267 that the traditional novel with its "closure" and plot development is impossible in modern literature. The appearance of a great number of novels employing montage techniques testifies to this fact.

The abandonment of the element of the plot is due to its fictive character which borders on artificiality. The principle of plot no longer matches the needs of the present moment.

Plot calls for the existence of the "protagonist of the novel," a central character around whom events and the fates of other characters in the novel revolve.

The individual protagonist is replaced with an anonymous person in montage, hence the use of impersonal form and the passive. This person is the representation of universal tendencies; he has the same role as the impersonal situation, the fatalistic role of exemplifying an impersonal process. In contrast, the individual protagonist in the novel had importance as such.

This approach to a person does not require assigning a name to the individual which is significant only when an individual character and his singular fate become the locus of our attention. Even if the latter is the case, the name is only a convention to which we are used.

The actual protagonist of montage is the course of life[3] with its intrinsic dialectic and two main tendencies, the biological (i.e. stable) and the social (i.e. relevant).[4]

Time takes the place of plot in montage. However paradoxical it may appear, time takes on the form of a chronicle and becomes the link between significant situations; thus, it begins to play the role of plot in the novel.

Moreover, time, which was usually the background for action, now takes part in action in montage. Time unfolds in transformations of nature, in its nuances and moods that lend themselves to being described in the categories of human life, in expressions such as the "contemplative" or "responsible"; apart from these, it appears to be an empty space. Different arrangements of time could be considered events—equivalent to intrinsic events and human fates.

The character of chronicle gives montage an epic quality.[5] And today epic is necessary once again. However, this need cannot be met through naïve realism, with the accidental nature of this genre which records banal "scenes from life," even though this type of realism appropriates the label "documentary" for

---

3 It should be noted that the protagonist of a montage novel, that is, "life," differs from the protagonist of the traditional novel, the individual. Walter Benjamin writes about the epic character of montage where life plays central role in his "Krisis des Romans." See footnote 2 to the essay "Romance of Dialectics" above.

4 See also Vogel's essay "The Romance of the Dialectics," where she discusses these two tendencies, the biological and the social, with regard to montage in Brunngraber's *Karl and the Twentieth Century*.

5 According to Walter Benjamin, it is montage that provides the novel with new epic possibilities.

itself. Likewise, the need for a new epic cannot be fulfilled through utilitarian realism which makes the creation of a program for life art's purpose. Similarly, Romantic realism—its program is based on proletarian literature—is not fit to meet this need, since it wishes to advertise only the "beautiful aspects of life." In turn, the term "Socialist Realism" is too broad and unclear. Therefore, it cannot become an aesthetic category, which would demonstrate the appropriate movement by its name alone.

The name for the essential style which aligns with contemporary needs is "Constructive realism." Montage which combines the documentary with the rigor of construction seems to move in the direction of such realism.

2. REPORTAGE

Reportage originated as an art form which claims to express the need for a new realism. It deals exclusively with the documentary element in life.

However, the instances of reportage until now have been close to journalism or naïve realism rather than art. Moreover, they have put themselves in the service of a single tendency—the class struggle.

There are two propositions in the definition, and in the program, of reportage which disqualify it as an art form.

1. Reportage is a reactionary art form, since its program calls for the reproduction of a certain unspecified "facticity."
2. It cannot literally fulfill its program, since there are no unambiguous or "documentary" facts and every fact in art is simply a product of interpretation.

The only type of reportage which could be considered an art form is the type which provides the abovementioned interpretation of life: the interpretation of class struggle as an inherent life principle which explains all the social and artistic processes.

In every other case, a range of journalistic descriptions of parts of the city, court cases, and the travel impressions—all the "scenes based on reality," the merely sentimental and accidental impressions previously called "feuilleton"—are now called "reportage."

Yet even when reportage appeared to be interpretative and to go beyond its own program, it nevertheless did not fulfil the requirements of the contemporary method of composition. While unsatisfactory as composition, reportage, however, could be used as a way to treat material in the constructive whole which I call montage.

3. STYLIZATION IN THE MANNER OF REPORTAGE

Montage in the visual arts, photomontage, deals with the partially ready-made elements of pictures and other juxtapositions taken from elsewhere or specifically prepared for montage. However, we often find arrangements of artistic elements which would be considered montage only by virtue of the way of their arrangement (as in Max Ernst's photomontage *Les malheures des immortels*).

Ready-made material could be used in literature in a similar way. Newspaper clippings, the lines from popular street and dance songs, a banal utterance from ordinary conversation, and rhetorical expressions supply us with such material.

The method of reportage comes into question for its artistic reworking of raw material into the parts of montage construction. In this case we may talk about the arrangement stylized in the manner of reportage. Such stylization depicts things from the perspective of absolute proximity, including their minute details—in an "objective" manner, which was the previous parlance, or, to use the current term, in a "matter-of-fact" way.[6]

The term the "facture of space" describes this treatment of matter best. The notion was introduced by the Polish artist and art critic Władysław Strzemiński. Every figure of space, form, and thing is a shaped space—the "facture of space"; space itself is the raw material.

Stylization in the manner of reportage presupposes the treatment of material as if it were a document, in the sense of the fiction of documentary.

4. THE PRINCIPLE OF SIMULTANEITY

The method of simultaneity is a direct consequence of recovering the multiplicity and polyphony of life. Such rehabilitation means that trivial, "small" events are important in the same way as those "big" heroic trajectories in life which record impatience and which are simultaneously empty in their pathos and rhetoric. The unemployed pass by the blooming acacias, and the acacias bloom

---

6 The term "matter-of-fact" originates from the name of the "New Objectivity" (or "New Sobriety") movement which emerged in the Weimar Republic. Franz Roh theorizes this style in art. Vogel mentions him in her other essays, for example in "White Words in Poetry."

while revolutions are in the making. The once stable and conventional hierarchy of experiences is abolished.

The method of simultaneity is not new. It was introduced by the Modernists. We encounter it for the first time in 1915 in the French poetry of Rivoire[7] and Apollinaire,[8] and in paintings by Delaunay.[9]

It could also be traced in the Surrealist writing of Breton, Aragon, and Tzara, and montage by Max Ernst.[10] Additionally, we find it in the novels *Manhattan Transfer* and *The 42nd Parallel* by Dos Passos and in the novel by Jules Romain *Les hommes de bonne volonte* (Men of goodwill).

The simultaneity of montage is grounded in another basic idea, difference from its abovementioned types. Such simultaneity is not the synchronicity of events in time and space, which would be different from physical spatial simultaneity, which can simultaneously incorporate multiplicity (as in Rivoire's and Apollinaire's work). It is also not about that simultaneity which is, rather, a method of composition and constitutes the background for action (as in the work of Dos Passos and Jules Romain).[11]

The logic of the arrangement of situations, their exemplarity from a specific standpoint, is decisive for montage. The fact that space can simultaneously

---

7 Andre Rivoire (1872–1930) was a French poet and dramatist. Vogel probably has in mind his poetry collection *Rêves et souvenirs*, which was published not in 1915 but in 1920.
8 Guillaume Apollinaire (1880–1918) was a French poet and an art critic, one of the most notable avant-garde figures of the twentieth century. Besides lyrical poetry, Apollinaire was also author of the study *The Cubist Painters* (1913). The poet develops simultaneity as a poetic method, which stems from his interest in Cubism in the visual arts.
9 Robert Delaunay (1885–1941) was a French painter who first painted in the Cubist style. He was one of the founders of the new style which Guillaume Apollinaire called "Orphism." See also Vogel's essay "The Genealogy of Photomontage and Its Possibilities."
10 André Breton presented Max Ernst's work (his paintings and graphic work, namely collages) to the Parisian public in May 1921 in the spirit of Dadaism. It is no coincidence that Vogel mentions Breton together with Max Ernst in her essay "The Genealogy of Photomontage and Its Possibilities."
11 The novels of Dos Passos were translated into Polish and were extremely popular among Polish readers in the interwar era. György Lukács writes about the novel-montage by Dos Passos in his classic text "Erzählen oder Beschreiben?" [Narrate or describe?]. Lukács notes that in the era of Naturalism the novel's protagonist is on the same level as the objects surrounding him, and it is the protagonist who gathers into a totality complex object images, money, production. In Dos Passos's work the characters do not have such ties; they do not participate in action, but only "stroll through the object-world of the novel." It is of note that Lukács published this essay in 1936 and Vogel published her essays on montage in 1937–1938, although she wrote and submitted them for publication in *In zikh* much earlier, as is evident from her correspondence with A. Leyeles. Lukács' and Vogel's ideas on montage seem to converge in time.

contain multiplicity is not as important as the space of inner experiences which simultaneously incorporates the different areas and contents, dimensions and directions of psychic events.

We can speak of the logical simultaneity of montage. (According to such a principle, for instance, two scenes could be arranged in the framework of the whole: soldiers marching in a perfect regular rectangular column and … flower shops with perfect azaleas. Their logic lies in the fact of perfection, which evokes a strange yearning for the stillness and freshness of new beginnings.)

5. CURRENT THEMES

We might strongly oppose it, yet life's material remains a theme in art. The decorative aspect is in a way included in every composition: treating life as a theme results in stylization.

The fact of life, which becomes a theme, also regulates its role in the artwork in terms of quantity and quality through the choice of specific spheres and features in life.

A similar conclusion surfaces from the previous attempt to introduce a socially relevant problematic into art. The failed attempts attest that a relevant problematic should occupy no more space in art than it does in life, since "life" should not be destroyed, as it is in times of war and revolution.

The second life principle—the stable and always relevant—could be alternatively called the "biological." A socially relevant problematic is justified as long as it can be linked to the biological element. The exclusive presence of relevant material leads to a naïve kind of realism—journalism and rhetoric. The hypertrophy of the biological element, on the other hand, leads to egotism and hermetic metaphoricity.

There is no good recipe here, yet there is a correct ratio between the two life elements. We should not renounce the artistic possibilities of the relevant problematic. Topicality could be introduced by the "mood of posters,"[12] which shows the beauty of things in a single dimension, without the depth of the perspective of reflection or commentary, without the context of other distant things. It is the specific beauty of matter-of-factness.

---

12 Posters or flyers and other types of inscriptions, such as advertisements, engravings on walls play a significant role in Vogel's poetics.

6

Literary Montage: An Introduction (1938)[1]

A MISUNDERSTANDING

A misunderstanding is inherent in the notion of "intellectual art." This prejudice originates in the Romantic worldview, in the postulate of the dynamic art of feeling which should capture experience in the process of its happening. Paradoxically, Modernism reappraised this prejudice with its seeming incomprehensibility. The point of view that you need to "understand" the new forms lead to the erroneous conclusion that the intellect participates in the process of their creation. Thus the "fiction" of art without the participation of "experiences" originated—the fiction of artificially contrived combinations. It was so far-reaching that Surrealism, which makes use of the irrational associative element, is considered "artificial," the product of intellectual combinations.

Like all poetic inventions, my "discovery" consists in showing the banal and the self-evident, and, therefore, the unseen.

I perceive things from a very close perspective. It allows me to abandon the conventional distance to the world of things. This distance is full of the interpretations which adhere to things, and, therefore, from our point of view, the interpretations and the things become indistinguishable—things are believed to be their interpretations. The optics of proximity allows one to overcome the clichés beneath which things have become buried over a certain amount of time. This optics makes it possible to see things outside the context of the interpretation and label attached to them.

---

1 See Debora Vogel, "Literarisher montazh (an araynfir)," *Inzl* [Bucharest] 4, no. 3 (1938): 6.

THE NOTION OF MONOTONY (CONTENT AND METHOD)

The notion of monotony stands in opposition to the worldviews of Impressionism and Expressionism.

Impressionism is rooted in the philosophical perception of reality as an assemblage of the transient combinations of impressions; therefore, it leads to a certain consumerist life program of making use of every moment. Impressionism adopts a stance of waiting and keeping an eye out for accidental "experiences" and "impressions."

Expressionism also demonstrates a consumerist approach to life. It treats things as concepts, rejects their concrete features, and works out the large, empty lines of abstract "spirituality."

It is no coincidence that the notion of monotony is combined with that of resignation. The latter means renouncing illusory, impressionistic colorfulness.

A few simple and stable movements which remain after such renunciation yield an image and a notion of monotony. Hence the dialectical source of the style of "cool stasis and monotony."

The notion of monotony has yet another social source—modern urbanism.

Based on the well-known psychological law—that a great quantity of speed and movement transforms into its opposite. The polyphony of the modern city passes into immobility and grayness. Even in terms of pure optics, multiplicity in the city merges into a gray static mass.

The motif of the mannequin and the mood of fatalism are also linked to urbanism. The similarity of a great number of gestures creates an impression of stereotypical machinic and serial movement. The mechanical element in the living body—the mannequin—is a person's figure with the functions of a machine. This machinic element in the living body represents the intellectual category of "fatalism." The method which corresponds to the lyric of cool stasis is called a cross-section. It signifies the stable schema of gestures and situations. This relative stability equals repetition. The cross-section of dynamic experiences features their inherently stable elements; therefore, it is static.

Monotony discovered as the structure of reality can become a program of life which rehabilitates everydayness. Therefore, this worldview is both hierarchical and heroic: it recognizes an intrinsic value in the laborious repetition of raw, everyday gestures, in the wonder of movement until its completion.

However, the next stage is the rehabilitation of all components—the great lines of life plans together with the monotony of life, its kitsch and pathos. The new stage is called

SIMULTANEITY (CONTENT AND METHOD)

The notion of simultaneity originated in different versions of the theory of Modernism. I understand simultaneity as the possibility of the coexistence of heterogeneous situations and experiences and the abolition of the hierarchy of things as a result. A type of the regularity and one-dimensionality of life, it may give an impression of stasis and monotony, and yet it is full of polyphony. A certain stasis of this polyphony has its origin in the eradication of hierarchy. This tragic worldview is due to its resignation—agreement with everything—in a way a modern Stoicism. Montage is its corresponding artistic method.

In my view montage is different from the program of passive reproduction in reportage. It also differs from Surrealist montage, although sometimes it appears to be similar. Surrealist montage originates in free, irrational assemblages of experiences, while this kind of montage is built on the logical principle which allows to combine different situations into a whole.

Singular situations are treated in a "realist" manner. I put this word in quotation marks because the realism I have in mind means stylization in the manner of realism—exaggeration in the choice of components and calligraphic precision in the treatment of details. (This realism is akin to "Magical Realism" which is the same as New Objectivity—the terms which the German art critic Franz Roh used in relation to a specific movement in painting). When Constructive montage-realism takes on the form of Surrealism, we might have another example of a quality which transforms into its opposite.

In terms of details which require further explication, I need to explain many quotation marks, especially in *Acacias Bloom*. Quotation marks indicate that an expression is a trite or stereotypical interpretation of a thing used only out of habit. In later montages, clichés recede into the background and give space to relevant material which is still raw, not yet overgrown with interpretations.

RELEVANCE AND MONTAGE

The current tendency finds its expression first and foremost in art through method. Yet the material, the theme, is also its carrier.

To outline the role of the theme in poetry more accurately, we need to establish the following: the theme may be hostile to the method, it may be altogether unfitting. It may also overtake the composition and force its own importance to the foreground.

We deal with the first case if the technique of Impressionism were applied to the theme of Laocoön's pain. The pathos and grand immobility of the pain do not match the technique which dissects reality into discrete, short-lived impressions.

The second case concerns utilitarian art, namely art which would like to inform and directly formulate a new program and rules for life. In this case, the style is not current, and the material will be reproduced in a raw and indiscriminate way.

The art forms oscillate between the two extremes. In the middle there is a possibility of agreement between method and material. This possibility is each movement's "privileged theme" (for Impressionism, with its reliance on mood, the landscape becomes this theme; for Expressionism—the city; and for the style of New Objectivity—the interior).

The privileged theme for montage is the polyphony of life. It embraces the eternal and the stable in the same measure as the immediate urgency of the everyday, of economic and political life. It makes it possible to discuss the most relevant events of the day.

The immediate material of life finds its artistic treatment in the method of montage—in the links between a situation and a plan. It means that everything belongs to life.

Unlike passive reportage which lacks a program, a constructive approach to the world based on logic belongs to the current tendency of our time.

Essays on Art, Artists, and the Applied Arts

7

Theme and Form in Chagall's Art: An Aesthetic Critique (1929/1930)[1]

ARTISTIC REALITY

Things do not have an intrinsic fate. They are fitted into a precise framework, into contours. The questions people ask about things create a story which we get from dividing things into groups based on our questions and demands. In this way, a specific reality revealed in the composition of form arises. As a rule, this reality is achieved through a reduction of the chaos of events and relationships—contained within everyday experiences and inherent in external fates or situations—to a unified rhythm of inanimate and animate masses.

This procedure simultaneously clarifies the role of the living element as raw material and the theme—mere matter in the artist's work—within a form's composition. However, we need to emphasize that the structure of this raw material is not accidental. This structure determines the specific rhythm of things in the new reality.

Hence the practical outcome for criticism. Firstly, an analysis of pure form leads to a determination of the type of form—mass, rhythmical line, and contour. Secondly, a description of formal types simultaneously determines the origin of a composition's essence in the theme. The formula of a specific reality is contained in mass, rhythm, and line, just as notions and words formulate this reality in a different way.

Analysis of the artwork's form yields the same result as analysis of the theme. We will demonstrate this through Marc Chagall's work.

---

1   See part one: Debora Vogel, "Teme un forem in der kunst fun shagal. Pruv fun estetisher kritik," *Tsushtayer*, no. 1 (1929): 21–26; part two: "Teme un forem in der kunst fun shagal. Pruv fun estetisher kritik," *Tsushtayer*, no. 2 (1930): 19–24.

I. ANALYSIS OF FORM

1) Scale. Artistic reality can be measured by the categories of the realm of life—scale, mass, and lines. By dealing with certain elements given at random and somehow understandable in our everyday experience, the construction of form differs from the realm of experience.

For instance, we are accustomed to the fact that a human being is smaller than a house, or that the size of one human figure compared to another is determined by a ratio which cannot violate certain boundaries as to what can be considered high or low. However, these measurements can be modified, and this modification will have an artistic value which lies in using the elements of scale for the purposes of construction.

Figure 2. Cover of *Tsushtayer* journal, 1929.

Thus, we come close to finding the key to Chagall's artistic method.

The element of scale in Chagall's work points to a key characteristic of his method—the use of uneven scale. Compared to ordinary size, Chagall's objects are enlarged or reduced; they enter combinations which are not justified by perspective or the realistic dimensions of space. The implementation of two-dimensionality for Chagall lies in the special treatment of scale. The foreground is enlarged, as are its objects, while people and things in the background are reduced in size, which produces the effect of a miniature—albeit caricatured—playfulness.

As mentioned above, the background is not always justified in view of perspective; sometimes it is akin to an imaginary dimension: an important person or a thing might not be at the center of the action, but somewhere in the margins. Sometimes the intent is to note the existence of a person or thing as such—not as something for or beside something else. The purpose here is to obtain basic weight, the essence of relationships, and the foundational rhythm of masses—as a result of the combination of objects or persons with other masses. Thus, foreground and background are "a trick" of sorts. Our naturalistic tendencies, like the inclination to see things in the foreground as larger than those in the background, are engaged here. One example is placing copies of figures reduced in a caricatural way beside the figures themselves in the foreground. (A Jew with an Etrog, and beside him a Jew, smaller in size, who also holds an Etrog on his head in the "Rabbi" painting.)

Single houses or groups of houses in the background are used for the purpose of enlargement or reduction. In the downsized houses which serve as the background for the human figures and events appears an element of the compartmentalization and playfulness. Yet at the same time the small size and the levity of the masses brings out their ornamental, accessory nature.

Figure 3. Marc Chagall (*Cattle Dealer*, 1912).

The specific dematerialization of mass and its ornamentality yields a formula emblematic for the direction of the tensions and rhythm of Chagall's constructions—the playfulness of all human events. The formula denotes the inner state in which things at the peak of tension pass into their direct opposites. Then the weightiest events can suddenly lose their weight. And vice versa, an insignificant object like a clock can become the most important of all.

The formula of playfulness explains the method of changing and reshuffling dimensions and the use of this method for formal purposes. The element of scale will simply be used to mark the significance or the insignificance of the represented object or person. The breakup of the mass of the human body and its limbs can perhaps be explained as an expression of this method. Likewise, the importance of one part in relation to other parts of the body at a specific moment will be emphasized through this method. This is certainly also the purpose of grouping separate limbs on various planes, which can be partially traced in Chagall's paintings.

One may doubt the originality or refinement of such a method of treating scale. This method can be considered essentially primitive, yet we always enlarge things or events which have a higher significance for us. But do we not travel the road of multiple hurdles and superstructures to finally arrive, or rather return, to this primitive means which we intuited before complicating things? Presently, we use a simple and well-understood element of mass size to formulate and express abstract dimensions—the significance of things and events for a person.

2) Weight. Like scale, the element of weight can be used as a formal feature. In this respect, Chagall introduces, perhaps unconsciously, two dimensions as well. This time it is a vertical two-dimensionality. Constructions like sitting, walking, or lifting human figures above the rooftops in a city, driving wagons at the height of the windows of houses, or on an imaginary road higher than a regular road exhibit this vertical two-dimensionality (in paintings like *Trip, In Vitebsk, The Cattle Dealer*). The artist overcomes the force of gravity by treating houses as blocks which are not rooted in the ground with their foundations. Likewise, in the case of the confusion and reversal of directions—passengers ride on top of trains, trees grow downwards or horizontally—it seems that the possibility of ignoring the gravity of bodies towards the center of the Earth as it is conventionally understood is expressed here.

Chagall's formal element of two planes and their simultaneity, or of opening wide the foreground to show the background, which to a certain extent recalls primitive the paintings of the Trecento era,[2] can be considered a way of

---

2   Trecento (1300–1400): pre-Renaissance Italian art.

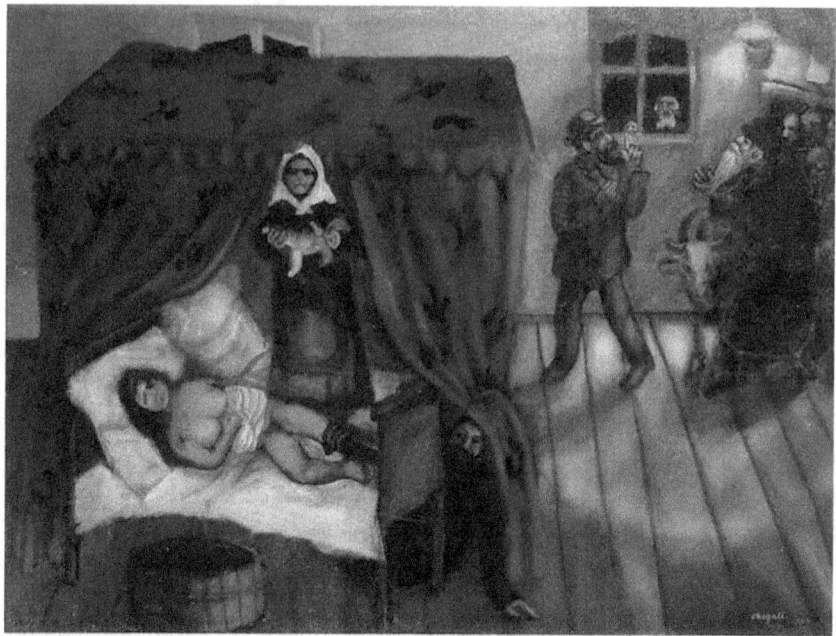

Figure 4. Marc Chagall (*The Birth*, 1910).

overcoming gravity. This is also the case when severed limbs are placed near a body in painting. Everything is shown in a way as if the scenes which in reality are divided into separate moments can happen simultaneously. Such simultaneity, or concurrence of scenes—which means their dematerialization to a certain extent—overcomes gravity. Things and events should be devoid of real mass to be able to occur in the same place at the same time.

Chagall's contour is indeterminate. It is not used purely as artistic material, rather the line frames the blocks. Line is treated here essentially as contour, hence the impersonality of the blocks. Inanimate masses can be both personal and impersonal like figures and faces. This means that the masses shown are like chess figures which point to something distant which is not identical or contained in them. Understanding contour also explains why the definitive and accidental physiognomy of beings and things becomes insignificant and recedes into the background.

The rhythm of line in Chagall's work is best described as the rhythm of deformation or bending. It manifests as a technique in the bent nature of blocks and bodies, or in a broken angular zigzag contour with its frequent expression of a brokenness and insecurity which borders on hopelessness.

When line expresses the rhythm of masses, we may speak about the zig-zag or bent movement which characterizes the masses included in the composition.

3) Color combinations. Beside dematerialization and the shift in the gravity of masses, the irrationality of their balance and the brokenness of contour, Chagall also has his color preferences—the choice of an irrational color palette. He chooses vulgar colors, like the green of grass and the countryside, the red of beets or the snowball tree, the empty and vulgar color of the lilac, etc. Color combinations are just as important as colors themselves. We observe a paradoxical and vulgar combination of colors—a bright green and an especially unharmonious red are combined on the canvas: half of the clothes, a house, and a sleeve are green, and the other symmetrical half is red; the faces are at times green, or the color of red rust at other times. For instance, in the composition of the *Cattle Dealer* painting, there is also a distant blurry blue, silk black, and the pink color of worms after rain.

And in these colors and their combinations there is a formal promise of reality where everything is possible: gravity transforms into playful lightness, and big becomes small. And where anything is possible, a person can wear such colors and be decorated in this manner.

This is what analysis of Chagall's form shows. Thematic analysis points to what extent the weight and rhythm of masses and the variety of lines and colors are an appropriate expression of the reality which Chagall showed in his paintings.

In the analysis of form above there are a couple points which the Russian critics Ephros[3] and Tugenhold[4] also consider in their study Marc Chagall.[5]

Ephros writes, "we are used to the fact that large is bigger than small, yet Chagall does not stick to this principle." Tugenhold adds, "Even Chagall's figures which come down to the ground contain an insecurity, a lack of balance

---

3 Abraham Ephros (1888–1954) was a Russian art critic, poet, and translator. He was the director of the Moscow State Jewish Chamber Theater in 1920–1926, where he invited Marc Chagall to work among others.
4 Yakov Tugenhold (1882–1928) was a Russian art historian and art critic. His main expertise was Western European and contemporary Russian art.
5 Vogel mentions the monograph—the critical portrait *Marc Chagall's Art* (Moscow: Gelikon, 1918) which Ephros co-authored with Tugenhold. During the course of his work as a critic, when censorship allowed it, Ephros turned to the work of his favorite artist Marc Chagall. His first article on Chagall appeared in *Novyi Put'*, no. 48–49 (1916): 60. Besides the mentioned monograph, he also wrote an article for the *Great Soviet Encyclopedia* in 1934.

after their long hovering in the air; it looks as if the gravity of the Earth does not have any power over these paintings, so large and light are they. ... Even houses and rooms are tied to the ground only with their lacquer."

Tériade,[6] the author of a famous study of Chagall's illustrations to La Fontaine's fables, also considers Chagall special treatment of gravity:

> [T]he unreality of such balance and the universe which maintains this kind of balance allows Chagall to offer us a poetic reality which can no longer be reduced only to phenomena. ... There are even no dimensions anymore ... there is only an unsurpassable lightness and ignorance regarding gravitation and the vertical. And yet his forms are plastic.

II. THEMATIC ANALYSIS

1. Themes in Chagall's work

Chagall's themes can be subdivided into groups according to two principles. On the one hand, there are everyday situations and events which disrupt daily monotony—birth, marriage, and death. The latter three enclose and frame all other life events with their tragic monotony.

On the other hand, situations can be divided according to certain thematic circles. Each thematic circle brings out the principal motif in Chagall's work—both the tragic and the wonderfully comic nature of our movements.

a) The Theme of Houses

In part, this is the motif of a single house or a group of houses, or houses which combine with the masses of human and animal bodies.

Each thing plays the role of showing the rhythm of events. Façade, the physiognomy of houses, becomes an expression of the rhythm of life for people who live in the compressed space of houses.

Ephros believed that "'national art' could truly exist ... artistic form is able to become the deepest expression of folk nature." See A. M. Ephros, *Profili: Ocherki o russkikh khudozhnikakh*, with an introduction by S. M. Daniel (Azbuka-klassika: SPb, 2007; reprint of the 1930 edition), 46. He noted the deep influence of the spiritual and cultural foundations of Jewish life on Chagall's work.

6   Tériade (Efstratios Eleftheriades) was an art critic, publisher, collector, and a friend of Marc Chagall.

This philosophy is evident in Munch's,[7] Vlaminck's,[8] and Utrillo's styles.[9] A comparison between Chagall's and Utrillo's formal composition will show the difference between the two worldviews. Utrillo's people live in dirty-pink and green whitewashed suburban houses. Like planets, these people circulate with quiet resignation among things and occupations. They carry inside the cheap sadness of hearts etched out on the back walls of suburban houses.

Instead of the quiet sweetness of resignation, musty suffering and the sadness of events appears in Chagall's work; instead of stasis and lyricism, there is the dynamism of life's tragic nature. The difference between the two artists is evident in their use of line. Utrillo employs a straight, quietly drawn, static contour line, while Chagall's line is an uneven, broken, and indecisive-schematic contour which abolishes the conventional balance of vertical and horizontal strokes and serves as a sign that movement in a straightforward direction is interrupted in the middle. All the tension which could be spread out on a bigger surface now gathers in one place— the tension of oppressive suffering which cannot be broken up or developed harmoniously.

The method of reducing the forms of houses and dematerializing them shows life's playfulness: anything is possible.

b) The Theme of Animals

In Chagall's treatment of the animal motif, we find the same conception: anything is possible.

Cattle live with people; they participate in human experience, and even take on a role different from the previously given one. In the *Small Birth* painting, a cow enters a house alongside guests, a pig eats together with a family; the face of a woman becomes similar to a pig's head, and both of them eat from one trough; a horse has the wily face of a human being; a calf—the face of a woman; while people besides these animals have impersonal and dull—one could even say—foolish faces.

---

7   Edvard Munch (1863–1944) was a Norwegian artist, graphic artist, and theoretician, famous for his painting *The Scream* (1893–1910) which became an emblem of Expressionism.
8   Maurice de Vlaminck (1876–1958) was a French artist, the founder of Expressionism among the Fauvists.
9   Maurice Utrillo (1883–1955) was a French painter, most notable as a master of urban landscape. See Vogel's poem "Suburban Houses" for which Utrillo's painting of the same name might have served as an inspiration.

In another comparison to artists who have also dealt with the animal motif, F. Mark[10] brought out the ornamental fantastic of animal bodies and their groupings: flattened bodies drawn in precise lines—mostly zigzag—are grouped according to the principle of symmetry, obtaining the look of ornamental surfaces.

In Emi Roeder's work,[11] the bulging ornament of a gesture originates in the delicate juxtaposition between two animal bodies which become lines meeting at a right, somewhat rounded, angle. Both artists used the animal motif because of its formal values and arrived at ornament as the artistic solution.

Chagall's animal masses do not simply decoratively fill the surface of the canvass. The literary theme of the proximity between the animal and the human sharing a similar fate is significant here; it was expressed by means of the artistic values of contrast or similarity.

The blurring of the line between creatures is the result of the perception that everything is possible and can pass into its opposite. The change of roles between a human and animal can be understood precisely in this way.

Only when everything is possible, can one blur masses and mix various creatures.

From this mixture of creaturely experiences originates licentiousness and the somewhat dirty suffering. The choice of animals is also symptomatic. Artists like F. Mark and E. Roeder and others prefer animals with associations of purity and mass—a horse, a deer, a tiger, and a cat. Yet in Chagall's work, animals—the cow, the goat, and the pig—are dirty, heavy, and vulgar without measure. [Perhaps a perception similar to the artist's resulted in the deification of the sacred heaviness of the calf in ancient Egypt.] A preference for unclean, disproportionate animals is also a result of the view that everything is possible, and anything may happen.

---

10 Franz Mark (1880–1916) was the representative of German Expressionism. Along with Wassily Kandinsky, he was one of the principal organizers of the artistic group "Blue Rider." Mark's paintings that include animal themes are: *Landscape with Horses*, 1910; *Blue Horse*, 1911; *Big Red Horses*, 1911; *Big Blue Horses*, 1911; *Horses Rest*, 1911/12; *From the Legend about Animals*, 1912; *The Tiger*, 1912; *The Tower of Blue Horses*, 1913; *Birth of the Wolves*, 1913; *Fate of the Animals*, 1913; *Foxes*, 1913; and others.

11 Emi Roeder (1890–1971) was a German Jewish Expressionist sculptor and artist. Her works were exhibited at the infamous *Degenerate Art Exhibition* that the Nazis organized in 1937 in Munich. After this exhibition the traces of her work and that of other artists vanished into Joseph Goebbels' Ministry of Propaganda. Roeder's works were found on a building site in Berlin in 2010.

Tugenhold turns his attention to the "dull eroticism" of Chagall's animals. He designates them with the categories of "sentimentality and tenderness," and terms like "sodomite"—"tender sentimental animals like a gazelle, or vice versa, those with the animal muzzles like a pig's head, and the heads of cows and calves which stick out from Chagall's interiors—symbols of sinful desire."

c) *The Human Figure*

The human figure receives a similar thematic treatment. The playfulness of the human being, a marionette in the hands of events, is represented through the dematerialization of its mass.

This dematerialization arises from freeing the body from any mass and heaviness, and also through an unnatural combination or severance of separate body parts and limbs, and the preferred method of enlargement or reduction of mass.

Everything becomes clear when conventional mass is taken off things, and everything can pass into its opposite. This freeing of human figures from heaviness is an example of the blurring of the boundaries between the significant and insignificant. And this is an example of when one no longer makes use of the symbolism of events or experiences, but exhibits the literal process of abolishing heaviness; the categories of significance and insignificance represent change and the reworking of the basic category of heaviness and lightness; they are symbols of these categories and of their application in the greater number of juxtaposed and complex events.

Compositions with figures over rooftops or at the height of the floor; lovers who hover in the air with strange, mad, and wry faces; children who move from floating in the air to their mother's embraces; figures with their duplicates besides them.

In the composition with lovers who float in space with lightness, there is something of the literary concept of that love which overcomes any oppression and obstacles in life. However, this content is unimportant. You can ignore it. From the point of view of a purely artistic perspective, the masses of people can be represented by very different volumes of mass, and the artistic content itself will stay the same. This content consists of the contrast between heaviness and the lightness; between the horizontal line (the cityscape) and the vertical (the human figures). This contrast is an example—and a simple one at that, not a symbolic one—of the transition from significant to insignificant, from the heaviness of human events into playful lightness—the playful possibility of everything.

The human figure in its coexistence with furniture and objects, with inanimate and foreign things, as well as the indifferent bodies which to an extent mean nothing more to us than living things, receives a different role. We are speaking of Chagall's interiors.

d) Interiors

There is no fitting designation for the compositions of rooms without ceilings. A fragment could be cut out from exterior scenes and fit into the frame of the canvas—it would be considered an interior rather than a street scene.

In such interiors in the larger sense, human figures receive very strange treatment. They don't have individual facial expressions, rather they are schematically general, indeterminate. Angular, these figures appear not as individuals with their own fate, and not even as types, but only as marionettes building and arranging their movements and gestures into an event—they must do everything they do. The rhythm of the event itself is important.

Besides rhythm, one may also observe deferred movement along the length with a zigzag line on the side; the collapse into a point, which is a response to the tendency of movement—and its superfluous nature. Life's grotesquerie, the next stage in the development of the concept of playfulness, is represented here in a piecemeal fashion.

However, the tragicomic nature of our life is hard to bear. One needs to find a way out. There is only one possibility here—acknowledgment of everything. This stance demands a certain attitude to life: one needs to find or even introduce wonder and sweet fullness into every comic and insignificant event.

Repeated in many of Chagall's compositions, the figure which provides an acknowledgement of everything in life is the klezmer.

e) The Klezmer

The klezmer is a figure which makes concrete the sweet melodiousness contained in the monotony of comically insignificant and repeatable events. This figure is simultaneously a witness to all events in the shtetl, as if in every event there is some colorfulness and fullness.

The klezmer observes everything, but not entirely in a passive way. He plays everywhere: at a wedding and a funeral; and also accompanies the simple work of a water carrier.

Perhaps there is a literary concept at work here—obtaining a positive outlook towards life through the figure of a playing musician. Symbolism which is too straightforward is necessary to recall the literary conception's significance, and, thus, may harm the purely painterly element.

However, the background of the composition abolishes the literary nature of the klezmer figure. The background controls the action in the foreground, which is comprised of insignificant events.

Only at times a musician appears as a figure in the foreground, with toy-like small houses in the background. In this case, the klezmer is an example of the reversal of values. Everything is represented as playful and insignificant in comparison to one thing—the person who plays music in the distance. Almost at the same time, the significance of the musician is also abolished by a second musician, a smaller copy of the one in the foreground who always accompanies important figures.

This diminution and duplication of figures has an artistic rationale: to take all the weight away from the first figure as the one less significant—the principle of that play which abolishes significance and turns everything into its opposite.

f) Theme in Its Essence

The theme of the fantastic comic nature of things appears without mediation once due to various represented events. These events are a disguise for the fundamental event—a mask taken seriously. However, it seems that sometimes people hide and play a role imposed on them; and so they play themselves, appearing in their own naked and unretouched form. Comedians act out the truth of human life—the truth contained in all our gestures yet retouched and buried under intellectual interpretations.

Here I have in mind Chagall's wall decorations for the Moscow Jewish Theater: the clowns in tallises, musicians with clowns' mannerisms, dancers with awkward legs and elongated bodies, dressed in striped and flowery velvet robes.

The heaviness and ugliness of the people's faces and looks negates the melodious lightness of the dance—it brings out the sad comic nature of the gestures which we all execute in such a way as if they were extremely important, while they are only tragicomic like the learned gestures of the clown.

This comic nature is retouched in life.

2. Form

Through the analysis of content, we arrive at the same formula that the analysis of the form yielded—the formula of the tragicomic playfulness of life.

This principal mood finds appropriate themes and form for itself. The artistic method of showing such playfulness consists in the fact that the inherent face of human events is worked out; this process makes things clear, which leads us to the border where the reality falls apart, and significance is transformed into its opposite, into playfulness.

On this border the sad comic nature of our movements from one thing to another is distinguished quite clearly.

3. Remarks

This study is an attempt at aesthetic appraisal conducted according to a specific principle. Progress and its formula demand the distillation and formulation of the reality which the artist represented with formal means, as far as he showed it with the help of artistic elements.

Therefore, it is not important whether the critical process of cognition only reproduces the formal method, or, in other words, whether the artist had the same thought process as the critic.

The artist considered the totality of reality including form, even though he thus surrendered the foundation to the work of the critic. The artist provides the critic with the substance and the material of reality similar to the way concrete things and events provide the artist with material.

The material of Chagall's work became the substance for executing a programmatic assertion, perhaps all the more appropriate since it is easy to distinguish between theme and form, the literary and the painterly, even though both principles are only two names for totality. Thus, it was easier to show that content and form are only two names for one thing, and that the sole artistic content lies in the form combination.

However, our discussion of Chagall moved into other dimensions. We have considered the artist from a literary point of view, even as we provided an analysis of the painterly side of his creativity. There is even difference of opinion here: we have considered Chagall as a poet, on the one hand, and as an intellectual, on the other. Wit writes: "Chagall's art cannot defy classification in terms of artistic composition, according to the instinctive necessity of form. ... Even though his art leads to problems of form, since it contains purely formal values, which are not controlled by intellect ... purely formal values are on two planes; they are not determined by the empty surface of the canvas, but by theme. Through content, Chagall is a poet and a storyteller ..."

K. Shwartz continues: "Chagall does not depict spiritual events, he depicts intellectual processes. In his work, the dynamic of expressionism becomes an internal dualism. The tendency towards gesture and ecstasy disintegrates into ambiguous analyses. Thus, he doesn't manage to delve deep into psychic processes in a convincing way. This is due to an intellectualism which went too far" ("The Jews in Art").

Rozanoff,[12] Karpfen,[13] Ephros, and Tugenhold also use literary categories in their criticism pertaining Chagall's work. In their analyses, they use superlatives, yet there is no recognition of the artist's merit when one considers him solely on the level of content; while the form—one's own creation—seeps into such criticism and surrenders painterly reality.

---

12   Vasily Rozanov (1856–1919) was a Russian art critic preoccupied with Jewish themes; he also made controversial statements on the subject.
13   Fritz Karpfen (1875–1942) was an Austrian writer, art critic, and feuilletonist. Together with Alfred Barr, Max Eastman, René Fülöp-Miller, and Louis Lozowick, Karpfen played a significant role in popularizing Soviet culture in the West, especially in the immediate post-Revolutionary years. He published a few volumes of his work as *Gegenwartskunst* (Vienna: Literaria, 1921–1923). The first volume was dedicated to Soviet Russia, the second to Austria, and the third to Scandinavian countries. He also wrote a work about art and kitsch. This topic was of interest to Vogel.

8

The Genealogy of Photomontage and its Possibilities (1934)[1]

> Montage is the contemporary epic.
> —M[ieczysław] Szczuka, *Blok*, 1924[2]

1. DEFINITION

The notion of "photomontage" originated in 1924–1925 to designate a new artistic movement which presented different "cut-outs from life" on a single background surface. These fragments are either photo stills assembled specifically for the purpose of montage (in Citroen's work),[3] or ready-mades used in a particular manner. Gradually, the photographic element was combined with elements of painting, facture, or form.

As a matter of fact, photomontage existed long before it was given a name and a definition. M[ieczysław] Szczuka provided one of the first definitions: "photomontage is a phenomenon of the mutual intermingling of the most diverse phenomena in the universe."[4]

Photomontage has a greater significance than might seem at first sight when we consider the seemingly playful combinatory work which forges a totality from newspaper clippings. Photomontage is a **symptom of the realist tendency** in art.[5] It had to go through various stages to reach its current one, just like any artistic form.

---

1 See Debora Vogel, "Genealogia fotomontazu i jego możliwości," *Sygnały*, no. 12 (1934): 9; no. 13 (1934): 9.
2 Mieczysław Szczuka, "Photomontage," *Blok*, no. 8–9 (1924): 108.
3 Paul Citroen (1896–1983) was a Dutch artist. His most famous work is the photomontage *Metropolis* (1923), which inspired Fritz Lang's film with the same title.
4 Mieczysław Szczuka (1898–1927) was a Polish Constructivist artist and the founder of the *Blok* journal.
5 All the statements in bold are present in the typography of the original article.

2. THE GENEALOGY OF MONTAGE

Artistic styles are not immediately perfect examples of the realization of an idea. They often appear as inconsistent, indeterminate textures mixed with other tendencies. The Cubism in Cezanne's Impressionism or the unnoticed geometrism in Seurat's[6] Pointillism[7] are classic examples.

We could trace the origins of photomontage to Cubism—in Picasso's, but especially in Braques'[8] and Marcussi's,[9] work. Compositions with newspaper clippings, labels on rum bottles or cigarette packs, which are often glued to the surfaces along with objects of a different order are examples of this technique. Likewise, the *papier collé* stage of Picasso's work, with clippings of paper attached to the painting, exhibits similar tendencies. In all these varieties, one may trace the idea of montage—with elements of heterogeneity and of daily street life—the tendency to show the reality of banal matters. Moreover, this idea does not diverge from Cubism, which represents, despite the worn label of "abstract art," a tendency towards concreteness, to the matter-of-factness in things framed within the bounds of a contour.

The principle of montage composition can be traced in every artistic movement. Szczuka's photomontage is based on the principle of balanced contrasts in **Constructivism**, which results in the machine-like, compressed, closed—as if in a constant vortex—rhythm of totality. The artistic principle of **simultaneity** put forward by **Delaunay**[10] is also present here. On the other hand, the principle of photomontage, and its characteristic worldview, finds expression in the seemingly exclusive formal principle of simultaneity.

In its literal meaning, photomontage appears equivalent to a worldview based on the concept of epic simultaneity which acknowledges the "objective" nature of the heterogenous facts in life.

There is also Citroen's "matter-of-fact" montage.

Another movement finds itself between Constructivism and contemporary photomontage. The 1924 program of Surrealism[11] contains the formula of

---

6   George Seurat (1859–1891) was the founder of Pointillism.
7   Pointillism (Divisionism, Neoimpressionism) was an art movement at the end of the nineteenth century. Its features include using points, unmixed colors and geometrical rhythmical composition.
8   George Braques (1882–1963) was a co-founder of Cubism. His work is characterized by a continuation of Cezanne's ideas, such as multiple perspectives, and an interest in geometry and decorativeness.
9   Louis Marcussi (1878–1941) was a French graphic artist and Cubist.
10 Robert Delaunay (1885–1941) was a French artist and the founder of Orphism.
11 The first Surrealist manifesto was was published in 1924. See André Breton, *Manifeste du surréalisme* (Paris: Éditions du Sagittaire, 1924).

"combining real elements into an unreal totality"—a montage of facts that do not belong together. The foundational assumption is that only this kind of montage yields factual reality. The term "unreal" used in relation to this reality and type of composition shows that it is not the construction of something which bypasses life, but, rather, the **subjective** "inner" reality of associations which may order the world for us. In the principle of subjective associations lies the difference in attitude towards the **objective, matter-of-fact order of things** which montage assumes by definition. The lyricism of Surrealism is replaced by the epic nature of photomontage.

There is a difference within montage: on the one hand, there is the "eternally relevant" element which originates in the consumerist attitude towards life in Surrealist montage; on the other hand, there is the social element which dominates in photomontage and transitions into proletarian reportage, as in Szczuka's graphic illustration to Stern's poem "Europe."[12]

The "Second Manifesto of Surrealism," published in 1930 by **A[ndré] Breton**,[13] affirmed that Surrealism was also a symptom of the tendency toward matter-of-factness and realism. In it, we read the following: "It is absolutely essential for us to act as though we are really 'part of the world,' in order thereafter to dare formulate certain reservations" (page 23).[14] The manifesto mentions Hegel on the matter of relating morality to the sphere of social life. There are also references to materialist dialectics in the example of a rose, "to lure 'the rose' into a movement ... where it is, successively, the rose that comes from the garden, the one that has an unusual place in a dream, the one impossible to remove from the 'optical bouquet,' ... the one that retains only those qualities that the painter has deigned to keep in a Surrealist painting, and, finally, the one, completely different from itself, which returns to the garden" (page 27).[15]

This description of the evolution of matter emphasizes that Surrealism is not a movement outside society. Rather, it is a movement which agrees with the revolutionary nature in the social dimension. This is sufficient proof that Surrealism is only one possibility, a certain concept of the concrete nature of matter; the concrete nature of social life is relevant only in one of its modifications.

---

12 See Anatol Stern, *Europa*, trans. Stefan Themerson and Michael Horovitz (London: Gaberbocchus, 1962).
13 See *Second manifeste du surréalisme* (Paris: Éditions Kra, 1930).
14 André Breton, *The Manifestoes of Surrealism*, trans. Richard Seaver and Helen R. Lance (Ann Arbor: University of Michigan Press, 1969), 137–138.
15 Ibid., 141.

All this attests that montage passed through certain stages until it started to reflect its definition.

3. A CONTEMPORARY LEGEND

We need to understand the tendencies elevated to the level of the singularly important, those which require socialization, through the **legend** of a certain era. Due to their raw nature for life use, these tendencies introduce some tension, hence their emotional quality.

"**Fact**" is the contemporary legend. Contemporary photomontage needs to become the equivalent of the literary genre of reportage and factual montage.

A question arises in art: Which facts are important? Notably, the seemingly complex "facts" which take up a large surface of life may turn out to be pointless for life itself, and also for form as a result, even if that fact is that a person is shot.

Another question is in order: Is there such a thing as a pure fact? Perhaps it is no coincidence that an individual fact—and even more so the selection of facts or their juxtaposition—suggest interpretation of the raw block of life, and, thus, perhaps there are no "pure facts"?

To deal with accidental material in illustrated journals and reproductions is not sufficient. These newspaper clippings are kitschy and shoddy; they are uncouth in their naïve, situational Naturalism. To believe that this is the way to capture "authentic life" is ill advised. We also need to question the statement that facts become authentic only in conceptualization—in a certain interpretation of the raw material of life. Only the principle of the "likeness of reality" makes from the reality of life a reality.

Mieczysław Szczuka's concept of photomontage as "contemporary epic," the "synchronicity of the multiplicity in space," is closest to contemporary tendencies (*Blok*, 1924). Montage on proletarian themes has the greatest chance to represent contemporary tendencies. This type of montage is most fitting for the photographic element of photography which envisions things "in a matter-of-fact way," as unambiguous, sharp, and one-dimensional.

The raw material of montage does not need to have been discovered by accident or come from photography. Montage where an element was created by the painter—in a way "as if" it were photography cut out from newspaper illustrations—generates true art (graphic work on revolutionary themes represents this type of montage).

4. EXPLANATIONS OF MONTAGE ARTWORKS

(a) Max Ernst, *Les malheures des immortels*, Paris, 1922.

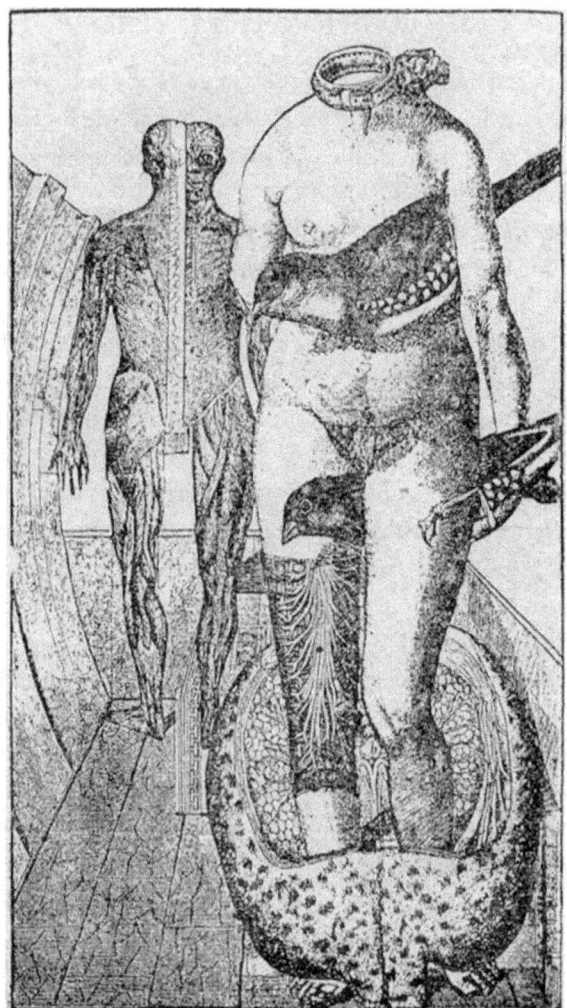

Figure 5. Max Ernst, *Les malheures des immortels*, 1922. [In: "Genealogy of photomontage 1"]

This is a Surrealist montage. The brutal, real elements of the fleshy female body and the naked muscles of the male body are divided by the line of the spinal cord into right and left parts, and at the same time—into front and back halves. The iron ring around the headless neck of the woman is accessorized with an intricate bow. In their totality, the birds and the turtle's shell create an unreal reality possible in associative realism. The material is painterly, not photographic, yet it is stylized in a way as if it were glued onto the surface. There is a tension of the strangeness of coexistence.

(b) Aleksander Krzywobłocki, *Photomontage*, Lviv, 1933.

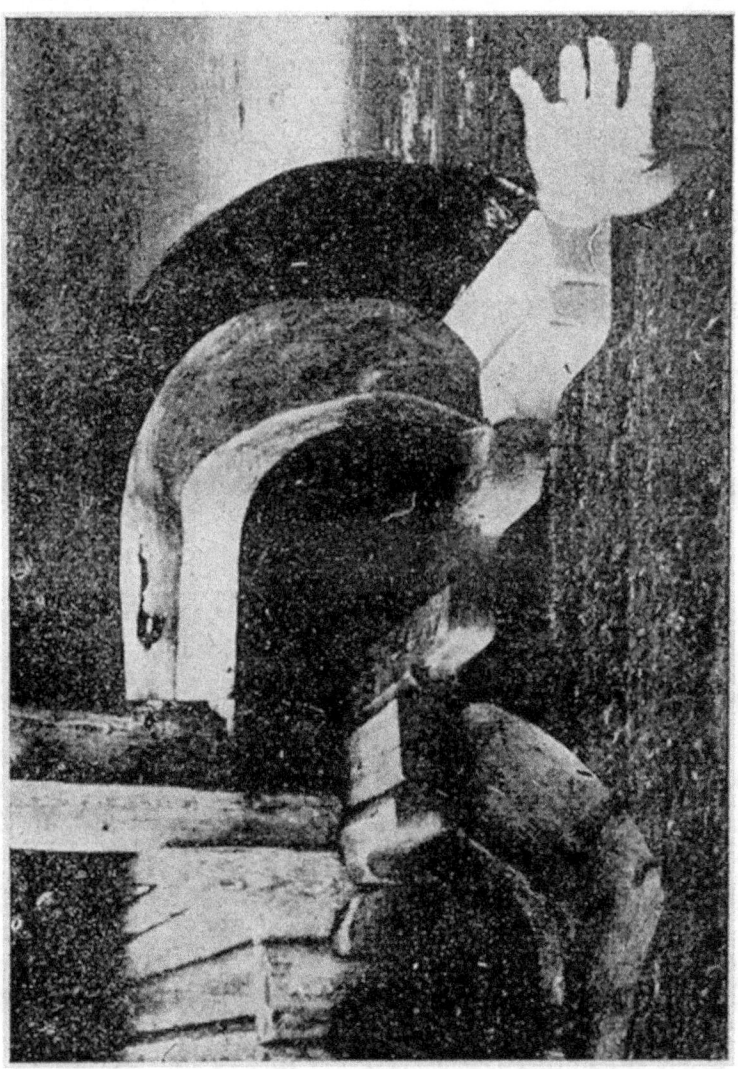

Figure 6. Aleksander Krzywoblocki, *Photomontage*, 1933. [In: "Genealogy of photomontage 1"]

This is a combination of photography of the authentic architectonic fragment which—as it seems—is organically introduced and completed with a human hand. The motif of the human hand which finishes the architectonic fragment of the column or protrudes from the wall is very common in Krzywobłocki's work; it represents the Surrealist element. At the same time, this is a Constructivist element, since it is used from the viewpoint of the mutual relationship of forms, their relatedness regardless of their distance from the sphere where they originate. As a result, a small number of combined elements and their type create a painterly impression. Likewise, Krzywobłocki creates an interesting montage of geometrical forms based on Constructivist principles. However, as an architect, he has a predisposition towards the architectonic element and a wonderful sense of its materiality.

c) Jerzy Janisch, *Photomontage*, Lviv, 1933.

Figure 7. Jerzy Janisch. *Photomontage*, 1933. [In: "Genealogy of photomontage 1"]

The Constructivist juxtaposition of the body and machine **with an emphasis on the relatedness of the two organisms**: the life of the machine visualized in a spinning circle has its equivalent in the circular organic forms in the open dissection of the human body. Both organisms are reduced to the meaning of machine. Hence, the Constructivist theme of formal analogy—the body like a machine. Furthermore, there is a Surrealist irony in using the blind sculpture (*Venus de Milo*) to represent the female body. The textural element of the bookbinding paper was also utilized.

d) Margit Sielska, *Montage*, Lviv, 1934.

Figure 8. Margit Sielska, *Montage*, 1934. [In: "Genealogy of photomontage 1"]

This montage is very painterly: it consists of a painted segment, gray forms (the ship), and colorful photographic forms. The selection of the various materials, the facture of the paper, and the use of textiles to express the contemporary tendency towards apotheosis of material—the texture of materials. At the same time, this conception recalls Cubist images and sculptures made from pieces of different materials and included in the painterly segments.

e) Otto Hahn, *Photomontage*, 1933.

Figure 9. Otto Hahn, *Photomontage*, 1933. [In: "Genealogy of photomontage 2"]

This Surrealist montage makes use of relevant elements like the fragments of a floating human figure, a part of a ship, and facture. The rhythm of smooth movement enclosed in figures—ordered fragments: a half-circle transforms into the compact static rhythm of the movement of swaying people. **The mutual**

continuation of forms is also a Constructivist idea understood not as a balance of contrasts but as the continuity of different forms, circular-fluid and angular. There is also the opposite mood here—the matter-of-fact and real rhythm of people at work transforms into the ill-defined rhythm of unreal figures. This is an external associative reality; its content and theme is belonging and connections between various forms and rhythms.

f) Henryk Streng, *Graphic montage*, 1933.

Figure 10. Henryk Streng (Marek Włodarski), *Graphic Montage*, 1933. [In: "Genealogy of photomontage 2"]

This is a post-Surrealist montage—the expression of a new concept of realism. A combination of abstract and wavy forms—almost baroque in their inert nature, which emphasizes the texture of matter, its corporeality, and the lack of outlines on the one hand, and on the other, a realistic human figure, copied and duplicated, needs to uncover the hard matter-of-factness of this figure and its angular literal gestures. Here the matter-of-factness of gestures is also underlined with the additional montage of shoulders near elbows so that they appear as stiff elements foreign to the structure, attached to the element of the body, elastic until the elbows. In this method, the older element of Constructivism is expressed—an immobility of sorts, the machinic automatism of the human figure. This moment was present in Streng's work in his Constructivist stage, and its lyrical element, the hopelessness of the human figure and its gestures, was retained in the artist's new realist stage.

9

On Abstract Art (1934)[1]

Art which makes use of geometrical elements is often called "abstract." Any evidence or assertions that, in fact, it is a tragic search for a concrete and secure foothold in a threatening and infinite space which leads to so-called abstract art are futile.

We will not consider whether this style is only a transitional stage in history, whether all the possibilities for the geometric style have been exhausted, or whether its continuation is at all possible. Yet it should be emphasized that abstract art is a product of the dialectic of form—the stage which art would have reached sooner or later. Abstract art is a logical result of how art has previously dealt with the question of balance. Abstraction also arises out of the whole constellation of contemporaneity. This latest and final stage of art provides simple and straightforward formulations of that which art has always offered in a concealed form. Paradoxically, the world of objects was art's smokescreen. With its inherent content, this world created a certain form of balance.

And once we enter the world of abstract art, we step into an unambiguous world without a mask, into the authentic world of the most important feelings in life. This world is revealed in a straightforward way—and perhaps it irritates at first glance—because it appears to be so difficult! We move in the world of things, where the categories of movement or immobility, the type and direction of movement, the weight, rhythms, and tensions, and even numbers and their rhythm, become concrete. These abstractions (in conventional understanding and perception) were treated here as if they were things accessible via the sense of touch and through visual impressions, as if they were bodies, landscapes, fruit, or flowers.

There are two main stages in abstract art. In the first stage, things are broken down into complexes of tensions and directions (in Cubism, Constructivism, and Purism). In the second stage, these tensions and directions of masses in movement become actual things which one takes into account, while

---

1   See Debora Vogel, "O sztuce abstrakcyjnej," *Wiadomości Literackie*, no. 25 (1934): 6.

naturalistic things and life-content are no longer considered. This was the case in Suprematism, with its black contour of the facture on the white surface. This is also the case in Unism—the most recent theory in abstract art which originated in Poland.

Unism currently finds its continuation and development in the artists of the Cracow group[2] and the Group of the Living.[3]

Yet there are traceable influences of other movements in Unism— [Fernand] Léger's Constructivism (in J[onasz]' Stern's work, for instance), or [Amédée] Ozenfant's[4] and [Charles-Édouard] Jeanneret's[5] Purism (in [Leopold] Lewicki's[6] *Bottles*). It is not self-evident that the Cracow group mechanically utilizes the guidelines of Unism or mimics compositions by [Władysław] Strzemiński and [Henryk] Stażewski,[7] two theoreticians of Unism. Rather, the artists find the formal guidelines of Unism independently of one another based on the dialectic of form. This conception corresponds to the Zeitgeist and the contemporary constellation. The original execution of guidelines, a certain passion and lyricism, and authentic feeling, all of which cannot be merely reproduced or forged, attests to the fact that the work of these artists is not simply an imitation. However, these works may be considered exemplary for Unism.

The theory of Unism was formulated by Strzemiński. We shall learn about its established guidelines to better understand its representative works.

The notion of "Unism" designates the unity of artistic forms and space— the unity of sculpture and space or the merging of forms of painting with the rectangular surface of the canvas. Space does not exist so that the foreign bodies

---

2   The Cracow group was founded by Leopold Lewicki, Stanisław Osostowicz, and Franciszek Jazwecki. The group's first exhibition was on November 13, 1932 in the building of the Professional Union of Polish Artists. The first exhibition of the group in Lviv was in October 1933, and featured Franciszek Jazwecki, Leopold Lewicki, Sasha Blonder, Maria Jarema, Stanisław Osostowicz, Alexander Winnicki, Berta Grunberg, Jonasz Stern, Zygmunt Gonsiorowski, Adam Maczynski, Henryk Wiciński, and Bolesław Stawiński.

3   The group of students of the Cracow Academy of the Arts called The Living was established in 1931. In their work, they combined formalism and sociopolitical engagement.

4   Amédée Ozenfant (1886- 1966) was a French artist, theoretician of post-Cubism, and founder of Purism in art.

5   The given name of Le Corbusier (1887–1965), a French architect, pioneer of Modernism in architecture, and a representative of the International Style.

6   Leopold Lewicki (1906–1973) was a Polish artist, illustrator, graphic artist, and member of the Cracow group. He lived in Lviv for a significant part of his life.

7   Henryk Stażewski (1894–1988) was a Polish artist, the representative of Constructivism in painting. He exhibited his works in 1921 together with Mieczysław Szczuka who is mentioned in Vogel's essay on photomontage.

of painted or chiseled forms can be inserted into it. Rather, space is material which demands and passionately longs for form with its menacing emptiness, which is unbearable if left unshaped. An artwork is, thus, an extension of space—formulated, composed, and shaped in a specific way.

"Every square inch has the same value in the composition of a painting. The primary properties of a picture—the quadrangle of its frame—are not only areas where forms which originated independently from these properties can be fitted. ... Rather, they are components of the image, perhaps the most important ones," says Strzemiński.[8]

Where does this postulate of the unity of space and artwork originate? And what does this theory have in common with the nature of art? Unism grants art a specific role and purpose—it becomes an answer to our urgent need for balance and boundaries in space. Space itself becomes the material which yearns for forms.

If we grasp these principles and their consequences, we will no longer be astonished when we encounter the rectangular surface of a canvas divided into smaller surfaces with shared contours, filled with diverse factures of many colors or a single color, or simply a monochrome facture, presented to us as an artwork. And neither will we be astounded at sculpture consisting of certain rectangular surfaces connected at right angles, like Katarzyna Kobro's sculpture.

We shall consider most works by the "leftist faction" of the Cracow group in this way. There are no conventional themes, including "interiors", "still lifes," or "landscapes." If there are any landscapes or still-lifes after all, they shall be understood metaphorically—as landscapes which solely consist of tensions and directions and result in an incomprehensible mood of stasis! The titles themselves are symptomatic: *Dynamic Directions*, *Interconnected and Adjacent Surfaces*, and *Facture Composition*.

At times these titles sound like mathematical tasks, and the paintings appear to illustrate an abstract problematic. In the series of paintings entitled *From Object to Surface*, an object has been divided into its surface components—a demonstration that these are intrinsic elements in a construction (Stern, [Alexander] Winnicki).[9] This is also the case when [Sasha] Blonder[10]

---

8   See Władysław Strzemiński, *Unizm w malarstwie* [Unism in painting] (Warszawa: Biblioteka Praesens, 1928).
9   Alexander Winnicki (1911–2002) was an artist and member of the first Cracow group.
10 Sasha Blonder (1909–1949) was a painter and graphic artist. His two main exhibitions in interwar Lviv took place in 1933 and 1936.

illustrates a transition "from standstill to movement," or offers an "analysis of circular motion."

These works seem to be too programmatic at times, as if they are programmatic illustrations of abstract questions in painting. Perhaps it can be blamed on a peculiar state of intoxication upon discovery of the fullness of a world of cool tensions and directions, and moments when boundaries are blurred between the conceptual formulation of cognition and plastic form itself.

Other compositions have more obvious origins in experience rather than in the program. Different juxtapositions and combinations of types of dynamism in Lewicki's *Composition,* or in his *Dynamic Directions,* result in saturated static ambiance. Consider also Blonder's programmatic composition *Analysis of Circular Motion,* where a similar mood of stasis is induced by a plastic configuration of the life of a circular line—a line which is everywhere identical and eventually immobile in its essence. Paintings like Lewicki's *Facture Composition,* or *Form Combinations,* or Winnicki's *System,* a subtly lyrical work, are undoubtedly exemplary for Unism.

Yet it should be noted that despite thematic similarities, despite the fact that the same motif is often utilized by a few painters, individual differences are distinct nevertheless: from the arithmetical vein in Stern's and Blonder's work to Lewicki's heroism and the deep melodious lyricism of Winnicki!

There is a need for a couple more remarks. Among the group members who make "subject paintings," we need to mention specifically [Stanisław] Osostowicz.[11] For Osostowicz, human figures are only a pretext to distribute the concentration of facture on a canvas divided into areas. Facture—stuffy, dense, coarse grained, dark red, and black—works on its own. It creates the mood of the stuffy and terse tension of immobility into which the gloomy houses and people on a stroll are submerged.

The unique sculpture by [Henryk] Wiciński[12] and Maria Jarema[13] comes close to Unism, since sculpture is thought as the shaping of space rather than block; they are, however, overly enriched with the life element, with more abundance of situations than Unist sculpture.

---

11 Stanisław Osostowicz (1906–1939) was a Polish painter and the author of many collages, advertisement graphics, and caricatures.
12 Henryk Wiciński (1908–1943) was a Polish sculptor; he created a concept of space forms which he called "the sculpture of perception."
13 Maria Jarema (1908–1958) was a Polish artist, sculptor, and scenographer. She worked with the experimental theater Cricot. With others, she formed the second Cracow group in 1957.

Finally, we need to reiterate the main point. Abstract artworks belong to a dimension which is different from finding joy in the similarities between objects known from life and their reproduction in paintings. On the one hand, emotions in such artworks are informed by the intellectual sensibility which triggers the deployment of the crystal-pure material of concepts; on the other hand, these artworks come close to works of music and their intensive, saturated, and authentic content which cannot be easily defined by the categories of life.

10

Henryk Streng, a Constructivist Painter (1937)[1]

Légerism—with its program of the stasis and balance of diverse life elements—was Streng's[2] point of departure. While comparing Léger's and Streng's Constructivist styles, we may come to the following conclusion: Léger's epic treatment of material gives way to Streng's lyrical method. Léger's epic arises from his treatment of equilibrium as the intrinsic content, from the method of objectifying this experience, detaching it from its source—to search retrospectively for exemplifications for the cosmic state of balance and stasis. When the experience of stasis becomes content in a complex of contrasting forms and things, it is only a secondary experience. And perhaps this derivativeness creates an impression of certain playfulness in Léger's work, for instance, in the assemblages of human heads severed from the rest of the body which are juxtaposed with keys in different positions.

For Streng, such positioning of experience inside things does not lead to a definitive break with the lyricism of this experience. The egotistical dynamism of experience is replaced with singularly objective, individualized cross sections of human life.

This difference becomes strongly visible in the treatment of the human figure. For Léger, the canvas surface is homogeneously filled with colorful rhythm and machine vibration, combined with the machine-like human body, seemingly subjected to this machinic rhythm—the body in balance regarded as a machine triumphs here. For Streng, the body is also broken down into such geometrical elements as a cylinder, cone, and various oval forms; and yet it ultimately fulfills the utmost sense of the geometrical figure and machine tempo—powerlessness and resignation. Helpless golems painted on signs in decaying

---

1 See Debora Vogel, "Henryk Streng—malarz konstruktywizmu," *Nasza Opinja*, no. 96 (1937): 6.
2 Henryk Streng (Marek Włodarski) (1903–1960) was a Constructivist artist, who used elements of Cubism, especially Légerism in his work, as well as Surrealism. He was the illustrator of Vogel's collections and a prominent member of the Artes group.

city quarters cling to the windows, gramophones, and bicycles, as if these were the last things granted to them life. They are tragically intertwined with banality. This mannequin-like quality of people constitutes Streng's Constructivism; it also becomes the fundamental tone in two subsequent stages in his painting.

The following painting is fresh in memory from the first stage of Streng's work—a head with a helpless smile and two round and smooth plums of eyes. Beside the head there are three stylized plums, steel blue, clearly outlined, and wise, like the eyes nearby. In this composition and in others, the "intellectual" principle of balanced contrasts becomes a worldview, according to which the boundary between the people and matter is eliminated, and the person becomes a mannequin, subject to the inevitable rule of life.

In his second stage, Streng worked in the style of Surrealism, and encountered one of the modifications of its form—the "plant" Surrealism of A[ndré] Breton. Through the principle of montage which Streng utilizes in this stage, he comes closest to the Surrealism of Max Ernst. At the same time, the principle of montage makes Surrealism kindred to Constructivism with its strict responsibility and construction. Surrealism's irrational element of uncontrolled associations only reinforces the lyrical and colorful elements; in place of perfect stasis, it introduces a bit of movement into Streng's work.

The unique montage of two torsi embracing each other juxtaposed with vine branches is one such Constructivist composition. These are torsos of musicians with bowler hats, full of tragic lyricism, with helpless and smug smiles attached, and a vine branch beside them. Irrational "encounters," "farewells to soldiers," blind torsos entwined with the columns on balconies, "families"—some of these are transformed into Goya's grotesque, others are broken down into a decorative motif, and yet other elements are accorded a realistic photographic physiognomy which only underlines the unreality of such compositions. Paintings devoid of objects which utilize only the quality of color also belong to this stage. Streng's Surrealism and Constructivism are brought into proximity through the unreal nature of montage.

The fatalistic stiffness of human dolls continues well into Streng's third formal stage—social realism. In this stage the mannequin attempts "to do" and "to change" something. However, it retains its earlier physiognomy—somewhat dull and stiff, helpless and angular, and its dull hard movements, all the while abandoning the previous generality of physiognomy which now becomes individualized, shaped in a detailed way, and treated with photographic precision.

Streng's realistic mannequin attempts "to do something." However, these actions contain a great deal of fatalism and sadness. Presumably, one reason for this is that it still does not use "mater-of-factness," and is thus limited only to the preparation stage. There is still a lot of Constructivist stasis in this new set of themes for Streng—in marches where revolutionary banners are held up and in the building of barricades. It is commendable that Streng works further with the fundamental rhythm of stasis necessary in equal measure along with the new Constructive realism and art which will last.

Static color, framed by hard contours, predominantly the steel blue, hard blue, tragic white, and the dark red from his Constructivist stage—is transformed into warmer color tones and polyphonic mosaic-like naturalist assemblages and a multiplicity of perspectives—which is yielded from the reciprocal flow of colorful streaks in realism.

Streng's illustrations of my Yiddish poetry collection *Day Figures* and my Polish collection of montages *Acacias Bloom*, and the artist's illustrations of the recent theatrical play by A[ntoni] Gronowicz[3] are not faithful text reproductions. They are original, and always correspond to the appropriate concept of form, to the mood of the whole work or of its singular parts. Streng stays true to himself, he does not illustrate texts in the realist or the literalist fashion.

---

3   Antoni Gronowicz (1913–1985) was a Polish American writer and dramatist.

11

The Dwelling in Its Psychic and Social Functions (1932)[1]

1

In their most profound and essential function, rooms struggle against space.

The following needs to be added to the statement which at first glance appears paradoxical and unexpected: as an element of limit and balance, a room is a negation of the menacing infinity of space; rooms are elements of stability and balance as opposed to those of chaos and the lack of support.

Not everyone is always aware of this hidden and intrinsic sense of the dwelling. Socialized and worn by habitual forms of thinking and feeling do not allow one to experience the original tremble of escape from the gigantic, empty, and boring space of the world into the cubic, compact space of a room; rather they make the dwelling self-evident and automatic.

This inherent meaning of a room is perhaps still sensed where it appears in pure form—where the dwelling fulfills the primitive function of the struggle against the element—as a defense against frost, heat, precipitation, and as a social institution which qualifies the human being as a member of ordered social life. One may thus infer that homeless people who are doomed to be "bound to the street" feel this almost metaphysical sense of the dwelling. In the gesture of the beggar who leans against a wall or a homeless person who leans on the dirty subway stairs covered in spit, there is something more than an urge or warrant to not obstruct communication. In their gestures, a primal fear of exhaustion and bodily annihilation is transformed and sublimated into a psychological escape from emptiness and the lack of balance; this anxiety is understood as psychological, even though it has the misleading name of fear of hunger. It is expressed in the search for a wall. The wall is a limit imposed on

---

1   See Debora Vogel, "Mieszkanie w swej funkcji psychicznej i społecznej," *Przegląd Społeczny*, no. 8–9 (1932): 208–217.

space. Stable in the chaos of change and transition, it can provide the sweetness of balance and confidence even if for a moment.

And like the defense against the element—the most embodied appearance of space—is needed, so did the fear of open, empty infinity become a stimulus for the persistent modeling of the first "houses."

Contemporary life, which is diametrically opposed to primitive life, contains an element which facilitates the appearance of the primal fear of empty space: mechanization and tempo. The monstrous space of the metropolis with the mechanized rhythmical movement of various cells—streets, factories, workshops—yields a threatening element of monotony and emptiness as a result. It leads to exhaustion which borders on a loss of equilibrium, introduces disharmony between the totality of rhythm and the lift of the biological rhythm of one unit. This disproportion demonstrates to the contemporary person the sense of the dwelling, just as the elements of hunger, frost, and heat illustrated it previously.

The human species, a certain international class which exists through time and uses the specific language of poetry, understands the sense of the dwelling also in the following way: people who search for a person on the city streets, and for unheard-of encounters, adventures, and fates, return to their dwelling tired by their search.

The function of a cubic space enclosed in the six walls of a room can be understood differently. Its function is to be a segment and a reduction of a great space, a condensation of its possibilities and adventures—to be an antidote to formless space.

2

The detailed form of this segment of space undergoes differentiation. It is a function of two variables: 1) the general line of direction of a given era—the style; and 2) the tendency of alignment of each rhythm of the street with the rhythm of the unit. This differentiation extends from the general line to the smallest details of an individual appliance.

A result of various rhythms brushing against each other, the interior is a form of a certain rhythm, represents it. It is achieved by the specific differentiation of the space of a room with the help of elements like the floor, the ceiling, windows, doors, and appliances.

"Insofar as shaping boundaries of space previously was primarily the subject of architecture, nowadays it is almost exclusively the environment for forming movements experienced by the person who uses the space. ... This is not just a physical-geometrical matter but also a psychological one. ... Impressions do not yet give spatial representations. Only thanks to the fact that the soul adds something from its treasury, the "experience of space" is created in effect. According to her temperament or mood at the time, a person emphasizes certain experiences ... and mines internal images. She then forms space according to them ...," writes Hans Poelzig[2] (*Innen-Dekoration*, vol. 11 [1931]).[3] Rooms exist for their dwellers. Their rhythm must correspond to the rhythm of life and the needs of their inhabitants. Thus, the stylization of the interior becomes comprehensible, the imprint of an era's artistic style on the appearance of an interior. The following postulate put forward for public consideration also becomes comprehensible: furniture does not have to be an unchangeable component of an apartment, a ballast which is passed on, an immobile décor on walls to which one needs to attend. Furniture has to be matter-of-fact and serve an outlined purpose. It also needs to be included as a component into the overall rhythm of a room and the dwelling. Yet this is already a matter of the contemporary interior.

3

The principal tendency of contemporary life goes along the line of simplicity. The simplification of the form becomes a cool geometrical line.

This yearning for geometricity can overcome a person in the same way as the need for overload, or the baroque. Moreover, we may assume that this is the most essential human tendency which is fundamental for the search of form in general, and that it simply wanders amid nongeometrical forms in search for its intrinsic form. Thus, multiple experiments with the interior yield the stage of geometricity.

This tendency is called matter-of-factness. Its postulate is to limit things to their most essential features—to elements which provide a rationale for their existence. These things are simple and, as a result, yield a simple line.

---

2   Hans Poelzig (1869–1936) was a German architect and scenographer. He was the author of the IG Farben project in Frankfurt-am-Main, the project of the trade hall in Poznan, and also the scenography for the film *Golem*.

3   See Poelzig and Franz Löwitsch, "Raum-Psychologie," *Innen-Dekoration*, no. 12 (1931): 456–458. This is a paraphrase of p. 458. Franz Löwitsch (1894–1946) was an Austrian architect, who published a series of articles in *Innen-Dekoration*, namely "Beitrag zur Raumwissenschaft." His works are collected in *Das Umfeld des Menschen. Die raumwissenschaftlichen Schriften von Franz Löwitsch*, ed. Marian Wild (Saarbrücken: AV Akademikerverlag, 2015).

This tendency consists of the yearning for equilibrium and stasis. Besides, the geometrical, matter-of-fact line of the dwelling facilitates a person's discovery of their own rhythm, or balance of individual movements, to soothe their need for coolness—against the mechanization and magnitude of the streets. The postulate of the "pathos of an empty wall"[4] is an ideal expression and illustration of this tendency.

Besides the yearning for geometricity, we also have another longing—a need for the fantastic, diversification, unpredictability, colorfulness, a negation of monotony. Geometrical figures are monotonous.

Previously this need for colorfulness, we are inclined to think, found its expression in the structure of a style: in the Gothic line of an angular arc and in the ardent variations of a single motif; in the heavy, stuffy baroque line and its precious materials; or in soft, toy-like, and perfected forms of Rococo swarming with surprising incrustations and embellishments.

It seems that the cold and factual line of the contemporary object, reduced to its actual volume and segmentation, and also the minimal number of objects which interrupts the pathos of the bare wall cannot meet the need for the fantastic. We need to add the "cold" action of the materials like colorless, cold steel and transparent glass as a frequent replacement of the soft and tender wood material which yields to color. The "schleiflak"[5] technique in the finish of wooden objects—in contrast to the lacquer of wood—is also an element of cold silence and simplicity.

In fact, the average consumer, who is used to the "warmth" and "coziness" (*Behaglichkeit*) of an old interior filled with bottles with artificial paper flowers, busts of famous men, and furniture with superstructures and embellishments, retreats before the coolness of the fashionable interior. ([Carl] Linfert[6] rightfully notes that many fashionable interiors become victims of instinctively sought compromise.)[7]

Yet a contemporary person knows that the fantastic of the geometrical line exceeds the apparent colorfulness of flourishes and additions—these become unbearably boring in their perception. Geometrical simplicity, on the other

---

4   See A. Sonne, "Die Wohnung eines Arztes: eine neue Arbeit von Fritz Gross," *Innen-Dekoration*, no. 9 (September 1931): 332.
5   The technique of multilayering and polishing lacquer.
6   Carl Linfert (1900–1981) was a German historian, art critic, and author of "Die Grundlagen der Architekturzeichnung" [The fundamentals of architectural drawing], *Kunstwissenschaftliche Forschungen* 1 (1931): 133–246.
7   Carl Linfert, "Der Innenraum von Heute," *Innen-Dekoration*, no. 1 (January 1932): 22–29.

hand, provides the tremble of novelty and of the new rhythm discovered inside, which may become the greatest and the most astonishing adventure in life. European artworks do not know the fantastic of geometricity. Rather, a commensurate geometricity is represented in the schematic form of triangle faces and immobile bodies in late Egyptian art.

The boredom of the fantastic of old reminds me of an anecdote which subconsciously encapsulates the contemporary sensibility. When I brought my books to the binder, I requested that the material for binding be smooth rather than boring fantastical paper. "Fantastical paper" was not a judgment on the spur of the moment, rather, it was a name which differentiated one thing from another; however, adding the word "boring" included a connotation of judgment. The binder pointed out this paradox to me. He paid attention that I called "fantastical" paper also "boring."

The contemporary fantastic has elements of that which Auguste Villiers de l'Isle-Adam[8] called "intellectual sensuousness"—sensuousness which colorless thoughts and schematic cold notions have for certain people. This notion is based on two principles: 1) the fantastic of ingenuity, from which we get the fundamental meaning of each object construed from the object's point of view; in such construction of the object's "soul"—the thing needs to be imbued with a great deal of the fantastic; 2) a large amount of simple elements in asymmetrical combinations; this yields a rhythmic totality, a melody expressed in the geometrical shapes of the object with a principal motif which, like music, develops in time, asymmetrically.

In relation to the first point, we need to cite Poelzig's astute analysis of the purpose of a tea table, as well as Willy Frank's[9] account on the different roles ... of a chair.

"The soul" of a tea table is like the drink served on it. To summarize Poelzig's analysis,[10] the fantastical lightness and aroma-like quality of an exotic drink, as well as restfulness and an element of dreaminess should be contained in a table.

In turn, a chair's shape depends on the two states in which people find themselves—the active and the passive—in Frank's opinion. Depending on

---

8   Auguste Villiers de l'Isle-Adam (1838–1889) was a French Symbolist writer, author of *Cruel Tales* (1883) and the novel *Tomorrow's Eve* (1886).
9   See Willy Frank, "Von Sitzmöbeln und vom Sitzen" [Of furniture for sitting], *Innen-Dekoration*, no. 2 (1932): 80; no. 3 (1932): 116.
10 See Alfred Wenzel, "Gruppierung um den Tee Tisch" [Grouping around the tea table], *Innen-Dekoration*, no. 9 (September 1931): 338.

need, a chair will look different. A soft, deep chair is fit for a state of passive consumption. In it, the whole body enters a state of rest and passive absorption of sensations. A working chair should have a different look: it needs to enable a compact and assembled posture, ready for activity and be somewhat forward leaning. This type of chair needs to be firm, since it keeps the body in tension. This is how a chair should look in a "lecture hall" which has to allow for a "logical conceptualization of thoughts," and also "a chair in the meeting room" which has to "allow a transition from the listener's role to the role of an active attacker," "the chair for meetings which has to keep a person in tension constantly."

The two analyses above exhaustively illustrate the principles of the fantastic which I call the fantastic of ingenuity. The fantastic in its current meaning which operates with the elements of colorfulness and surprise is added and to the fantastic of the imagination and of the asymmetry in the style of matter-of-factness. This fantastic can introduce a necessary sensuous tension of each thing in a creative way based on the facts and psychological needs. It enables the excessive individuation of the universal line of style. These reflections will be considered in a separate section.

4

The simplicity of an interior cannot be mechanical. The simplicity needs to have a soul.

There are some ultra-Modernist dwellings which look like exhibition halls and schematic showroom interiors rather than spaces where a unique person lives and moves. These rooms are impersonal, schematic, and lacking in individuality; they firmly hold on to the newest ... [sic] fashion trends. It is obvious here that fashion is not a deeply felt internal need but rather a canon of snobbishness. Such rooms embody the mechanism of simplicity, but they are not a living expression of its soul.[11]

This personal touch is first and foremost color. Color is the soul of a thing and its language. To reject its anthropomorphic qualities and sensuous touch means rejecting important means of shaping. For example, with frequent use, the absolute whiteness of a wall becomes boring and exhausting regardless of its brightness. Walls ask for color. The monochrome surface of a wall uninterrupted by any pattern or design can fulfill the need of pathos and balance. But mono-

---

11 See Ludwig Neundörfer, *So wollen wir wohnen* (Stuttgart: Franckische Verlagshandlung, 1931).

chrome needs to have color. It is even more important since it is understood now that which needs to be accentuated in a room is the space itself, enclosed by walls, floor, and ceiling.

"The shaping of the dwelling starts with color. Color defines a space not only from the point of view of dimensions; it relates the space of a room to a person. Colors have the qualities of moods."

The following examples are listed according to Neundörfer's book[12] who refers to Steinfels' work *Farbe und Dasein*;[13] as well as Kandinsky's book,[14] and Goethe's *Theory of Colors*.[15]

Yellow. It is the brightest color after the color of light (Goethe). In its pure state on elegant material, it works brightly and warmly and excites. Yellow is passionate; it rises like the voice of a trumpet (Kandinsky).
Green yellow. Yellow with admixtures appears under clunky paint or because of adding blue to make the color cooler. As a result, it yields a jarring quality—"yellow from envy."
Blue. Blue is related to shadow. The deeper its shade, the more profound a person's yearning for infinity. The color incites a striving for purity and transcendence in a person. The brighter it becomes, the more distant it is (the color of the sky). (Kandinsky). Green blue is hard and cold. Ultramarine is full of internal restlessness.

These few examples illustrate the range of possibilities and significance of using color in shaping the dwelling. Color may represent the principal tone of a room's function—for instance, the "mysterious, live stillness" of cobalt captures the mood of a library. Color may also express the principal mood and constant mindset of the inhabitant; or it could be reserved for a particular mood which surfaces at a certain moment of mood fluctuations.

Besides, there are also individual perceptions of the qualities of mood expressed by color which oscillate between extreme values. All of this could be used. Color is a person's most special possession.

In addition to the walls, ceiling and floor—a lacquered hard wood, a colorful linoleum, or carpet, doors, windows, and furniture are objects here.

---

12 Ibidem.
13 See Wilhelm Steinfels, *Farbe und Dasein. Grundzüge zu einem symbolischen Weltbild* [Color and Being. Characteristics of the Symbolic World Picture] (Jena: E. Diederichs, 1926).
14 See Wassily Kandinsky, *Über das geistige in der Kunst, insbesondere in der Malerei* [On the spiritual in Art, in particular in Painting] (Munich: R. Piper & Co, 1912).
15 See Johann Wolfgang Goethe, *Zur Farbenlehre* [Theory of Colors] (Tübingen: Cotta, 1810).

Another fashionable guideline of Purism is the elimination of all pictures from a wall (however, sometimes adding an ad hoc picture combined with a wall is allowed). This postulate makes sense if it is directed against the hopeless cluttering of a wall with colorful reproductions in gilt frames juxtaposed without any direction and inserted as if absolutely by accident where there is no furniture, or where there is an empty wall between windows which "asked for a picture." But this Purist prohibition is misplaced when one deals with original artwork which corresponds to the likings of the inhabitant—his favorite artwork, as long as this artistic piece is not inserted "anywhere" where there is vacant space with no furniture. This artwork must have a specially allocated place in the space of the room.

The idea to hang certain artworks for a limited amount of time—as long as their impact does not become dulled by long habituation, so that they are continuously useful for the inhabitant—is rational. It was suggested for the first time by the forerunner and genius in many respects, Cyprian Kamil Norwid.

"Should not architecture and painting be in harmony?" asks the founder of the Purist movement in art Ozenfant.[16] "They will be in accord if they originate from one spirit. ... This spirit is called the sense for structure. ... The sense is revealed in the reflection that everything should relate to an axis, regardless of whether the axis is real, dynamic, or spiritual; the aim is to reach a completed order of totality."

Grouping elements of objects is also important as an expression of personal rhythm. As is well known from the analogy in painting, various groupings of the same elements yield various rhythmic tensions, various contents of rhythm. Psychology poses the question of the quality of form (*Gestaltqualität*) or contents, which demonstrates that the contents of totality depend on the arrangement of a certain number of elements. The character of the dwelling is like a human facial expression which cannot be reduced to the structure and actions of its separate elements—the nose, lips, eyes, the forehead, since these may be shared by a few different individuals—rather, this character is in a conceptually elusive relation, arrangement, composition. The physiognomy of the dwelling is also a result of an instinctively executed configuration, while the space of a room is ideally adapted to it. Styles bear the imprint of such arrangements in quenching, charging, and filling every inch of free space with objects without a plan, while simultaneously introducing the principle of the boring

---

16 See Amédée Ozenfant, "Wie stehen die Baukunst und die Malerei zueinander?" [What is the relationship between architecture and painting?], *Das Neue Frankfurt*, no. 4 (1928): 66, 67.

symmetry of the old-fashioned dwelling. The spacious matter-of-fact grouping of things, the horizontal line, and the fantastic of asymmetry are expressions which flow out of arrangement.

Inconspicuous objects like bottles or vases—but not empty ones—are useful for the individual design of the dwelling. Matter-of-factness demands them to fulfill their function—to contain live and artificial flowers. Artificial flowers are, in turn, adapted to our need for regularity and coldness. Thus, they are made from cool and smooth celluloid and are cut out into geometrical shapes.

5

The title of the article is "The Dwelling in Its Psychological and Social Functions."

The psychological conditions of shaping the dwelling which we considered until now form the basis for specifying the dwelling's social significance.

The cubic space of a room shaped in a certain way is an important social factor if we take the productivity of human labor and the sense of equilibrium achieved through it as measure. A proper room helps discover a lost balance and fills with a sense of the fantastic and fullness, adapting us to further energy expenditures.

Every person experiences both the positive and negative influences of the dwelling on their mood and work productivity. Yet we don't realize it enough, not wishing to be susceptible to the "external affliction" of the dwelling. ... This kind of carelessness has dominated society, a consequence driven by the specter of internal catastrophes.

People have never burnt out so quickly as nowadays. (We obviously mean life in cities, but the effects are felt even on the peripheries of life most distant from world centers.) Mechanization, in addition to hyperproduction and competition, demands constant tension and energy. Even where such factors do not come into play directly, a person is exhausted through the search for new forms of thought and life—ever more significant and truer—instead of the worn thoughts which no longer provide a feeling of *raison d'être* in life.

The cold steel dwelling adapted to the yearnings of the contemporary person successfully fights with the despondency which often originates quite unconsciously in a stuffy room which was not aired, and which is filled with impersonal, accidental things. It originates in the the arrythmia of chaos and the tightness of a space which is too deeply infused with the breath of foreign life, a strange, chaotic, and crass soul. (These rooms are advertised for "one or two men, or for a childless couple. ...")

The dwelling has another social function which is of interest because it consists of "inversion." To an extent that in the first stage a person shapes the dwelling, the roles are reversed, and in the second stage the dwelling begins to shape the person. It may cultivate a person's instinct for a way of perceiving things and a certain type of thinking.

For instance, when there is an influx of geometrical elements every day and for a long time, one may get used to operating with them in transmitting internal experiences. This may educate a modern person.

Somebody who is familiar with geometrical elements from childhood on will later not turn away from a series of forms and conceptions related to this element. Familiarity with this element facilitates an understanding of the totality which has been difficult until now and demanded previous analysis and habituation to the material of composition. Habituation to the geometrical element enables comprehension of the totality of a work of art.

Today the dwelling plays the role of a landscape in the life of a modern person. Like nature previously, the city and its cells—factories, workshops, and interiors—now supply a person with the elements for processing thoughts and forms.

The cityscape of iron and concrete, and the steel-glass landscape of the dwelling diversified by the soul of color and asymmetrical melodiousness, replace the green landscape of nature. The eternal need for romance has now shifted its point of gravity from the chaotic interior of nature to cold and ordered human compositions full of balance and measure—cities and houses.

Literature in the field does not pay enough attention to the educational role of the contemporary interior.

12

The Legend of Contemporaneity in Children's Literature: Fragments (1934)[1]

A few recently published children's books encourage me to shift the question from "everydayness" as a literary motif to posing the question of contemporary "legend."

Legend surpasses any specific reality insofar as it exhibits the longing for perfection and the unity of a certain element; where this element—realized in life without a plan and yearning for glorification—is elevated to the element of "wonder." Legend distills the extract of the tendency of a certain era and presents it in absolute colors and names.

What concerns the abovementioned motif of surrounding reality and production, is the place where the question of "legend" is posited, perhaps only in insignificant nuances. However, they are factual ones.

Previous books by [Franciszka and Stefan] Themersons (*The Post* and *The Birth of Letters*)[2] rehabilitated the banalized and mechanized everydayness around us like writing or communication—matters which are settled and viewed as self-explanatory, so that the "wonderfulness" and poetic nature of these everyday life companions need to be discovered anew, their poetic value uncovered from a thick layer of habit and unavoidable dullness. A new book by Themersons *Our Fathers Work* (Warszawa: Gebethner and Wolf, 1934) needs to be considered a legend of our times.

---

1   See Debora Vogel, "Legenda współczesnośći w literaturze dziecięcej. Fragmenty," *Przegląd Społeczny*, no. 3 (1934).
2   See Stefan Themerson, *Poczta*, illustr. Franciszka W. Themerson (Warszawa: Wydawnictwo tygodnika "Płomyk" 1932); Stefan Themerson, *Narodziny liter*, illustr. Franciszka W. Themerson (Warszawa: published privately by Themerson, 1931).

It is a legend of work in its various modifications represented by occupations. There is the question of urbanism with its legend of "glass houses"; a legend of cities-gardens, weaved in the most ordinary way into a passage about a gardener's occupation, as well as the question of pacifism like in this sentence: "children from all over the world will live in these (glass) houses." Illustrations by Franciszka Themerson again become an indispensable element of the totality; they influence with their suggestive colors and inventive montage. Stylized as posters, they cut into the text with their wide, simplified surfaces. The board with a tailor's sign *of a suit divided into parts* is especially perfect. As for the poetic text—as was previously indicated in the title—it privileges the male gender in the representations of professions and could lead to a false division of the world into men as workers and women as consumers. This does not correspond to the image, or the legend of modern times.

The legend of pacifism which uses the motif of the similarity of the way of life—its identical nature on different continents and across various geographic latitudes—is perfectly represented in Ewa Szelburg-Zarembina's[3] book *Our Brothers*, illustrated by Jadwiga Gladkowna and Edward Manteufl (Warszawa: Gebethner and Wolf, 1934). It guides the reader through various countries and different areas in the city like the industrial district, and the reader concludes that life is similar everywhere and that there is a closeness between people. The illustrations, montages of types of physiology, dwellings, typical occupations, natural backgrounds, and ambiance, work in the same way as the text.

This book begs comparison with two recently published books in the *Father Castor's Albums*[4] series by the French publisher Flammarion. One book is called *I am Making Masks* (*Je fais mes masques*), and the second one—*Everybody Has a Home* (*Chacun sa maison*).[5] Both books share a similar philosophy with E. Szelburg's book. There is an assembly of colorful masks (the child has to put them together from pieces using directions and projections in the book). There are also descriptions of houses, customs, typical animals, and commodities from a child's surroundings in all countries and the means of communication which aims to bring the French child closer to distant indigenous, African, or Arab

---

3 Ewa Szelburg (1899–1986) was a Polish writer of both children's books and novels.
4 *Paul Faucher. Albums du Père Castor* was a series of children's books.
5 Nathalie Parain, *Je fais mes masques*, illustr. Nathalie Parain (Paris: Flammarion, 1931). See also G. Deffontaines and Paul Faucher, *Chacun sa maison*, illustr. Khem (Paris: Flammarion, Paris, 1933).

children.⁶ The construction of work consists in the text and in the detailed illustrations scattered all over the book in separate squares which need to be cut out.

Books like these are designed to encourage the child to engage in the activity of montage—in concrete interaction. They approach legend from a concrete angle and from the side of children's literal and makeshift work. From this perspective, the Polish author's book is a very complete and closed work; it is a ready-made montage which suggests an idea rather than a literal demonstration of the idea of work.

A juxtaposition of the two types of books from the artistic point of view ends in favor of the Polish authors. The French books' textual and artistic level (Nathalie Parain is the author of the illustrations of the masks) is falsely adapted to the imagined primitive nature of the child, while in the Polish books, the child's world is stylized, elevated to the poetry of facts. These albums are also symptomatic thanks to their yearning for literal interaction.

Among the Flammarion books, there are two books with a special significance symptomatic for our time. One of them is *Play with Plants* (*Je fais mes jouets avec des plantes*) with Ruda's illustrations;⁷ another *Circles and Squares* (with Nathalie Parain's illustrations).⁸ These albums introduce the rule of geometrical shapes discovered by the contemporary plastic arts. Any object, animal, or human body can be made from these shapes. Here are a few main shapes in the branches and the fruit—cones, acorns, and chestnuts—which allow one to assemble birds, animals, and people and create complete stories; the same can be done with the circle and square.

The second book by Ewa Szelburg which is significant in this respect is *Travel in the City* (with the illustrations by Antony Wajwoda). This book should be discussed only in superlatives. It is constructed in a way that the source of the legend is integrated through montage into a description of a city scenes. For instance, in the first poem the author pays detailed attention to materials ("stone houses," "shiny tin"); factories and workshops are described as "the most important buildings in the city." These are the "enchanted palaces" of the new

---

6   Besides these children there is also a little Slovak and Japanese girl, an indigenous child, and a French boy. The French boy is dressed as a city dweller, while the others wear traditional costumes which allows one to recognize them easily.
7   Vogel means Lida Ruda, *Je fais mes jouets avec des plantes. Créations des enfants de l'Institut Bakulé présentées par le père Castor*, illustr. Ruda (Paris: Flammarion, 1933). In the afterword to the book the authors write, "We don't want our readers only to make toys from plants, we want you to truly research the world of nature and use your imagination. In this you will find a rare joy which not many adults experience, the joy of creativity" (26).
8   See Nathalie Parain, *Ronds et carrés*, illustr. Nathalie Parain (Paris: Flammarion, 1932).

landscape—the city; the new legend is expressed by the apotheosis of the gray workshop, it does not shy away from the colorless or dirty factory landscape.

The similarity between *Travel* and the idea of the latest book by Themersons is the rehabilitation and foregrounding of "prosaic," "trivial," or "harmful" professional work considered as such not too long ago, which people longed to escape by fleeing into a wonderland. Moreover, in Themerson's book every kind of work is made equal in value—blue-collar work is placed together with so-called higher-level work like the actor's job for instance. This only becomes possible when work is considered as the formation of something, then the hierarchy is abolished. The difference between the two books is in their composition: Ewa Szelburg introduces the plot element of "further development" by connecting separate scenes by taking the streetcar to where one needs to go in the city. Likewise, the author takes into account not separate professions but the totality of life to which also belong the fantasy of travel and rest.

The legend of the city is present here—it wishes and knows how to speak to our need for the fantastic which does not require old-fashioned embellishments. This fantastic is wonder in itself. To get a colorful image, there is no need to add anything from "fantasy":

> Many lanterns so wonderfully
> light up the streets
> silver, yellow, and red.
> The lights of the ads and the strings of windowpanes
> cast their light from above.

Exoticism is unmasked in depictions of an indigenous boy who goes to school and only comes to his village home on vacation in *Our Brothers*. We also read in the book about Numbu, an ordinary boy very similar to us, who gets tired from collecting the bones of elephants when he meets white people "who have come to learn and describe a black person's life and later show it in a movie to other white people in a distant land." What a powerful antidote to books like *Nick of the Woods* and *Africa Speaks!* ... [9]

This new type of book ... opens new perspectives on life and on feelings; it initiates new types of psychic states which deal with the concrete element—until now believed to be an accidental element in life.

---

9   See the Polish adaptation of the book by Robert Montgomery Bird *Nick of the Woods* and the book and the film *Africa Speaks!*

Essays on Socio-Critical Issues

13

Courage in Solitude (1930)[1]

"You ask if your verses are good. You ask me. You have previously asked others. You send them to journals. You compare them with other poems, and you are troubled when certain editors reject your efforts. Now (as you have permitted me to advise you) I beg you to give all that up. You are looking outwards, and of all things that is what you must now not do. Nobody can advise and help you, nobody. There is only one single means. Go inside yourself. Discover the motive that bids you write; examine whether it sends its roots down to the deepest places of your heart, confess to yourself whether you would have to die if writing were denied you. ..."[2]

With these words Rainer Maria Rilke responded to a young poet. And these words should become the life slogan of every adept of the arts for the time in life when the desperate search for validation from outside is no longer a means to numb his own insecurity and push away the responsibility from himself to burden others.

Would you have to die if writing were denied you? Rilke suggests asking the question. He means writing, and not necessarily publishing. Publishing is merely the last act of the play called the artist's life, as necessary as sewing the last stitch on a piece of clothing or putting an address on a letter. Publishing is justified when the work is necessary and socially significant for a specific time. The actual justification of the artist's existence, however, is to be found in his work—in the creation of a world system from the material of words, or lines, and colors.

A question emerges: when would the artist's inner world be capable of existence? Or rather, when would it have objective value? When this world is singular and historically necessary is the answer.

Formal plagiarism, which always grows out of the plagiarism of experiences, has neither objective value nor does it negate the dialectic of forms, which is merciless and continuously demands new forms of life and art.

---

1 See Debora Vogel, "Der mut tsu zayn eynzam," *Der Morgn* [Lwów] 4, no. 1223 (1930): 7.
2 Rainer Maria Rilke to Franz Xaver Kappus, Paris, February, 17, 1903. *Sonnets to Orpheus: With Letters to a Young Poet,* ed. and trans. Stephen Cohn (Abingdon: Routledge, 2000), 173.

The objective phenomenon becomes subjectively known as the desire for new meanings of things. Furthermore, it becomes impossible to deploy the well-known yet worn-out categories anymore. Forms exhaust their meaning, and the artist's greatest compulsion or preference is to shape. She cannot feel the rhythm of shaping until she repeats foreign forms. The compulsion to form has the same meaning as the discovery of a new expression which would be fitting for a specific time. This requirement does not come from outside. The origin of the internal distress due to the impossibility of living without a life system is similar to the decision to search for new forms.

Oddly enough, this search for the new meanings of things is at the same time a search for oneself—for one's own singular and individual categories.

It seems paradoxical, yet it is very hard to see things in a unique way, even though every person is singular. It is as difficult as the courage to free oneself from every convention.

Freedom from the conventional—and even the most original worldview or form becomes conventional when it is repeated—is as difficult as it is simple to fit our life into the framework of the conventional and trite mode of thinking.

However, the requirement of singularity and originality should not be understood as irresponsible play with contingencies and moods to one's own liking. Every unique world is an amalgam of the inner possibilities and the external material of phenomena. The components of this amalgam originated in a specific environment and historical mood. Due to the portion of objective life material, the artist's subjective world is not entirely divorced from the totality of life—it is neither residual nor marginal. The secret lies in how to combine objective necessity with the subjective singularity in a thing—the singularity which justifies the existence of the objective new form and prevents it from becoming superfluous, since it is not the only one. It is possible to plagiarize the current form—not only past forms.

Therefore, the artist would be well advised to be a human being with his own desires and experiences, have a job or occupation, since this creates a strong bond between an individual on the one hand and things and relationships between things on the other …

Rootedness is a specific form of life and a lifestyle, as well as a singular, unique approach to the world of things. It affords a security which no criticism or editing may provide. It gives the calm and persistence to wait and search further rather than hold a view only because it is validated from the outside.

One more piece of advice may serve as consolation, helping the adepts of the arts to be patient because they need to endure solitude at least for some time in their career if not their whole life. Art critic K[arol] Irzykowski formulated this advice in the following way: "There is no solitary thought which will not reach another person at some point who will surely pick it up and understand." This certainty might help in the solitude which should be accepted as a necessity.

14

Exoticized People (1934)[1]

1

In this essay I will discuss [Kamil] Giżycki's book *The Whites and the Blacks*.[2] The novel will serve as a starting point to reflect on the complex questions around the notion of "race" in general. We need not embark on a journey to discovering the black continent in Africa; we may discover the "black continents" in the heart of Europe as well.

2

Let us begin with a couple remarks about Giżycki's book. I believe that the artistic merit and the social significance of this compelling travel narrative are greatly overrated. An article by Zbigniew Grabowski published on June 24 in *Wiadomości Literackie*[3] is an example of such an overly favorable assessment. This review compares Giżycki's unassuming account of current affairs in Francophone Africa with Céline's tragic book *Journey to the End of the Night*,[4] which represents a specific thesis and a unique worldview. Moreover, Grabowski's comparison does not favor Céline, which can be gleaned from the following statements: "Céline is a city dweller to his core, one might even say that he is a city rat intimidated by a large open space. He feels uncomfortable in the African jungle whenever he encounters the infinity of forests and sky. … By contrast, Giżycki is a person who is comfortable in an open space and perceives the washed-out basin of an African river in a natural and optimistic way."

---

1   See Debora Vogel, "Ludzkie egzotyki," *Przegląd Społeczny* 8, no. 7–8 (1934): 150–159.
2   Jerzy Giżycki (1889–1970) was a Polish writer and diplomat. He published his travelogues in the book *Biali i Czarni*, 1934.
3   *Wiadomości Literackie* was a social-cultural publication in 1924–1939 in Warsaw.
4   Louis-Ferdinand Céline is the literary pseudonym of Louis-Ferdinand Auguste Destouches (1894–1961). He was a French writer and doctor. He published the novel in question in 1932 as a debut, which brought him fame.

The fact that Céline approaches the theme or rather the notion of the black continent in a section in his pessimistic novel is no justification for reading him and Giżycki in a similar vein. For Céline, a colony in Africa, a battlefield, or a Parisian suburb simply constitutes a background and a landscape. These are occasions and possibilities to posit a thesis about human life and people in general. For Giżycki, however, the French colony becomes a theme for a short story, a fascinating travel narrative. The reader finds here accounts of the beatings and exploitation of Africans alongside cheerful and quick-paced descriptions of successful crocodile hunts. There is absolutely no hierarchy or contrast, the descriptions grouped together are completely devoid of any logic of form. Beside the story of the fate of an African woman, her belly cut open on an operating table, there are narratives of historical events in different African tribes, stories about their kings, and anecdotes regarding their customs. From time to time the author condescendingly pontificates using a tone of light and gentle irony about these "dumb heads" who are so "foreign" to him!

Unlike Giżycki, Céline treats every event as a pretext to depict life's tragic nature—the eternally tragic nature of humanity and life perspectives.

Thus, comparison between Giżycki and Céline is superfluous. Giżycki's book may only be judged in terms of its social relevance; it does not meet the criterion of presenting a novel worldview or form. Likewise, the book is too gentle to be an expression of condemnation of certain actions or a protest against them; the lighthearted tone of the narrative does not bring into sharp focus the outlines of injustices on all continents—both in Africa and in Europe.

Nevertheless, the book has achieved resonance. It pulls at the heartstrings which compel us to speak about it, constantly articulating issues which one wishes to conceal—in the politics of imperialism or settler colonialism, or in the allegedly even more dangerous politics at work within the mechanism of the body and soul. The irrational fear of the foreign in relations between types of men needs to be articulated in language.

3

It might seem unbelievable, and yet it is true: one does not need Africa to exoticize people, reducing them to beings of incomprehensible mentality, whom one only approaches with mixed feelings of pity and contempt. It might even be unclear whether pity is only a milder form of disdain. One may exoticize

Jews in a similar way as one exoticizes people of color: "Yarmulkes on heads swarming with fleas, snotty noses, mothers' shawls across their backs, worn-out shoes, and a sad defiant tune hovering over their heads like a strange multilayered curse from which they don't understand a single word." This is how Wanda Melcer[5] describes the "dark continent" of the Warsaw *kheyders*.

The next best thing—a sequel to the exotic "lovers of murdered girls" after the Warsaw brothels of course—is the new sensation: exotic Jews!

My concern here is not to defend the *kheyder* system of education or religious customs that might appear to some as "barbaric." These would be overcome by life itself and through the emancipation of contemporary Jewry. My intent is also not to criticize or defend the Talmud, in which besides pure scholasticism (and it is well known that scholasticism is not a purely Jewish creation; it would suffice to consider questions like this one: "how many angels fit on the tip of a needle?" which were used to educate the young non-Jewish minds), you could also find authentic life and social wisdom. This is not what I seek to defend, just as the intent of the author of these reportages is not simply to critique. Perhaps she herself is not fully aware of the unconscious motivation behind her statements.

One such concealed driving force—and every Jew will see it similarly—is the othering and antipathy which hides under the smoke screen of pity rationalized as the need for the "white civilizing mission"—a gesture of pity for all the black continents of the world!

This secret aversion is unmasked in the emotionally charged expressions—slurs regarding the circumcision of the newborn male like "cliptip," or descriptions of voices as "loud and pesty," etc.

I do not merely criticize statements which some might even support. Rather, I identify the symptomatic—whether these descriptions are subconscious for the author, perhaps even written in good conscience as a pretext to express an irrational feeling and aversion towards otherness in concrete terms. Thus, we read these expressions as text to get at the heart of what is behind them.

"The evening melody," the "sad defiant tune" stands between us. Would we ever succeed to eliminate this difference?

---

5   Melcer's reportage cycle is entitled *Czarny ląd – Warszawa* [Warsaw: Black continent]; two parts from it were published in *Wiadomości Literackie*. [Vogel's note.] Vogel cites the second part of this reportage by Wanda Melcer (1896–1972) who was a Polish poet and publicist.

4

This psychological response to otherness does not stem from the realm of the rational; we shouldn't search for it in the realm of "opinions," or judgments.

Approximations of facts and agreements between different worldviews—class, occupational, theoretical, and artistic approximations—are possible and occur in our conscious emotional life.

However, there is something which divides us in our approaches to the same issues in life. There is something irrational radiated by the consciousness which lends a curious coloring and rhythm to the latter. Perhaps the quantity of components, and the repeatability of sensations and psychological outlooks is only transformed into a different quality here; perhaps all of this is due to different blood and body types—a thesis based on certain reflexes in life and not fully refuted, even as it is strongly questioned in theory.

History and our immediate experience suggest the following explanation for the above-mentioned feeling of otherness. The identical life circumstances, which anonymously shape the fates of the entire generations, create a certain sensibility—even more so when they fall into fertile soil—a predisposition to feel and react in a certain way. When I invoke the identical "life circumstances" acquired throughout generations, I do not exclusively speak about ghettos but also about the thousands of hurdles imposed by society, as well as the anomalies of psychic life, and the vagrant lifestyle of nonbelonging, to which a people without a land—at best a continuously tolerated minority—is subjected. From the point of view of refinement and layers of psychological life, these abnormalities, which result from a life of a constant lack of security, sometimes take on a positive, at other times a negative form.

This intrinsic fate binds a human group into a totality. In this whole, the similarities between a group's members are noticeable, although individuals, their characters, or views strongly differ. Thus, the commonality of the external fate shapes the identity of the intrinsic human fate in the sense of predisposition to specific reactions to life events—the significance of life circumstances is minimalized while the structure of psyche becomes decisive, for a certain type of fate in life.[6]

Nothing can reduce the extent of the influence of this fate. On the contrary, it is defined, and its grip becomes stronger through the background of repeated circumstances. Therefore, may it be that our external fates lose their significance after a certain time, and that the internal fate acquired over centuries

---

[6] The notion of "intrinsic fate," introduced in psychology by Eduard Spranger, is very fruitful and noteworthy. [Vogel's note.]

determines the course of life of an individual, which results in the fact that in all circumstances we always remain the same and draw certain conclusions by reflex while our neighbors who are in the same environment come to absolutely different conclusions about life?

And perhaps it is true that everything else is a lie, an artificial feeling which comes from group assimilation. This is akin to the feeling of satisfaction which a person who is usually sad experiences when he unexpectedly finds himself in cheerful society—to fight against the wall of isolation and solitude which grew around him because of his otherness, his only weapon is to become similar to his surroundings if he wishes not to remain lonely. He makes an attempt—he adopts cheerful facial expressions at first. Slowly, he is strongly overcome by a mood which was foreign to him and starts to believe that he actually feels this way. And only when he "no longer needs to fit in," when the irrational aspects of his personality could again surface, he realizes that he is hopelessly sad in fact.

This does not mean, however, that the abovementioned community generates no worldviews and perspectives that will be quite like the creations of "others." However, in these creations, the sign of otherness, of difference in inner fate, is visible—an unspecified quality which makes one group different from another.

The burden of sadness gives a certain coloring even to the most monumental and heroic, optimistic and constructive views. It is precisely this otherness—the "sad defiant tune hovering over their heads like a strange multilayered curse"—which invites the other to speak.

What I write here might appear very reactionary from the point of view of the psychological theory which proclaims the absolute "plasticity of dispositions," as well as from the perspective of the theory of social class, according to which the transformation of societal form leads to the abolition of all national communities and their replacement by different versions of class mentality. This "reactionary" view, however, allows for a radical one.

The irrationality of othering neither excludes mutual understanding nor proximity on the level of rational consciousness. The social phenomenon which considers people as exotic beings, and the phenomenon of "race-based" dislike should be eradicated.

5

Othering between types of people can take on various shapes, all of which, however, are merely types of antipathy.

The fact of a communal sense of animosity becomes clear when we understand its structure and agree with Ribot's[7] thesis that aversion is a kind of loathing. In all stages, it is the body's defense against the foreign, the other, and the harmful, even if only considered as such.

The thesis about otherness established here is linked with the fact of communal dislike explained through this more or less conscious feeling of foreignness or otherness.

"It can happen that in the face of mystery, the unknown, which may lead to a misunderstanding, self-preservation spontaneously takes over," Ribot writes in his study on aversion.

Before speaking about aversion or enumerating the stages of this feeling, we should consider the degrees between neutrality and the dislike, the latter a lighter form of aversion, its initial stage.

An example of the above phenomenon is the reflex of mistrust. A relatable reflex: one doubts that in certain circumstances—best described as a lasting sense of insecurity—a person can develop in a natural and normal way, whether this person may attain certain values. The doubt is whether this person's whole existence is not accidental or abrupt in terms of growth and development—an ephemeral creation prone to decay. Groups of people with a settled lifestyle and all the minimal necessities develop a negative reflex of antipathy to anything which is accidental.

A more strongly defined and logically justifiable form of this othering is the misunderstanding and restlessness associated with it. Agitation always appears because of a confrontation with the foreign, the incomprehensible, thus, the person retrospectively connects the symptoms of unrest to an imagined source, inferring that certain things and people are essentially foreign.

The unrest exists until those othered do not wish to dominate, do not threaten us directly, and do not harm our *psyche* and *physis*. If that were to happen, we find ourselves in the territory of aversion. Thus, Ribot's profound interpretation of aversion will be of use for us here.

In the framework of antipathy, Ribot distinguishes a range of stages and forms. The simplest form—revulsion—appears in the plant world. It is an

---

7   Théodule-Armand Ribot (1839–1916) was a French psychologist and philosopher. Vogel later cites Ribot's *Problèmes de psychologie affective* [Problems of affective psychology] (Paris: Felix Alcan, 1910); in Polish, *Z zagadnień psychologii uczuć*, trans. Henryk Swierczewski (Lwów-Warszawa: Księgarnia H. Altenberga; E. Wende, 1912).

organic antipathy, the instinctive defense of an organism against harm. This form of aversion does not typically evolve further; it is contained in its initial form "despite further developments in consciousness and communal life, through which the antipathy becomes more intellectual and refined."

Instinctive apathy is a higher form of antipathy than revulsion. Ribot defines instinctive apathy as "absolutely unreflective," it is "ruled by the spontaneity and stability of instinct." Of note is the emphasis that this kind of aversion is hereditary. According to Ribot, this type of antipathy is an inherited trait which we primarily encounter in the animal world and among children.

Antipathy among adults is based on specific knowledge like:

1. intuition, which is widely considered to be knowledge established by logical leaps (Ribot speaks here of "feeling rather than cognition");
2. reflection, based on which "something which began as a light aversion ... is gradually strengthened and completed through the addition of other elements, and a series of observations or deliberate judgments."

This form of antipathy acquired through the logic of the force of judgment and reflection is of great significance for our purposes. It results in a feeling designated by Ribot as "collective antipathy." Only its source remains instinctive and unreflective by way of exception, yet as a rule, this antipathy tends to find its own justification in the logic of reflection.

"When an individual antipathy becomes collective, it transforms. It then becomes less based on an instinct and more on a commonly held belief which is not devoid of reflection. This reflection seeks to justify itself; it strives to become somewhat rational."

Cases of collective antipathy based on instinctive reaction are rare, as, for instance, "among primitive peoples that apart from any fear feel profound aversion to everything foreign. Even civilized people—primarily those who are less refined and educated—have an almost natural antipathy against the customs, language, and views of a different people."

An analysis of this impersonal form of aversion—directed against a family or a national community, political parties or classes, literary or artistic schools—is the following according to Ribot: "it corresponds to existent affection ... a collective antipathy takes on the form of suggestion, affection, imitation, or participation ... psychological unity is essential here, without it the antipathy remains individual."

The second important point is that antipathy is acquired, "it originates from the options which are available; it arises within the individual under the influence, and through the pressure, of those like him; it is influenced by upbringing, tradition, and customs."

Thus, we have discussed the basis for our conclusions and generalizations. We also need to mention the factors which encourage the emergence of antipathy according to Ribot.

Ribot subdivides these factors into the intellectual factors and those which are based on feeling. The first universal intellectual factor is a lack of plasticity—one can neither empathize nor understand that which is outside of his own personality.

The second intellectual factor is a one-sidedness of intelligence, not in the sense of a feebleness of mind, but rather in the sense of a one-dimensional perception of things. This intellectual stance can also influence emotional life and become a "natural source for instinctive aversions."

We need to consider one more thing: what are the arguments, how is the logic of antipathy, which is based on reflection, construed?

In fact, there is a constantly recurring and unchanging argument: the collective towards which one feels antipathy is inferior. This alleged assessment of the inferiority appears here as sufficient grounds and an adequate justification for disgust and contempt.

Ribot writes, "Most human communities tend to exaggerate their virtues, their collective belief is shaken by the opposing belief which restricts their own belief or negates it."

Tarde[8] makes a similar claim: "the most important instinct of collective conviction is the insurmountable primary pride that every tribal community—regardless how negligible the number of its members—takes in its alleged superiority over its neighbors."

This primitive reflex is used with an unexpected sanction and theory in a very developed culture in the twentieth century. It provides alleged evidence that Jews are not only different from Aryans, but that "through the former every race is negated"—or, in other words, every structure and style. The ideologues

---

8   Gabriel de Tarde (1843–1904) was a French criminologist, sociologist, and social psychologist who wrote *Le lois de l'imitation* [The laws of imitation], 1890.

of racism define Jews as the "anti-race."[9] From the psychological point of view, this theory is nothing more than a sanctioned reflex of primitive membership in a community which considers another community as inferior. The former fears that its own beliefs are allegedly threatened through the existence of another belief system. When the notion "belief" is replaced with the modern concept of life "values," or "ideals," this yields an unsophisticated psychological basis for the overpowering theory of racism.

I mention psychological facts here to show that the question of othering and enmity among races, nations, and classes can also be illuminated from the psychological perspective, rather than just from the anthropological point of view. The psychological interpretation sheds light both on the sources of the mass reflexes and on the theory which grows on the basis of instinct.

Moreover, when antipathy has a certain social significance, when an aversion to specific forms of perception and thinking contributes to a crystallization of opposing forms, recklessly allowing them to be realized as the only possibilities in the world, we must fight against this aversion, and especially strongly when it results in sheer negation, without offering a positive program.

The knowledge of the reflexive character of the societal antipathy which manipulates judgments to induce or strengthen instinctive disgust can be helpful here.

If these judgments which are prejudices were modified, the reflexive source of mass antipathy would be refuted and rationalized. This seems to be within reach in terms of the tasks and possibilities of educational and other social systems.

The outlook is grimmer regarding instinctive aversion—the defense mechanism against the foreign which is perceived as threatening and harmful. Can we rationalize it in its existent otherness? And even if we could, must this initial stage in which the foreign awakens aversion and rationalizes itself in subordination to the "other" continue? There are examples of the irradiation of feelings through judgments and convictions. One knows just as well that otherness may be in the same measure a source of affection, in the sense of sensitivity and being comfortable with something which is so vastly different.

The irrationality inherent in diversity and otherness should not become an obstacle for understanding. A common front should be created in the rational world of judgments and worldviews. The particularity of judgment does not

---

9 The notion of *Gegenrasse* was introduced as part of Arnaud Schikedanz's (1892–1945) antisemitic program.

depend on programs and, therefore, cannot be viewed as a vice or virtue on its own. Quite the opposite, in the perspective of a lifetime, it could be considered as an aesthetic law of diversity and plurality of forms of life.

Meanwhile all the dark continents of Africa, America, and Europe are waiting for refutations of prejudices which present themselves as logical judgments. These are condemned by authentic humanity which calls for understanding and the rejection of pity and interest in exoticizing.

15

Lviv Jewry: A Précis for a Monograph about the Jewish Quarter in Lviv (1935/1937)[1]

There have always existed centers and peripheries—elasticity and strength, life which flows in quieter, somewhat flattened waves. This pertains both to Lviv Jewry and to the Jewish quarters all over the world which are always found on the margins, off the main avenue in life.

A stroll through the streets in Lviv makes one succumb to an illusion that the center of the city is surrounded by the two half-circles of Jewish streets. However, these streets form the only half-circle in the city from the east to the north. And as the city radiates south- and westward, the Jewish side streets calm to a standstill, crowded and pressed against each other in two larger compact groupings. Only parts of these streets continue in the foreign and elegant quarters. The grotesque figures of junk peddlers—sellers of old bottles, clothes, and scrap paper travel quite far. They shout, "I buy old rags, dresses, clothes, iron!" and "Exchange your old dishes for new ones!" ...

The long apathetic Krakowska (Cracow) street[2] connects the two groups of side streets. It is an artery of sorts for the node of streets in the south of the city: Boyim Street, Serbska (Serbian), and Blakharska (Tinsmith) streets become deserted and empty in the direction away from the city. Who would have guessed that they are so close to the downtown core!

The ancient gates with the ornamental decorations, the wonderful baroque of Rynek (Market) Square: the lion, split in half, serves as a cornice, a chimera, and a vine ornament. These are the gates to the long shopping arcades. Upon

---

1   See Debora Vogel, "Lwowska Juderia. (Ekspozycja do monografii żydowskiego Lwowa)". This article originally appeared in *Almanach i leksykon Żydowstwa Polskiego* [Lwów] 1 (1937): 89–98. It also appeared earlier in a Swedish translation from the German manuscript "Judekvarteret i Lemberg" in the Stockholm journal *Judisk Tidskrift*, no. 8 (1935): 318–325.

2   There is an interactive map of all Lviv's city streets at different historical periods. See http://www.lvivcenter.org/en/streets/streets/.

seeing the streets, we might say along with the Yiddish poet [Reuben] Iceland,[3] "It smells here of cinnamon and cloves."[4]

Figure 11. Golden Rose Synagogue.

However, another type of reality does not allow us to consider life as decoration. In the tragic light, we behold something else. This tragic perspective illuminates decay and grayness, movable racks and bare hands with "commodities"—a dozen cheap ties, handkerchiefs (ten pieces for one zloty), hairpins, and safety pins—all of these become stark clear. An improbable scene is repeated multiple times a day—the commodities for which one has not paid "taxes" are confiscated.

And here is Serbian Street again. The street's cool gates smell of mold, old iron, and memories. The openings of the gates are supported by vaults with slate pillars; these are decorated with ornaments of keys and set square stones. Small

---

3 Reuben Iceland (1884–1955) was a Yiddish poet, originally from Galicia, a member of the Modernist group Di Yunge [The young ones] in New York.
4 Citation from the poem "Tarnow" in *Fun mayn zumer* [From my summer] (New York-Vienna: Unzer Shayer, 1922), 73.

shops, small wooden shacks so tiny that the merchant and his wares barely fit inside, are crowded within the gates. As a matter of fact, this cityscape is dreamy, as if out of a sad and hopeless fairy tale.

After we circle multiple times around these strangely helpless street curbs, filled with a mixture of exoticism and brutal everydayness, we enter a courtyard of a residential building on 27 Blakharska (Tinsmith Street). Here we find Golden Rose Synagogue[5]—one of the oldest synagogues in Lviv. Crooked pillars support its walls, a single leaf ornament adorns the main entrance, and one can see a beautiful Renaissance altar inside. This synagogue was built in 1528; it has its own legend and splendor. They say that a beautiful Jewish widow Rosa sacrificed herself to free the synagogue from the power of the Jesuits, and then committed suicide in the temple which was later named after her.[6]

Figure 12. Serbska Street.

---

5   Di Goldene Roze, also called the Nachmanowicz Synagogue and Turei Zahav, was one of the central synagogues in Lviv, and the oldest synagogue in Ukraine. It was destroyed during the Nazi occupation. Now in the place of the synagogue, the remnants of which are part of the UNESCO heritage, there is a memorial complex called The Space of Synagogues.

6   In 1606 the synagogue was confiscated by the Jesuits; the Jewish community bought it back in 1609. Various legends about Roza Nachmanowicz can be found in Majer Balaban's book *Żydzi Lwowscy na przełomie XVI i XVII wieku* [Lviv Jewry in the 16th and 17th centuries] (Lwów: Nakładem Funduszu Konkursowego im. H. Wawelberga, 1906), 178–181.

Let us return to Krakowska (Cracow) Street to reach another group of side streets. This group of streets is dominated by Dragon Street at their core—one in series of streets with names straight out of fairy tales. Yet it is still far from where we are, and before we go there, we still need to walk on other pavements, and encounter other faces and fates.

Figure 13. Boyim Street.

Zhulkevska Street comes next. It is an expressionless, flat, and banal street—half provincial, half urban. (A one-floor residential house with wide gates—dirty and derelict—stands on this street. There lived my great-grandfather sixty years ago. Known as the "silk Jew,"[7] Reb Nissan Süss,[8] a Kabbalist, received a secular education. An author of treatises and a publisher, he must have radiated an aura of quiet solemnity. On business days, he wore his satin coat and a round sable hat—perhaps as an expression of the festivity which always kept him company. He is a representative for of a whole generation an lifestyle, where a way of living and the pleasures available to a person permeated his limited everyday walks and experiences. It was a kind of life in a satin coat which was not at all disturbed by the fact that the border of ghetto where the Jewish world ended was very close by.)

Figure 14. Selling of fish (corner of Starozakonna Street).

From Zhulkevska Street, diagonal streets radiate onwards in the direction of Słoneczna (Sun) Street. The narrow, crooked, and deserted side streets are shaped as four concentrated rings. The last one of these is Słoneczna (Sun) Street.

Where does this name originate? If your path takes you to the area, you will barely believe that this sober and sedate street serves any other purpose than that of quickly passing through. It triggers absolutely no associations with beauty. And

---

7 A *zaydener yid* in Yiddish means a person with a noble character.
8 Avrom Nissen Süss (1789–1905) was a printer and publisher in Lemberg.

Figure 15. Pedestrian gate, Market Square 18 Boyim street.

yet it is truly sun drenched when you stroll from the direction of narrow, dreadful Łazienna (Bath) Street, or from Pod Dębem (Under the Oak) Street.

In the east, Słoneczna Street meets Theodor Square which they call "Paris" in the suburban jargon. It clearly dominates the whole area, this empty nonregular place with a few suspect human figures. This is a district of *shund*, the shoddiness of life, the peddling of commodities, an area of insecurity and trinkets, similar to Berlin's Alexanderplatz, or Paris' Montmartre, only a Jewish one … full of oppressive sadness and disbelief, and lacking a wide decisive gesture, as well as the chutzpah of secure and stable existence.

Noisy and restless Kazimierz Street is to the left of Słoneczna Street; it leaves the last glimpses of the Jewish quarter behind and "leads into the wide

Figure 16. Golden Rose Synagogue.

world"—to streets which are wider and more comfortable but also dull and banal. They are not even overly banal, only "renovated"—they have lost their soul with this new luster. These worthless, confused, and indecisive streets now

Figure 17. At Zbożowy square.

imitate regularity and simulate normality. These are Alembek Street, Kotlarska Street, and Berek Joselowicz Street. (On one of the streets, Kotlarska Street with its empty and flat building facades, in number 14, my grandfather Jacob Ehrenpreis[9] spent long years of his quiet, good, and studious life. He married one of the seven daughters[10] of Süss who is now buried in Stockholm Cemetery. Jacob Ehrenpreis, "the Jewish Hartleben,"[11] was the author of popular commentaries on current topics of his day, including the Beilis[12] and the Dreyfus affair, and the Russian pogroms. A printer and publisher, he lived primarily from his writing; his Jewish treatises were printed in thousands of copies and disseminated

---

9   Jakob Ehrenpreis (1848–1916) was a printer and a publisher.
10 Vogel means her grandmother Chaya (Klara).
11 Conrad Adolph Hartleben established the publishing house A. Hartleben Verlag in 1804, which existed until the interwar period.
12 Mendel Beilis (1974–1934) was a worker who in 1911 was accused of the ritual killing of a Ukrainian boy. Beilis underwent two trials which became internationally known and were observed by Jewish communities worldwide. In 1913 Beilis was found not guilty, yet his case revealed prevalent antisemitic stereotypes.

all over the Galician province. This is a fragment of life of an old Jewish family in Lviv—the lives and works of its members unknown to the larger world.)

From this world of the bastard ghetto streets and their attempts at emancipation and assimilation, we are led by a longing to return to the ghetto. Słoneczna Street brings us back. We come to the square in the middle of three areas, between Zhulkevska Street and the wild Theodor Square.

Figure 18. Dragon streetview of Cracow Square.

It is a hot June afternoon. Spellbound by the charm of this awkward miniature game, one strolls the streets with colorful names. The white restored house fronts, polished and austere, glance at the passerby. Although these buildings look more miserable and accidental, more so than in Boyim or Serbska streets, we may ask: why all this shininess? The renovations are not helpful. They are only a hurdle to deciphering the true soul of the buildings.

I look for Smocza (Dragon) Street. I want to see it in the weary afternoon hours, so similar to the street's soul. ... I look for it in the street tumult of Lamana (Zigzag), Lazienna (Bath), Starozakonna (Old Testament), and Gęsia (Geese) streets. I imagine that I am walking in a completely foreign city. Perhaps an illusion of foreignness helps to decipher the meanings of these street names. Finally, I find the street, and it is disappointing, as was to be expected. Its name does not correspond to its banal and crooked houses or toy-like signs. The pictures on the tin surfaces illustrate what wares are available in the shops in a straightforward and primitive way. What does a "dragon" have to do with all this?

Figure 19. Tailor from Dragon Street.

We may be disappointed but cheerful after all. The disappointment calls us to order, it helps us overcome the false exoticism which we cast as a veil over life in foreign cities and streets. This life is an ordinary life, a schema known since days of old—life moving between the poles of birth, marriage, and death, and a constant balancing act to prepare for what is to come. This is the life schema which Chagall discovered in his shtetl scenes from Vitebsk.

The likes of "Dragon" streets have a sobering effect on us. The "Dragon" streets stage a protest against offensive exoticism. They protest with their ordinary inconspicuous appearance and gray objectivity. My visit to exotic Dragon Street in Lviv's Jewish quarter comes to an end.

Figure 20. Dragon Street (corner of Owocowa Street), 1937.

Illustrations by Jozefa Kratochwila-Widymska.[13]

---

13 Jozefa Kratochwila-Widymska (1878–1965) was a Polish painter, graphic artist, and sculptor. She was educated in Vienna and lived in Lviv.

16

A Few Remarks on the Contemporary Intellectual Elite (1936)[1]

1

This short essay will not consider the sociological question of whether professional intellectuals as a group constitute a separate social class. (Such consideration would be justified if the work typically associated with a profession were to serve as the criterion for dividing society into classes.)

The focus of this essay is to provide justification for the specific sensibility of the intellectual elite, a certain type of awareness and approach to social issues, as well as grounds for the transformation of the existing form of society. Rehabilitating such a sensibility seems to be ever more relevant, since the contemporary intelligentsia appears to have lost faith in its abilities and frequently attempts to enter the ranks of the proletariat.

"To enter the ranks"—a colloquial expression which has recently gained currency—is difficult to define by a more precise term, since the process it describes is vague in its essence. If we speak exclusively about economically conditioned assimilation, above all to the ranks of the unemployed proletariat, then a programmatic longing for lowering the standard of life would be an artificial and naïve imaginary digression. (Such a concept turns up in disguise from time to time when one conceals her origins or does not allow herself the "luxury" to meet the most essential needs, etc.) Neither do we speak here about the motto of "working for or beside the proletariat," a program which in its previous formulation, "working for the nation," is already long past, as are the first socialist and positivist slogans. This slogan sounds so sentimental and, thus, unacceptable at a time

---

1 See Debora Vogel, "Kilka uwag o współczesnej inteligencji," *Przegląd Społeczny* 10, no. 6 (1936): 114–121.

when the importance of the proletariat in its historical role and necessity has been defined.

The only meaningful "entrance into the ranks of the proletariat" is in terms of spiritual assimilation—the adaptation of a sensibility and engagement with questions. The basis for this tendency is justified; it is a reaction grounded in dialectics, and a real necessity.

2

"Democracy is the idea of the century," Krasiński proclaims in his *Ungodly Comedy*.[2] Today such a proclamation can only be made regarding the role and significance of the proletariat. To understand a social class as "the idea of the century" means to consider it exemplary for the main tendencies and ideals of an era. In fact, the type of work performed by the proletariat—the direct processing of raw materials, as well as the hardness of feeling, and the asceticism associated with them—embodies a contemporary legend, the legend of production and construction.

The need for Constructivism in life—secondary, unadorned, and concrete—is a secretly impulsive force. It encourages the intellectuals to search for support from the proletariat, to ally themselves with the social class which by its way of life actualizes the legend of the time. It is the intelligentsia which creates the schema, basis, and values of the legend.

The abovementioned is justified in terms of the historical dialectic and the biological longing for life. Both are pitiless and brutal. Life saves itself by all means available; it has its own definitive arguments. Nonetheless, the illusory grounds for justification, or smoke screens, and excuses cannot be stopped entirely.

One such smoke screen is the cause of "social justice" and the struggle for the disadvantaged social class often presented by the intelligentsia. It may be considered undisputedly essential for an ethical-sensible way of being, however, it does not have justification, whether dialectical or biological, which would be at all times valid. It has a sentimental, and even "petty bourgeois-decadent," charitable aftertaste.

It is not a matter of "injustice" here—an abstract and incomprehensible concept from the historical point of view, but something much more

---

2   *Nieboska Komedia* is a Romantic play by Zygmunt Krasiński, published in 1853. Its main leitmotif is history and human fates that do not depend on providence. The book is an allusion to Dante's *The Divine Comedy*.

important and ruthless—the necessity and the right of the historical dialectic. The decisions made within its bounds are devoid of feeling. From this point of view, today the proletariat is a social class with historical potential for the future.

An intellectual experiences this evidence and motivations only in theory, and not in terms of direct interactions in life. From this stems the misunderstanding regarding the question of "the intellectuals entering the ranks of the proletariat." The error comes from disregarding the form which social arguments take on in the life of the intellectual. Hence, another misunderstanding which should be formulated even though it is ubiquitous and straightforward.

3

The misunderstanding can be formulated in the following way: the historical value of the proletariat does not always match its actual spiritual physiognomy; "the idea of the century" does not always correspond to reality. One of the possible causes is the nonhomogenous structure of the social class which we universally call the proletariat today. Part of this social class has very petit bourgeois and shoddy needs, illusions, or yearnings. The cult of film stars, the homeliness of lampshades, the comfort of silk stockings all emerge as its ideals, which is understandable in view of the grayness of a life devoid of any gentleness.

The Soviet writer Leonid Leonov[3] depicts these petit bourgeois ideals in earnest, without any ironic undertones. He enthusiastically describes the long hours which take up a whole afternoon spent listening to lectures and light music on the radio. This passive and consumerist ideal justifiably seems boring and unproductive for an intellectual who constantly lives in "Faustian" tension, on an eternal search, and in unrest.

The program of "Romantic Realism" in proletarian art is also petit bourgeois. According to this program, art should only consider the "beautiful sides of life," since life offers too many hateful and filthy aspects. Here there is a certain petit bourgeois longing for coziness and comfort which is carried over into the programmatic province of art. The tendency to consciously falsify representations of life with the intention of providing psychological comfort—as in the case of artistic harmony—is petit bourgeois and decadent.

---

3   Leonid Leonov (1899–1994) was a Soviet writer who was considered a master of Socialist Realism. He was nominated for the Nobel Prize in Literature.

Such tendencies point mostly to the unenlightened proletariat—the colorless and expressionless types whose only merit is that they are hungry, never worked, and are not prepared for any kind of work, who now mix with the unemployed proletariat. However, in the case of the conscientious and creative proletariat we need to deal with a yet another misunderstanding. The intellectual formulates the program—one that is allegedly necessary for the proletariat—a kind of art with the themes and forms specifically cut out for it. In this program the intellectual tasks himself with creation which would serve the supposed needs of the masses, and with decreeing himself as allegedly the closest to the perceived will of the masses.

Admittedly, any conscious proletarian does not agree with such approach to his needs. Rightfully, proletarians perceive it as a humiliation when they are told that only certain areas in life should be of interest to them. Since the proletariat's purpose is to take the place previously occupied by the intelligentsia, it strives to grasp the most complex content—not merely the "simple," set in an seemingly accessible form. Thus, proletarians instinctively appreciate what would be considered complex and incomprehensible works, not only revolutionary art which formulates the needs and programs for the proletariat.

As for the misunderstanding above, experience seems to be undervalued, both in life and artistic experience, even though it is crucial for grasping the specific forms of life and artistic notions.

We forget about the dialectic of forms, the historical proof which makes clear to us how naïve and false it is to allow ourselves to be guided by simple instinct when we would like to grasp certain artistic and life questions. This naïveté, already abandoned in the Soviet Union, belatedly takes root in our country, and manifests itself to the greatest degree in cases when one despises professional expertise and relies on raw primitive feeling.

All these misunderstandings interfere with the life of the intellectual elite to a larger extent than heretofore believed. They cause the intelligentsia's confusion, its distrust in its own worldview and the decision to subordinate itself to the needs of another social group—even though such perceived demands are pure fantasies. This artificial search for the approval of the proletariat translates into the abandonment of their own intellectual worlds, and the emergence of questionable cultural values as a result. And yet we recognize that it is possible to have different formulations of needs in life and of social arguments. Both can reach a common denominator and strengthen or emphasize one another through parallels.

4

In the *Bells of Basel*,[4] L[ouis] Aragon claims that the intellectual will never be able to grasp a proletarian's soul, since he does not know the difficult and monotonous labor of the proletarian. His claim contains pejorative irony which is true of the intelligentsia and its attempts to enter the ranks of the proletariat.

In his outstanding book *The Impossible People*, Béla Balázs[5] courageously points to the at times strange motivations of revolutionaries which might appear totally incommensurate with responsible work for the revolution.

Individuals led astray in search of inner adventures; those for whom a toothbrush becomes an excessively irksome symbol of reality; the decadent, sentimental, and exaggeratedly refined Romantic who does not know what to do with her life—all of them are suddenly presented with the possibility to make something out of everydayness; and they hold onto this concrete possibility with the grip of a drowning person. Distributing illegal communist works may take the outline of concrete activity which makes the life meaningful.

Therefore, it is neither a conviction in the right thing, nor a theoretical belief, a mode of questioning, nor a desire for a new order which stirs people to action in this case. Rather, it is a silly need for adventure in life which here suddenly takes on the form of a controlled activity. Thus, working for the cause of communism is no more than a psychological adventure—Balázs accounts for such possibility and rehabilitates it.

One could say that such reasoning is decadent, moreover, one should not reckon with these people because they are not the ones to create a new social order. However, such a judgment is unjustified: finding happiness and purpose in life can be as strong a motivation as hunger or exploitation. This concerns people for whom the main stage for events in life is the so-called soul and its adventures.

We might even claim that these purely idealistic reasons are more obsessive and have a more lasting effect, leading to more radical activity than the reflexes of hate or revenge. The mounting questions without answer, "How should one

---

4   This novel (1934) was part of a series of social novels under the umbrella title *The Real World*. *Les Cloches de Bâle* depicts the period from the Basel antiwar congress (1912) until the beginning of WWII. At the center of the novel is the interaction of various classes in French society, namely the proletariat and the intelligentsia.

5   Béla Balázs (1884–1949) was a Hungarian writer, film theoretician, and screenplay writer. This novel was published in 1930 in German. The Hungarian version of the novel appeared in 1965.

live?" and "What should one do with one's life?"—considered as "luxuries"—can become larger than life. They may loom so large that even death may appear too small a price for life; it may become a ransom, a risk that one takes in a transaction which has a chance of ending well.

The intellectual sensibility is to experience even such problems as hunger and unemployment in this way. Therefore, the intelligentsia plays a significant role in working towards social transformation.

When I give examples of this "intellectual" sensibility in my montages *Flower Shops with Azaleas* (*Acacias Bloom*, Rój, 1936), I am certain that the whole social group, of which I am part, perceives these issues in this exact way.

This sensibility can find its expression in such statements as longing "for the full roundness and the mild melancholy of rectangular objects,"[6] for elastic metal, cool and still glass which may incite to revolution. Perceiving unemployment from its "poetic" side is another such impulse. One may say that one lacks vaulted, great space, instead space may be only perceived as expressionless, "flat like potato peels."[7] The space might also lack the noise of "things yet incomplete and unprepared,"[8] which may document well that "life is indispensable after all, and there is no time to be wasted."[9] The exaggerated perfection and completeness of things serves the same purpose. The flawlessness of things testifies to the fact that there are no other tasks and aims left in life.

The ironic notion of dexterity used to mock the intellectual should be revised. The typical motivations for this group will be rehabilitated in terms of intensity and authenticity. Neither the proletariat nor the intellectuals benefit from the abnormalities that have grown as if on a foreign body. Only grotesque structures which belong nowhere and are realized in this dubious way remain. This strange and troubling phenomenon comes to the fore as especially crass in the case of artistic production—both in the psyche of the artist, and in the type of artistic creation.

We may observe the grotesque split of an artist degraded by his petit bourgeois origins into two types of personalities, the programmatically proletarian with a seemingly proletarian sensibility, and another one, no more "intellectual" than the first, boring and sentimental-bourgeois sensibility. The latter is expressed independently from the first one, mainly through eroticism. The

---

6   See "Ships Carry Gold" in *Flower Shops with Azaleas*, p. 235.
7   See "Life is Undertaken from the Beginning," p. 246.
8   See "Houses with Hard Rhythm," p. 225.
9   Ibidem.

impossibility of harmonizing the two tendencies, which we may call the social and the biological, attests to the artificial nature of the corresponding thought process of intellectual assimilation with the proletariat.

(E[lżbieta] Szemplinska's[10] poetry offers an interesting example of such ambivalence. Another poet, K[adia] Molodowsky,[11] attempts to reconcile both life tendencies: on the one hand, the biological tendency—the form and symbolism of a "saffron day in July," and on the other, the social tendency—the form and symbolism of *Dzhike gas*.[12] Eventually, the poet rejects the poetic mood of the saffron day which results in self-accusation: she, the poet who wears yet-unworn shoes, walks amidst the people in Dzhike Street, and "writes poetry." Thus, she must be different from the people she meets).

This approach gives rise to an insufferable type of literature—melancholy and sentimental self-accusations—pure egotism in an era of objectivity and collectivity, a self-centeredness which should have been overcome long ago. The poet repeatedly places her torn and sentimental soul at the center of her poetry and affectively requires that it be reckoned with. Romanticism, long outdated, and its corresponding cult of the individual, appears again and again.

Upon consideration, such a programmatic stance shows the ideological camp to which the writer belongs in a straightforward way; it serves as a basis for the classification of the writer as the "proletarian" or the "bourgeois-fascist."

However, the writer "belongs" only insofar as she is able to express the needs of her contemporaries and grasp new social and individual realities. The artist becomes contemporary only by proposing a certain construction of reality rather than by virtue of program, party membership, or political beliefs.

We need to investigate the notion of "contemporary art" further. The "contemporary" is often defined directly—through themes and questions from proletarian life—and indirectly, through the creative process itself which envisions the proletariat as the consumer.

Two mistakes are evident here. This type of art is mainly produced by "intellectual" writers (the Soviet Union is an exception), for whom this area

---

10 Elżbieta Szemplińska-Sobolewska (1909–1991) was a Polish poet. In 1939 after the Soviet occupation of Lviv, she was the editor of the *Literary Almanac*, an organ of the Writer's Union.
11 Vogel wrote about Kadia Molodowsky, her visit to Lviv, and her poetry in her review "Kadja Molodowska," *Chwila*, no. 4265 (1931): 9. See also Debora Vogel's essay, "White Words in Poetry."
12 *Dzhike gas* was one of six poetry collections by Molodowsky. It was published in Warsaw in *Literarishe bleter* in 1935. The collection depicts the life of the poor Jewish quarter, in particular a city street in Warsaw.

is terra incognita. As a result, the theme is slightly exoticized—a burden from which one needs to free oneself. The second fundamental mistake of the above-mentioned artistic conception is that it barely considers the intelligentsia itself. In this view, the intelligentsia is unimportant and marginal, significant only when it becomes akin to the proletariat. This is also the reason for the intellectuals whose lifestyle is not taken into account in art, to search for footing in a sphere where there is a responsibility for human life and fate.

To summarize, the intellectual sensibility and perception can be rehabilitated only when we recognize the otherness and the value of the raw materials with which the intellectuals deal—the raw materials of thought and feeling, which correspond to the raw materials with which the proletariat deals.

I have accounted for the arguments and interests on both sides of the issue to provide proof that identification is an unnecessary artificial process which falsifies the multifaceted nature of life. However, this does not mean that the significance of the proletariat as a historical class is denigrated. Quite the opposite. If we grant the intellectuals the power of creation, insofar as their artistic production is analogous to that of the proletariat, then we highlight both the importance of the proletariat as well as clearly define the position of the intellectuals.

Both social groups meet on the level of the legend of production and processing of raw materials. Raw materials in a literal sense become firm geometrical objects with clearly outlined contours, which are introduced into systems of forms and concepts (the "raw materials of the psyche").

Part Two

"An Attempt at a New Style": Poetry

Selections from
Day Figures (1930)

Figure 21. Cover of the first edition of *Day Figures*, 1930.

17

Preface to the *Day Figures* Collection[1]

The rule of boredom is ruthless, it reveals itself not only in the events and experiences, but also regulates and measures the course of the life of forms.

Gradually, boredom can be a style. This means that the form combinations of a certain kind are exhausted. The forms may become exhausted like things and events. Then they are transformed into the gray surfaces which have lost their contours and their colorfulness and fantasticality. And, thus, they say that a worldview has been exhausted—it has reached its end.

Boredom comes in this way. The fact of life and the combination of forms do not possess the rhythm and the excitement of experiences anymore. Without this boredom, any attempt at a new style is incomprehensible. Here lies the origin of my poems.

Modern plastic arts grasped the fact that the surface, line, and color are simply the elements of a distinct reality constructed in a composition. In poetry, the word acquires the role of line and color. Yet the word is too strongly bound to the rationalized life. The word is too much of a carrier and mediator of needs and orientations in life. Therefore, it is difficult to justify and make comprehensible the role of the word in poetry. It is simply an element in the construction of a specific reality.

I consider my poetry to be an attempt at a new style. I find analogies to modern painting in these poems.

Simplifying the seeming multiplicity of events and reducing them to a few simple, angular and repetitive gestures—to monotony and cool stasis—is a tendency in Cubism in general.

Such simplification originates in the realization that complexity and multiplicity are simply an addition and a superstructure. However, a schematic geometrical figure contains that which is unchangeable. This is noticeable when

---

1   See Debora Vogel, *Tog Figurn. Lider* (Lemberg: Farlag Tsushtayer, 1930).

the complexity we attach to a few things and events reaches its highest tension. Then it can suddenly turn into its opposite, a geometrical surface, a gray ascetic line. The geometrical figure is the principle of the monotony with its repetition of one contour.

A new type of lyric can arise in this way, a lyric of cool stasis and geometrical ornamentality with its monotony and rhythm of return. This lyric may replace the dynamism, or melodiousness, which until recently has been regarded as the single principle in poetry.

The monotony can become a distinctive mark of style. It could be analogous to the rhythmical monotony of an ornament. This monotony is derived from the monotony as a theme. It unfolds as a method of working with the certain simplified objects, situations, states, and the names of things that return in a few combinations. The following formal means originate in this theme, the counting of things and situations, the use of numerals as graphic signs to replace certain similar things or perhaps even the same thing which is simply repeated multiple times.

It is difficult to attain the multiplicity and the colorfulness when you want to limit yourself to the real and lasting elements, to a couple of angular, unhewn blocks of situations. Therefore, this cool geometrical ornamentality could appear as cold and overly measured when compared to the style full of metaphors.

However, as K[arol] Irzykowski answered the accusations of his "lack of warmth" once, "you should be very hot in order to be so cold."[2]

This collection of poetry should set an example of this kind of lyric, the lyric of that which is static in life.

It would be a misreading if you were to believe the poems to be an artificial experiment. Such a formal attempt is a necessity, attained and purchased by the trials of life.

---

2   This answer by Karol Irzykowski (1873–1944), a Polish writer and literary and film critic, addressed the criticism of Stanisław Leopold Brzozowski (1878–1911), a Polish philosopher, writer, and literary critic who reviewed Irzykowski's novel *The Hag* (1903).

18

Rectangles (1924)

DAY FIGURE

A gray rectangle.
A second. A third.
Seven times the tin rectangle opens.

Yellow sun. Red sun.
On one side, on another:
the day-rectangle has closed.

Gray tin birds hover.
Lumps of soft dough with two hands and two feet
roll in the gray clay of light.
Four times a day.
Yellow sun on one side of the rectangle, on the other.

A first month of stiff tin flowers,
a second, a third month
of sticky tin flowers, hands and clothes.

How many times it has opened
how many times closed,
the tin rectangle
with the yellow sun-circle on both sides.

CROSS SECTION

Many days have passed by in the glass sphere.
Many suns, on two sides
many dusks, twice a day.

126 | "An Attempt at a New Style": Poetry

Figure 22. Henryk Streng's illustration for "Rectangles" from *Day Figures*, 1930.

The day is a rectangular lump.
A block with two suns times seven
is called a week.

Seven times: a yellow light. A blue light.
Seven times: a yellow sun. A white sun.
You count days unused.

And again you count:
a second week, a third, a fourth.
A block with thirty suns: a month.

Three months of blue skies and sticky sprouts
three months of yellow metal flowers, birds, and clothes
three months when everything is the same
and three with white days flat as paper.

And nothing comes.
How many times have the sprouts sprung up
how many times the white paper days arrived.

STILL LIFE IN COLD

Half a year
days are in green twilight
as in Flemish paintings of green cold.

Half a year
nights drag on for twelve hours.
Long like bodiless days.

The day is a glass-colored length
divided into two halves
by a flat red circle.

Between four gray walls of the world-rectangle
board-like bodies rise

flat wooden logs on two feet.
Every twelve hours.

Nothing more happens
in the glass rectangle
with yellow stars, white stars.

Faces become flat panes—
colorless glass quadrangles like days.

And dull-wooden watery-yellow four sides:
pieces of flat boards, like wooden-yellow nights.

WHITE SQUARES

Weeks of white
three months of white day squares.
Every year these three months come
with the seven day count in a week.

Every day the snow stuff from the gray sky is gray.
The suns are red: red moons.
Every day is a square with a blue edge of a night.

Seven times a week
the day is white, the sun red, all bodies.
The streets are without length.
On the first street a white house stands,
on the second street one, two, three
white houses, gray houses:
heavy and light bodies. Cold bodies.

Seven times the four-sided figure comes.
You ask again
for the second time
why lift your feet, why lift hands.

STILL LIFE IN GLASS

Between two white gray bulging scales of the world
hangs the glass fruit of space
with a white creased paper kernel
of a stiff angular sun.

Every day the white kernel sits in the flesh of glass,
bodies revolve, with faces like cool flat panes,
and glass birds come and go, like lumps of identical days.
First dusk. Second gloaming.

Until a colorless flat rectangle of sound falls
out of the glass containers of bodies:
like a long sigh of glassen shards.

Now all encounters sound monotonous:
like spheres of colorless glass,
like flat panes of liquid glass.

Like a long sigh of cool glass.

STILL LIFE WITH SEAGULLS

Out of the fragrant lead of sea, which ebbs and flows
countless times
Between two suns—

round grayness comes over seven days.
Seven days: seven gray pearl beads.
Falling one by one: the first bead and the seventh.

Gray paper shells of seagulls
ebb. Flow. Ten times in a row.
Twenty times.

With the dawning of the dawn
until the dusk.

With a cry, so round
and monochrome gray like a bead of a day.

How can the yellow star roll every day
how can blue waves and shells of seagulls flow
and people lift their legs
when every day is a single bead
floating on the surface seven times a week.

FLAT DECORATION AT NOON

Gray paper rectangles
colorful rectangles
gray houses. Colorful houses.

In front of paper squares, red-colored circles tighten.
Red dahlias
angular and stiff like paper, like busy people.

And yellow circles: small tin suns
with a pungent smell of oil
stand lost, like people at noon.

Houses dahlias sunflowers
are circles in the first street, in the second street
from five in the morning. For a week. For ten and twenty years.

Light dolls with glassy eyes
in green and white window frames
now stick out their white and yellow faces:
triangles of white and yellow cardboard.

Glass drops of the elliptical eyes in green windows
follow tin angular streets.
The metal sphere of sticky heat seals the stiff streets.

In the yellow light glass resonates
for two hours.
Each day is lost.

THE TWELFTH HOUR IN A DAY

The space is a sphere of glass
filled with clay-yellow light.

Three white apple trees
shed flowers: tin circles.
Two lumps of bodies
raise hands: four yellow wooden logs with fingers.

And a clay mass with hundreds of feet and hands
is pressed into a firm angle of a cube
out of the sphere of clay: one time and another.

Then the tin voice
of a shabby red music box rings
the monotonous clang of glass panes of days
and circular streets
which flow into the house where you live for twelve hours.

The sweet tin rhythm of equal days
is like the shabby red music box.
It mixes with a shard of sound: where to?

Now you don't count the squandered years anymore
their yellow glow is a thousand years old.
Everything should be as is.

The red music box of days should rewind
its tin cheap melody.

SUN IN THE YELLOW STREETS

The houses are tin-yellow squares
scattered on a blue cloth.

In angular streets of stiff yellow metal
it smells of sticky light
like viscous tin
and watery glass.

The sun is an orange sphere of glass
Between tin-yellow leaves of houses
on the tin platters of the streets.

In metal streets
a single body circles:
a yellow sun.

The sun-body is
a sweet weight
like two breasts filled with white milk.
It is a lighter weight
like falling flower circles of white fragrant tin.

Where should you go
to another body with hands and feet.
The sun is a body. A hot body. It drags around the streets.

AUTUMN DECORATION WITH PEOPLE

Inside blue glass fruit
on the wallpaper of the sky
a gray, a dirty-pink, a lime-green house
is painted.

Ribbons of gray-pearl sweet milk
flow under
they are streets with figures of smiling yellow tin.

The figures have sweet gray flecks of eyes
the same color as the streets
where everything is always the same.

They have heavy golden-velvet flecks of eyes
the color of long streets after many months
of aimless strolls
with multiple returns.

PARCHMENT LANDSCAPE

Gray strokes of rusty triangular leaves
painted on yellow parchment.

On the parchment street platters
golden leaves smell
of rotting things.

And wooden figures shrouded in copper garments
circle slowly on round parchment plates
where no one ends up anywhere.

Four weeks
are repeated three times.

Now nothing can happen anymore
and everything should be as it is.

AUTUMN SKETCH

In the gray zinc plate of the world
gray strokes of squares
are etched with a cold needle
three four five house-boxes.

Made from citrus-yellow cardboard
(the color of abandoned things)
three female heads stick out from the misty windowpanes
of the tin tray of one day,
seven tin trays of a week.

Gray sweet milk of equal days
trickles thirty times
thirty times thirty

into the three citrus-yellow plates of faces
into glassy circles of eyes
that become sweet flecks of grayness

Like the milk of days, when you don't want anything anymore.

IN THE WINDOWS

At six in the morning
red, yellow, white window shutters open.
At six at night
colorful window shutters close.

At six in the morning
citrus-yellow, clay-brown, chalk-white faces
cling to
the red, yellow, white frames.

In the flat glass windowpanes at noon
yellow and white faces become rectangles
and people cling to the four angles of days.

Seven times
yellow squares of walls
with faces white and yellow go outside
seven days a week they go away.

Seven times
a red pane, a yellow is pressed into a frame
like longing.

The world of many weeks is a square wall
that goes up seven times a week
with rectangular suns of citrus-yellow, clay-brown, chalk-white faces.

Faces days weeks are rectangles
Lime-yellow, chalk-white.

Figure 23. Henryk Streng's illustration for "Houses and Streets" from *Day Figures*, 1930.

19

Houses and Streets (1926)

GRAY STREETS[3]

The streets are like the sea
they reflect the color of longing
and difficulty of waiting.

They are gray now
like pearls of renunciation.

And citrus-yellow faces
in pale-yellow house windows
fade out
like pale transparent lanterns
that go out at 4 in the morning.

In the milky-gray streets
you don't count lost days anymore:
they run out like thick sweet milk.

Faces are extinguished with the color of renunciation
like gray streets with yellow lantern moons
which want nothing anymore.

GRAY HOUSES

One gray house.
The second gray house.
A third and fourth gray house.

---

3   This poem was published in French in Joseph Milbauer, ed., *Cahiers du Journal des Poetès*, Série anthologique, Collection no. 20: *Poetès Yiddish d'aujourd'hui* [Brussels] (1936): 85.

Go together
one day. A second day.
7 weekdays long.

They stretch 60 or 100 feet.
For 12 hours.
The first day. The second. The seventh.

Lights go on. In the first house. In the second.
Lights go off. In the first house. In the second.
7 o'clock at night. 10 o'clock at night.

The second day
they stretch again another 60 feet
two three four gray houses.

SUBURBAN HOUSES

After Utrillo[4]

In the watery pink house they sell:

$$tobacco \text{ and } cigars$$

a cheap watery scent for evenings of desolate people.

And on the street corner—
you can get coffee: a thick brown drink
which caresses you softly like the blue tobacco smoke.

Sad, long strokes of an inscription
on the tin sign with a purple-lacquered figure
sway for seven days: The House of Pretty Gabrielle.
The memory of your broken heart could be clouded here. One evening and another.

Until you see a cynical sign nearby:
Old Bedding

---

4   The French painter Maurice Utrillo (1883–1955) painted many versions of *Le cabaret de la belle Gabrielle à Montmartre*.

For Sale.
Two helpless hearts punctured with two arrows,
sketched with a pencil
hearts forever broken.
And their story etched in crooked strokes.

Seven days of a first week and a second,
two banal hearts are painted on the wall
with the lines written beneath:
You are the most beautiful memory of my life—
and an added clumsy chunk of a sentence:
You are my life's misfortune.

SUNDAY OF SUBURBAN HOUSES

Before the lime-green car-repair workshop
1 red wheel is on the ground
and a yellow car with 3 red wheels.

In front of the yellow house, the first and second gray houses
three, four, five lumps of yellow clay with glassy eyes
sit the whole seventh day
wheels have nowhere to go:

and no car drives in, no car drives out
of the windowless red garage-house.

But Monday at 6 in the morning
the green repair shop, the red garage,
gray houses, cars with 4 wheels and clay lumps with feet
move a few yards farther away

the sphere of space is large again
it can take in houses, cars, bodies.

LAMENT ABOVE COURTYARD WALLS

The rear walls are not guilty of anything
of not having been whitewashed even once,

only smeared with fatty black and yellow paint
with cynical advertising slogans.

On the other side a 1000 suns
rise up every evening. At 4 in the afternoon
round electric eyes already open. Red, aquamarine blue, yellow orange.
They shape elastic bodies with breasts, as do people's searching eyes.

But here 7 days a week a flat sun hangs
and caresses cynical advertisements.
And maybe, as a result, a legend of the single yellow sun
can still rise.

BIG CITY SUN

The big city sun is smaller than the moon
and smaller than each red lamp
and every orange or blue lamp-sun
that lights up every night at six.

Yellow and red lamp-apples flicker on
glaring brighter than the succulent sun-orange.
You can count them like days running out,
days extinguished in the blue night, like suns.

And somewhere there are more lime-white houses
red window shutters green window shutters open and close
and the windows open and close
as does the yellow sun.

And there are also back walls
painted muddy green and bleak red
where hearts are drawn in red and blue chalk
along with etched lovers' goodbyes.

It could be that here one still needs the sun.

THE CITY SUN AND THE CITY MOON

Seven times a week,
who counts it
a yellow sign hangs above gray-block walls.

Seven times a flat lantern climbs the blue sphere
it seizes every day:
among a thousand red and yellow lanterns the thousandth and the first.

Why does the yellow sun still rise,
why the white moon
above thousands of citrus-yellow blue cherry-red suns.

Who counts them
on the day with a thousand red green yellow suns
in the night with a thousand red green yellow suns.

A POEM ABOUT THE COLORFUL LIGHTS OF ADVERTISEMENTS

A poem about the colorful lights of advertisements
in red yellow blue letters
about the flat angular suns of written lines.

The colorful strokes of shoe and fur ads
are a poem written by a gentle poet
on the gray cardboard of city walls.

The cherry red glows and draws like another body.
The aquamarine blue caresses like an inexperienced hand.
The citrus yellow cools with its metallic light.

The red blue yellow bodies of lines
can change around for twenty-four hours.
And rise five or ten times a day.

Under the electric suns of advertisements
there is no point in counting days.

You can only absorb the colorful body of light
breathe in the glowing smell
and go around in circles.

In a rectangle. In a circle. In a parable.
Four times a day. Five and ten times a day.
Countless times you go
from one body to another
led by the colorful round eyes of lamps.

HOUSES AT NIGHT[5]

Night streets would be lost
and we would be abandoned
if not for the houses.

They stand on the streets.
And, like us, perhaps wait
for a second body.

So you can compare them to bodies,
a gray house with red light inside
and the second gray house. With yellow light.

The first house is like
a transparent light body,
which can still long for something
that could have come but didn't.

And the second house is
a robust body with sweet light kernels of longing
of thirty evenings a month filled with waiting,
a house, which has given up the wait.

And you still have someone to go to
in the bodiless glass city globe.

---

5   A slightly different version of this poem appeared in *Tsushtayer* 2 (1930): 25.

A WALL WITH FLYERS IN THE RAIN[6]

Today the rain has covered gray houses with a second coat of paint
with its hidden color gray.

You are far away.
Now everyone is.
And one cannot turn to anyone.

I lean back
against the wall of fliers covered
with citrus-yellow and orange-red papers.

Today the rain has washed off the heat.
The crimson letters read:
in cinemas today
a film about the red ballerina.

The red strokes are caressing hands
hands that fall heavily
on hot bodies of yellow paper.

In the midst of ten gray houses
the board wall is covered in yellow and red
a single hot colorful body.
And you can unite with it
as if with a human body
that is now distant:
unreachable.

THREE HOUSES

Someone has painted little rectangular boxes
with the color of rare fruit

---

6   "Plakant-vant in regn" appeared in *Tsushtayer* 2 (1930): 25. An English translation of this poem by Adrienne Rich appeared in *A Treasury of Yiddish Poetry*, ed. Irving Howe and Eliezer Greenberg (New York: Schocken, 1969), 236.

figures circle from morning till night.

In the cherry-red house
the days are stuffy like the flesh of waiting.
You can enjoy the day, like glass lamp-cherries.
And everything could still happen to the bodies.

In the orange house
thirty layers of thirty gray days settle
and become the glassy fluid
of days, when everything is the same.

But in the citrus-yellow box
where you live, after seven years of waiting
the days become flat glass panes,
the nights cool glass fruit.
And you know: nothing can happen.

After seven counted years, the days become clear panes
like quiet glassy joy.

STILL LIFE WITH HOUSES AND LANTERNS

In a flat paper rectangle
yellow tin boxes stand
with figures of red porcelain.

And between hot bronze leaves
the lantern lighter hangs glass-fruit
round oranges and oblong citrus ellipses
of fragrant colored glass.

To lean against the fragrant tin of houses.
And eat the cooling flesh
of red glass oranges
of yellow glass citruses
with their sweet light-kernels in the middle.

GLASS FLOWERS

The moon is a white cherry blossom
smelling murky with the sticky longing
of seven years.

And the lanterns
are yellow tulips of glass
planted in the first, second, third street.

Yellow glass
smells of cool hands
and amber beads of renunciation.

You can go onto the first street.
Onto the second.
Let drops of blue moon flow into yourself
that smell of sticky longing,
and the coolness of yellow lantern-glass.

What more can happen each evening:
only the distant smell of sticky waiting,
only the cool glass-fragrance of renunciation.

PRIMITIVE LIFE IN THE CITY

Can you live like a blue mountain,
like a green river,
between lamp-suns and moon-ads
under cherry-red orange-yellow leaf-green city suns?

Cool water flowing through a pipe, steel-fragrant
and the water of glowing air with the yellow metal smell
can be like a caressing green body of a river.

And pot-bellied fruit of
the sun-cherries, sun-oranges of ads:

like golden apples, cherries, plums,
cool down the body with their glass bodies.

You go down every street
like a river flows: for twenty years and for a hundred.
Like a mountain stands: for twenty years and for a hundred.
Seven days a week.
Seven times the same street.
For the seventh time a thousand suns, blue and red.

Until the yellow walls with fliers and colorful lamp-suns
fall out of the round hall of the night city.

And you are not lost anymore, and you go
embraced by tender hands of fliers
caressed by hot lamp-bodies
for two or three hours.
Until you go back into a flat rectangle of a room
and go out: like a yellow sun. Like a white moon.

STREETS AND PEOPLE I

You can live like a street
like the yellow one,
tin ribbon moving
seven days a week
between foggy-gray, coffee-brown, orange-red houses.

Six in the morning
the yellow window of the street opens,
embarks on a long journey
from the first house to the second.

Four times a day
you walk to the second house and then back
to the first.

At night you turn onto a clear street,
lean against

ten yellow lanterns
longing for another.

Ten lanterns
lead the blue street to the second.
Two three four crystalline hour-long clangs.

And you become a tired street,
which returns to a foggy-gray, coffee-brown, orange house
and wishes no more
to be an empty world-globe without length.

STREETS AND PEOPLE II

From round yellow streets of twelve o'clock
and rectangular streets of milk-gray autumn material,
and flat paper streets
mixed with bodies
like wax apples, a paint is mixed.

In the yellow street
the fleshy yellow metal of waiting burns.
Hard beads of thirty renunciations in a month
fall silently from the gray street.

And the flat white street
reflects the sad paper of happiness
of daily walks in the second street.

And one becomes a yellow street
gray and white paper street.

Houses and Streets (1926) | 147

Figure 24. Henryk Streng's illustration for "Tired Dresses" from *Day Figures*, 1930.

20

Tired Dresses (1925–1929)

WEARINESS

Today again is
the fifteenth day of the month.
Many times the fifteenth of a month has already come
many times the next fifteen days have gone.

Every year apple trees blossom
and again the trees yellow
and the chestnut tree in front of my window glows red.

Seven years have gone by
since I began counting unused years.

What will happen this year? What the next?
What for the coming years:
nothing comes.

Years do not count.
Only days are there:
a single day that returns a thousand times.

THE EIGHTH AUTUMN

I have counted autumns
for seven years
again the trees are red and yellow,
and nothing comes.

Now I do not count anymore
the sun is a hot body that drags through the streets.

The lanterns caress.
The yellow and red posters caress.

And the houses are
sad bodies
you can go along with them
three or four hours.

Nothing can come anymore,
everything should be as is.

THE RED FLOWER

Of a fire-red flower
that has blossomed overnight
in the home of a lonely person.

Where does the fire red come from
now when the sun is a circle of flat paper
that goes down at 3 in the afternoon,
between the four white limestone walls,
where no one comes in to stir
the solid fluidity of waiting.

And perhaps the fire-red flower that
waited for seven years to bloom
comes from the oppressive climate of the house,
where for seven years someone has
relinquished every single day
one or two hours in.

Until it ignited with renunciation:
as seven years of waiting for the flower come to an end
in a dark wave the heavy color of flames.

A POEM ABOUT AMBER

Yellow amber is a tear of a tree
which mourns the golden beetle.

It smells of sticky resin of yellow days,
when everything can happen,
and of gray matter of days,
when it's all the same.

In its cool cracks
sticky sighs of thirty days
lie enclosed
sticky drops of renunciation.

AUTUMN DAHLIAS

In a flask of blue crystal glass
three tea-yellow dahlias stand in my room.
They are in bloom for the second time now.

They bloom for the first time
as if made of stiff tin:
like angular people: like busy people.

And when they bloom for the second time
they are as if from still porcelain,
the same as people that carry around in the vase of their body
thirty gray water pearls
of unused days.

With the watery smell of abandoned days
like hard drops of renunciation
in the cool crystal glass of thirty days.

YELLOW LANDSCAPE

Somewhere in hot yellow-red sand
a loamy river idly flows
with the sticky smell of tired yellow leaves.

In our place dahlias bloom for the second time.
Thirty days of hot sun glow yellow three times,
like round oranges from foreign, idle lands.

You can glow once again
with the hot metallic color of waiting
like a murky-yellow dahlia which blossoms for the second time.

Until the body becomes a stuffy pearl in an idle yellow river,
with a sticky smell of tired rusty leaves,
of the metal of waiting,
of your sweet body.

RUSTY-RED DRESS

Rusty paint-sap
covers the threads of my dress:
so I wear the color of an autumn leaf.

There are many thousand threads in a dress
and to count them: every thread
is tired like rust from three and six months of waiting.

How tired must be the material
woven with tiredness-threads
like a tree in autumn. Like my body.

With a rusty-red dress on
I am a tired chestnut tree in the month of October,
in November.

ABOUT THE AUTUMN DRESS

I have imagined a dress for myself
of a lost murky-gold color
of late blooming flowers in October.

It is now the month of October.
Dahlias bloom for the second and third time.
I can go out again in the glass streets of a round city,
for the second and third time:
something should come from the streets.

But nobody comes.
Neither the first week. Nor the second.
And I have counted this way for seven years.

ON THE DRESS OF MOURNING

Today it is the fifteenth day of Tammuz again.[7]
The sphere is yellow. The sun is spherical. The sun is yellow.
Again one of three months when anything can happen.

Today I put away the black dress
I have worn every day for twelve months
the rigid dress made of black material.

Twelve months were
as one month.
Neither the first half of the day.
Nor the second.

But a gray block:
from one dawn to the next.

Now I want to have many days.
Many months. Many bodies.

ON LONGING[8]

Today I've bought yellow cherries
they smell watery like longing.

The cherries never grow old.
These cherries are sixteen and seventeen years old.

Today I am like a yellow cherry
I feel again the somewhat empty taste
of wandering at night in the city streets
with yellow lanterns.

---

7   The Hebrew month of June–July.
8   An English translation of this poem by Adrienne Rich appeared in *A Treasury of Yiddish Poetry*, ed. Irving Howe and Eliezer Greenberg (New York: Schocken, 1969), 238.

Every evening something might happen in the world.
Something might come
from so much walking
so many people do daily.

Yet as in the previous year
and two and three years before
again, nothing happens.

I have only understood the watery taste
of longing.

CHERRY-RED SUN

Yesterday the sun was cherry red.
A big cherry was the sun
that smelled of yellow metal heat,
a pungent metallic smell.

In the white cherry garden of an evening
the red sun-cherry exploded.

I have sniffed the sticky flesh
of lost evenings and unused days
like the smell of a big sun-cherry
with a pungent smell
of yellow and rusty-red weary metals.

MOUNTAINS AND FRUIT

Mountains are pot-bellied fruit
placed on a flat platter
of gray fog.

At times they are long plums
of see-through cheap blue:
fruit with a watery flesh of longing:
people who can still wait.

And at other times they are heavy gray glass apples:
Cezanne's solitary apples,
lonely people in the first, second, third streets
desiring nothing more.

LOVE POEM

It was not a yellow day when everything could happen
nor a blue evening, when someone runs out of waiting—
when you came to me—

but a gray afternoon
between two dull identical days.

And wet snow fell, tired
like the tears of days of abandoned people
that don't want anything anymore.

Only then did you come, only then.
Why does everything always come too late?

FAREWELL

It is the fifth autumn
since we began counting the autumns together.

Too many times
we parted
in a yellow glow, in gray stillness.

Soon days of Elul[9] will come again.
And the stuffy grayness
that doesn't want anything anymore.

Once again we want
to walk alone.

---

9   The Hebrew month of August–September.

To walk the same streets
and never meet.

A LOVE POEM

But today I came to see you,
just fifteen minutes too late
I came to the garden
quarter to one
we agreed to meet
at half past twelve.

You, day in day out—
how long can someone part forever
and again decide on a time to meet
and walk side by side somewhere far away.

And you are a hot human body
with two slender hands that caress.

But alone I walk in circles
in the glass streets of the night city
and allow a yellow wall with flyers to caress me
my whole body kissing the scarlet flesh of crimson letters.

Will I be able to live
without your two slender hands,
and two hungry eyes
accompanying every quiver of my body?

WEARINESS OF WAITING

Twenty-five years circling around—
will feet not grow weary?
Twenty-five years I have walked along the same streets.

I've walked the streets
and not once have I met you:
neither on the first street, nor on the second.

Now you must come.
Now I no longer want to ask who you are.
And take my lips. Take my colored words.

3 POEMS ON WAITING

1
How long can one linger near a window
or stroll in the streets, yellow, gray, and blue
and wait until you travel from a city
three hours away
from mine?

A person can wait a whole year.
For eleven o'clock.
Yet you don't come
the first week, or the second.
Every week that ends
is seven times awaiting you.

I have paced out the streets in search of you:
the yellow street at noon
when somehow everything is lost,
the street at three in the afternoon
when everything is like everything else.

And the evening street of glass
where a yellow wall of fliers
could become a second caressing body.
First street. Second and third.

And I went back into the streets,
where I met twenty bodies, fifty bodies—
but not you.
Where were you.

2
I have worn out
all my dresses
waiting for you.

I put them on the first time
took them off the last time
in a month of sticky sun, in a month of tired leaves

in the evening garden
a chestnut red dress,
ready to wrap me
soft as velvet.

The rust-gold dress
for the month of tired leaves
and bleak flowers' second blossoms.

And a coral-colored dress,
in which I look like a cold coral
in the glass sea of afternoon streets
with a smell of the seaweed of bodies.

Never again
will I worry what dress to wear for you.

3
The blue of my eyes
flows out after you.

Slowly trickles out
like a sweet fruity wine of longing, aged for seven years.
Every evening you don't come
the blue turns a murky yellow.

This evening I stopped
waiting. Yet I wait.
Wait and wait still.

Every evening my body becomes
a porcelain vase
wanting to spill the fragrant oil
of its longing.

And when no one comes
the waiting slowly trickles out,
until the very last drop.

HORSE I[10]

You are light and supple.
Like a young horse.
You laugh. You can laugh.
Then you lift your head high
like a young horse, sniffing out a beaten path.

Today the snow is soft,
breathing of fragrant oats.
And anything could happen to me.

I want to show you how to tempt me:
tell me about all your lovers.
Or perhaps you have had no lovers yet?

Were they dark-blooded, sturdy like cows,
or slender and supple like the stems of flowers,
or do you prefer a body's soft roundness?
Or perhaps porcelain dolls,
with lively eyes, eyes like raisins?

Someday you'll say this about me:
I met her one night.

---

10 In the first version, the poem's title was "Du bist laykht un beygevdik" [You are light and supple]. It appeared in *Tsushtayer* 1, no. 1 (1929): 37. It was also published in Hebrew in *Al neharot: tish'ah mahazore shirah mi-sifrut Yidish* [By the rivers: an anthology of Yiddish poetry], ed. Shimshon Meltzer, Dov Sadan, and Moshe Starkman (Yerushalaim: Mosad Byalik, 1956), 25.

It was the fifth day
of some week
in a month like all the others.

A year-old young mare, burning
to be consumed
by fragrant snow oats,
and perhaps also by me.

HORSE II

Brown horses in yellow streets
streets with hard iron clamor,
with the yellow speed of falling wall-squares,
splintering the world into a thousand shards—

Horses loving on roads that don't cross—
what more can they do than brush their necks
and wearily breathe in the fragrant smell of oats coming from their bodies?

Then the stiff contours of two bodies melt away
into a fantastic melodic ornament,
where solitary angular surfaces, wedged and silently bent towards one another
rock in a play of lines of sad necks and limbs
on the white paper surface of tiresome days.

Sometimes we are such horses
we are nothing more:
only with moist eyes, and necks in angular embrace,
wearily, we inhale the sigh of a long sad conversation,
which broke out from somewhere

a place
in the glass globe of our loneliness.

OF MOUNTAIN WIND

Of mountain wind a colorless poem like gray straw flowers
of yellow September grasses breathing in tiredly,

of dry silver thistles that smell like white paper,
of the four last summers and four autumns:

In four summers three months
come with thirty abysses of yellow color
when you search for things that have never been,
and days that respond with flat glassy sounds.

And four times the autumn has come
with still rectangles of transparent days
framed by see-through streets that
go nowhere.

Every summer
every autumn the waft of grass drags along,
mixed with the smell of silver flowers,

with the shiny smell of gray metal days
that have come now.
After four years of waiting.

POEM ABOUT THE RIVER

One year after a second.
Two years. Three years. Four:
the river flows.

Three years ago I was on its banks,
three years ago everything still needed to happen.
Now nothing can come of it anymore.
I know: it should always be as it is.

And as before all the days of three long years
the river wants nothing, only to flow.
After all the days of three long years
I want to be a still life like a still river.

In twelve months so many similar waves flow.
In twelve months so many similar days go by.
One can go by many times in a day:

from one street to a second,
from one body to a second:
just like a river.

Sometimes the river is blue. Sometimes lime yellow.
Days are light like the color blue. And heavy like lime.
One day. A second.

PRIMITIVE LIFE[11]

You can live like a mountain.
Like a green river.

A thousand years the mountain stands.
A thousand years the river flows.

The mountain is blue: a pomegranate.
Or gray. When fog falls.
The river is green or blue like the afternoon sky.
At times lime yellow. Like unused days.

The days go by: from the yellow sun to the white moon.
Weeks go by: when the sun comes up for the seventh time.
Months: when a round moon rises for the second time.

Out of many days in a life,
a part flows like a blue river, light in the distance,
a part stands heavily in one place like gray mountains in fog.

MY DWELLING

With pearl wallpaper I covered
the four walls of a room

---

11 This poem was publishing in French in Milbauer, ed., *Cahiers du Journal des Poetes*, Serie anthologique, Collection no. 20: *Poetès Yiddish d'aujourd'hui* [Brussels] (1936): 86.

where my days pass
and which is my dwelling.

Today I want to be alone:
alone with a long evening.
Without you. Without anyone.

But today the street before my windows
is covered with the wallpaper
of the sweet tired wool material
of gray.

And I go outside:
to walk on a tired street
in order to return once more
to the cool pearl shell of my dwelling.

A POEM ABOUT EYES

Eyes can glow like two hard chestnuts
two hard kernels of sadness
in the yellow tin frying pan of the streets.

At times they are two still dates.
Dates of heavy drops of waiting,
which draw you to empty streets with yellow lanterns.

Until they become velvet brown specks
and fall heavily, like sweet drops of renunciation,
onto streets, lanterns, and bodies,

from which nothing can come anymore.

Figure 25. Henryk Streng's illustration for "Tin" from *Day Figures*, 1930.

21

Tin (1929)

A POEM OF COLORS

The white is flat:
a usual house seen from up front,
a boring house where nothing happens,
a flat paper rectangle, which wants nothing.

The gray is long and round.
You have nowhere to go, so similar are the houses.
And you go. Go impatiently along streets
until the street grayness gives out
and closes round the dwelling where you live.

The yellow elastic heat tin,
the tin yellow is deep.
Like the distance of things that do not return.

THE COLORS OF THE BIG CITY

The city is a flat tin sign
with artful glass oranges and lemons:
and electric lamps from colorful glass.

The cherry red is long. It carries the history of waiting
and goes out in a sigh-flare
of the pale yellow flame of resignation.

The orange red is round and deep:
a bulgy lamp, sweet and extended,
a glass bell jar with unused years.

The citrus yellow is the color of flat coolness.
It extinguishes stuffy elliptical lamps of waiting
and round lamps of murky abandonment.

With a rectangular glass pane of gray days.

A COLORS-POEM IN SUMMER

Sand yellow. Vermillion red. Coral red.

The streets are sand-yellow silk.
Rooftops are vermillion drops on a yellow cloth.
Begonias—drops of red lacquer.

In streets women circle—slender vases
deeply embraced in hot sand-color,
(the sand-paint smells of yellow leaves)
in the warm sticky begonia red,
in the glass coolness of coral red:

yellow and red caterpillars.

The body of the sand-color,
of the sticky glass-red
burns in city streets. Big sun.
Nothing more happens.

A PANORAMA OF PAPER FIGURES

The paper is flat and light.
This poem about the flatness of its watery color
about the cheap sadness of its flatness.

Paper dolls
in green-lacquered windows,
in red-lacquered balconies
that smile with a flat cheap smile

down on busy streets at twelve o'clock:
like white paper rectangles
with their sadness of stiff angular surfaces.

Paper faces of the shoemaker and barber mannequins
sway behind the sticky-yellow glass:
behind the window-case pane of a seventh day in a week,
their rich-yellow clay bodies under zinc arms,
with a stiff tin cover on top of hair.

And the figures of retired officers
that flatten themselves, not knowing where to go:
flat quadrangles on the round world panorama.

With round vermillion lips a tin figure cries out:
the spherical panorama with paper dolls, the round panorama!
Every day from eight in the morning until eight at night you can admire
figures that artificially circle
and are not pulled by the strings of longing.

COCKROACHES

As if made from black lacquer paper, so flat:
black paper ellipses.

Paper wants to be flat,
overgrown with the flatness of boards of a table.
Like a face of a person retired from life,
who wants nothing anymore:
only to be a watery sheet of paper
glued to a colorful backdrop.

Cockroaches want to be flat:
like beer-brown boards.
Like paper.
Not wanting anything. The board should want.

A POEM ABOUT MILK

The milk is stiff, watery, and sweet, like paper:
white milk is paper oil,
the oil of sticky day drops.

You can learn the sweet stiffness of renunciation
from the stiff sadness of milk paper
enclosed in the right angles of a jar.

The paper is sweet as white drops of milk
the drops of resignation
and their sticky joy

flowing in angles
as the sweet paper milk
in the rectangular tin jar of days.

THE MILKMAN

A month has thirty days.
Thirty times:
gray street, long street, narrow street.

Days are sometimes sweet like white milk,
flat like quiet milk stains.
Or crushed into sad drops like curdled milk.

Life is a paper
milky fluid
in the gray tin can of a day,
in seven cans
in thirty cans.

And rolls of cheap white calico
with the sticky odor of sweet milk
and watery days, unused.

From this calico you can cut
seven pieces
thirty pieces—
and the material always remains the same—
milk-flat, milk-sweet, and sad-stiff,

like a face which is glued
for the seventh time
to a white frame of a door,
to a brown frame of a door.
A third door. A third street. A fourth.

A GLAZIER

He was the same as other people
who know nothing about white gray glass:
about the flat drop of sameness
in a frame
of white-lacquered window
like a gray block of longing
lying in a day-rectangle of the colored dough of encounters.

He has installed the window panes:
in a gray house with white window frames,
in a white house with gray shops.
The first window pane. Second. Tenth.

The panes are flat and still, like rectangles.
The panes are colorful tears:
it is the color of watery joy.
Glass has a rhythmical smile
like a person after seven years of waiting.

Now his face is a transparent glass pane
which takes into itself
streets. Houses. Circulating bodies.
And a flat drop of sameness,

which smiles measured with watery joy:
everything should always be as is.

A TINSMITH

Tin is helpless and lonely.
Like milky-blue paper flowers
in a room garishly whitewashed.
Tin is sad and stiff,
like a dull bent rod
like a sticky mass of boredom
and forgotten fleck of joy
of plastered stiff figures when they enjoy a clumping walk.

Tin is colorless
like the seventh day in a week,
it can only smile. Sweet and stiff.
Like people who don't want anything anymore.

And when the smeary dusk has come—
In the tin triangle of a face
a sticky heat wave arose.
And he smiled like tin: helpless and sweet.

THE ORANGE SELLER

The oranges are round and fleshy
they smell of cool glass,
fantastical glass of night lamps.

And the tin is flat and sticky.
Sad as a stretched-out paste stain.
Helpless.

Every orange seller from the glass street
was once a tin figure on a sign:
you could tell from the silly stiff body
and two drops of blue-lacquered tin

that merged on his face
with an uncertain sadness: two flecks of eyes.

And he traveled around with pot-bellied oranges
every day from eight in the morning till eight at night.
He weighed the fragrant roundness of red fruit
on the tin hand scales,
caressing the sweet weight
laden with a thousand glassy sun-drops.

Exclaiming and selling
the sweet glassiness, the round fullness.
Until he could only smile helplessly
at the round oranges similar to the colorful space of encounters,
at the people who bought from him
red spheres of colorful spaces.

He has become helplessly flat
as the tin figures on the lacquered sign
that smile foolishly with their tin flecks of eyes
and foolishly cry with their lacquered flecks of yellow-red orange tears.

SIGNS WITH KEROSENE BOTTLES

Two old-fashioned female figures with cinched waists
pour tedious greasy
smeary oil
into narrow bottles of cool glass.

In angular cubic bottles painted on the tin sign
the sticky oil transforms
into a still glassy substance,
falling with the sad thump
of resigned geometrical figures.

And the helpless tin figures are sketched
on the flat sign of the world
cast in angular bottles of similar days

an oily stretchy substance
of measured steps through banal houses,
of fantastical strolls in the city streets.

And the dull day
of gray and colorful strolls
becomes a clear glassy substance,
which flows rhythmically enclosed
in the cubic bottles of seven equal days,

sad like the mass of rectangles
and like stiff contours of renunciation.

SIGN: ORANGES

Among the signs showing helpless sacks of flour,
bottles of stiff oil and drab black shoeboxes

tin mixes
with red-lacquered oranges,
with yellow-lacquered lemons and brown dates.

And a white-lacquered person
praises his merchandise with a foolish smile:
plump red oranges,
cool yellow lemons and bright dates
of flat tin and thick lacquer.

Flat tin material of lacquer oranges and lemons
can transport to an unfamiliar fantastical train station
your swaying figures in the yellow ribbons of streets
which go on a fantastical walk bored, sad like ellipses, forever yearning,
your measured walk like the soul of bored stiff rectangles
or circles quietly resigned …
the time of the artificial tin oranges has come …

On every street they sell
sweet red oranges,

cool yellow lemons and brown dates
of flat tin and colorful lacquer.

SPHERES OF GLASS

Yellow spheres of voluminous lamps which between bronze-red leaves
are like long sighs, a remainder of days
fantastical as ellipses.
And like contained oval spaces
with encounters that fall on the streets, like heavy drops of color.

Round lamps can be large tears that come on days
monotonous as spheres:
when you walk and wind up nowhere
on streets as dull as circles.
Lines of circles have given up longing.

But in lonely streets decorated with lanterns
on evenings that are forever lost
the round glassiness of lamps is fragrant.
With their clear flowing coolness:
sweet coolness of rectangles
and strict odd numbers.

Then the breath of round glass caresses
with its cool dimensions
of geometrical figures, figures forever calm.

METAL

Gilded tin,
which seems cut into sheets,
smells sharply of sticky sighs of abandonment.
Days of bronze heat are fragrant with elastic yellow tin:
yellow scorched days, burned until they are sad tin
days when unfathomable things happen.

The smell of gray steel is angular.
Like a banal limestone-white house with flat figures.

The smell of gray steel frames colorful encounters
in a still frame of similar days,
in rectangles of sweet gray color.

And the sad gray tin smells murky.
Helpless days smell like tin,
when you no longer know,
and suddenly remain standing with a foolish smile
in the midst of ten or twenty years of waiting.

MATERIALS

You can live like porcelain and like wood,
like flat paper material and old wily tin.[12]

The smooth porcelain of pink dolls behind the quiet windows of a barbershop
lives without encounters that make us sad
so the porcelain can smile down
on the solitary streets of yellow tin,
on the streets of gray tin—
like round dolls with glassy elliptical eyes.

And the blunt yellow wood
with the helpless angular body
yearns for lightness.
It goes after the colored encounters in larger space.

And at times people understand the soul
of resigned stiff paper material:
and you let the days pass one after another
with their usual banal encounters
in white-lacquered rectangular windows
in flat houses with attached windows
white-lacquered.

Only later you grasp the stiff gray tin:
tin is an old material, of pure sameness.

---

12 The same size font as in the original.

Like a person who has lived for many years
tin becomes familiar
after seven and more years of waiting for things
that only happen once,
that are forever squandered
in houses with banal windows, painted lime white
on the second street and a third.

And you become a tin figure
on the flat sign of similar days
and smile helplessly at everything that comes along.
Like a red-lacquered mannequin on a shop sign.

Selections from *Mannequins* (1934)[1]

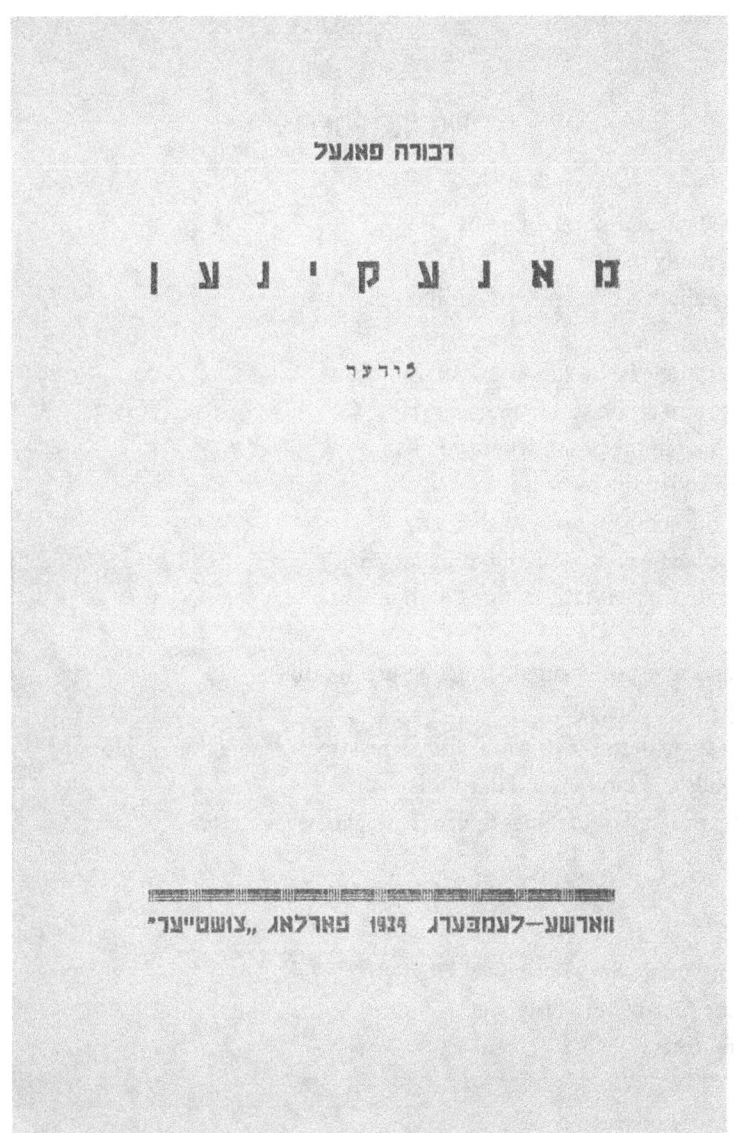

Figure 26. Cover of the first edition of *Mannequins*, 1934.

---

1 See Debora Vogel, *Manekinen. Lider* (Varshe-Lemberg: Farlag Tsushtayer, 1934).

22

Mannequins (1930–1931)

FIGURE POEMS[2]

I[3]
When days cannot be different
from exactly these
the rectangle is the figure of our life.

The rectangle is the soul of sweet monotony
when there is one street for every day
beginning in the house where you live
and closed in the same house
when the sun hangs on another side.
The rectangle is the soul of renunciation:
gray train cars pass the stations with one kerosene lamp

gray and blue pots hang on the lime-green walls
a gray pot, a blue, a gray …
train cars with milk jars travel above the streets where the fog blooms
and walls and tables stand in rooms
and by the walls and tables figures with glassy eyes

II

But the square does not travel
into the melancholy distance
of one street.

---

2   The original "Figurn I–V" [Figures I-V] appeared in *Tsushtayer*, no. 3 (1931): 23–26.
3   Kathryn Hellerstein included an English translation and an in-depth analysis of this poem in *A Question of Tradition: Women Poets in Yiddish, 1586–1987* (Stanford: Stanford University Press, 2014), 144–145.

The square fits the whole of life
in leaden lumps of days
squandered from the beginning, always.

You can stay in the house where you live
since nothing can happen
in the second house.

Why walk onto the second street:
a square surface of sweet monotony
is life, is the world.

III

A colorless street goes around the city
in the pale circular street
ladies in blue gentlemen in black circle
all houses are the same
on that circular street.

Why walk into the melancholy distance
of a circular street
when everything which may be
happens in every house.

One encounter may take place
and a second …

The city is the soul of a circle
the circle is a tired body
which gave up the wait
for a thousand colorful things
which had to happen.

The gray house on the first street and the second
is the most colorful thing
out of all unknown fates in distant streets.

IV

Sometimes a round tin pot is
melancholy like a boring person.

In many houses servant girls scrub large floors
and soldiers in blue march on the streets
and on soldiers' stiff uniforms
on soldiers' blue uniforms
there are four shiny round buttons.

In shop windows sad paper dolls
present cornflower-blue dresses
and smiling porcelain dolls
exhibit wavy hairstyles
every inch
a wave of black and yellow tin.

And red and blue streetcars
take tired passengers
back to the flat house where they live
each under a different number.

First stop. Second stop. Third.
BROAD STREET ... LONG STREET ... GARDEN STREET ...
GARDEN STREET ... LONG STREET ... BROAD STREET ...
First stop. Second stop. Third.

A large sphere of gray sameness
is life,
is the world.

V

Between the pathos of gray lead bodies
that wish for nothing
there is an ellipse of a single body
which still awaits encounters in city streets

The ellipses understand circulating planets
and all solitary people
who renounced waiting.

The ellipse is the yearning of space
and the colorful distance of fates.

And when everything is lost
then perhaps you need to return
to the sad yearning of ellipses
which always wish for something.

Many days in large space.
Many people. Many unknown things.
A wide road goes from one day to the second:
the fantastical road of renunciation.

CIRCULAR LANDSCAPE[4]

In rooms angular like renunciation
in white and whitewashed kitchens
brass pot-oranges ripen
blue long plums of pots.

And bottles like cool lemons, quiet glasses
open their resigned bodies
for pensive tea from foreign lands
and coffee, hard like resignation ...

Outside circular streets flow
train cars carry sweet white milk in jars
and needless breasts full of sweet milk
bend over sweet gray jars.

---

4   An English translation by Anna Elena Torres is in *Pakn Treger: The 2015 Translation Issue* (Spring 2015/5775), https://www.yiddishbookcenter.org/language-literature-culture/yiddish-translation/circular-landscapes-poem-dvoyre-fogel. Anna Elena Torres discusses this poem in her article "Circular Landscapes: Montage and Myth in Dvoyre Fogel's Yiddish Poetry," *Nashim: A Journal of Jewish Women's Studies & Gender Studies* 35 (October 1, 2019): 40–74.

Suburban streets open window shutters
with silvery round kerosene jars
and circular oily herring barrels
and sacs of grits and brown kasha.

And on pavements and squares
round hats of black gentlemen sway—
people have lost their fates somewhere
and stroll.

What is longing … what is renunciation …

HERRING BARRELS[5]

Round like the world and the city
are the five hooped herring barrels
in the grocery shop
at 20 BROAD STREET.

Five round wood barrels
with fat gray salted herring

    50 Groschen   Each   *50 Groschen*
           Fat herring
        At Joshua Schimmel's

and on distant glassy seas
narrow ships sail laden with fish
—fish gray and velvety like an autumn day—
ships sail in blue, cool distance
of resigned landscapes of steel …

And on hot seas
of blue cobalt and ultramarine

---

5   First published in *Yidish. Vokhnshrift fun der yidisher kultur-gezelshaft* [New York] 1, no. 6 (1932): 8. The English translation by Zachary Sholem Berger appeared in *Eleven Eleven Journal*, no. 10 (2011).

ships sail laden with oranges
with fleshy bananas and stuffy dates ...

ships sail from brass landscapes
where the sun is a large metal ball
where in streets elastic like gold tin
everything happens as if for the first time, as if necessary.
Fantastically as if from nowhere
like experienced, overripe bananas. Like oranges.
Like people with squandered fates.

WOOD MERCHANTS

A hundred yellow boards and two hundred
in a blue glass bell jar with yellow sun.
Yearning from five in the morning
in the circular distance of a city
with a thousand distant colorful things ...

Yellow boards near fantastical days
with encounters like colors and gray renunciations
which open and close
like a blue day and anthracite night.

And when nothing else can come
you are again, as always
in the boring train station of timber depot
where wooden logs with feet wait.

Dull watery eyes of wood merchants
and angular wooden lips
now lick the colorful noise
which sticks to drifting boards:

just as things which did not come
later stick to dresses and fingers
when you return from the absolutely
unnecessary trip you took.

DOLLS[6]

She stood for a long time
like a half act of porcelain
behind a milky windowpane
BARBER'S SHOP—BROAD STREET—15.

She was kneaded
from red porcelain dough
of women's bodies by Rubens
and seduces with two pink breast-apples
as if with round shiny eyes.

With half-open eyes
the porcelain smiled
smooth and watery, as if enchanted
by everything which happens in the world
on the second, the other side of the window.

And on the other side of shop window
elastic dolls stroll
with sweet long almonds of eyes
and agile hands and feet.

Dolls with a movable heart
carry glassy pupils of eyes under eyelashes with mascara
and a carmine smile of Chameleon brand
and faces of smiling porcelain.

At the same time
pink dolls at fifteen Broad Street
show their lively breasts like round apples
and sadness like squandered happiness.

---

6 The original version appeared in *Oyfgang. Zamlbukh* (Warszawa: Varshe Press, 1931), 160. The Polish version by Vogel was published in *Nasza Opinja* 5, no. 85 (1937): 11.

HORSES AND TORSOS[7]

For Chirico[8]

It is a misunderstanding that they keep their eyes open
tragic horses on Chirico's paintings
instead of hollow openings—the eternal eyes of sculptures.

The horses' manes fall all the way to the ground
made from brown stone and white marble
like Doric and Ionic capitals.
Their feet are four hard columns.

Near the old temples dedicated to gods
are aged oaks
with stumps of walls and blind torsos.
O the helplessness of old temples
of torsos with chopped hands
of blind horses with curled manes …

In the barbers' shop windows wax dolls
smile blindly like ancient torsos
which come from the wide world
with a tragic decision: to pass …
yet they cannot pass
the torsos with two blind eyes.

Let us make barbers' shop windows in the old temples:
a window with blind torsos, all-seeing
a window with torsos in trendy hairstyles!

And proud horses with stone manes,
let us display them in the spaces of glass and iron
where they showcase Fords and Citroëns.

---

7   An English translation and in-depth analysis of this poem is in Kathryn Hellerstein, *A Question of Tradition: Women Poets in Yiddish, 1586–1987* (Stanford: Stanford University Press, 2014), 145–148.
8   Giorgio de Chirico (1888–1978) was an Italian painter active in the Pittura Metafisica and Surrealist movements. He is famous for his empty cityscapes and themes inspired by Classicism.

Whatever happens is blind
like an ancient torso
with chopped hands
and hollow openings instead of eyes.

MANNEQUINS[9]

Three round dolls from pink porcelain
lost, they smile behind glass cases
like sad tin, like paper

they lift one pink arm
they lift the second pink arm
they lift the first arm …
They wear blue dresses with frills:
this year blue is the trend …

The world is a porcelain merry-go-round
with linen blue skies
and with skies from elastic gold tin
where glued stiff black gentlemen
and elastic blue ladies
have nothing else to do
but smile with their blue-lacquered eyes
and contoured carmine lips.

First street second street a third …
Every two minutes a rotation and it goes again …
Until a second paper sun
rises on linen skies.

And you can do nothing more
but smile foolishly at everything …

---

9   Originally published in *Literarishe bleter* 9, no. 27 (1932): 428. Anna Elena Torres discusses this poem in her "Circular Landscapes": 40–74.

A POEM ABOUT FURNITURE

Rooms can be abandoned like people
rooms wallpapered with resignation
where between quiet tables and china cabinets
melancholy ensnared fates once took place.

Then the furniture spins out
from its angular solitude
entirely strange stories hidden:

about melancholy oak wood
and red mahogany which is yearning in the great distance
and velvet ebony that wishes for nothing.

Brought from distant places colorful
fiery carpets from blue Smyrna,
allow caresses
of tired hands and tired leaves.

Finally stove tiles open
with a long incomprehensible story
of things lost from the beginning …

An empty room
and a large abandoned city
are filled with colored fates.

WATER

Water flows over thousand-year-old stones
water stands in wells three hundred feet deep
and in large banal kitchen pots.

Mountain water is like a drama full of pathos
like the cool joy of everything there is
like life after long years of waiting:

O, white stones, o, the flow …
The sky is blue and the walls—gray …
The sky is sweet like an almond …

And in round tin kitchen pots
lye water lives, fatty like boredom
sad like flour and people
who cannot live on nothing.

But in the evening, when everything is lost
lively waters stand in glasses:
brown coffee, brass tea, orangeade

bitterness of yearning
colorful distance of foreign lands
and aromatic coolness of abandoned days.

In coffee shops in bars in hallways
in angular rooms with furniture
you drink slowly
and do nothing more
bitterness of yearning
and sweetness of life

through a thin straw
of a silly glass of orangeade
with a slice of orange in glass …

TWO METALS[10]

Red brass is a fantastical tear of the Earth
shed in a moment of great happiness
when you have everything
there is to have.

---

10 Originally published in *Oyfgang. Zamlbukh. / Ojfgang. Almanach literacki* (Warszawa: Varshe Press, 1931), 159.

Elastic—like autumn streets
of red and yellow colorful fabric
which promise much
and enchant with wily parchment
like with unknown fates—

brass is the soul
of days when everything is possible
in banal rooms
in streets with nothing
but blue air and yellow lanterns …

But gray tin is saddened
and helpless.

Sad like boring people
gray people who cannot live
on nothing
on blue air
or warm lantern lamps …

HOUSES

Vermillion roofs: drops of warmth.
And whiteness gathered in crooked rectangles
white which is flat and without sweetness
here becomes a sweet sigh …

Leaning against walls
leaning against an oval of the street.
O, the street would close in a circle
and finish its course so still
if the houses agree …

But the houses don't want death:
the houses simply want to draw one breath
to rest—by the gray sea: by the street …
And they are enticed further by the bend of fates …

Just for one breath
the walls crowd together perplexed
before the great sea of stillness
which suddenly surges around them.

CITY GROTESQUE BERLIN[11]

Purple is stuffy like squandered life
and like a lost fantastical thing
all evening and all night long
purple circulates on a gray wall.

And orange advertisements on a second wall
open with distant avenues,
like well-known cities and houses
you cannot leave.

Until a citrus-yellow landscape refreshes us
with the glassy coolness of resignation
with the wisdom of rectangles and cubes—

in purple orange-red citrus-yellow letters
entangled fates are written:

    UFA-FILM[12]
    Hotel Stadt Lemberg[13]

---

11 Original publication as "Shtot-groteske" in *Tsushtayer* 3, no. 3 (1931): 26. Compare this depiction of the city through the lens of the film and montage and Walter Ruttmann's 1927 film *Berlin. Die Sinfonie der Großstadt* [Berlin: symphony of a great city].

12 The UFA film company (Universum Film Aktiengesellschaft) was established in 1917. It existed in Babelsberg, Germany, until WWII. The studio made commercial films with famous stars like Marlene Dietrich, but also propaganda films, including Nazi propaganda. See, for instance, Klaus Kreimeier, *The UFA Story: A History of Germany's Greatest Film Company, 1918–1945*, trans. Robert and Rita Kimber (Berkeley: University of California Press, 1999). See also Sigfried Krakauer's "Calico World," "Film 1928," and "On Berlin's Picture Palaces" in *The Mass Ornament: Weimar Essays*, ed. and trans. Thomas Y. Levin (Cambridge, MA: Harvard University Press, 1995).

13 *Hotel Stadt Lemberg* was the German and Austrian title of the Hollywood film *Hotel Imperial*, directed by Mauritz Stiller, and starring James Hall and Pola Negri. It was the first film made in the US by UFA. The action of the film takes place in Galicia during WWI. Its 1927 worldwide premiere coincided with that of *Metropolis* by Fritz Lang. See Andrij Bojarov, "The City

=UFA=
written in purple stuffy letters
and nothing else is written
in the color of lost things ...

=the=chaste Susana=the chaste=Susana=the=[14]
flows by in orange light bulbs
goes by a hundred and a thousand times.
Today a large audience
can tremble before hidden distant things
in front of breasts tender like transparent apple blossoms
and bellies slender like costly pearl mussels
of=the chaste Susana=the chaste=Susana=the

very late and suddenly
the noble color of resignation is revealed
the full of pathos landscape in citrus yellow
on a red wall of the sixth floor
   VACUUM CLEANER
      AT FRITZ WOLF'S
         FOR SALE
THE=THE BEST=THE MOST DURABLE=VACUUM CLEANER=
written in the noble color of resignation
in glassy color
of days full of pathos like gray rectangles
which suddenly and unexpectedly
revealed
the color of ordinary lemons ...

    Name Game," in *Montages: Debora Vogel and the New Legend of the City* (Lodz: Muzeum Sztuki in Łódź, 2017).

14 Richard Eichberg's *Die keusche Susanne* (1926), starring Lilian Harvey and Willy Fritsch, premiered on November 11, 1926 in the UFA Palast am Zoo in Berlin. Vogel lived in Berlin at the time of writing of this poem.

23

Drinking Songs (1930–1932)

DRINKING SONG I[15]

Today the time has come
the time of drinking songs has come
for we are sad unto death.

What then can you do
when sadness takes hold of you
like a coral reef with a thousand hands
on this side and on the second side
what can you do then …

When you cannot live without people
yet you cannot live with them!

Then you should sit around the table
women should dress in soft velvet
men should bring hot lips
and caressing hands sad hands.

And you should set crystal glasses
glasses from cool amber, from red beads—
and drown in the sticky drink
in the drink from grapes and kisses.

And nothing more
and do nothing more
well, what else is there to do …

---

15 Originally published in *Der Morgn. Dos naye togblat* [Lwów] 5, no. 1133 (1930): 11; also in *Unzer Bukh* [New York] 5, no. 3 (1930): 79.

DRINKING POEM II[16]

Waiting.
Waiting until in the first street and second street
the windows of houses bloom yellow and red.

Waiting.
Waiting until sad windows
fade behind heavy curtains.

How many fates are now played out
behind yellow window panes,
so helpless and sad
and lost forever.

In all rooms
behind all lit window panes
 people sit at tables and against walls
and nothing happens in the rooms
and it's all that could ever happen.

From the distant streets of the whole world
human fates have returned
into the room where they live.

The time of drinking songs has come
because nothing can come from the streets.

DRINKING SONG III[17]

Our drinking song is sad.
Like life. Like death.

What then should you do
when nothing comes from the great number of streets
and when everything that happens
is the same.

---

16 Originally published in *Morgn* [Lwów] 1246 (1930): 8; also in *Unzer Bukh* [New York] 5, no. 3 (1930): 79.
17 Original publication in *Unzer Bukh* [New York] 5, no. 3 (1930): 80.

When nothing comes
one year two years and three
you should repeat every day a hundred times
a helpless poem for life:

what else can come then
what else
but the brass chestnut tree every autumn
but ordinary people on banal streets,
in uninteresting rooms with walls and with tables
what else can come.

When everything is fragile and very rare
like transparent and fragrant porcelain
the cold earth waits with five feet space
and nothing waits, death.

Empty streets are more colorful than nothing
and everything that comes is more
than nothing, than death.

Let us sing a wine song to life,
which is sad like death.

DRINKING SONG IV[18]

And the day with a hundred streets should fade
the streets of all cities measured
by hundreds of tired feet.

Only now you can strike up a drinking song
only now.
When you should not wish for more.

Let us light yellow lamps
you can extinguish them whenever
and get ready with a frothy drinking song

---

18 Original publication in *Unzer Bukh* [New York] 5, no. 3 (1930): 80.

on the second day which will come
which is not yet lost and squandered
when something can still happen …

Tomorrow the round sun-lantern
will count us once again
one more lost day. And life
in which nothing happens …

DRINKING SONG V[19]

You should now prepare a song
for the saddest hour of the night
when cold star-suns fade
when sweet wine pours into red glasses
and you slowly fade. Like a moon. Like a red sun.
From sheer weariness.

What else then remains for us in life
than that which is like death

like a day and a night and a day.

Let us close our eyes and go.
Let us go twice a day and a hundred times
into the houses a couple shades of gray
into the houses where nothing happens …

And stiffly press the hands to the body.
Not send out superfluous hands
into the streets, where you would never
always—find not that …

Let us drink up the last hour
soon the yellow space with streets will come
where you should always wish for something
always …

---

19 Original publication in *Unzer Bukh* [New York] 5, no. 3 (1930): 81.

DRINKING SONG VI

Now the night sighs for the last time
with the rustle of poppy-induced sleep.

Let us prepare for the melancholy
of everything that can come in a day
dancing.

The sixth drinking song drunk
to the blue glass of the night
should be called the dance of rectangles.

One step. One step. One more ...
in straight line couple and couple ...
And now once more two diagonal steps—
and back: one step. One step. And one more.

Stiff rectangles are sweet
and they never get jammed tin-like
with the shard of lament: not that ...
with the grate of a word: why ...

Red glass suns in the hand
a metal shine of stiff clothes
And a long glass sound resonates
from one hall to the second dance hall ...
One step ... one step ...

And now to be scattered quiet around the hall
like withered red autumn leaves—
who remembers lost years ...
One step ... one step ... and one more ...
First street, second street, third street ...
First room with tables and walls ...
Second room with four flat walls ...
Red sun on one side of the house, on another ...

What else can come, what else ...
Stiff rectangles are sweet.

AUTUMN MOTIF I[20]

Once again streets open
with boulevards of fantastical fates
once again they promise everything.

And you set out into the streets
all the roads are as if one road
and you can neither escape that street
nor tiresome company:

lanterns, which hide the last flare of waiting
behind the smile of indifferent glass lips
and go alone, it does not matter where to …

And proud trees with incomprehensible
colorfulness of great weariness …
And street cars which return to depots …

Until you are infected with the mood
of the melancholy company
in the brass autumn salon
with the weariness of lost things.

Leaves fall. Tired leaves.
Red leaves. Yellow leaves.

AUTUMN MOTIF II[21]

Now nothing will come anymore
you should not wait for anything anymore
and everything will be unnecessary and for no one.

Above the evening unfolds
a long roll of a costly melancholy scarf
embroidered with patterns of lost things.

---

20 Original publication in *Der Oyfkum. Khoydesh-zhurnal far literatur un kultur-inyonim* [New York] 6 (June/July 1931): 7.
21 Original publication in *Oyfgang. Zamlbukh*, 158.

And vast navy blue nights are studded
with distant shimmering moons and unknown things
which perhaps can still happen. Perhaps.

But in parchment streets which are for no one
things which did not happen fade into nothing
colorful phantoms on the backdrop of gray waiting.

In front of the windows stand rusty-red chestnut trees.
They smell like wax. Like the red wax of things
lost from the start, always.

AUTUMN MIST

Today grayness is unnecessary
the sweet mist, rain carpet
leaves are a wet coat of rust on the sidewalks.

The leaves do not hang on the trees anymore
waiting for fantasies in brass—
only in the previous week the sweet mist was needed.

From now on everything that happens is unnecessary.
Like time. Like imitated life
full of insecure yellow leaves of attempts.

You should not get involved in things
since everything is lost from the start
and everything comes late and uncertain …

LOVE VERSES (1920)

1

They met at a time
when one could not live without the other

yet they had to part.

2

And so it had to be

they encountered each other when
a person does not know yet, inexperienced
what the other can give

wishing everything, not knowing what
wishing all of life.

3

Those who belong and love each other
rarely stay together in life.

Hear out why,
you who will once love

lovers want to give more and take more
than is allowed and possible in life.

4

Passerby, do not be saddened
about the loss of a beloved

a long way of losses
goes around the world
there are so many days in life, so many women and men.

LOVE POEM

You are quiet and slow
like a very long raft
which carries fragrant fir logs
from the mountain in blue mist
to a distant city with lanterns

through days with yellow suns
through days with gray skies.

You are sad like a raft
quiet and sad like happiness.

Years will pass by with you
who remembers the lost years …

INSCRIPTION ON THE MATZEVAH[22]

In memory of Judith Maltz[23]

The one who rests here under this headstone
has never been preoccupied
with colorful things in life.
What is life …

Her days are fitted into the angular frame
simple like matzevahs.
Life is heavy from mere grayness
what is life …

SHOES

In memory of my father[24]

The first drops of yellow noise fall onto streets
red fatty chestnut blossoms fall

---

22 This means "tombstone." One version of this poem appeared in *Unzer Bukh* 5, no. 3 (1930): 82; another version in *Der Morgn. Dos naye togblat* 5, no. 1185 (1930): 7.
23 Judith Maltz (1900–1929), the daughter of David Maltz and Miriam Ehrenpreis, was Vogel's cousin. She was an active participant in Lviv's Zionist youth movement Hashomer Hatsair, and from 1919 she lived in Palestine.
24 Anselm Vogel (1874–1927) was Debora Vogel's father. He was the principal of Baron Hirsch High School in Bursztyn, the town where Debora was born. In Lviv, he was the principal and a teacher in the orphanage for Jewish children on 8 Zborowska St. After his death, Debora Vogel and her mother, Lea Ehrenpreis (1874–1942), worked in the orphanage.

and white apple blossoms. And sighs.
Birds hover.

Soon people will put on shoes
black shoes, brown shoes …
Many will go down
Zhulkevska Street
all the way to the muddy Bernstein Street …

The feet no longer belong to him
neither does the body to a pair of feet without shoes.

Yet under the bed two black shoes
stand, still going someplace
shoes with a thousand wrinkles
and two abandoned twisted heels

two worn-out black leather shoes
that know the pavement of Zhulkevska.

24

Shoddy Ballads (1931–1933)

A BALLAD OF A BLACK BOWLER HAT[25]

He came in a hat
a round stiff and black one
and with the round hat in both hands
he looked for a long time at the tips of his shoes.

And the hat danced in his hand
perhaps foxtrot or blues or tango
the bowler hat round at the edges
was a very foolish look …

She held her breasts stiffly
thirty days with him—boring tin days …
and foolish figures on the signs
also send a greeting with their round stiff hats …

Later they walked hand in hand
A walk—a film—a dance—
and he said to her: sweetheart
caressing the brim of the bowler hat.

And again the word fell …
that is: no—you're going away—forever …
… why—perhaps after all—now so suddenly.
… the bowler hat dances a sad sweet tango.

Later he went into the street
he walked so far, like never before

---

25 This poem also appeared in *Oyfgang* 2, no. 7 (1934): 11.

and the coat he wore was metal
and the hat stiff like tin …

Then all the blue streets
all bridges passages and doors
were covered with bowler hats
all men understood him …

So his happiness was squandered
a person in a black bowler hat
… thirty days with him were boring
like round foolish hats …

A BALLAD ABOUT A TRASHY NOVEL[26]

And so it came about
as they write in potboilers
with invented ludicrous fates …

He remained forever
the best memory of her life.
Yet he was always
her life's greatest misfortune.

Couldn't live with him—couldn't live without him …
Why did you break my heart …
And the heart is forever broken
as they write in cheap novels …

… and life is squandered. Long as melancholy
as they describe in these stories.
What does the word "squandered" mean …
Yet everyone understands it.

In every street and house
delicate ladies, stiff gentlemen carry

---

26 Originally appeared in *Literarishe bleter* 10, no. 11 (1933): 171.

shards of broken hearts
cut out from trashy novels ...

And sweet ladies cut out from wood
and stiff wooden gentlemen
imitate a shoddy novel
its title: life, happiness, and death.

A BALLAD OF A BROKEN HEART I

It began with a heart.
As usual, with a broken heart
just as every misfortune
she couldn't live with him, couldn't live without him.

His soul was like a color,
it existed in the world only for her.
He said, besides you, I had nothing
nothing at all in the world ...

Couldn't live with him, couldn't live without him ...
O happiness ... O happiness ... O happiness ...
She had to leave him
and she was his treasure and happiness.

Then all the strangers
came from the streets dragging
her lips hands and breasts:
O happiness ... O happiness ... O happiness ...

How hard it is to approach the other.
Perhaps after all ... once again ... one more try ...
O happiness ... O happiness ... O happiness

A stranger gently touches two breast-apples.

A BALLAD OF A BROKEN HEART II

… And in the end it happened
like in strange old-fashioned novels
when you love unhappily until death …

He called her a landscape …
A foreign land with unexpected cities …
He called her a sea.
"His soul was like a color
of sweet velvet autumn days
and destined only for her in the world …"

Then small markets with acacias
became theater props
with hidden, melancholy fates …

And it probably had to happen
it was perhaps quite necessary and yet unnecessary
until it actually happened …

They couldn't live together, yet couldn't live apart …

A BALLAD OF A BAD LOVE

It would have been a thousand times better
if he didn't come
if they didn't meet each other
among thousands people, he and she …

No green leaves and no sky
no blue morning and no evening
since that time …

It happened as it usually does
with happiness
it amounted to nothing
between them, o happiness …

They hid their feelings
perhaps he doesn't love ... or she doesn't ...
As it should be ... only him alone ...

Later the memory remained
(compared to yellow leaves)
the memory is perhaps too little
and words like you, my happiness

why does the sentence incessantly appear
it would have been better
if they didn't meet each other ...

A BALLAD OF PARISIAN SQUARES[27]

In the Place Pigalle in Paris
they loved and died
and changed lovers every night
and sang about short-lived happiness ...

In the Place de Sebastopol and d'Orleans
people stood by the lanterns
they enticed each other with glances
and with tired words and hands.

And in the Place and Rue de Montmartre
even the skin grew weary
like gray fur and waiting heart
and the cocktail was sweet like death ...

... O the saddest happiness you
when love becomes a poem ...

Circular squares of Paris
are filled with incomprehensible fates
where love is a little poem
sweet and shoddy like life ...

---

27 This poem also appeared in two journals: *Lid. Shrift far lid un iber lid* [Los Angeles] 2 (1934): 15 and *In zikh* 15, no. 6 (1934): 176.

A BALLAD OF PARISIAN STREETS

Coming from the Trocadéro—
the Place du Trocadéro is like a wall
the Seine flows flat
and the Eiffel Tower is the vertical
flooded with Citroën ads.

From Mirosmenil, from the crowded Place d'Orleans,
from the Place de Grenelle and La Motte
from the well-worn subway stairs,
from boulevards with advertisement for Cadum soap

narrow streets with fate
glued to the front walls,
where our happiness and misfortune
do not have a lot of time
to find the rear walls.

A street like Campagne-Première
Moulin de Beurre
or withered streets of Montmartre.

In the Campagne-Première there is a bar,
a green bar "Pelican."
There the window shutters are always closed
and you don't know what happens inside.
O, nothing happens
after all what can happen … one more cocktail …

On the closed white window shutters
large red and green bellies dance
on thin legs, with faces like raisins.
O, you dance when nothing else can happen …

Here is Montmartre and the Place de la Concorde
they are both in Paris.
The Place de la Concorde is for the assured and intoxicated,
Montmartre is for the lost lives—

And in the end Moulin de Beurre, this street—
Moulin de Beurre where suddenly you don't know,
why you came here in the first place ...

And what is this little word—"life"
which everyone seems to understand ...

A BALLAD ABOUT THE SEINE[28]

The mist was like soft velvet
the blue Parisian fog—
was like a boulevard
a blue pavement of Paris, the big city.

And the Seine landscape was a postcard
with a red sentimental ship
and a river of ultramarine.
O, where is this ship suddenly from
the ship which quickly traverses the sea
and transports gold sardines?

And a vagabond with curly red hair eats herring
and the herring is sweet gray like the sky
in a landscape with the crimson ship.

The bridges over the Seine
bridges full of pathos
and sentimental ones
with the tragic gesture of an arc
and bridges of pointed sadness
from iron ...

Until you come to one of them
saccharine and shoddy like life
the bridge plays bashfully and accidentally
with a couple of clumsy chords
the banal comedy of abandonment ...

---

28   Also published in *Lid. Shrift far lid un iber lid* 2 (1934): 15.

And one should gently pass by
the twenty bridges over the Seine
as if they were life …

Life is continuously too much …
And you should return to it
to the crimson ship with sardines
to ultramarine rivers and people …
… wasted time … what a pity …

SHODDY BALLAD PARIS

And one can forget the color
the style and even the material
of your necklaces clothes bridges
Paris, you are the city of colorful kitsch.

And one can forget the velvet
of sidewalks and pavements
Paris Berlin Stockholm
and cities I haven't seen—

when you live in a country
which is covered with fields
where cities are like fields
of yellow boredom and purple potatoes …

O, potato flowers have a sweet and subtle smell
and the horizon is not bedazzled
with boulevards of city fates …

But somewhere there are quick-paced cities
where the sticky subways
can be like sweet dates
and like cooling white linen.

And you long for a city where people
are fatigued and happy
sticky subways and pavements
and a thousand colorful shapes

materials people and bridges
over the green Seine.

BENCHES ALONG THE CHAMPS-ÉLYSÉES BOULEVARD[29]

On the Place de la Concorde in Paris
cars dance a mechanical ballet
around the ceiling of cool glass.

On all Parisian stars of squares
Opéra Étoile Madeleine
a sea of steel car waves flows
the gray Baltic Sea of Paris.
And on the boulevards the rivers of cars flow.

The boulevard des Champs-Élysées is like a city
and the twentieth floor of the boulevard
is a city of cold neon.
Near the Champs-Élysées the Seine flows
the Seine is of elastic steel
the Seine is like a tragic decision.

Over the Champs-Élysées cold neon flows
on the Champs-Élysées cars flow
hunched tender benches surface suddenly
from wet fog
from blue air and yellow straw
O, here you can grow tired like a tree.

Corridors of blue air and fog
benches of blue air and fog
and nothing more
pieces of life became entangled
in the benches of blue fog
on the paintings by Annenkov.[30]

---

29 Originally the poem appeared in *Yidish* [New York] 1, no. 18 (1932): 5.
30 Yury Annenkov (1889–1974) was a Russian Expressionist painter who lived in Paris. He painted Parisian suburbs.

Life is a gentle passage
through the blue corridors of Annenkov
over the steel fields des Champs-Élysées
with the pieces of tired souls
glued to straw benches.

Life is to be washed away gently
from the foggy benches
from the steel shells of cars
you just need to touch gently
the neon advertisements
and life.

BALLAD OF A STREET WALKER I[31]

And why exactly a ship with eight sails
which should come for you from afar
a red-haired streetwalker from the "Three Penny Opera" … [32]

Dressed in black scarf
—the scarf is very much like satin—
in long black shimmering socks
with red suspenders to be taken off.
"dressed in silk and satin …"
and black was her color of choice.

Days pass by on the plush red sofa
the sofa can be like a beloved
she had a lover in a bright coat
he forgot her, maybe it should be like that …

And then dressed in black
everything still had to happen.

With another girlfriend he forgot her
the girl in purple pajamas
just like that, according to a trashy novel.

---

31 See Ekaterina Kuznetsova's and Anastasiya Lyubas's article, "The Image of Streetwalkers in Itsik Manger's and Debora Vogel's Ballads." Forthcoming from *In Geveb* in the fall of 2020.
32 This is an allusion to the song of the Pirate Jenny in Bertold Brecht's *Three Penny Opera*.

But he never knew
neither he nor anyone else
that she waited for a ship
the ship with eight large sails
the ship of brass and cobalt
like the sea with unknown continents ...

O what a slender queen—O!
Even though she forgot Apache ...

O, sweet happiness of waiting
for the ship with white sails
which still promises everything
like days on the plush red sofa
when no guest comes to visit ...

BALLAD OF A STREET WALKER II

A ballad of a street walker
with the brass name Maia[33]
who showed her body
and her very sad heart
in a suburban play in Paris.
Admission: three francs and higher ...

It is a port. Perhaps Marseille. A lantern
an illuminated window and a door.
On the doorstep a pink dress opens
the dress belongs to a woman
and the woman utters just one word:
come ...

And as for the money
she was paid

---

33 This might be a reference to Francisco Goya's *La maja desnuda* and *La maja vestida*.

she did not want any pearls
satin dresses or pajamas
she didn't need glittery accessories or gold
just a piece of ordinary happiness
just a bit of ordinary life ...

O, gray paper boxes with red florins
a present to the new girl for pajamas—
that girl cut her hair
after the first kiss on the neck ...

... and the dress opens further:
a loose fit, buttonless, and guest-friendly ...
O where does one get happiness, foolish happiness ...

A sweet woman with her hopeless life
more or less like all of us
one more attempt: you ... come ...

In sticky middays and out of nowhere
wax girls in the windows
crochet delicate pink bras:
... two stiches and three ...

In the port by the gray sea
in the port by the sea of blazing blue

at night there was shooting again
the Apache shot his girlfriend
the girl in purple pajamas
somebody tapped with five fingers
the melody of every sad life ...

But the most important thing is still to come
and you should prepare for it
with a nicely fitting bra ...
... three stitches and two ...

LEGEND OF GOLD SHIPS[34]

Sometimes the sea is dreamy cobalt
at times it is melancholy ultramarine

and gold is warm and soft
or midday distant.

Europe departs from Cherbourg
Georgic sails from Liverpool
and a confused ship called *Manhattan*.

The ships carry gold over the seas
round like tedious life
circular pieces of luster and happiness.

Later in banks and exchange offices
lay heaps of sweet longing
in Federal Reserve Bank in New York
in Union Bank in London and Madrid
things and fatal fortunes
and the happiness of the world: the event …

If there was no gold in the world
people would invent it
as a sign for life and fortune.

The sea is cobalt
the sea is ultramarine
over the sea carriers of gold pass
ships with oranges and herring
nobody knows about the gold transport
anonymous and fatal.

---

[34] The English translation by Anna Torres was published in *Dibbur*, no. 5 (Spring, 2018). Torres discusses this poem in her article, "Circular Landscapes: Montage and Myth in Dvoyre Fogel's Yiddish Poetry," *Nashim: A Journal of Jewish Women's Studies & Gender Studies* 35 (1 October 2019): 40-74.

Why is gold carried in crates
our yearning and our fortune
and not under open sails
solitary and proud like legends ...

LEGEND OF BANKS[35]

From semi-official memos we learn
that on March fourth, nineteen thirty-three
the gold reserve in the Federal Reserve Bank
amounted to four billion dollars.

And greater even than the value of bills
was the heap of yellow gold
a half billion more ... O, what fortune! ...

It happened in the proud skyscrapers
of New York, Detroit, and Chicago
in the classical stillness
of walls. Glass. And steel.

The piles of gold lay
like rich earth
like difficult fortune.

You couldn't believe
that this could be
that gold can lay
around in heaps needless
like crooked rich soil

until you touched it,
felt gold blood in the world.

Then for three long weeks
gold escaped into the world

---

35 The English translation by Anna Torres was published in *Dibbur*, no. 5 (Spring, 2018).

from bank houses and offices
but order was upheld
gold was replaced by bills
and securities.

Seven billion dollars
now flooded the world
to maintain the world balance.

Now the banks could be opened
securities are traded
for fabric
clothes houses potatoes

And the world once again has fortunes …

LEGEND OF SILVER[36]

Silver is a resigned metal
silver is mild and faraway
like pearl gray and weary dusks.

Silver is indifferent
and, thus, very melancholy
like someone who doesn't believe in anything.
Always at a distance from life.

And so silver was not reckoned with
in the world economy in nineteen thirty-three.

But people cannot live without gold
which buys trades and sells
the sweet usefulness of our life.

---

36 This poem appeared in *In zikh* 16, no. 11 (1935): 196. The English version by Anna Torres was published in *Dibbur* 5 (Spring, 2018). Torres discusses this poem in her article "Circular Landscapes."

Life is traded for commodities
for clothes, shoes, potatoes
with money
who wants to live without money …

Gold takes the first place
what other metal is so warm
and connected to life …
Silver takes second place
silver is an indifferent substance …

But the proud gold was scarce
and there was more desire in the world
for the warm red gold …

Then silver also lived
its proud and grotesque legend
a piece of silver for a piece of life
a piece of life is needed for silver
things obtain fate through silver …

When financiers
large corporations, oil companies, factories
which belong to Fords Deterdings and Kreugers
just give a wink what have you …

Then even silver
the pale distant metal body
can entangle the world with fates
in the genre of a new legend …

25

Afterword to *Mannequins*

Sadness is a decorative element in life. All of life can become decorative. It happens when a heroic raw schema—to which the multiplicity of events is reduced—reveals the arch-scheme of monotony. Then one must return to interpretation, the "superstructure" of a couple of raw facts in life. In effect, the surface of life is filled with events. It becomes an ornament that does not leave any space for monotony.

The raw concentrated three-dimensional block of life becomes flat two-dimensional décor. However, with the decorative arrangement of life without the residue of events, there emerges a psychological constellation of reckoning with the somewhat available ready-made things that "should happen." Hence, the only possible state is waiting for the ready-made possibilities and "experiences" which can happen, yet do not.

Therefore, the decorative worldview leads to the consumerist one. I say "consumerist" because we wait for and are nourished by ready-made experiences that are independent of us.

The poems in the *Drinking Songs* and *Shoddy Ballads* sequences in the collection are expressions of the decorative-consumerist worldview. The *Mannequins* sequence represents Constructivism and is the continuation of *Day Figures*.

The dialectic of content unfolds according to a wonderful Hegelian principle.

THESIS: the raw schematism of life; coolness and heroic monotony; the monotonous figure of the rectangle as sign and symbol of the rhythm of life; moods and events best classified by the names and contents of the geometrical figures—the arch-scheme of the round and rectangular. The psychological transposition of the two principles is the following: dynamism—waiting—a transformation linked with an image of an elliptical line; and stasis—the stillness of mass—an unchangeability which includes the monotony of repetition, associated with the symbol and the figure of a rectangle.

This scheme of life corresponds to Cubism. Constructivism is the continuation of Cubism. The principal issue here is the exposure of the opposing tendencies in life, which assume the shapes of the bodily and the machinic. Crossing and mixing the limit between the two principles—the machinic, or the mechanical, and the organic, or the living—creates a mood of stasis, with an added ingredient of the wonderfulness of life.

ANTITHESIS: the tragedy of monotony and the arch-scheme of the rectangle. The blind circle of things, the blind circle of events of the soul, where two opposing and singular possibilities seem impossible, since none brings happiness.

SYNTHESIS: the rehabilitation of that which is possible and within reach—"life." This entails the rehabilitation of monotony and kitsch—the material of all of important events.

Now, the time is ripe for a new thesis—a raw and hard arch-scheme of life is necessary. Thus, the presentation of the decorative-consumerist formation requires an explanation.

Perhaps it can be the following: every constructive life-formation transforms into a decorative one.

It might be entailed in the moments which reveal another side of everything in life—the endless sadness. Subsequently, the decorative principle will be rehabilitated as something that always belongs to life.

Part Three

"Marching Soldiers and Blooming Acacias": Prose

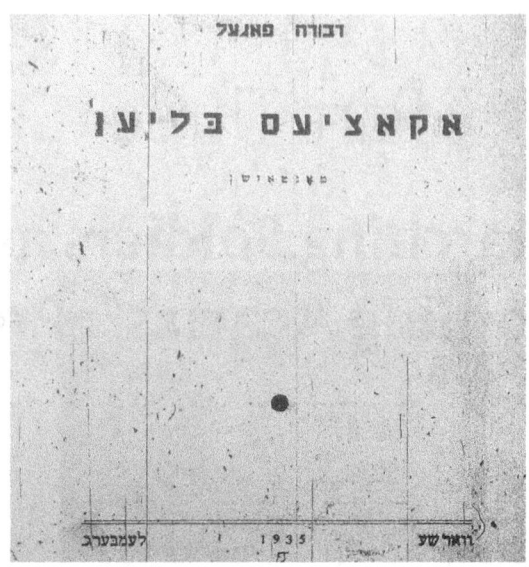

Figure 27. Cover of the first edition of *Acacias Bloom* (Yiddish), 1935.

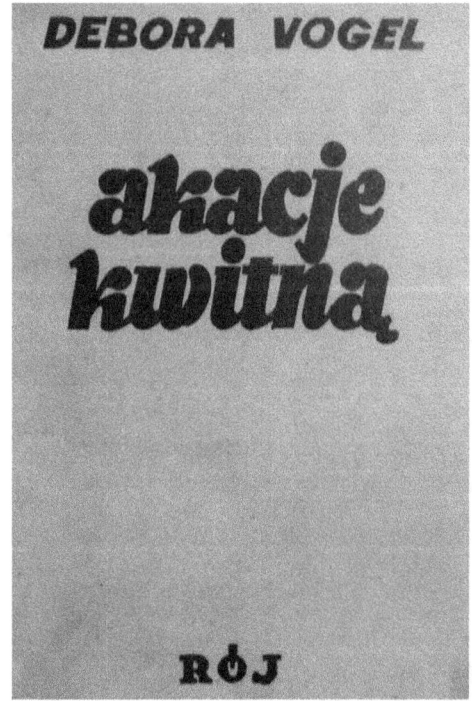

Figure 28. Cover of the first edition of *Acacias Bloom* (Polish), 1936.

Selections from *Acacias Bloom: Montage* (1935/36)[1]

---

1 The original in Yiddish was published under the title *Akatsyes blien. Montazhn* (POL: Varshe-Lemberg, 1935). The original in Polish, *Akacje kwitną. Montaże*, with illustrations by Henryk Streng, was published in 1936 by Rój Publishing House in Warsaw. The second edition of *Akacje kwitną. Montaże*, edited and with an afterword by Karolina Szymaniak, includes original illustrations by Henryk Streng. The new edition, which was published in Cracow by Wydawnictwo Austeria in 2006 features some additional prose pieces that Vogel published in journals, which Karolina Szymaniak translated from Yiddish into Polish. The present English translation is from the Yiddish and Polish texts.

Figure 29. Henryk Streng (Marek Włodarski), *Still Life*, 1930.

26

Flower Shops with Azaleas (1933)[2]

1. STREETS AND SKY

That day, the streets reflected the sky. And the sky was gray and warm. And when the sky is gray, the streets are matte[3] and sweet, like a warm gray sea.

The people who found themselves on the street that day were dying for some kind of encounter. *Like once before.*[4] And finally, an awkward and inexplicable longing emerged to immerse themselves in an elaborate novel, even an old-fashioned one.

Surely, the novel had to open with the following sentences: "That day ..." and "on a gray day with streets like gray seas, [the calendar date comes here], a man in a gray coat and a black bowler hat strolled along L. Street, reflecting on his life up to that point ..."

The novel had to start in that style and everything in the *romance* novel[5] had to begin with a similar effect, since there is a *suddenly inexplicable* demand for that now. And the novel would recount the course that life could

---

2   The sequence of mini-collections in this translation follows the reverse chronological order of the Polish original publication—from *Flower Shops with Azaleas* (1933), and *Acacias Bloom* (1932), to *The Building of the Train Station* (1931). The sequence in the Yiddish text is chronological—the mini-collection written in 1931 came first, while *Flower Shops with Azaleas* (1933) appeared last.
3   In Polish the epithet is "tired" (*zmęczony*) rather than "matte" (*mat*) in Yiddish.
4   The sentences, words, and expressions in italics indicate discrepancies between the Polish and Yiddish texts. They are mostly additions to the Polish edition of 1936, which do not appear in Yiddish unless otherwise indicated.
5   The word in the Polish text is *romans* (romance novel), which is different from the word used in the beginning of the sentence, *powieść* (novel). The Yiddish text uses the word *roman* (novel) throughout.

take, *what could happen throughout the course of an ordinary life,* and how fates are made out of nothing: out of blue air, tacky boredom, and a single banal encounter.

And like a matter still not settled—though it has been experienced for many years—a long-forgotten sentence began to gnaw: "How does one live?" The question was just as banal as it was before, as ignorant of its own banality as it was the first time.

Meanwhile, on the streets as gray as the sea, the new *romance* novel of ordinary life had begun, as yet unnoticed by the many passersby.

The streets in that novel smelled of elasticity, of glass, and of walking. They smelled, also, of something unusual: the hardness and roundness of objects.

In the streets of that novel, sticky space hardened into things of unusual kinds: spheres and flat planes, mostly gray and white.

The appearance of dense canvases of white space is treated like an event. Walls occur in this novel, thick like longing and sweltering heat. Walls: whiter than in reality, melancholy white or hard white.

And there are surfaces—spherical, square, and rectangular (in everyday nomenclature: dresses, furniture, pavement, and figures). *People from this novel live with things like flatness and roundness—white, gray and colorful. They wait for these categories as if for the one-and-only adventure.*

And so the first chapter of the novel begins more or less in this way: "In gray skies, walls rise, smooth like satin. Walls rise, similar to lacquer or paper. Figures walk the streets, figures taken from the *romance* novel called Life."

2. STREET DUST

Meanwhile in April, the first month of sticky leaves and still middays, the following event happened. On the outer edge of the pavement a handful of dust whirled and vanished into the dim air, very low, perhaps two feet above the sidewalk.

This unassuming event that had happened last year and the year before seemed to prove that everything returned to normal and that it will continue further in its prescribed order and according to the established rules.

And surely, this event became important all of a sudden, since much in people's lives was already irretrievable.

The same incident was the beginning of a whole series of events that have taken a completely unusual turn. And something other than usual became important.

With that, an annual series of banal events ensued such as: sticky, lacquered heat, aimless walking on the streets; cobalt streets[6] and longing for textured things; different things, round and angular, square, hard, sticky, and elastic, as well as encounters, similar to fragrant metals.

Finally: the story of "happiness squandered"—that's how this matter is called—already well known and usual in the chronicles of life. Every year has a predetermined plan of happiness and something squandered.

A flaxen handful of dust emitted a fragrance of yellow heat and hidden possibilities.

And there was no more time to be wasted.

3. HOUSES WITH HARD RHYTHM

The hard noise and speed of things yet incomplete and unprepared can document well enough that life is, after all, *meaningful and* indispensable, and there is no time to be wasted.

And so it follows: in flat[7] and inconspicuous textile, glass, paper, and metal factories, the sweet[8] and elastic matter of life is produced. And sweetness (one also calls it energy), seeping drop by drop, since seven in the morning, is like a machine that recycles the syrupy boredom *and the languor of the world* into hardness and into events.

For some time, white stillness fell on one factory and then on another. At first like a block, heavy and sticky, and then, after some time, like a sad and helpless paper mass.

In the spring of 1933 a number of factories came to a standstill.[9] In the streets, however, one could see people who had too much time on their hands, those who have forgotten what exhaustion is.

They sat on the benches in the alleys, on sticky blooming middays. They sat on the benches in the boulevards, at *the gray hour of* seven in the morning. In the early damp mornings, in the navy blue evenings, with flowing

---

6 In Polish, "cobalt 'gardens of evening streets.'"
7 In the Polish text, "gray."
8 "Warm," in the Polish text.
9 In 1931 strikes were widespread all over Poland. On March 6, 1933 in Łódź there was a general strike by textile workers which lasted until the end of March; over 100,000 workers participated in it.

rivers of electricity; above them: the triumphant Ford and Odol[10] toothpaste advertisements. They hover over the shop windows with wares, women's clothing shops *with the wonderfully sounding names and alluring lines, Jean Patou and Molyneux* and the *rows of* ties—*the most elegant of which is the Rekord* brand. Then they stroll further. At first one's feet did not want to go, later they kept walking without stopping.

They sat on the street benches and studied the gray concrete of the sidewalk. They did not pay the slightest attention to the sudden popping of tree buds with small sticky leaves.

Meanwhile in the factories the machines stood still: sad like bored people *and like paper goods*, blank and expressionless like undefined and *empty* longings.[11] *People who have nowhere to go at seven in the morning.*

And in this way the first month of sticky buds passes, the month of blue, light, and nonobliging mood.

4. SPRING AND HAT BOXES

Meanwhile, spring surged with canvases of lush greenery, which later, upon closer observation, split into fingerlike chestnuts and lilac leaves, unassuming and "similar to human hearts."[12]

A sea of greenery surged in front of the windows of houses and streetcars. Approaching noon, it swelled like a sea of gray water only to calm with noon's arrival, and it froze into a clump of greenness in the evening.

And in this way the second month of sticky buds and blue air passed.

At that moment—although also now, as usual, for essentially no clear purpose—people decided to "live." And everyone understood that word *life*.

And one started to prepare for the days when the heat blooms like a round, stiff, glass flower just as one prepares for a long-awaited encounter.

So people treated the event of greenery as an encounter with life itself, which was—how typical of that time—represented by the lacquered and helpless heat and unheard-of possibilities, as was typical.

But just as usual, this event took on an unexpected, if banal, course, namely:

---

10   Odol was a famous brand of cosmetics and products like toothpaste. It was founded by the German businessman Karl August Lingner. In the 1930s, the brand had a factory in Lviv. Stefan Banach, a mathematician at the Lviv School of Mathematics appeared in one of the advertisements for the brand.
11   This word appears only in Yiddish.
12   The quotation marks are in the Polish version only.

Figure 30. Henryk Streng, reprint of illustration from Debora Vogel, *Akacje kwitną. Montaże* (Warszawa: Rój, 1936), 20.

Suddenly all the sidewalks and squares were covered with the flaxen cardboard and paper of hat boxes from women's millinery shops, just like the pink petals of chestnut trees cover the gray streets of June.

On the sidewalks and squares spun female torsos—ancient torsos *with wavy hairstyles* without eyes—on the waves of lush greenery and the multitudes of miscellaneous *unusual* delicate things, which were happening all around, and which were to change shortly. *(The blind hollow eyes of ancient torsos—busts from hair salons, and the women's busts on the streets—look out for life. They strive for unknown shivers of happiness and its unknown possibilities.)*

That which was within people's power was being done: they made arrangements to receive what had been prepared for life. And it turned out that porcelain torsos with breasts are capable of receiving life properly only if they are wearing new, as-yet-unworn dresses. But the fashion that year, *1933, was coarse-grained* and thick *materials in which one could still sense the aesthetic of the longing of raw materials.*[13] As for the colors: warm chrome and matte contemplative sienna.

On this occasion, perhaps for the first time, people discovered the incomprehensible but indubitable effect of as-yet-unused elastic materials. It was noted that they helped to forget the decaying things, which nothing could help anymore.

So, for that reason, they could help one live.

5. GRAY SEAS AND SHELLS OF HEARTS

On the shore of the Baltic Sea poplars are greening in the yellow sand. On the gray seashore a thousand shells lie. The water surging with grayness and life spit them out.[14]

In the gray sea of *summer* streets, it suddenly reeks of stuffy seaweed. The odor makes one anxious,[15] like sudden and hidden possibilities. It is already summer.

Then people understand that life which renounced "waiting"—this is how people denote an element of helplessness, hardness, and sentimentality[16]—is colorless and flat:[17] a gray seashell, spat out from the *stuffy* sea of longing.

Then people want "to long" once again; completely helpless like before.

And suddenly in the streets the large leaves of matters lost start falling. It becomes apparent that one can be late for some irreversible matters of life. Later nothing happens as if for the first time.

On that day when the streets are like seas and mirror the gray sky,[18] one can wish for nothing more "than what is at hand."

On a day like this nothing can be done about the sadness of missed opportunities.[19] And yet: there are so many days in life, so many people.

One must forget: there is always something waiting for us in life.

---

13 The italicized text is according to the Yiddish version. "[T]he aesthetic of longing of raw materials" has a different wording in Polish: "the longings and anxiety of raw materials and life." It also appears after the sentence about colors.

14 The Yiddish version of these two sentences is the following: "(On such days poplars become yellow on the shore of the gray Baltic Sea, a hundred shells lie in the sand, plucked from the sea of grayness.)." This sentence appears in the text in brackets as the second paragraph after the sentence "It is already summer."

15 In the Polish version, "the odor introduces anxiety into the streets."

16 In the Polish version, "helpless and sticky heaviness."

17 In the Polish version, "sad and barren."

18 In the Polish version, "On that gray day like the heavy Baltic Sea in flaxen light."

19 This sentence in Polish is: "On that day, when the streets are like the seas and mirror the gray sky, nothing can be done about the sadness of missed opportunities."

6. RAINY DAYS

Then came a series of rainy days. According to the calendar, the days were supposed to be as though composed of yellow lacquer, which sticks to the fingers and to the soul, and of incomprehensible vastness, when everything takes on an unexpected meaning.

But this year a shabby and dense grayness enveloped the days. And once again one needed to lean against the dazzling wall of posters as if pretending to wait for someone with whom one had arranged a meeting, although there was no one to wait for.

And certain afternoons and evenings were just like in an old-fashioned hit song where one "waits forever, waits again, without knowing what one is waiting for."[20]

Figure 31. Henryk Streng, reprint of illustration from Debora Vogel, *Akacje kwitną Montaże* (Warszawa: Rój, 1936), 25.

---

20 In Polish, the words of the song are: "you need to pluck happiness like sour cherries until time is lost and the charm is broken."

These were unmistakable words, which recalled the sticky and resigned odor of dresses worn until threadbare. And which recalled the withered and helpless situations: when one bears them in the soul one cannot live.

But on those rainy days in 1933, people rehabilitated the thing and the fatalism, which was occurring to people at that moment. And, as usual, when things were already so banal, an event happened so far removed from life it was as if it were altogether fictional.

It was also noted then that even the figure of heroic life, which had been associated for some time with the figure and melody of a rectangle, now bore a drop of melancholy in the gray elongation of its lines *and its sad repetition*. Perhaps life requires a drop of melancholy?

And so unexpected possibilities became stories of "broken hearts," of "*walking the* streets that want nothing more" and "waiting for life." It was as if all of that belonged to life now.

During those days, gray from the rain, a tango with the following lyrics played every evening for the whole month in the Femina bar:[21] "It is all, or nothing at all …"

7. FLOWER SHOPS WITH AZALEAS

In the city of blue grayness and five million legs, there are also shops with huge, flat, spherical flowers.

Azaleas in the flower shop on the Boulevard Montparnasse in Paris are perfect. Their color is like that of salmon or oranges; in fact, they reflect a hundred shades of noble smoked lox or round oranges.

Azaleas from the Boulevard Montparnasse in Paris no longer need the drawn-out and contemplative fragrances of the ordinary flowers. They could be made of satin, odorless brass: they have poured their whole soul into the color, which is *incomprehensible and* full of sad experiences, like brass itself.

This event takes place in the summer of 1933, at the same time as the other events described here.

A great sadness suddenly passes through the bustling Boulevard Montparnasse, a brass sea of melancholy. It seeps—no one knows how—from the shop filled with azaleas.

The day is gray *and sweet*, one in a series of gray days. People search for hard objects to hold in their hands; *they search for gray walls, and the walls*

---

21 This is an allusion to the Femina bar (1 Johannesgasse, Vienna) or the Berlin bar Ballhaus Femina, as suggested by Anna Maja Misiak.

of dazzling billboards, for distinct and unambiguous events. And this thing, which is taking place here at the azalea shop, in fact, completely resembles something known for a long time, a usual thing, but for a long time one could not remember where this dull and colorless burden had come from. Until suddenly one knows that what is happening now on the Boulevard Montparnasse always happens when a thing is settled and when nothing can be done about it anymore.

In front of the shop with the *melancholy and yet hard* brass azaleas that have no fragrance, as if they had tried on all possible fragrances, life suddenly becomes like a long, gray stretch where everything is already settled and everything that was supposed to happen has already passed.

And suddenly, perfect things and sweet encounters and elegant azaleas the color of lox[22] become unbearable. And suddenly one desires houses, formless and too large, filled with things and people. One desires "missed opportunities" and "failed romances" and "unhappy loves."

The weed of longing grows and spreads, the longing for things full of coarse solitude and for the bleary burdock leaves of unrest.

And like the grotesque tagline of a pulp novel, the following sentences form: "Among perfect things there is no longer a place for life. … This is where abandonment and *dull* sadness come from, which goes hand in hand with every nice thing. That's why people need a bit of raw disorder and *coarse* abandonment in life in general …"

And who would have thought that these far-reaching conclusions would have stemmed from unimportant azaleas, as if made of sad brass?

Yet that's how life works: the most meaningless things remind us of the most important things in life.

8. SOLDIERS MARCH ON

That summer, which came at last, was unusual and inconsistent with the calendar.

It started and went by without yellow heat, without flies, and butterflies. *It did not have deep avenues of heat when suddenly everything is feasible, nor glass stillness where everything is lost.* And yet it happened. It could be recognized from the green of the trees, which grew darker. Later, from the spotty yellowing of the chestnut trees.

---

22 In Polish: "orange azaleas."

(Such a summer was hard to reckon with: people allowed the leaves to darken and yellow again, and "hearts"—what an old-fashioned word—*to be vessels which* spill over missed opportunities.)

It appeared as if the sight of the course of life was lost, like the undecided and dull summer.

And yet a few weeks ago, as happens every year at this time *of sticky leaves*, people had decided to "live." And now it was as if this decision were absolutely obliterated from memory. And people wished for nothing and did everything without conviction, not engaging fully, as if unsure of what had to be done at this moment and how to proceed.

Later, on a particular day, an odd urgency: to accomplish everything that belonged to life.

And it was formulated in exactly that way: "to figure out life."

And into this atmosphere of catastrophic excitement an event entered. It unambiguously expressed that the world stood, nevertheless, on its ancient, predetermined, and well-grounded place, and that it was always possible to "come back to life."[23]

Figure 32. Henryk Streng, reprint of illustration from Debora Vogel, *Akacje kwitną. Montaże* (Warszawa: Rój, 1936), 36.

---

23 An allusion to Hegel's absolute idea, *Rückkehr zum Leben*.

Soldiers march in the streets. They march in big rectangles of blue grayness, the gray of a warm November day without sun. They have soldiers' uniforms. On their coats: precisely four polished buttons.[24]

Attention: now the left leg goes up. Next: the right one. Then each leg returns to the pavement at the rigid, right angle to the street. And it transpired as if the soldiers were contemplating something very important with their feet, perhaps the flat, angular event of this march of large, blue rectangles composed from the soldiers' uniforms *and polished buttons.*

On a particular predetermined day, otherwise the same as all other days, in the same place, the blue rectangle gushed with a coarse fountain of voices: for the most part, they sang a tango adapted to the rhythm of a march.

That syllogism of marching was no more or less significant than any other event. And it comes as no surprise that it can be treated with the full, *sweet*[25] resignation that life deserves: as a self-explanatory thing.

And so one does not know what can become important in life. Each matter can differ from what it is supposed to be; it can become important in a different way from its meaning: like the rectangle of soldiers which helped to "come back to life." To some extent, the whole process resembled everyday life.

Jasmine, acacias, and finally linden bloomed in turn.

And once again there was "too little of life," just as before, when happiness determines its measure. This is what the blue rectangle of soldiers accomplished. It played the role of joy that summer devoid of heats and flies.

9. SHIPS CARRY GOLD

Everything that has taken place so far happened in the summer of 1933 in the following way.

Everything was authentic. And as important to people as life, although the world was then full of events belonging to a quite different series and order.

These events contained the fate of matter. In fact—and it could not be defined otherwise—it was about regulating the helpless matter that had been bearing on people's fate. From time to time the weeds of disorder overgrew the

---

24 In the Polish version this paragraph reads as follows: "[S]oldiers march in the streets. They march in big rectangles. They have soldiers' uniforms of blue grayness, the gray of a warm day without the sun. And on the soldiers' blue coats there are four polished buttons, precisely four round buttons."
25 This word appears in Yiddish only.

world, and then strange and blind needs *and passions* descend on people: the needs to rearrange and rework, to regulate life. Such a time had come.

At first the event took such shape.

Under the shabby door of a house in Biedermeier style, 28 Skarbkovska Street, the unemployed wait. On every first and fifteenth day of the month, they come one by one, in alphabetical order. They go up the wooden, winding, worn-out stairs. They wait awhile. They wait through an uncountable period of time, the time until life can be seized.

Meanwhile, the kings of *fat* oil, coal, and matches do not know what to do with these sticky materials *and with gold; with happiness,* and with life. There are too many things in the world for them, and nothing to be done with the surplus stock.

Then something happens that illustrates to what extent something can become more important than what it usually is and how it pertains to life—as in the case of the Parisian azaleas and the marching soldiers.

At that time, it turned out that somehow, for some period, *the stalks of weeds* and the dirty stacks of commodities had drowned out the world's supply of gold. At that time, the country of America, a landscape of concentration and *hard* balance, started to take away its gold from the unbridled and wanton, soft and pathetic Europe.

Berengaria, Liverpool,[26] *Georgic sailed from the European ports. One unruly ship was even called Manhattan.*[27] Nobody pays attention to the nameless transportation.[28] In that whole incident, what may turn out to be of most importance was the landscape of red gold over the *fantastical* cobalt of the sea, full of incomprehensible yet definitive contents.

And yet people do not see that yet. The sticky residue of days spent processing the shabby and fat, expressionless and filthy matter of life for the pearls on foreign women sprayed with Paris Twilight perfume,[29] still permeates the unemployed near the Biedermeier door.[30] They are permeated with the tacky

---

26 In Polish. In Yiddish the sentence reads: *"Berengaria, Georgic,"* and two other ships.
27 This addition is in the Polish text.
28 In Polish there are two sentences in place of one sentence in Yiddish. The Polish reads: "The red metal is transported over the ocean in 250 unshapely chests which encumber the holds. Nobody pays attention to that nameless and fantastical transportation; nobody thinks that gold is exchanged for commodities: dresses, shoes, and potatoes."
29 Soir de Paris was a perfume by Bourjois (created by Ernest Beaux, the creator of Chanel No. 5), which came out in 1928.
30 In Polish this phrase is "sprayed in an unknown place on the dress."

and flat odor of boredom and bitterness, rigid like a burdock leaf. *They do not yet sense happiness, which is ubiquitous where there are hard things with a fragrance of metals and movement.*

It is, apparently, still not important to the planned epic of life, and it waits until everything excessive is resolved. However, the thing that will happen shortly is angular[31]. *It is already contained in the tacky air of standing near the door of the office for the unemployed; it ferments in that empty action of standing sealed off from the rest of the world.*

It comes shortly. It takes on a shape of the nagging longing for gray noise, for the helpless sweetness of flat things, for the full roundness and the mild melancholy of rectangular objects.

Then there will be no more time for the questions "Why?" and "For whom?"

10. CALENDAR SUMMER

And in the end calendar summer has come and one could return to the usual order of things. And it was no longer necessary not to fall into some fatal series of events, *which strayed from a foreign dimension*, from some *marginal* time, which fits nowhere and differs from itself.

Melancholy towards everything, which is inherent in life, belongs to the plan for these days. These are the days from wise and sad brass *and from helpless lacquer.* And this kind of life has come.

Now these weren't distinct any more: the *eternal* brass helplessness of man and the sweltering heat made of *tacky* lacquer; decaying things and blooming acacias; walking along round squares and the yellowing of leaves.

Lush, green leaves, blocks of fragrant colors, and things lost now finally belonged to themselves. And again, they could be called by a name, taken from an unusual and unused terminology: the days of sad metal dresses,[32] hands, and flowers. Metals, lacquer heat, and round squares[33] have in themselves the same helpless and sweet rigidity. And the whole summer was as if made from yellow and gray metals.

People were now somewhat happy. That's how the thing we call happiness looked like.

---

31 In Polish it is "apparent" rather than "angular."
32 "[S]tiff metal dresses" in Polish.
33 In Polish, instead of "round squares," "strolling around the streets and squares."

Only people of whom they say that "the bottom fell out from their lives" could not even experience sadness. And during a particular summer,[34] one of the particular stories happened to them, an incomprehensible and silly story, out of which ordinary life is made.

11. "HEARTS FOREVER BROKEN"

The following thing was happening in life: it was guided—even though not everyone was aware of it—by a rectangle, a figure of heroic life and gray encounters. It was like a gray surface,[35] full of monotony, concentrated, hard movements, and sweet melancholy.

That summer, however, an element of roundness began to be tolerated: it took on the appearance of soft flesh and senseless events; longing and waiting. It manifested like the need for senseless events.

And suddenly it becomes apparent that happiness is needed for life. At the same time, it turns out that there are plenty of passersby on the streets[36] who have "broken hearts."

They stroll aimlessly on the streets. They touch strangers' hands and leaves. If they happen to be women—they change hats and dresses—this or that material, *coarse-grained or satin*; this or that *stuffy* color, *or cold blackness*.

And yet, they "can't live." Yes, exactly: they cannot live. What stands between them and life is one trifling thing that had to happen but did not end up happening. It had to give a drop of happiness, always needed for life.

That summer one started to pay attention to the "heartbroken" people, as they wanted to be, more or less like all of us, an illustration of one of the many possibilities in life.

Banal hearts, pierced by arrows, hearts from Utrillo's[37] pale pink walls and all the rear walls of the city apparently belong in equal measure to life, just like walking, happiness, and the *yellow*[38] chrome leaves of Pelikan brand paint[39] in the months of October and November.

---

34 "During a particular summer" appears only in Yiddish.
35 In Polish it is "long."
36 In Yiddish, the phrase is "passersby on the streets"; in Polish, "people."
37 Maurice Utrillo (1883–1955) was a French painter noted for his cityscapes, especially the streets and buildings of Montmartre.
38 This word is only in Yiddish.
39 Paint of the Pelikan brand was of high quality. From 1898, the company organized poster contests, in which many artists took part, to advertise the quality of the product.

Figure 33. Henryk Streng, reprint of illustration from Debora Vogel, *Akacje kwitną. Montaże* (Warszawa: Rój, 1936), 49.

12. MOUNTAINS AND RIVERS IN THE YEAR 1926

That wonderful adventure with the contemplative cobalt mountains and rivers of cold-water metal could happen yet again, especially a few years later when one is "forever broken by life."

Then mountains could be again like plums in blue fog, which resemble *the person's* watery longing. And mountains in gray fog are like apples that, in turn, have to be compared to desolate people in the afternoon city streets. And rivers could be, in turn, like hard decisions, and not undecided drops of color.[40]

Then the following happens—and who knows how it comes about—one "belongs to life," and, moreover, one "can forget." *Does it come from the fact that mountains stand in place and rivers flow for thousands of years, and yet they "live"*? Or from the fact that mountains and rivers are like hard and tragic decisions? Or that they want nothing more, since they already have everything: blue air, gray fog?

---

40 The color is defined in Polish as "drops of blue."

And so it turned out that one has to rehabilitate that which people who are "utterly broken" have called the "escape into the mountains."

And the following thing became very likely, which before had an aftertaste of sticky hopelessness: the thing with people *who take away our life, not knowing what to do with their time*, preoccupied with themselves, constantly dissatisfied people.

The most important matter is now: happy people. Only they "live."

13. "LIFE"

And then when it was settled with the term "happiness" (out of circulation for a while), it was time for the most confusing term, although everyone seemed to understand it, namely that soft word: "life."

It started the following way: the day smelled with the glassiness of October. The leaves were already yellow. The sky was warm and blue; the streets were gray.

A tango refrain was coming from the Femina bar, 72 Karmelitska Street:[41] "who cares about our love if not you and I; who is our love going to hurt if both of us are sad. …"[42]

In a moment and without a comprehensible reason a lady in a soft suit remembered, like a few other passersby in rigid bowler hats and bright coats, that "life has to be lived, as much as one can," and that people have not tended to their lives, with years lost and possibilities squandered.

And so it was phrased, everything that happened to people on that glassy October day—*that one needs to use life.*

This was the beginning of a long *and difficult* treatise on life, although these matters turned out to be well known and long settled.

The treatise was composed in a cheap and vague style. The dreamers are used to utilizing this kind of style; people striving for "perfection"; people who want to master "spiritual experiences" from the higher "hierarchy of souls *and their intricate adventures*," those who discover with huge aplomb and ecstatic transfiguration things already discovered and long settled. (In our living conditions these are mostly hairstylists, manicurists, waiters—*people condemned to foreign lives on the other side of the shop window.*)

---

41 In Polish, "37 Karmelitska."
42 This quotation is from the tango "Kogo nasza miłość obchodzi." Its text and music are by Marian Hemar (1901–1972). It was performed by Hanka Ordonówna.

This style uncovered shoddy shades of life—*which inevitably appear and as if it were their sign*—with muslin sweetness, brass hope[43] for "that which has to come."

Yet this fact did not stir acrimony or aplomb. Since at the time people got used to treating muslin and brass sweetness[44] as those things which make up life itself.

14. TREATISE ON LIFE: CHAPTER ONE

It simply suffices to go out into the streets, into the amber October dusk. Then, between four and five in the afternoon, life is always "broken," regardless of what happens to us.

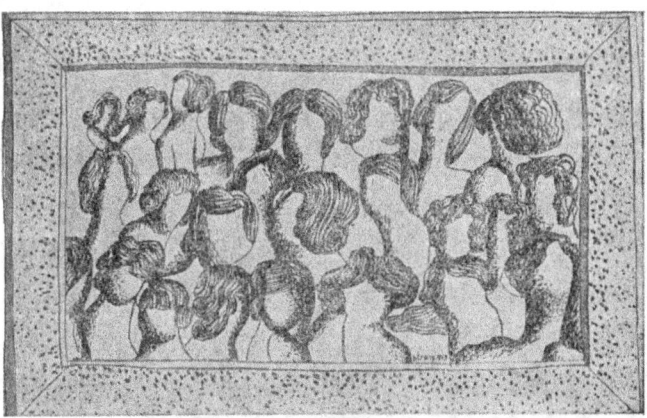

Figure 34. Henryk Streng, reprint of illustration from Debora Vogel, *Akacje kwitną. Montaże* (Warszawa: Rój, 1936), 57.

In Salon de Beauté, 25 Karmelitska Street, a manicurist appears to be made from wax *and with a high hairdo*, like a typical doll from 1924. A hairdresser has a wavy hairdo scented with Milles Fleurs perfume, and the owner of the salon is like a heavily retouched photo of a woman circa 1900, with a deeply cut waistline and a stiff underwire collar, the latest fashion of the early 1900s.

In the yellow dusk between four and five o'clock,[45] the owner of the beauty salon on 25 Karmelitska Street—unceremoniously and without

---

43   The phrase "muslin sweetness, brass hope" in Yiddish is "muslin hope" in Polish.
44   "[H]elplessness and brass sweetness" in Polish.
45   In Polish, "in the warm amber dusk in October."

paying any attention to customers—asked her employee: "What is it that I am living for?"

As if answering the question, the manicurist under the purple lampshade swayed at that moment and gave the lady in black[46] an aluminum bowl with water for her nails.

Then, with a lot of noise and imagination, the hairdresser started working on one *wavy* hairstyle and then another one, with particular thoughtfulness, tending to every single wave.

In turn, a female apprentice began to arrange and set up canisters with black and brown henna, *with incomprehensible haste and* making unjustified noise.

And so a cheap sight with a woman on it, and rigid tins with hair dye, pointed to a conclusion that it's useless to "live in the world." And how could it be otherwise in this setup and under these circumstances?

And so it always started with a question, "Why should one live?" That's how the course of every single life began and the autumn treatise on life.

Figure 35. Henryk Streng, reprint of illustration from Debora Vogel, *Akacje kwitną. Montaże* (Warszawa: Rój, 1936), 59.

15. FROM THE SECOND CHAPTER OF THE TREATISE

"And yet life is worth living."

And so the second chapter of the treatise—and of life—began.

---

46   In Polish, "in a blue dress."

It is an ordinary summer, and sticky, wide and thick matter of the world ferments with promises, aromas, and possibilities. It is divided up and segmented into different lumps: thick blocks, flabby and shapeless; tight and elastic like waiting; and flat, insignificant, anonymous layers of brass, and scraps of wide, self-important life-matter, *almost obscene* from the excess of assurance.

All of this falls into things: smart contours[47] of bodies and breasts; weeds, leaves, walls, bottles, and events. And then there is a reason to live in the world.

In the city park alleys, heavy torsos with round breasts stroll. They cram chaotic layers of body curves in brocade corsets the color of flesh or apricots.

There is too much of the body. The body has the smell of wide *summer* leaves. It sparkles with possibilities.

Then the old ladies in dresses that are too wide and loose, especially sagging around breasts, look at the torsos, as well as people who "cannot live."

And then one can be sure that all the passersby think about one and the same thing: that life flies by irreversibly. That single honeysweet day, full of a thousand possibilities and promises, is slipping away.

Then the heat is bronze; the world is a metal seething ball of heat; and life is worth living.

Figure 36. Henryk Streng, reprint of illustration from Debora Vogel, *Akacje kwitną. Montaże* (Warszawa: Rój, 1936), 62.

---

47 In Polish, "all this falls into caressing and soulful contours."

16. THE THIRD SENTENCE OF THE TREATISE

The month of October, made fully from brass and grayness, lends itself to treatises on life. It entices into the gray area of concepts—perhaps also because they are too similar to the gray and contemplative October avenues.

And simply against this background and under these circumstances *in October*,[48] a banal sentence of the treatise becomes understandable and acceptable: "One needs to go through life."

(Life can be like a foreign street in a city one has known for a long time. The houses have flat and square facades: contemplative houses. The corners of the houses are slightly rounded in a velvet way. There are also balconies, round and absolutely unexpected. On the sides of the walls there are unnecessarily low, almost near the pavement: *semi-circular stems swinging from the trunk of the wall*. Nearby can also suddenly be a gray, coarse, protruding house with nondescript dwellers.)

On that already gray October afternoon hour, Sh., a carpenter of styled furniture, walks from Horodotska Street and along Karmelitska Street; he is on the way to Teatynska street where he has to get an order for a room from a lady in cobalt lacquer. A few steps ahead, there walks a woman in a matte bronze suit, coarsely textured, and mildly contemplative; she wears a soft felt hat which is the same color as her clothes.[49]

The lady in matte bronze walks as if floating, lightly swaying on her nicely arched legs, with her step poring over every gray board of sidewalk, lost in thought.

And it is clear that she left the house with a plan for a long stroll in accidental streets.

Karmelitska Street in Lviv is always full of pastel sweetness, as if it were intended for "aimless" walks. Along one side of the street, a whole mild, white wall connects right to gray or blue sky, standing upright, it is itself a piece of the *gray sky*. It is free from the facades of houses with their variety of vibrating souls, which introduce into the streets the undecidability of the mood, and, eventually, an absolute disarray, usually part of this mood.

---

48 The month is only specified in the Yiddish version.
49 This paragraph is quite different in Yiddish; it does not include a carpenter. Rather, it provides even more detail about the woman passerby: "On that gray afternoon hour, a woman walks on Karmelitska Street. This lady in a matte bronze suit is absolutely gorgeous. Her complexion is the color of bronze tree bark, strung on a pink apricot. Her eyes are also the color of bronze tree bark. Her outfit is made from a mild contemplative material, and the perfect line of a soft felt hat is the same color as her clothes."

The walking is "without a purpose," if seen from the viewpoint of "settling" some matters in life. In fact, it always has an aim, even when it does not fully lend itself to a certain conventional, recognized, and established life necessity.

In this case, for instance, strolling might be about the need to "forget." To forget, let's say, a thing that cannot be undone, which floods your memory, like a river, or an unpredictable passion at the moment when you glance at the white wall or chrome chestnut trees.

This lady in a matte bronze suit is absolutely gorgeous. Her complexion is the color of bronze tree bark, strung on a pink apricot. She also has beautiful brown eyes. And thanks to the lady in bronze and sentimental Karmelitska Street, cheap delights and needs of the soul are expressed, delights and needs which we always prefer to "forget." Then yellow-honey, twilight falls, and it becomes impossible to go on living. …

Karmelitska Street has almost no *car or horse-drawn transportation* traffic. It is no highway providing access to the outlying centers of life. It is a street meant for exhausted and frustrated people. Rare cabs have their permanent clients: women going to the maternity ward in the hospital on Kurkova Street. Bodies frantic, with concealed enthusiasm at the thought: in a few hours they will become mothers.

Every other lady in a bright coat standing under chestnut trees[50] peers into every passing cab. A light residue of sadness and sweetness falls on her face, and she looks like a crumpled autumn leaf.

At that time on the street there are a few passersby walking hastily and absentmindedly. Such walking offers no opportunities. It does not allow for studying the singularity of the street where the bodies and dresses of passersby exude elasticity and something akin to a sense of life. Apparently, these couple-passersby wish for nothing more than to cover the length of the street as soon as possible. In that afternoon hour falls a stiff departure from occupation *or a return home from the office.*

And from the Femina bar, 23 Karmelitska Street,[51] a tango refrain plays: it is either "all or nothing at all. …" It plays the whole of October.

Then the passersby find inside themselves layers of experiences, coming out of nowhere, like a commentary on the latest life wisdom: it's either nothing or everything at once.

---

50 In Polish it is the "lady in a bright coat under the chestnut trees."
51 In Polish, "37 Karmelitska."

According to the formula, "nothing," however, is no allusion to the dull, burdock vegetation of the soul. The greedy consumption of events and fates is also out of the question, *or the mood of "waiting for good fortune."* It is simply a dysfunctional nomenclature, which history and events have already left behind. It resembles, however, the hopelessness of that time in life when to find one's sense of direction, one utilized such notions as waiting or resignation.

Meanwhile the sentence means something completely different: the last, third sentence of the treatise, more or less. The sentence, which in other contexts sounds like "walking through life."

And so we are about to finish the autumn treatise on life.[52]

And it's too bad that this sentence is repeated in the refrain of the "gutter" song. Everyone feels, after all, that these words are as serious as life itself, the same in all circumstances, even if in a cheap attempt to pull at heartstrings. ...

And so we reach the end of the autumn treatise on life. At the time it is always the end of October, and the yellow and rusty leaves smell of raw paint and the melancholy of things coming to an end.

The commentary on the last sentence in the chapter of life reads: When a person puts great passion into things chosen and rare, he rarely finds what we call happiness. Then he is either: 1) "broken," when that which should have happened does not happen; or, 2) "has too little life," when everything happens as it should.

Karmelitska Street. A long, yellow-amber dusk[53] fills the objective commentary on life, always hasty,[54] with unexpected vaults, *and convex*[55] colors with a hint of sadness. It saturates with sense and sweetness the flat avenue of notions,[56] which lasted for yet another year.

The dusk was nothing out of the ordinary, at its usual time in October. The dusk was pastel and gray, full of incomprehensible promises, while sadness fell from the chestnut trees, walls, and faces, along with wide crumpled leaves.

Yet today nobody cared about that first sentimental part of the evening. Today the evening unraveled the second layer of its matter: avenues, *incomprehensible in this season,* and hazy in the gray dusk of October.[57] They

---

52 This sentence appears here only in Yiddish. In the Polish version it appears after the next paragraph, after the words "even if in a cheap attempt to pull at the heartstrings."
53 In Polish, "a long dusk of October afternoon."
54 In Polish, instead of "hasty," the word "unpredictable" is used.
55 In Yiddish "full."
56 "the horizon" in Polish.
57 In Polish, "hazy in the blue dusk."

were full of coarse events, hard metallic aromas, and the nameless scent of walking, unworn dresses, and objects.

And the streets were full of clay and pungent smells: full of promises of things, raw and detestable like weeds, which should bring that incomprehensible happiness.

17. OCTOBER EVENINGS

Chestnut trees grow in the round designated places on the streets and sidewalks. Only now they are noticed.

Red and ochre-yellow, they hide the blue and *velvet*[58] gray of October space. Only now one sees them: the heaps of warm yellow paint.[59] The corner of "Governor's Walls"[60] is rounded. So is the corner of Karmelitska and Ruska streets.[61] On these corners now rustle flat paper masses of the wavy brass and warm chrome: chestnuts.

On evenings like these, every house is flat and somewhat dull. *The squares and the streets, on the other hand, are fantastical, like unexpected halls, full of vaults and the elasticity of bodies in movement, filled with the unfathomable contents of encounters among people.*

On that honey-yellow evening, a boiler burst in the "Gentleman" metal works factory in Lodz, "causing the deaths of dozens of people"—the newspapers inform us as usual. And undoubtedly, things were happening in the world, more important than this evening, things able to change life itself. Meanwhile those chestnut trees make a person a graft of grief, like a yellow leaf, crumpled by dusk and the smell of grayness.

A rounded sidewalk corner is then like a thing which does not return. One has to enjoy it like life. On an evening like this, there was nothing left to do than circle around the mild arcs of gray sidewalk curbs once again, a few more times.[62]

---

58 In Yiddish.
59 "[C]hrome" in Polish.
60 This is a place name in the city of Lviv in the Polish version of the montage. In the Yiddish version it is the "New Square."
61 The current street name. In Yiddish it is "Boyim Street."
62 This paragraph is different in Polish: "On evenings like these, there was nothing left to do other than circle around the mild arc of the gray sidewalk with the golden chestnut. The arc of the sidewalk was like a thing which passed by irreversibly and which needs to be used like life itself and like gray dusk with yellow lanterns."

This was a wonderful and unvalued event, like an encounter, incomprehensible in its meaning.

And then later when you returned to the rooms where you live, you tried to understand that incomprehensible event, which can take up the whole evening. Then, unexpectedly, that whole process took on the shape of the following sentence:

"Chestnut trees were warm from yellow paint.[63] The streets were velvet gray.[64] The curbs of the sidewalks were softly rounded."

One could only say this much about the curbs.

The story of one of the most colorful events in the whole year came about in this inconspicuous way.

18. LIFE IS UNDERTAKEN FROM THE BEGINNING

Meanwhile October passes. Then the transparent November comes.

Silence, sticky and pungent like weeds, still hangs over the factories. Newspapers columns are full of the news of further layoffs. Among people you feel the tacky odor of calico and the soft, pleasant smell of fabric, the cold touch of glass, and the sad stickiness of oil.

This deprives people of a big elastic space and instead leaves them in an abandoned space, flat like potato peels.

At the same time there are more advertisements for maternity hospitals in the newspapers: women's bodies are like trees, they bear the most in November.

And so a new series of history ensues.[65] And like every year in this season, as usual, it is full of its own matters of incomprehensible and time-consuming importance. Yet no one can tell what is so important about them.

You take up life exactly where you left off a few months ago.

Exactly at a point when a yellow, metallic summer starts. And control over human fate is interrupted, when you expect something from finished things and events, which life holds in store for us in certain measure.

On that undertaking of an interrupted life—as if nothing happened at the time—the year ended, signed by the date of 1933.

---

63 "[F]rom yellowness" in Polish.
64 In Polish: "the streets were the velvets of matte gray and ambers."
65 In Polish, "life."

19. FLAT PANORAMAS OF LIFE

Between November and those weeks[66] ebbing with waves of forgetting, unused possibilities, and greenery of Pelikan brand paint, stretch three months of flat avenues of white.

These three months cannot be taken into account at all: flat and expressionless, absolutely deprived of any panoramas, backgrounds, or views.[67]

In that landscape there are no baroque trees *and leaves*. And burdock leaves of *human* madness do not define life.

That *strange* prospect of a pause in life does not promise much of anything anymore. In fact, the opposite comes to be: things, once started and initiated, lie like a deadweight inside of us, fermented and sour. Thus, we may bring to an end the chronicle of the period at hand.[68]

It was a usual year. And all the banal stories *of each year* repeated themselves that year, as if there was nothing more important in life. Namely, the green heaps[69] of leaves and of waiting; the lacquer, sweltering heat and the sweetness of walking; the pink lumps of blooming chestnut trees and "frustration." Every year has its own plan of happiness and some lost cause. This thing is integrated as if it is an ordinary process into a stable course of the year, *into a series of adventures like streets with people and strolling*.

There, however, where we are right now, in the middle of November, the world stands at the peak of perfection: it is like a monotonous soldiers' march, shimmering with a million polished uniform buttons.

The gray street scenery[70] is as if made from the perfection of monotonous things. (Twice a year this grayness of the streets and the sky appears: in the middle of November *like now*, and sometime *at the end of April and* at the beginning of May when the first dust appears on the sidewalk.)

And sadness falls simultaneously with the drops of leaves (terra rossa, Pelikan brand). It is an incomprehensible melancholy[71] which we suddenly discover in the perfect rectangle that agrees with life.[72]

---

66 In Polish, it is "spring" instead of "those weeks."
67 This sentence in Polish reads as follows: "These three months cannot be taken into account at all: flat and expressionless, they are devoid of perspective, a large space of abandoned things and the round depth of promise and possibility."
68 In Yiddish instead of "chronicle of the period" it is "year."
69 In Polish, "waves."
70 In Polish, instead of "gray street scenery" there is "scenery of seasons."
71 "[S]adness" in Polish.
72 In Yiddish the phrasing is slightly different: "discovered in the middle of life brought to an agreement with a heroic rectangle."

And in the end, as a conclusion to the treatise on life, it turns out that a person is a vessel for sadness, which is predetermined and necessary for life *and that everything is as it should be*. At the moment, the sadness is hard and metallic, and at another time extensive and fragile.[73] As usual, everything ended with a sentence: life is worth living.

The great treatise ended in such a banal way: life is worth living for its hustle and bustle. However, we know this event of the illuminated streets, full of the rustle of feet and conversations, and construction which smells of rawness of pungent lime, dense clay and concrete;[74] and shops with rigidly formed regular stacks of attractive textiles or helpless calico, and all the places where heaps and the noise of things are hoarded in large quantities.

Everywhere where heaps and hosts of things are gathered, it reeks of the elastic and lengthy smell of life, which is unlike any other fragrance. It contains an inherent atom of sadness.

20. COMMENTARY

Meanwhile November continues.

The remainder of life, attempts and frustrations, awakened by *the gray landscape of* November, gives two more commentaries on life.

In their style they resemble objective sentences of systems, *which do not need any scenery*, written in a geometrical way. It is not clear who would make use of these sentences, and in what circumstances.

This is the first commentary. In life, all things are in proximity to each other, without any rule or system, similar to the abovementioned narrative:[75] the green leaves and experiments with life; the heavy drops of raw matter and happiness; the gray and circular streets without a distinct purpose;[76] and the passion for grayness and contours *once and forever*.

Gently and evenly textured, events fill up life. The weights and contours, colors of different texture and finish[77] that would be called things and experiences: an advertisement for Odol toothpaste would be a continuation of the event of the blooming acacias.

---

73 In Yiddish "velvet."
74 In Polish "brass."
75 In Polish "chronicle."
76 The phrase "gray and circular streets without a distinct purpose" is, in Polish, "aimless strolling."
77 The "colors of different texture and finish" are not mentioned in Polish; instead, the expression is "weights and contours of the incomprehensible material of life."

The rough and tacky matter of events holds its hard secrets which deal directly with the dirty matter of life; they know the way to colorfulness.

"One needs to know the hidden secrets of matter:" this is the first commentary on life.

21. SECOND COMMENTARY

This is not yet a novel we feel passionate about, in a sudden and sweet way, then, at the very beginning of the year, on a day of gray skies and the streets like *gray seas and skies*.

Yet life in every future *romance* novel would be handled this way: as a chronicle where everything belongs and where there is no plot development.

The chronicle knows no events that would be more important than others. Here everything is important and necessary *for life* in the same measure.

The chronicle does not single out the sharp contours of tragic experiences or the blocks of resignation. Here everything appears as part of the plot and without hierarchy. Hence the monotony—sometimes unbearable repetition.

Life is like a chronicle: a block, anonymous and unpretentious. Only upon closer examination can the sticky and wanton mass of life be divided into singular fates and details. Just like in June or July, one divides a block of green into individual stems and leaves.

At any point, life can be put on hold and then picked up: like a chronicle of the year, interrupted in the month of November, made from copper brass, sad and fantastical, "like life itself."

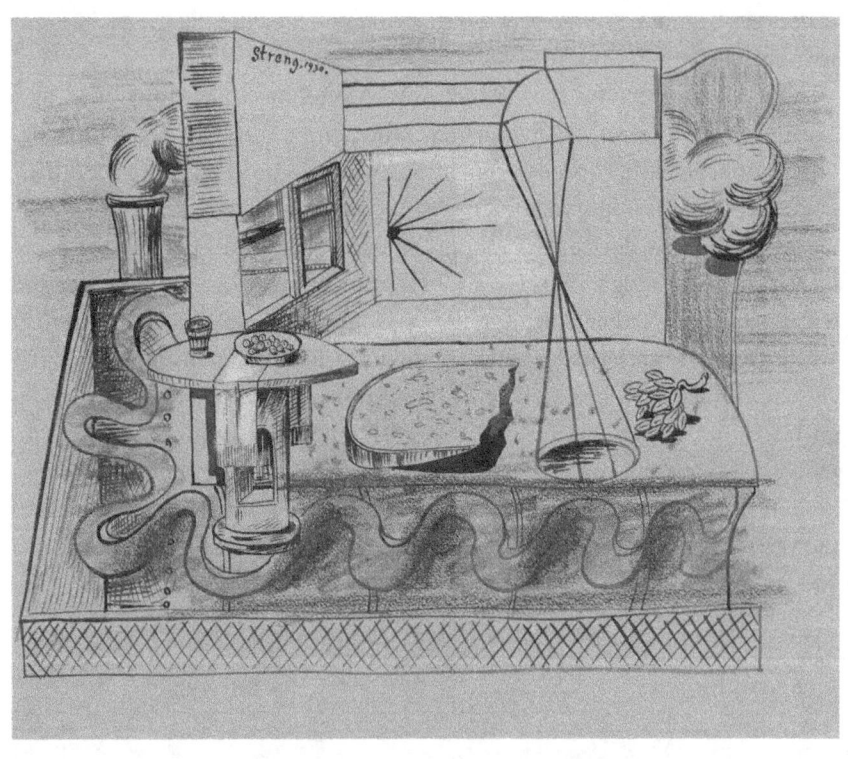

Figure 37. Henryk Streng (Marek Włodarski), *Still Life*, 1930.

27

Acacias Bloom (1932)

THE NEW LEGEND[78]

1. The Mannequins are Unmasked

It all began this way. Suddenly and unceremoniously, a mechanism of the mannequins, wound up by the coiled spring of longing, unmasked itself. It brought about events cheap and shoddy (i.e. "life …") which happen like sweet fate, and banal encounters—like a singular and colorful adventure.

And so it turned out: all the stories with "things squandered" and "years lost"; all the stories of "hearts forever broken", all of that was simply cut out from an old-fashioned *romance* novel, trashy and very funny.

As if wound up, dolls—the rigid men in round bowler hats and the elastic ladies with cinched waistlines—attempted to approach each other. In essence, this was the main event in life. Before one's eyes, figures lengthened (such lengthening of one's waistline and face was called sadness and also frustration).

Then something strange happened. Suddenly colorful events—at first not considered fate—started to recall flesh, raw flesh in the butcher's shop, full of unrest and ill-considered passions.[79]

Those "fatal and colorful fortunes," stories[80] and encounters, now were like *continuously* unfinished and bland things, with a indistinct, sickeningly sweet, and intrusive odor, like over-fermented dough *and sticky goo*. Even people now seemed formed from dough, the sticky dough of longing. They let their passions ferment like lumpy pieces of dough.

It completely fell apart in one's hands, like a shoddy commodity, important and pathetic, a long and always sad event called "life."

---

78 This excerpt appeared in Yiddish as "Akatsyes blien. Di naye legende," *Inzl* [Bucharest] 1, no. 1 (1935): 9.
79 In Polish, "unpredictable," or "erratic."
80 In Polish, "adventures."

Figure 38. Henryk Streng, reprint of illustration from Debora Vogel, *Akacje kwitną. Montaże* (Warszawa: Rój, 1936), 89.

And at the same time the stuffy purple disappeared from advertisements and city lamps, as well as the red *of frescoes* which is usually weaved into incomprehensible and unpredictable adventures *in the streets without people*. Finally, the pathetic citrus-like yellowness, *fantastical like cubes and like the steel Northern seas*—the color of cold resignation—disappeared as well.

In the *plump*[81] pomegranate of the *night* city *with the kernels of lanterns*,[82] red and blue neon appeared.

That red and blue were cold like steel. The cold steel started to dominate the city.

And so, the new legend of the city began.

---

81 In Yiddish.
82 In Yiddish.

2. New Raw Materials Are Needed

Longing is the sticky material of life events.

Sticky, dissolute materials, full of soft, faint whims, excluded from life, were now to be eliminated from the whole production process.

Their place was taken by large drops of concentrated grayness of different weights and moods. Among them was the light and somewhat melancholy grayness of concrete, and the hard machinic grayness of iron and elastic steel, and the fantastic brass grayness which wants everything to be only as it is. Finally, there was also glass, an awkward drop of big colorless consistency.[83]

At first, from these artificial materials of grayness, one managed to extract slices of things, hard and weighty like fate.

Round and smiling porcelain entered the new order of life, although the porcelain possessed a remainder of helplessness.

In the midst of the concentrated grayness, red brass represented a drop of banality and sentiment, always needed.

The boring and altogether sad[84] material entered its most perfect stage in life, its predestined segment of the artificiality.

It was now equivalent to a life that is not lead anonymously, to a responsible life, already forever freed from the exuberance of ceaseless changes *and events*,[85] marked by an unbelievably emotional *and fantastical* monotony.[86]

3. New Mannequins Rise

Then a soul of materials was discovered in people:

A soul of helpless porcelain.

A soul of wood and paper.

A soul of iron and a soul of brass.

At the same time, various types of doll-like mannequins walked out *into the streets* from the shop windows. Here, a woman's head with a drop of porcelain sadness, or a drop of *arrogant*[87] licentiousness, all upon request. There, a doll walked, half of it made from a melancholy which cannot be taken seriously

---

83 In Polish, "an awkward drop of a large, colorless, and already cold tear."
84 In Polish "shoddy."
85 In Yiddish.
86 In Yiddish.
87 Only in Yiddish.

since it is so unsure of itself, so undecided about whether to wear a mask of happiness or to perform a scene of sadness in a light pink dress. Oh, and those pieces of dresses of limestone pink with shades of blue belong to that whole intricate matter of life. ...

And there was among them a pear-like head with the round lazy eyes of Picasso's woman, and an indecisive, lost mask the color of withered roses and greenery.

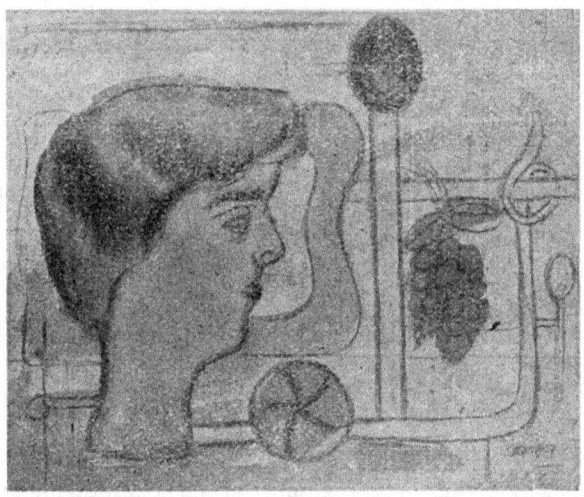

Figure 39. Henryk Streng, reprint of illustration from Debora Vogel, *Akacje kwitną. Montaże* (Warszawa: Rój, 1936), 95.

(It was once painted by Toulouse-Lautrec,[88] and now represented anew by Pascin.)[89] And all these torsos, bent left and right, present a singular and an unusual event: an updo, with waves every one or one-half inches, no randomness or whim here. A brass sea of hairstyles goes up and down, its rhythm *measured and* constant like fate.

In those dolls even melancholy was crammed into hard *and balanced* contours: brows tattooed with black henna, lips contoured with carmine Chameleon brand lip liner, and two symmetrical rouge touches of blush on the cheeks.

---

88 Henri de Toulouse-Lautrec (1864–1901) was a French painter and graphic artist, known for his posters for the Moulin Rouge.
89 Jules Pascin (19985–1930) was a Bulgarian-born American artist, famous for his paintings of women. He was most active in the Parisian circles.

And through that rigid ornament of contours *and surfaces* penetrated not a single atom of licentious flesh. And moreover, in the hard contours near the body, there was the so-called soul. It entered fully into a composition with the rigid body[90] and did not stay apart from it.

Only one of the drops remained in motion: the black, gray, and blue drop of the eyes.

Then the heavy drop of the eyes started presenting all the possible shades of the precious material of melancholy, *which already belongs to life.*[91]

4. A Few More Types of Humanlike Dolls[92]

However, these were not the most important dolls. The most important mannequins were those that presented the souls of materials: the souls of wood and paper, porcelain, brass, and iron.[93]

Paper is rigid and flat, without prospects. The paper is sad like people who cannot deal with anything in life; *it is like white-blue milk and the big pink flowers of calico.*

Figure 40. Henryk Streng, reprint of illustration from Debora Vogel, *Akacje kwitną. Montaże* (Warszawa: Rój, 1936), 99.

---

90 In Polish, "it entered fully into a stiff ornament."
91 In Yiddish.
92 In Polish the title is slightly different: "A Chapter about Mannequins: Continued."
93 This sentence does not appear in the Polish version.

Wood, on the other hand, is sad like *helpless people,* uninteresting people *who do not know how to live from nothing: from the navy-blue air and from life itself.*

People with the soul of wood or paper:[94] one can see them *on the street* and in the shop windows of a photographer's salon. They order pictures from a *chuppah* wedding ceremony: ten or twelve at once, for all the relatives, and as a memento for themselves. They carry out a program of life: everything that belongs to life, in its prescribed order and time.

(When is the proper time? For that, one has to rely on life.) However, nothing is ever figured out in life: death also remains.

5. A Few More Examples of Mannequins

Iron's soul: the soul of happy, parallel running rails. *The soul of* machines, focused and clear, wonderful in their painful working of screws and springs. Such are the fates of those without a worry in the world. And other fates: those of elastic rails, hard rivers, and the soft, insecure landscape of life.[95]

Figure 41. Henryk Streng, reprint of illustration from Debora Vogel, *Akacje kwitną. Montaże* (Warszawa: Rój, 1936), 102.

---

94 In Yiddish.
95 These two sentences are different in Polish: "People with souls of iron walk through the soft and uncertain landscape of life, unentangled in the stuffy matters of fate."

Those who were similar to brass have already spoken their minds: let everything be as it is now. The *gray* brass is experienced *and sad because of that.*[96]

People with a porcelain soul, in turn, were constantly amazed and smiled helplessly.

Mostly women were close to porcelain and paper. Men, however, were related to iron and brass, or to wood, dull and inexpressive.[97]

6. Necklace, a Lyrical Intermezzo

The street mannequins from *pink* porcelain adorned themselves with colorful feather necklaces. Over the twisted cones of breasts, a round bustle surged. A rustling the noise of glass, wood, and steel. This metallic bustle lay over soft contemplative materials;[98] *over the contemplative black of velvet and the pensive materials of the terracotta brand.*

Where are the red coral necklaces that resemble a hundred hands?[99] There are also no pearls of pensive gray skies[100] and melancholy gray seas. ...

The new necklaces from steel and glass are cold, like a foreign thing, and like life without luck.[101]

The women plunge into the caressing metallic bustle. In this way Leda once sunk into the tender fluff of a swan.[102] In this way Max Ernst's[103] women (blind, fleshy, brutal) are caught in-between brass birds, blind and monument-like ideas.

Now the women with the cold porcelain soul let themselves be caressed by cold metals and hard silent glass. And what are velvet pearls, monotonous like life itself, when you could have glass jewelry, full of possibilities, glass, which

---

96 In Yiddish.
97 "Helpless" in Polish.
98 In Polish, "over the melancholy bronze of folded material."
99 In Polish, "Meanwhile the red necklaces torn off from a hundred living, warm, and dissolute arms disappeared from the streets and shop windows."
100 "[O]f pensive gray skies" in Yiddish is "quiet like a steel day" in Polish.
101 "[W]ith no luck" in Yiddish is changed into "when we wish for that which is" in Polish.
102 This motif was pursued by multiple painters, among them Peter Paul Rubens in *Leda with the Swan* (1598) and Polish artists—such as Tadeusz Styka *Leda* (ca. 1920) and Jerzy Hulewicz *Leda* (1928).
103 Max Ernst (1891–1976) was a German painter, graphic artist, author of the three collage novels, constructed from Victorian pulp literature, including *The Hundred Headless Woman, A Week of Kindness, A Little Girl Dreams of Taking the Veil.*

can be a *sweet* window pane or a bead? What are the stuffy tears of emeralds and rubies, and their own life, concealed from us, full of the weight of the earth and sadness?

On 20 February 1932, the newspapers reported the closure of the largest diamond mine in the world, in Kimberley, Canada. It was done, apparently, under the pretext of unfavorable conditions in the diamond market.

And so, it was agreed that diamonds were no longer needed. And velvet tears of pearls, emeralds, and rubies that lead their life independently from us, were not needed either.

Meanwhile the shop windows were full of artificial necklaces. Artificial beads can be fitting for the one of many days of life.

7. Apples, Lemons, and Oranges[104]

Until now we have not understood fruit. We saw in it pulp, whimsical matter, pulsating and delicate (just like Renoir's bulky women, as if they were made from apple pulp,[105] as if they were painted with the red complexion of apples.)

However, apples have a hidden soul. And so do all other fruit, like oranges—*round spaces*, or lemons—*beings made from a cold and glassy fluid*—*are not what we take them to be. Round fruit is, in essence, very different from the literalness of pulp*[106] *its brutal licentiousness, and its indeterminate whims. It turns out: fruit is not as it seems.*[107]

We discover that shiny lacquer and thick, shiny oil paints are rather suitable for depicting the hidden souls of table fruit: every pulsating matter.[108]

It has become manifest that painted and lacquered fruit on canvasses represents the actual soul of round fruit: its sweet roundness.[109] *And so pulpy fruit with bodies full of unrest became unnecessary.*

Near the fruit, on the shop signs, figures smile. They look into the world with the round drops of blue lacquer. They smile with the blue paint of the sky, of

---

104 In Polish, "lemons" instead of "oranges."
105 Renoir (1841–1919) painted women with round bodies and glowing complexions.
106 Yiddish "pulp" is different from the Polish version which is "matter."
107 This sentence is only in the Yiddish version.
108 In Polish this sentence in different: "You discover that shiny lacquer and thick shiny oil paints are rather suitable for depicting the bodies of fruit, rather than sticky and soft material."
109 In Polish: "The painted and lacquered fruit presents the soul of the fruit: sweet roundness."

every July afternoon, when even the sky is made from lacquer, hard and shiny, and so is it.[110] *And so cold-and-shiny-lacquer fruit entered life.*

8. Plates and Glasses

Then it turned out that until now we also did not understand porcelain tableware.[111]

Three[112] times a day glasses and plates enter the company of people, the order of human life and its gray events. *Three times a day they fill colorless houses with the definitiveness of still roundness.*[113]

Meanwhile they stand in china cabinets? They lay on racks and shelves, waiting for when the quarter hour strikes, when people need their cold soul: the sweetness and fullness of the round contour.[114]

And it is not known: is it a contour of the *transparent* porcelain—with a drop of balance upon request? Or is it perhaps a blue, endless body of air, which hardened into the white roundness?

In the *round*[115] contours of tableware a large space lingers for a moment, shaking off its cool magnitude, which for a minute became the roundness of the plates or still glass, and went further, heavy with new possibilities.[116]

And here lies the importance of unpretentious tableware and its fate in the world.

This revelation happened during a *wonderful*[117] time when the legend of "geometrical events" arose.

9. Mountains, Trees, and Seas

From afar mountains are like lonely apples[118] and blue plums, a land and a horizon.[119]

---

110 In Yiddish only.
111 "[P]orcelain tableware" in Yiddish is "soul of cold beings from glass and porcelain" in Polish.
112 In Polish, it is "five times."
113 This sentence is only in Yiddish.
114 Appears only in Polish.
115 In Yiddish.
116 In Polish this sentence is the following: "in the contours of the tableware large space lingers for a moment, shaking off its cool dust of magnitude and roundness, and it goes further, stone and tragic, heavy with new possibilities."
117 Only in Yiddish.
118 In Polish "pomegranates."
119 In the Polish version "a land and a horizon" becomes "a solitary and grandiose land."

Close up, however, they are like piles of helpless earth, overgrown with the banal greenery of trees.

And trees grow, dissolute, like the weeds of mountains. Under sharp, restless, and always dissatisfied angles, a vertical trunk propels itself upward, baroque heavy blocks of branches and leaves, heaps of leaves and flowers.[120] Trees in green fill out all the space with fleshy wanton unrest.

Meanwhile rivers invariably flow for a thousand years. And seas live according to the number seven. Seas and rivers do not spread like weeds, they do not overflow like clay or tacky longing.[121]

The concrete city sea of streets, and the concrete landscape of walls—plants with trunks and branches of verticals and elastic horizontals—live according to the river's rhythm of tumult and *according to the number of* the gray sea: This tumult is according to a number and monotony, endless and definitive.[122]

The streets are a sea of concrete with waves. Or a river of gray tumult. The walls, however, are the gray plants of hard verticals and elastic horizontals. A gray right angle is mild, reconciled with life.

Here fates do not grow into weeds of solitude, since there is no place for that. Instead, fates get stuck against the walls of a giant cube, they tighten, penetrate, and disperse into measured intervals, irrevocably and irreversibly, like the waves of transparent rivers and gray seas.[123]

10. Meanwhile, in the Peripheries of Life ...

In the peripheries of life, one could still mark space, one, two, three floors high. In the evenings this space was only as high as the shop windows which were

---

120 Instead of "heaps of leaves and flowers" in Yiddish, the Polish version is "heaps of greenery and color."
121 This paragraph is different in Polish: "Meanwhile the rivers invariably flow for a thousand years. The seas sway in a measured way. The seas and rivers spread like weeds, they do not overflow like clay or longing, surging like a block of green tree. The sea lives according to number seven; the sea lives in the hard gray troughs of the earth. And it is full of everything."
122 This sentence is absent in the Polish version.
123 The last two paragraphs are completely different in Polish. "Under the mild angle, which seemingly agrees with life, a landscape of the vertical and horizontal grows; it is strong, full, and saturated with the balance of simple angles. The gray plant of the walls and windows fills the flat field of days with events. In that landscape human fates cling to each other, like the hard angles of enormous blocks made from multiple walls; they overlap, penetrate, and move away during measured intervals of time irreversibly and irrevocably. Like the waves of gray seas and transparent rivers. In that landscape there is no place for useless hands and hearts. There is always something to be done here with an unnecessary heart and two superfluous hands."

lit up, the only thing that was higher was the blue heaviness. Later, at seven at night, at the very beginning of the stuffy muddled night, the space is as if closed, along with the extinguished lights in the shop windows.[124]

In the cobalt darkness[125] the space got its voice again later: it sprouted around the yellow glass flowers of lanterns. Then a flat circle with a dormant possibility lured with a view of fatal and sweet things, caressed with the melancholy of missed opportunities.[126]

Later, in daylight, one stated that *the fantastic*[127] glass flowers *of the night*[128] or *the glass fruit with sad kernels*[129] are *old-fashioned*[130] gasoline lanterns, and yet one waited for unheard-of encounters.[131] And so life passed.

11. At the Center of Life

Meanwhile at the center *of the world* everything followed the proud rhythm of monotony. A classic city grew: a wonderful tree of verticals and horizontals. The world brimmed with gray coolness as if with a precious material. And life continued without the fermented, red weeds of passions, without the blunt, milky weeds of yearning. And the most fitting pattern for life was the figure of the rectangle.

Many adventures, including longing, fatigue, and hard resignation, had their pattern in gray figures: in the ellipsis, circle, and square.

Yearning stretches into distance to close upon itself in a *mild arc of* the ellipsis. Fatigue is engrossed in its own matter, *full of dense and immobile* monotony like a circle. And resignation is hard, monotonous,[132] and as if once and for all—*like a square*.

Raw and uncontrolled movement vanished from the world. Why move things and feet when in every place there is everything that there can be?

---

124 The two sentences make up one sentence in Polish: "In the evenings this space was only as high as the shop windows which were lit up, and it closed at the same time with the shops at seven at night, at the very beginning of the navy blue, stuffy night."
125 "In the second part of the night" in Yiddish.
126 In Polish: "then it was a flat circle and fatal possibility. ... It caressed with stuffy melancholy, lured with a distant possibility of things forever lost and some distant things which may still happen."
127 In Yiddish only.
128 In Polish only.
129 In Yiddish only.
130 In Polish only.
131 In Yiddish, "fates" instead of "encounters."
132 Only in Yiddish.

The street is gray like the sky, and yellow like the sun. Later again, dark blue like the sky. A person waits. A gray thing waits. The sun hangs on the one side, and on the other.

And then later, when everything had already happened, the soul of the world got its voice in the following fact, *for example*: every day—as if nothing happened in-between—a certain number of feet were positioned in the streets, set into motion by the question of old: how should one live?

As if nothing happened in-between. Thus, the soul of the world was discovered: motionlessness.

THE FALL

12. Kitsch Overflows the World

… until artificial and cheap commodities have turned up for sale. And like all unimportant things, these irrelevant commodities were the first signs of change. They flooded the markets like the pink blossoms of chestnut trees flood sidewalks and like intrusive sickeningly sweet longing floods the lives of boring people. A strange thing happened with these commodities: they doubled and increased unceasingly, as if they mutually fertilized. There were already too many of them in the world, and yet they increased, *becoming all the more similar*—fantastic, as if upon request, with *cool*[133] simplicity upon request, according to a template.

And one could not contain the wild, released kitschy commodities. One could buy: shoelaces, black and brown, ten pennies a pair, ten handkerchiefs—the fine batiste—just for one florin. (All commodities *on the market* now had the same price, irrespective of what: ten pennies a piece for every product. Ten pennies a piece.)[134]

The following things were available: *stands for cacti*, stands for iron from braided wire, gadgets for the quick and secure tying of ties, devices to quickly thread needles, curling irons for quick wavy hairstyles, a ready wavy hairdo in five minutes.

And above all, *for everyone: the world-renowned*[135] tangos "Rebecca," "Your Love," "Autumn Roses," "You Say You Love Me to Death"—for just ten pennies.

---

133 In Yiddish.
134 In the Polish version, the second sentence in this paragraph comes first, and the first sentence appears as the second.
135 In Yiddish.

Figure 42. Henryk Streng, reprint of illustration from Debora Vogel, *Akacje kwitną. Montaże* (Warszawa: Rój, 1936), 118.

And these commodities are sold with such *fiery* pathos, and such bitter gravity, as if kitsch played the singular and essential role in life. The world stood in well-tied shoes, black and brown. Under the beds of people who recently passed stood black-and-brown shoes, black shoes, which, it seemed, were still used for walking.

13. Calico Surge

In the millinery shops, stacks of thin, cheap calico piled up, in flowery or striped patterns. The patterns were in vulgar and, at the same, time fairy tale colors, including *a mixture of*[136] snowball tree red, violet, and grass green, or *sky*[137] blue, dahlia red, or red orange. ...

The calico was stiff, dry, and without pulp. Sometimes it tried clumsily to be something else: soft silk, or fleshy velvet. Yet its luster was flat and stiff, lifeless.

And the cheviots had an even crispier texture: they broke into sharp angles, and crumbled into dry, angular surfaces. And no color would hold on the stiff fabric threads, to make them elastic with a sweet stretch[138] or *cool* contemplation of color, which bounced off from the fabric like stiff[139] lime, hence their *sad and* inconspicuous appearance.

---

136 In Yiddish.
137 In Yiddish
138 In Polish "allowance."
139 In Polish "dry."

Now these are completely off the market: plush velvet, wavy silk, and caressing woolen cloth. Colors, including elastic autumnal bronze, cool and fantastical coral red, sweet steel gray, vanished.

Flocks of the porcelain female dolls entered the shops with the calico and cheviots.[140] They shoved each other, and loudly, rustling, and in unbelievable haste, they bought all the flowery calico prints and all kinds of striped cheviots.

The world was flooded with kitsch: derivative creations, by-products of cold and compressed things; contorted masks *torn away from faces and*[141] which distanced themselves from their patterns and decided to lead their own independent, carefree, and irresponsible life.

And life overflows with kitsch: a caricature of the world *of the verticals and horizontals* which could be mild[142] like October grayness or pompous and *lofty* like leave-taking and like a single meaningful event in life.

14. Intermezzo: Coffee

And in distant Brazil, Java, and Argentina,[143] they threw into the cobalt sea millions of pounds of coffee, 3,900,000.00 kilograms in 1932.

In large, flat fields the oval drops of coffee harden.[144] Later they become a savory drink, velvet and bitter, like a gray day in October and November,[145] *consistently permeated with the fragrance of foreign cities, where one observes when the strolling happens as if for the first time.*

One drinks coffee on a blue[146] evening with yellow lights and doomed things. Yet black people from Brazil, Canada, and Argentina[147] don't drink coffee. And neither do the whites who work in factories and mines.[148] Only a few thousand people drink coffee in the whole world *between the steel Northern seas and the cobalt Southern waters.* For what, then, are the miles of shrubs which may be unnecessary, just like a person?

---

140 In Polish the fabrics are not specified, the shops are simply "textile shops."
141 Only in Yiddish.
142 In Polish "sweet."
143 In Polish, it is "Sumatra."
144 In Polish this sentence is slightly changed: "In the brown fields, miles long, with a copper circle hanging in the air, there harden gray oval bodies of coffee."
145 "November" appears only in Yiddish.
146 "[G]ray" in Polish.
147 "Brazil, Canada, and Argentina" in Yiddish is changed to "Brazil and California" in Polish.
148 This sentence in Polish is "And neither do the whites from the factories in Europe."

Coffee, however, is not obtrusive; it is not like weeds which overgrow uncontrollably. Coffee gathers the aroma of billions of hard ovals, billions of sweet ellipses, *of the geometrical figure of yearning*.[149]

Coffee should remain in the world:[150] these oval drops cannot be treated like weeds.

Thus, the tired hands of blacks caress the plants, and later send them as a gift *to the golden border*[151] over the cobalt sea.

15. The Next Chapter of Decay: One Seeks Adventures. ...

And it started all over again. One started to seek adventures in the city streets. One waited again, like once before, for silly encounters, which were somehow important.

One wanted to be there only for someone else. One would wait for an *unusual* fate: a whole banal, wanton, restless fatality, the so-called "colorfulness of life."

Certain types of people were rehabilitated who were not current at the time of heroic grayness—people preoccupied with an incessant *and inexhaustible*[152] search for happiness; those with "broken lives," and those who don't "know how to live without people," *even for the duration of one evening*. (In their lives, experiences meant nothing; frustrations did not play their role of unmasking "happiness.")

In these people's lives only one thing fermented like a wanton and bad dough. Until the person became like a poisonous weed, overgrown and obtrusive, and grew unceremoniously fermented stems and shoots of their life story and the sticky leaves of their "experiences."[153]

Now one began to reckon with these people.

And suddenly, at the tables and against the walls, there sit elastic ladies with their sad, cinched waistlines and rigid gentleman dressed in black bowler hats. And yet again, one anticipates the day "when something can still happen."

Here and there a gray color, a hard decision, a fate of renunciation creeps into the world. However, these things and matters awakened only sympathy with their helplessness amidst longings, tacky and overflowing like dough. The

---

149 Only in Yiddish.
150 This part of the sentence appears as the full sentence at the end of this part in Polish.
151 Only in Yiddish.
152 Only in Yiddish.
153 In Yiddish the sentence is slightly different: "Until the person became like a raw poisonous weed like burdock and grew the wide, fatty, and annoying leaves of a tacky life story and the sticky dissolute weeds of 'spiritual experiences.'"

unnecessary ballast of aimless and rounded gestures which imitated the gray heroic gestures of life took their place. And these movements and situations were light *like colorful and carefree balloons.* One cannot even take into account such occurrences, although they are very similar to the wonderful adventure of life.

ACACIAS BLOOM. ...

16. The Circle Closes

And the cause of everything that has happened so far pointed in the direction of life being so perfect and motionless, and so definitive.

It turned out that the perfection of things is unbearable. The perfect things were too gray and monotonous, freed from all expectations and from every memory.[154]

Everything was too perfect and too planned, and there was nothing else to do in the world. Unfinished things became a necessity once again.

Somewhere raw materials waited. Succulent, heavy, insatiable. *In the tropical, bronze countries. In the hot sand of California. In the mountains of the gray Urals and Scandinavia, with dense fog like blossoming buds covering everything with the petals of a gray veil.* Somewhere the fates waited. Colorful, silly, and yet singularly important.

And there, where the poor and flat soil could not push out from itself, a lot of fantasticality and brass colors—there was sticky clay, bland sand, and colorless rubble—happiness.[155] And all things and encounters possessed everything once again, as if for the first time.[156]

One comes back to "life."

17. Acacias Bloom

Suddenly acacias bloomed in the market. Then they filled all the streets with the sad smell of things that were possible yet did not happen.

---

154 These two sentences are slightly different in Polish: "And it turned out that people cannot bear heroic monotony for a long time. The gray ornament of days was too tragic, devoid of waiting and memories."

155 The same sentence is different in Polish: "And there, where the poor and flat soil could not push out from itself a lot of the fantasticality—there waited sticky clay, bland sand, and colorless rubble—inconspicuous and devoid of any possibilities, these materials were like events."

156 The same sentence in Polish: "Unknown matters waited in hiding, and they promised everything as if for the first time."

All of this happened in June, *one of the three months of the sticky odors which harm our hands and our hearts.* The leaves were fleshy and bright green. The green fullness of leaves filled all windows and days.

Then the linden blossomed, they smelled of everything: the history of such blossoms is nameless.

And in this way the time of big and important events started—*sad and fatal events of intermittently incomprehensible importance.* "Fatal encounters" appeared again, as well as "unhappy loves"; sad happiness—unattainable—and yet "happiness."

And again, acacias bloom. They bloom for someone. Such events are incomprehensible, pulling us into regions from where it is not easy to return; and where happiness[157] lies in big heaps—like leaves on a branch, and flowers; where the street lanterns are fantastical "glass flowers" or "glass fruit"; and the gray skin of the evening—a velvet tapestry.[158]

In that region happiness is unknown. There, a person gets entangled with other people, and she can no longer live with them, yet she can no longer live without them.

18. Autumnal Conversations

Then the months of flax suns and brass leaves arrived.

In the dimly-lit streets it smelled of bitter fried jam and leaves.

And in a strange way that odor reminded of regular fates and ordered lives.

Then a series of the unending conversations began; they were incomprehensible like "life itself."

These conversations were about the autumn leaves in need of gray rains and sweet, still fogs in order to yellow. The topic was precisely these sweet, *gray rains* and the long-lasting velvety fogs which envelop the leaves, still green and weak, so that they eventually shrink under the sadness of gray mist.

Unusual and overlooked matters then received attention, for instance, the same leaves are still green when covered in gray mist, but they are rusty red in the chrome afternoon light. The gray walls become white from the silence on the lead sea of the sky. The walls are light, like cartons of fluffy paper with rectangles of celluloid on days of blue sky. They only imitate the concrete walls.

And these conversations clearly replaced very important and delicate matters that had to be settled right away, with no delay, such as the confessions

---

157 In Polish "all the possibilities."
158 Instead of "velvet tapestry," the Polish version is: "like the blue ambiance of foreign cities."

Figure 43. Henryk Streng, reprint of illustration from Debora Vogel, *Akacje kwitną. Montaże* (Warszawa: Rój, 1936), 134.

of lovers; incomprehensible happiness, and the matter of how a person should live, which never seems to be settled.

And, in fact, nothing was done. Yet it seemed as if at the same time a lot was being done, that is, everything which could be attained in life.

And suddenly people felt responsible for life: a similar thing to what was happening to the leaves, which at the moment had a hard and responsible smell, happened also to people.

And so it began again: things and fates originate in life. They spread and become details of different situations, expectations, and frustrations. They increase with an unexpected sense and roundness.

In this way life is rehabilitated, its sweet shoddiness, which always begins with "a broken heart," and ends with a resolute decision "to live", which in the old-fashioned, trite terminology would be called resignation.

19. Potato Fields

The potatoes smell[159] of small stiff flowers.

The purple and white potato fields have a sweet and a somewhat raw smell, like clay. And the miniature flowers are like stiff *purple*[160] calico, if a little scattered.

---

159 "[B]lossom" in Yiddish.
160 In Yiddish.

And it is good that the purple and white potato fields smell of calico boredom. It's good that events and raw materials[161] swell with tedium.

Around the world the sticky material of boredom is waiting. It is awaiting its fate. Just like fantastical *and yearning*[162] brass and succulent iron, and the usual, literal material of clay, *out of which a man can be molded.*

The sticky and raw material of life awaits its fate: there is still something to do in the world.

You only need to live up life[163] which accumulates everywhere in large heaps *and increases.*[164]

It grows like the crescent of the new moon. It takes in fermented juices from weeds that appear out of nowhere, perhaps out of the blue air? From banal[165] encounters? From squandered days and lost things?

---

161 "[E]vents and raw materials" in Polish is "finished and raw things" in Yiddish.
162 Only in Yiddish.
163 Instead of "life" in Polish, it is "boredom like a singular precious material" in Yiddish.
164 In Yiddish.
165 "Fatal" in Yiddish.

Figure 44. Henryk Streng (Marek Włodarski), *Keep*, 1929–1930.

28

The Building of the Train Station (1931)[166]

1

There is a lot of space in the world. Needless, helpless space.

Oh, space that is flat and slow. Boring like a large board floor, scrubbed with lye, like the circular landscape of a calendar Sunday that features people who have misplaced their fates, even if only for a few hours. *And they go for a stroll.*

Space is dull like people with their squandered lives. Space is heavy, like life without fate.

Space sheds large, hollow tears. And these tears are for no one in particular.

There is too much space in the world. Something has to be done with all the shoddy space of the world.

2

A part of the field where the new train station will be built is covered with purple thistles and yellow buttercups at the moment.

The buttercups and thistles have a smell of sweet calico boredom, of white or flowery calico.

Legs walk in the space full of the calico smell of large red flowers. The legs wear black and yellow shoes; in haste, they push away the soil, the legs brimming with the sweetness of the earth, heavy like happiness.[167]

What are they doing in space? Oh, we need to reduce the needless length of the world by one-third, or even one-half. But the steps drag the round weight of the world a few feet further, they drag the naked matter with its lost cause of life, and with the second and unknown matter of death.

---

166 Excerpts from this collection (1, 2, 6, 7, 11) appeared in Polish as "Budowa stacji kolejowej," *Sygnały* 2, no. 10/11 (1934): 29.
167 In Yiddish "legs, heavy like the earth and happiness."

Let us stand still. Like trees.

Trees know nothing of fear or death.

Trees live as if inside the four, *sweet gray*[168] walls, as if in the reduced space of a street or a room.

Let us build streets and houses. People need streets. People need walls, windows, and balconies.

Let us build stations. Stations with parallel rails embracing the world. Stations divide all the world into distances.

There are no rails yet in the field with the boring yellow buttercups and watery-purple thistles. There are no walls. There are no balconies or windows.

3

Two miles from the construction site the soil lays in heaps. The needless, wild, parasitic soil.[169]

It grows like wanton weeds in large piles which we call mounds. Nobody needs the soil, it belongs nowhere.

And here, where the station is supposed to be, there is only a crooked, scrawny field with yellow buttercups and purple thistles, and there is no dense black soil for the track beds. So you need to move whole squares of inconspicuous bronze and black soil somewhere where they may be needed.

Who said that there is any sense *and a purpose*[170] in this? Why move a thing from one place to another? What happens in the world at large when we move so many things every single day?

But nobody thinks of asking that here. People drag iron pushcarts, filled with bronze and black soil. The people are oxen, they are horses, and camels.

People caress the red-hot iron of pushcarts and the sticky, stretchy soil with the skin on their bodies. With much affection, people take and bring back the soil, which sticks to the body and sky, to the scrawny field with the yellow buttercups. Iron pushcarts with bronze and black soil roll lightly, as if dancing.

And the skin on the bare trapezes of shoulders glitters in a bronze-like fashion, like fragrant tree bark. And the crooked bronze roots of arms and hands tear themselves away from the yellow-clay air and grab the red-hot cradles of iron, as if these were the only and last things in life.

---

168 In Yiddish.
169 In Yiddish it is "decisive" rather than "parasitic."
170 In Yiddish.

Like bark, the sweltering heat is bronze. The heat is about one hundred degrees or higher. And there is nothing in this section of the field with calico flowers—only iron cradles of earth. They are like happiness, the greatest happiness which always turns out to be the greatest misfortune. They are like the fate we await. And like the flat bowls on ancient Egyptian bas reliefs, full of booty for a winner or a god.

Figure 45. Henryk Streng, reprint of illustration from Debora Vogel, *Akacje kwitną. Montaże* (Warszawa: Rój, 1936), 147.

The 50,000 cubes of soil were brought to the construction site of the new station.

Then the large trapeze bodies of the brown and black soil arose. This soil was dragged from a distance of a few feet all the way to this place. And measuring tape calculates the souls of the trapeze bodies of soil, brought by people into an irresponsible section of the field with the sweet calico flowers. And people, even out every unnecessary cubic inch of the earthwork, they polish it like glass and like fragile coral, they polish the brown, sticky, and listless earth.

That section of helpless space covered with yellow buttercups and thistles until now, becomes later a land of hard track beds and fantastical rails. Then it can provide the elasticity for tired legs and hands that have nowhere to go.

Thus ends the chapter about the raw material of the soil and its fate at the time of the building of the train station.

4

The earthworks manager.

He is the earthworks manager. He does not have a name. The name is unimportant here.

He says to hurry. He oversees. He counts the relays.[171]

Come on, people ... come on ... come on. ...

Every ten minutes—a half mile of tracks is installed. Every half hour—a relay. *Sometimes even only twenty minutes per one relay.*

And almost every hour a new stretch of track bed, a new mound.

Quick. ... Quick ... quicker ... come on.

In a light, dance-like manner *of sea foam,* iron pushcarts filled with clay and sticky soil roll like tears of heavy soil. *Oh, to make the thin field yield velvet tracks, luminous from sheer mass, like an event, and the ornaments of identical roads of gray melancholy.*[172] *They roll so lightly like transparent sea foam.*

These are the track beds, *still a wild section of the field* waiting for measurement and tape. And the *fantastical ornaments of the elastic iron* rails long to run their course at a slow space, *for the circular run of two cold parallel lines.* And the walls long for a vertical.

The walls say to hurry up and rush, to suck the marrow out of bones to the point when people blacken, dry up like tree bark, from a worry which could persist until death.

Oh to make the velvet track beds glittering with the verticals and horizontals of walls from the fields, fragrant with calico! And the streets: ornaments with a motive of grayness, ornaments with a motive of sweet melancholy.

Not everyone will understand this; tracks and highways have to be like fate which happens only once in a lifetime. Every wall and corner of every track bed lights up like a colorful adventure in the boring field with the purple thistles.

The track beds have to be smooth like velvet, like a gray day in October. The rails are elastic like longing; the gray walls are hard like tragic decisions.

And so it happens that the skin of hands in anticipation, the skin on the whole body, and the velvety skin of track beds tremble when they touch accidentally.

The first relay ... the second one ... the twenty-third ...

---

171 In Polish: "He oversees. He counts the relays. He says to hurry."
172 This sentence appears only in Yiddish.

One hundred degree heat, eight hours of work, and twenty-three relays. ... Every twenty minutes a relay: a record set! A rare record.

The track beds grow in the field with the purple thistles, the earthworks blossom, the world is filled with glittering track beds and hard inflexible rails, like a hard river and a tragic decision.

Amid the world of the *even*[173] tracks and *glittering* rails, a huge belly swells, it outgrows itself like large, round, and coarse weeds.

A world of verticals and horizontals, and carts with soil rises monumentally around the human body, heavy *and sticky* like yellow clay mixed with water.

5

There is a separate world of raw materials. A world of thick, sticky, pungent materials.

Time is one of the raw materials: it is a pasty, dirty, wanton raw material.

Time is the heavy body of boredom and monotony.

The engineer at the construction site of the station, or any engineer for that matter, processes the raw materials, including the repulsive matter of time. And so the walls, streets, and passages arise.[174]

The days of other people are crushed into the shimmering drops of encounters, into the colorful sand of words. The colorful vases of encounters and fate which arise as if out of nowhere.

The world of cold verticals and horizontals is different. They are constant. They make space steady. They are made from everything, like a block of resignation, which includes everything.

The vertical and the horizontal grow very slowly. The walls rise very slowly, like a sticky leaf of burdock the round grayness of tardiness arises: every brick is measured against the other one, and every row of bricks against the other row, molded with the velvet of patient lime and caressed for a long time.

The bricks are all the same. The bricks are the cubes of red color. All the bricks have the same measurements of 10 x 5 x 2 in.

The walls grow from bricks. The growing walls know only of two longings—upwards, in the direction of the yellow orb of the sun—the longings

---

173 In Yiddish.
174 In Yiddish, "railroad tracks."

of trees and of grass; and downwards—where weights are pulled, along with all the weary things *and our hands, when everything has been lost in life.*

These two longings of the vertical are constant like the sun, darkness, and life.

The slowness of unfinished walls is called boredom. Trees, grasses, and life contain that kind of boredom. It is the same with people which have something to do with the world of slow matters. (This kind of life is represented by the rectangle, chosen out of all the geometrical figures; it repeats the sweetness of the square and of every week, hence its lengthening.)

The engineer carries inside himself the soul of the slow walls. The soul of the eternal vertical.

At the peripheries of this growth there are days without fate, marginal and irresponsible, weightless like hollow bricks.

And everything that happens on these days can be either that or something completely different.

6

There is a separate world of raw materials.

A world of fatty, pungent, and wanton materials.

Raw materials are awaiting their fate.

They are stacked in large heaps all over the world. Like weeds. Sticky, corrosive, wanton, and heavy to lift from their long waiting.

Raw materials want to be numbers and figures. Raw materials wait for measure and contours: it is their predestination and fate.

The body of raw materials is thick and helpless, a piece of large, gray weight which makes your eyes well up with tears, like a large floor scrubbed with lye, and like a life without luck.

But the soul of raw materials is very delicate and fantastical. You simply need to mine for the hidden soul of matter.

There is the sticky clay lost in life.

Concrete is gray, corrosive, and as if made from nothing.

Velvety lime is full of patience.

Brass, experienced and melancholy, is like a person who wishes that which is in life.

And iron is hard like tragic fates.

The hidden formula of these souls can be discovered on all construction sites.

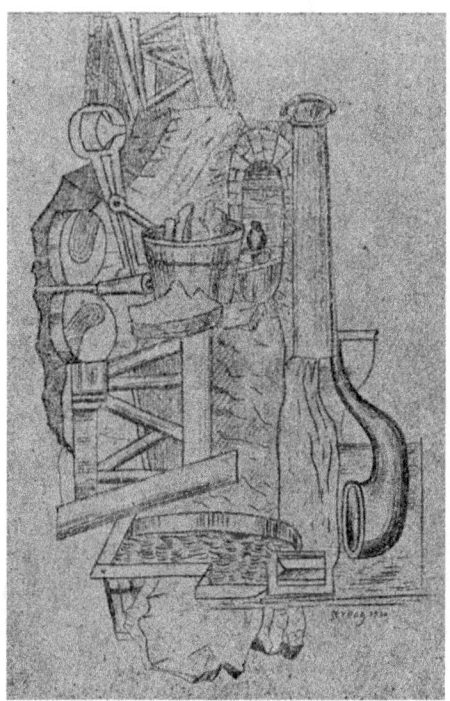

Figure 46. Henryk Streng, reprint of illustration from Debora Vogel, *Akacje kwitną. Montaże* (Warszawa: Rój, 1936), 157.

7

Clay. Clay is heavy and helpless. Like happiness or misfortune. Clay-yellow is the color of lost causes, just as citrus-yellow is the color of cold resignation. We are shaped from clay: our two legs and hands mobilized once, then fall down a hundred and a thousand times in the same place. When one thing is lost in our life—the whole life is squandered.

They burn bricks from the sticky raw material of clay—*the red*,[175] angular cubes measured and numbered: 10 × 5 × 2 in. Their red color is hard and somewhat stiff.[176]

Bricks are transparent *and full of glassy sound,* hard and resolute like busy people: thing-like people whom you might compare to stiff blossoms, red round dahlias.

---

175 In Yiddish.
176 In Yiddish, "blind."

Bricks are absolutely unlike clay: they have a clear and transparent soul of a dough-like, wanton, hopeless body of clay.[177]

8

Concrete. Concrete is mixed from slimy cement and the gray and odd fragment of monotony.

Then comes rubble, a helpless and sad body, *like kasha*.

Water, which kneads the hollow seeds of rubble, sand, and cement, is also colorless and unlike anything else.

Likewise, concrete has to be boring like worn-out happiness. When you see concrete—you start to shed tears.

That goes for its body. But the soul of concrete is usually very delicate and fantastical.

Above the round Earth concrete ceilings hang—one, two, hundreds and thousands of ceilings; streets with the arcades and pavements of concrete run their course. In the streets the white and gray walls are proud trees of concrete. And the city is full of the gray matter, the sight of which hurts like endless flat fields of purple thistles. And like *all of* life.

It is a velvety day in October. The sky is a hue of blue without a name, a color which only appears when everything is lost. And the leaves are brass; and, like brass, they are *elastic with* melancholy. However, the avenue, walls, and pavements are sweet[178] gray *like evenings with dim lanterns*.

The grayness of concrete. The brass of leaves. The nameless blue of the sky.

And the matter of gray, brass, and blue[179] is played out in the oval salon of autumn.

It begins like this: the nameless color of the canvas of the sky—the color of possible things—paves the streets and promises everything as if for the first time.[180]

And when nothing happens,[181] then melancholy falls on people like the large, red, and yellow[182] leaves of squandered things. Brass leaves *with a lasting fragrance* fall from the trees. As if brass inundated the soul.

---

177 "Helpless body" in Polish is "bodies" in Yiddish.
178 Only in Yiddish.
179 Instead of "blue" in Yiddish, it is "sky" in the Polish version.
180 In Polish, "and then everything could still happen."
181 In Polish, "and when nobody comes."
182 Instead of the enumeration of colors "red and yellow" in Yiddish, the Polish version makes do with the word "colorful."

The whole time grayness awaits, leaning against the concrete *of walls and pavements. It lurks in the alley, which is like a vast, sad sea.*

Concrete is boring and pungent like weeds. *Yet grayness needs concrete.* The grayness of October and November[183] cannot live without the concrete *of walls, vaults, and pavements.*

Grayness smells like walking. Rusty leaves smell of life. Then you see, as if for the first time, the flow of the red rectangle of a streetcar, it shimmers like warm crimson. And then there is nothing else in the long streets; there is only that crimson rectangle.

The rustling brass in grayness is deep and taken out of life.[184]

How arrogant and banal is the juicy green of summer trees—a cynical advertisement for old furniture hung in the fiery landscape of gray steel. And that greenery is tiresome like a person without fate. And it turns out that only *melancholy* brass lends itself to be shaped into leaves in the landscape of *gray plants*—walls.

Grayness is important for life. Grayness cannot live without concrete. And it happens that in the *October* city streets, concrete is no longer a boring burden *and a helpless being,* the sight of which hurts like the sight of a field with calico flowers. Here they have discovered the fantastical soul of concrete, the formula of its hidden life—arcades, walls, and pavements.[185]

The formula of its life was also found at the construction site of the train station. It can be found at every construction site.

9

The sad[186] brass of a roof.

The big quiet tiles of glass *in windows.*

Furnace tiles, astonished: the green, yellow, red *squares of* tiles.

And the angular boards of floors and doorframes.[187]

All of this fills with balance the soul of calico fields, which are yet indecisive. Just as the first furniture[188] fills rooms with the still-lingering, empty, wet

---

183   November appears only in Yiddish. It is the second time that Vogel uses both months together. Even though the names she uses are "October and November," one cannot help but think that she must be thinking in terms of the Hebrew month of Heshvan.
184   This sentence in Polish is the following: "The rustling brass in grayness is dense with the matters of life."
185   In Polish, "streets, walls, and arcades."
186   In Yiddish, "melancholy."
187   In Yiddish, "and the angular boards of floors, windows, and doors."
188   In Polish, "equipment."

smell of fresh paint. Just like the first adventure and the burden of fate gives constancy to the circular rooms of time.

When the rooms are already there, they wait for their fate: furniture. They wait for the horizontals of tables and cabinets, and the verticals of chairs and wardrobes.[189]

And a strange plant of horizontal and vertical lines, a geometrical tree of surfaces and contours, walls and furniture—classical and proportional—increasingly grows in density.[190]

Until it completely fills out the place, as if predestined for purple calico flowers with the elastic facture of things—events. And only then will the world become round; *only the world of ready-made, dense things, caressed by measure, is round*. Like the globe—monumental and perfect.

Now it can be embraced with the hard caress of the *glittering* parallel rails:[191] the juicy grayness of a single motion for the many days in life.

The first day. The second. The seventh.

10

And when everything is ready and finished in the calico field with the indecisive purple and butter-colored flowers, there comes a chapter of the glassy melody of life.

Usually it happens in November.[192]

Ready-made things and settled matters[193] ring like glass and melancholy. Everything which has stiff[194] contours and the shape of a rectangle or a cube is gray with sadness; since it is once and for all.

That is why tailored dresses that hang in wardrobes reek of *glass* melancholy, as does the furniture of yearning mahogany or oak which stands against the walls; yearning is achieved in the lives of experienced people.

The motionless walls which reached their prescribed measure; the track beds, caressed by the tape measure; the rails wonderfully parallel, including in all rounded places and arcs; and people's souls for whom this empty place with

---

189   In Yiddish: "They wait for the horizontal of the drawers, and the vertical of the tables."
190   In Yiddish: "Soon we will allow the wonderful growth of surfaces and lines to grow; the geometrical tree of the walls and furniture."
191   Only in Yiddish.
192   Only in Yiddish.
193   In Yiddish, "fates."
194   "[P]ermanent" in Polish.

purple thistles and buttercups was their fate of the last three months—all resonate with melancholy in the completed train station.

From now on nothing more happens in the space with the calico vegetation.[195] The boredom *of life* was processed here—the helpless and monotonous body of materials. The hidden soul of time was discovered here—the tacky body of monotony: hard things, events, and happiness.

And in a week or maybe in a month from now glittering train cars will pass through the new station. They will stop for a short time, carrying people from one place to another. Just like the soil is carried from a place where it is not needed to a place where it is needed. (People are constantly and forever awaiting their fate—just like heavy and fatty materials.)

The train cars are identical. So fantastically identical as only numbers can be. And grayness. And in the end it turns out that monotony is the fate and the predestination for which people wait their whole lives. They grow heavy and full of helplessness from this long wait, similar to dense raw materials.

This short chapter in the history of people's longing for mass and numbers *and monotony* ends here.

11

Praise be to coarse, sticky, dense raw materials. To all of them, scattered around the world like sticky weeds,[196] waiting for their *history and* fate.

Praise be to the unpredictable, irresponsible fields of purple calico vegetation, fields of the large burdock leaves of boredom.

Praise be to the life which is like a large weed-like leaf of boredom and the raw block of *fatty* clay and fatty pungent cement.

There is the origin of things in them, things that shine with smoothness and measure; they smell of fresh firmness, the elasticity of metals, and walking.

The completed train station praises the freed, dough-like raw materials, dissolute like boredom, all the materials used in its construction.

It is November and the construction of the train station comes to an end.

---

195 In Polish, "thin."
196 In Polish, "insipid."

Part Four

From Lviv to New York: Letters (1924–1940)

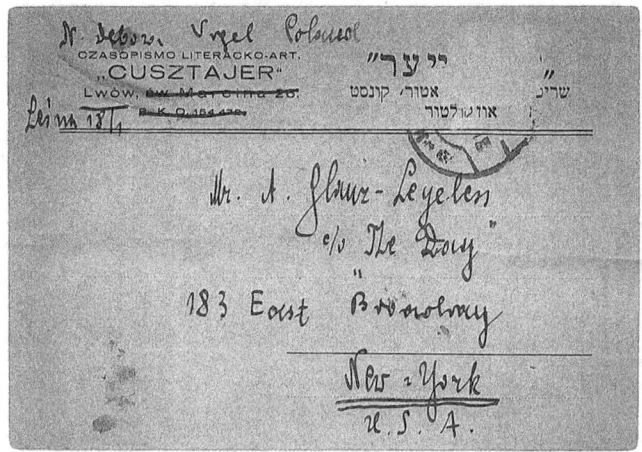
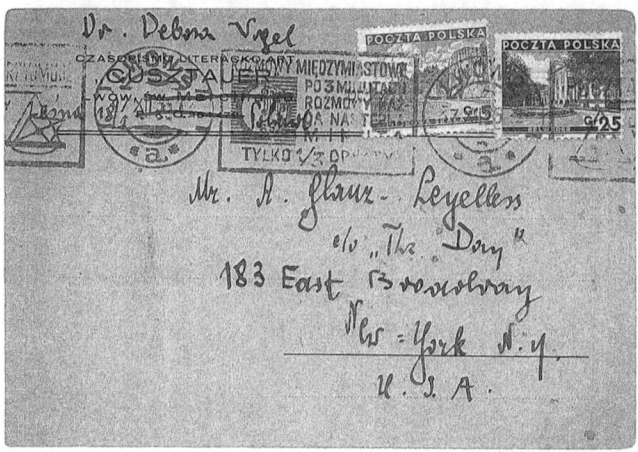

Figure 47. Postcard to Aaron Glantz-Leyeles, January 4, 1937.

Lviv, May 2, 1924
To Marcus Ehrenpreis[1]
[One page, original in German]

Dear Uncle,
Today I am writing to you with a question, or rather a request for a piece of advice.

I would like to publish my poems which I wrote in German, which I cannot do here [in Poland]. I am forced to stay here because of the difficulty with my passport and also because my exam will take place at the earliest only after the holidays (my professor will not provide the decision regarding my work earlier). I would like to find a publishing house in Germany, or in Vienna.

If you are in contact with any publishing house, perhaps it would be possible for you to ask if the publishing house would be at all inclined to publish my poems; then I will send you some of them as samples. Naturally, it would be good for a critic to recommend them which might make the publisher inclined regardless of the value of the text.

I do not know anyone personally; I could send my poems at best to someone whom I know as an authority only by their name. I am certain of the value of my texts which I would not show to you without this awareness.

Please write back, and greetings to all

Dosia

To Marcus Ehrenpreis

[Side notes on a letter from Lea Vogel, original in German]

Lviv, March 14, 1929

My dearest,
I am truly ashamed of not writing to you. You should not think that it is just a phase when I say I cannot bring myself to write. Besides working in the orphanage,[2] and the school,[3] in the newspapers, and a monthly journal, to which I contribute, there are lots of nonprogrammatic events such as thousands of possible

---

1 Marcus Ehrenpreis (1869–1951) was a Hebrew and Swedish writer, a translator, a Zionist, and the chief rabbi of Bulgaria (1900–1914) and Sweden (Stockholm, 1914–1951), as well as Debora Vogel's uncle. He published *Judisk Tidskrift* in Stockholm where Vogel published articles predominantly about various artists. For more on Marcus Ehrenpreis, see Steven Fruitman, *Creating a New Heart: Marcus Ehrenpreis on Jewry and Judaism* (Umea: Universitet Umea, 2000).
2 Debora Vogel's parents were in charge of the orphanage on 8 Zborowska Street in Lviv.
3 From 1929 Debora Vogel taught at Jacob Rotman's Hebrew Seminar in Lviv. She taught psychology and literature, namely Yiddish literature.

and impossible meetings to endure (the plague of meetings), papers, illness (Mom often stays in bed), and relatives who become very upset[4] when I don't visit them for months, etc. I am currently preparing a lecture about Chagall's art. I have also published an essay about Else Lasker-Schüler (in Polish).[5] I will send it to you. I am preparing for a trip to Palestine. Kisses and hugs to all of you. Dosia

PS: Dear Uncle, why haven't you answered the editors of *Morgn*?[6] They have pleaded with me to communicate how urgent this is.

There's another request on my part. I am traveling to Italy and I will be spending a few days in Rome. Mom would like to ask you to send your card to the local rabbi in case I need something.

To Marcus Ehrenpreis
[Four pages, original in German]

April 23, 1929

My dearest,

Today again marks our usual deadline for showing signs of life to each other. This long period of time always passes very quickly because we live in incessant, strenuous, and unregulated work. There is always something else which needs to be done, not a single day off. I am single. Even though I am young, I am quite tired, and Mom is exhausted. We are already thinking in earnest of stopping working here if it is not organized in a better way; we need to find someone to help Mom with the housework.

Mom has been very sick for two weeks. They treat her for blood sugar, but that is not what's wrong with her, there's something else. Today she feels better, and I hope that she is going to be well in a few weeks' time.

I should be going on my tour of Palestine now. Yet I obtained my passport in vain. Mother's sickness does not allow me to go, perhaps I could still do so in May.

Today's *Morgn* included a long report about the Jewish community in Stockholm and your work there, dear Uncle. Perhaps you already know about it. The article was written by someone who stayed or is currently staying in Stockholm (his name is Grasovsky).[7]

---

4   Here Vogel uses the Yiddish word *"broyges"* in German.
5   This essay was never found.
6   *Der nayer morgn* was a Yiddish daily in Lviv.
7   See "Di renesans fun shvedishn yudentum-a ferdinst fun M. Ehrenpreisn," *Der nayer morgn*, no. 749 (April 24, 1929).

What are you writing now, dear Uncle? How is everyone doing? Why don't Miri[8] and Dori[9] write to us?

I wish you happy holidays (I remember all the "preparations," the backstage of these holidays) and kiss you cordially,

Your Dosia

PS: Many greetings to Zosia. I have enclosed a card with the information about the painter. Please purchase the reproductions of his paintings for me as we agreed before. Miri, please show your aunt Zosia the National Museum[10] and the Liljevalchs Exhibition Hall.[11] I need these reproductions for an essay on modern art.

Many greetings and kisses to you and to dearest Zosia.

Mama is doing better.

To Marcus Ehrenpreis:
[Two pages, original in German]

November 6, 1930

My dearest Uncle,

There was a lot of extra work lately, many visits and meetings, so I simply did not have time for letters. You have probably found the letter which we had written to Miri.

What's wrong with the beloved Aunt? Is it sciatica again? My beloved Aunt, I wish you a speedy recovery.

Now that the Hebrew seminar has resumed, I am teaching a few courses there. However, we are still hanging in the air because we have no money. We are experimenting with having classes only this month for now. This is the fate of the only Hebrew institution in Lviv!

Dear Uncle, I am sending you the article about Bruno Schulz[12] and the next volumes of *Tsushtayer*. Please write to me whether the measurements of the reproductions are acceptable for your journal. If they are, I can send you the prints (all 3 or just 2 of them), and it will save you making new ones. However, if the reproductions are too big, then you could also make new prints from these.

---

8   Miri (Miriam Nathanson, nee Ehrenpreis, 1911–2006) was Ehrenpreis's daughter and Debora's cousin.
9   Dori (Theodor Saul Ehrenpreis, 1909–?) was Marcus Ehrenpreis's son and Debora's cousin.
10 The National Museum in Stockholm includes collections of painting and sculpture from 1500 to 1900.
11 Liljevalchs Konsthall is a Stockholm art gallery which hosts three large exhibitions dedicated to art and design every year.
12 This article appeared in *Judisk Tidskrift* in November 1930.

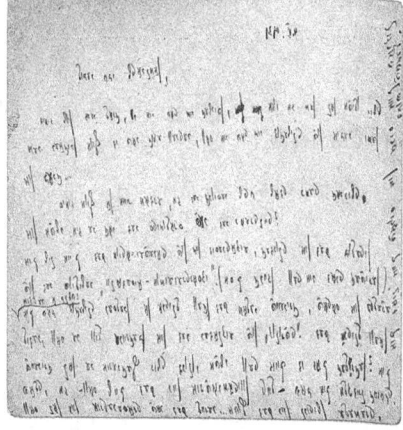

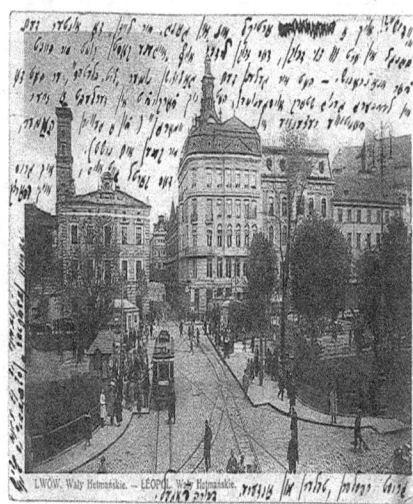

Figure 48. Postcards to M. Starkman, May 4, 1931; June 14, 1933.

How is your health? Are you writing something new?

Cordial kisses to all,

Dosia

Dear Uncle, please proofread the translation of your secretary. I would also like to ask you to return my German manuscript to me.

I and others who are interested won't understand the Swedish text!

Meanwhile, I am sending you my new picture, I look so nice after spending time in Zakopane![13]

To Moshe Starkman[14]
[Postcard with business address on the letterhead]
Tsushtayer shrift far literatur, kunst un kultur
Pismo literacko-artystyczne "Cusztajer"
26 St. Marcin Street[15]
P. K. O. 154.472
[Original in Yiddish]

May 4, 1931

Dear Mr. Starkman,

It has been quite some time since you have last written. I can no longer respond to the couple of good words you sent me over the oceans and mountains. ...

It is indeed strange that, generally speaking, great distances do no harm, perhaps they are even an invitation to proximity?

I am sending you the prospectus of my dissertation, which was printed in the *Bulletin of the Polish Academy of Sciences*[16] (there are a lot of mistakes there). I have a request to make. I sent an essay about the painter Feuerring[17] with

---

13 A resort town in Poland.
14 Moshe Starkman (1906–1975) was born in Galicia and lived in New York. He wrote in Yiddish and Hebrew, was a lexicographer, and published an edited volume *Leksikon fun der nayer Yidisher literature* [Lexicon of the new Yiddish literature] (Nyu-York: Alveltlekhn Yidishn Kultur-Kongres, 1956–1981).
15 The address of the editorial office of *Tsushtayer*. The building which housed the editorial office belonged to the parents of Rachel Auerbakh, one of the editors of the journal. St. Marcin Street currently has the name Zhovkivska Street in Lviv.
16 See "Znaczenie poznawcze sztuki u Hegla i jego modyfikacje u J. Kremera," *Polska Akademia Umiejętności. Sprawozdania z czynności i posiedzeń* 32 (1927): 10–11. The abstract of the doctoral dissertation in German is "Der Erkenntniswert der Kunst bei Hegel und dessen Modifikationen von polnischen Denker Joseph Kremer," *Biulletin International de l'Acadéomie Polonaise des Sciences et des Lettres*, nos. 1–3 (1927): 41.
17 Compare Vogel's short text on Feuerring, "Maks Feyering," *Tsushtayer*, no. 2 (1930): 57–58.

pictures of some of his works which he would like to submit to the editors of *Tsukunft*[18] to Ressler.[19]

He cannot publish the essay on Feuerring anywhere, perhaps you would be more successful at that? I believe that in respect to the purely informational side of things, I have written everything that is of interest … only there is no critical element. Thank you in advance.

Yours cordially,
Debora Vogel

To Moshe Starkman
[Postcard (Hutsul Types, an Old Hutsul Woman); Original in Yiddish]

Mr. M. Starkman
c/o Yiddish Culture Society
130 East 17 Str.
New York, NY, USA

Kishau, July 9, 1931

Dear Mr. Starkman,[20]
Your letter was forwarded to me in Kishau, where I am "getting some fresh air." Before I write a proper letter to you, I am sending you a card with many greetings once again.

These greetings from a remote Jewish shtetl in the mountains are worth something: they bring with them the air of scorching yellow heat, of sweet sad evenings when people sit on benches in their houses, and of hot nights with humid winds and the smell of withered yellow grasses. Unsolicited, I am sending you my longings, and the longings of the women sitting behind cool doors and embroidering these yearnings into artful "follettes"[21] for days on end. (You surely know what a "follette" is?)

PS: I sent the two poems for *Oyfkum*[22] to your address. Ressler has some other poems you could publish somewhere if you wish to take it upon yourself.

Many cordial greetings,
Debora Vogel

---

18 *Di Tsukunft*, the oldest Yiddish literary journal in New York, was first published in 1892.
19 Binyomin Ressler (1901–1983) was a Yiddish writer, dramatist, and actor, who contributed to many Yiddish publications, such as *Der Morgn*, *Literarishe bleter*, and *Di Tsukunft*. From 1928 he lived in New York and worked for the press there.
20 In this letter and in all the other letters, Vogel addresses Moshe Starkman as "comrade Starkman."
21 A follette is a large scarf, triangular in shape, and was fashionable in the eighteenth century.
22 *Oyfkum* was published from 1926 until 1938 in New York.

To Moshe Starkman
[Business letterhead, one page in Yiddish]
Tsushtayer shrift far literatur, kunst un kultur
Pismo literacko-artystyczne "Cusztajer"

September 15, 1931

Dear Mr. Starkman,

I have been waiting for your promised letter. We are constantly talking in superlatives about you, especially regarding your ambassadorship and your person. We think of you "lovingly" here. The stagnation, however, has become somewhat greater, and the overall sickness affects our production as well. We sit, stand, or stroll the streets of the city of Lviv, and wait, wait for ... dollars. And this reminds me of Ilya Ehrenburg's[23] remark about the "gulden" (in *The Life of Cars*)—the wonderful, fantastic, poetic sound of this word ... this is the sound which dollars have for us. Without them, there is no joy in the world—more specifically on 26 Marcin Street, in the editorial office of *Tsushtayer*.

To state it even more clearly, we write poems and essays, we work like *lamed-vovniks*,[24] and one beautiful day—whether a winter day or a blue summer day—we will discover ourselves even if nobody from the wider world comes to discover us.

Please pay attention to what I say, since "there is a grain of truth in every joke," as an old saying has it.

To finish my laments for today, I would like to ask you something. I sent three of my poems to the editorial office of *Tsukunft* two months ago ...

Please write back. Wishing you all the best,
Debora Vogel

To Moshe Starkman
[Two pages, original in Yiddish]

Lviv, November 18, 1931

Dear Mr. Starkman,

Your last letter arrived a while ago. (It arrived exactly in time for my marriage on October 11,[25] and your "*mazl tov*" greetings were very appropriate for the occasion. I have not changed my mind about the abovementioned marriage, as you may see.)

---

23 Ilja Ehrenburg, *Das Leben der Autos* (Berlin: Malik Verlag A. G., 1930), 27.
24 According to the Talmudic legend, the thirty-six righteous ones (the *lamed-vav tsadikim*) live in the world and support its existence.
25 The wedding ceremony of Debora Vogel and engineer Shalom Barenblüth (1896–1942) took place on October 11, 1931 in the Reform Synagogue Tempel at 14 Old Markek Street in Lviv. The synagogue was destroyed by the Nazis in 1942.

In the meantime, I have received a letter from Mr. Ressler. Besides other information, it is very clear from this letter that the evening dedicated to *Tsushtayer* was not quite successful. Please do not be saddened; you have done everything in your power, and with a little bit of money here and there, I am certain we will be able to launch the publication after all. (By the way, Ressler writes that *Tsushtayer* is the best Yiddish journal right now. What do you say to such a compliment?)

Thank you for the information from the "battlefield" pertaining my poems. I hope that when one poem is published black on white, you will let me know.

What happened to your *Oyfkum*? You promised to send us each volume, and I have already thanked you and others in advance.

I have also written some prose recently and … plan to publish it in the new volume of *Tsushtayer*. We shall see how it goes.

I am planning to travel to Paris at the end of November. I long for colors and painting, and in a month's time, I will be traveling to the capital of colors.

We are also planning to travel to America in 1933 if it's true that the trip is as inexpensive as they say. Are you planning to come to Europe? How grand! Jews need no cities; we use continents like cities, as is the case with Greding or Kopychinec.[26] The entire world, what do you say? A few days ago, we received a quarterly journal from Africa. Well, enough of the small talk for now.

Best greetings to you and all the comrades,
Debora Vogel

To Moshe Starkman
[Two pages, original in Yiddish]

Lviv, January 10, 1932

Dear Mr. Starkman,

I obviously owe you a letter. As I am taking care of some other correspondence, I am reminded of writing to you.

I returned from Paris a few days ago. I stayed there for five weeks absorbing the painting and the city colors, as well as the wonderful pace of life. Paris is indeed a symbol of always-triumphant life; it allows for no stagnation, no "shrinking to one point" (I cite myself here). For the second time—after my travels to Berlin and Stockholm[27]—I felt how wonderful a big city can be and

---

26 Kopychinec was a Hasidic court in Galicia.
27 Vogel lived in Berlin from mid-October 1926 until the beginning of January 1927; afterwards, she left for Stockholm to visit her uncle.

how it draws me to itself and excites me. I have already decided that I want to test New York in this respect. In a year or two, you will probably meet me on the streets of New York ... if I'm able to save some money for the trip. Walkowitz,[28] a painter I met, has also encouraged me to travel to New York. He is such a thoughtful person, a profoundly talented painter. I would like to write something about him and his art.

Well, what else is there to say? I met many people, including some French writers and painters. I was at Chagall's and gave him *Tsushtayer* (he was very much surprised that Jews already engage in art criticism). I also had a poetry reading, I read from my published collection as well as some new poems. The evening was "hugely successful." An art critic, Chil Aronson,[29] introduced me, you must know him from *Tsukunft* where he wrote about Soutine[30] and others. His insights into my work were so profound and captured the essence of my poetry so well, about which he spoke so enthusiastically that I was truly touched. ... He will also be writing an introduction to the second collection of my poetry to be published by *Triangl* in Paris (the publisher of Einhorn's *Violet*).[31] At present, I have no money for publication, if only the costs were not so high. I do not feel good about borrowing fifteen dollars from *Tsushtayer*—I "deposited" the money there myself which came from subscriptions. Should I do it? By the way, all the French publishing houses print this way: they do not publish more than 250 copies, 200 of which are always pre-ordered. Is there a similar practice in America? I am not sure if it is like that here. The poor hide their poverty from the neighbors. ... What do you think? Can you print something in your publishing houses, for instance, for 50 cents per collection, even a luxury edition? (15 francs total.)

Everyone likes our *Tsushtayer*. Even the French writers. I have advertised the journal, and I think that the fourth volume will "sell" in Paris. And yet, will we reach the sacred number four?!

Oh, I must have written too much. Today I am as chatty as ever. Please send my cordial greetings to Ressler and to other friends.

Cordial greetings,
Debora Vogel

---

28 Abraham Walkowitz (1878–1965) was an early American Modernist painter born in Siberia. He created more than 1,000 graphic works of the dancer Isadora Duncan.
29 Chil Aaron Aronson (1898–1966) was an art critic and head of Galerie Bonaparte in Paris.
30 Chaim Soutine (1893–1943) was a Belarussian painter, affiliated with the Paris artists' colony La Ruche.
31 David Einhorn, *Violet. Lider 1925–1930* (Paris: Triangl: 1930).

To Moshe Starkman
[Postcard (Lviv, Hetmanski Valy)
Original in Yiddish]

Mr. M. Starkman	Dr. D. Vogel
Yiddish Culture Society	Lviv,
130 East 17th street	18 Leśna street
New York, NY, USA	

July 7, 1932

Dear Mr. Starkman,

I owe you a letter. First, I have some news; second, I want to thank you for the volume of *Refleksn*,[32] even though I don't fully agree with the tone which dominates in the journal. I believe that we need to draw our own conclusions from the sad fact which you also address: there is neither the space for polemic nor are there partners for it. One has to be content with positive achievements, since polemics might not always be fruitful. Thank you for sending me the third volume of *Yidish* which features my poem. I am currently rewriting my first prose text which is a "reportage" of sorts. I wrote it a year ago and would like to submit it to *Yidish*!

Another essay is on its way to you. We don't have enough publication venues here. "Self-publishing" poetry seems to me anachronistic today. Have you read the Galicia issue of *Literarishe bleter*? It had a strong resonance here in Lviv—it sold out and got a positive assessment in *Morgn* (from Hamer, you probably don't know him).

There is no more space on the postcard, I am sending you cordial greetings. Please greet Ressler, Teller,[33] and others,

Debora Vogel

Please send along future issues of *Refleksn* when they are published.

---

32 *Refleksn* was a journal which was published in 1932 in New York; one of its editors was Moshe Starkman.
33 Y. L. Teller (1912–1972) was a poet and journalist who lived in the US from 1921. He wrote in Yiddish and English. His minimalist style of writing can be compared to that of Vogel.

To Aaron Glantz-Leyeles[34]
[Two pages, original in Yiddish]

Lviv, February 27, 1933

Dear Mr. Glantz-Leyeles!
I know that there are more important problems in the world today than publishing or not publishing the things which were written. Nevertheless, it is difficult to keep silent constantly, especially when you sense your own relevance, having managed to capture the essential contemporary dialectic of life within the dialectic of your artwork.

Three months ago, I sent the editorial staff of *Yidish* a fictional reportage under the title "The Building of the Train Station." Did you have a chance to read it? I would be very much interested in your feedback, and I would also be very happy when you publish it (the piece is already dated, it is almost two years old—high time that it not be "forgotten"). My work entitled the "Mannequins: A Chronicle" is somewhat more recent—it is a year old. Here I attempt to reproduce all the markers of the distant possibilities and forms of movement in the reportage manner stylized as chronicle, and I believe that my attempt was successful. My new poems also move in the direction of reportage and objectivity. And a specific genre, which I call "shoddy ballad," is born out of this meeting, out of the clash between straightforwardness and pathos. I am sending you some of these ballads for publication in *Yidish*.

If I had money I would publish—with no regard to my overall circumstances—a collection of prose and poetry. But I have no money.

You may interpret this letter simply as a few words written to someone whom I trust. With many friendly greetings,
Debora Vogel

To Moshe Starkman
[Three pages, original in Yiddish]

April 18, 1933

Dear Mr. Starkman,
This letter took me so long because I was waiting for a photo, not just some picture, but a portrait[35] which Witkiewicz, a painter and writer who also happens to be my

---

34 Aaron Glantz-Leyeles (1889–1966) was a poet, essayist, and theoretician of literature who together with Y. Glatshteyn and Borukh Minkoff founded the literary journal *In zikh* and the Introspectivist movement in Modern Yiddish poetry.
35 The best-known portrait of Vogel, painted by Stanisław Ignacy Witkiewicz, pseudonym Witkacy (1885–1939) who was a Polish artist, photographer, writer, and philosopher.

friend, painted of me four years ago. This picture of the original might be of some interest. It is a well-deserved thank-you for your support.

What a lovely gift is the review by Mr. Greenspan, and his deeply original method of approaching the poems. To make a table out of a stool, and then criticize the said table that it is not at all a table, and a bad table at that.

And the task to name banal and real things with the existing hard and shiny words which I believe to be universal for all modern poetry was usurped only for the domain of "proletarian art"!

Meanwhile the definition of "proletarian art" is not so simple, even though so-called proletarian poets feel so sure of themselves in this area and have reduced their program for life to a simplicity which borders on emptiness.

Let me turn to another matter: my trip to New York. You should know that I am serious about it. I would simply like to ask you if you also meant it in earnest when you offered to reimburse me all the costs. You should also know that I have no money. And that is the whole problem. Without a doubt, we should use the opportunity which is now presented to us at the Chicago Exposition.[36] The costs involved are $200 for the round trip and a one-week stay in America. It is very cheap but at the same time a lot when one … does not have the money. Yet I am taking this project seriously regardless! And oh, how the wonderful city of New York draws me to itself! And the prospect of travel sounds very exciting in general!

Here in Lviv we had a poetry reading which we advertised with posters in advance. … The evening was a great success, and people could see that poetry is always necessary, even when some demagogues would like to prove that now there is no place for poetry anymore.

I translated some poems by the Franco-Jewish poet André Spire[37] into Yiddish. Can you suggest where to publish them?

Best wishes from my husband and me,
Debora Vogel

---

36 Vogel means the World Exhibition in Chicago which lasted from May–November 1933 and from June–October 1924.

37 André Spire (1868–1966) was the leader of the Jewish revival movement in twentieth-century French literature, a theorist of poetic language, a literary innovator, and a committed Zionist. Compare Spire's views with those of Marcus Ehrenpreis, Vogel's uncle, who believed in the synthesis of Jewish and Swedish culture. Vogel translated Spire's poems from French into Yiddish.

To Ezekiel Brownstone[38]
[Postcard with business address, original in Yiddish]
Tsushtayer shrift far literatur, kunst un kultur
Pismo literacko-artystyczne "Cusztajer"
Lviv, 26 St. Marcin Street
PO Box 154.472.

Lviv, June 12, 1933

Dear Mr. Brownstone,

I am sending my poetry collection to you. Soon I will send you my second prose and poetry collection to be published shortly. If only money wasn't so scarce! I did not get a single penny from the sales of the first collection. It was still Kletskin[39] who was selling it. I only received an insignificant amount of 25 Złoty (around $3)!! This is what we call our "book market"! It is the same with the field of criticism here. Thus, your work in the *Lid*[40] is excellent and much needed. I would like to write a review for the *Nayer Morgn* in Lviv about the two chapbooks we have received from you and later send the review to you.

It would be so great if each chapbook included a page or two of translations from the Yiddish poetry into all foreign languages (French, German, English), or they could even be alternated. What we lack is ... advertisement: no, not the noisy self-promotion, but other literatures getting to know us, promotion which is also undertaken by the better-known and established literatures. I think one can find translators and recruit them for this effort (I myself can translate from German), and that's it. If a new journal, a continuation of *Tsushtayer*, is published in Lviv, I would like to try to include a translation supplement there as well. Let me know what you think about the idea!

Meanwhile I am sending you two ballads and ask you to publish them at the same time, perhaps even in the next volume, under the joint title "From the Series *Shoddy Ballads*."[41]

By the way, is it possible for you to sell a few copies of my book in a bookstore (for fifty cents)?

Please write.

Greetings from Debora Vogel

---

38 Ezekiel Brownstone (1897–1968) was a Yiddish poet and the publisher of many journals; he lived in Los Angeles.
39 Boris Kletskin (1875–1934) was the founder of the very prestigious Kletskin publishing house in Vilna.
40 One of the journals which was dedicated to poetry and poetics which Brownstone edited in Los Angeles.
41 See "Balade fun dem sen-taykh" and "Balade fun pariser pletser (fun dem tsikl *Shundbaladn*)," *Lid* (May 2, 1934): 15.

To Moshe Starkman
Tsushtayer shrift far literatur, kunst un kultur
Pismo literacko-artystyczne "Cusztajer"
Lviv, 26 St. Marcin Street; c/o Dr. Debora Vogel
PO Box 154.472, apt. 1 bld. 18 Leśna
[Original in Yiddish]

Mr. M. Starkman
c/o Yiddish Culture Society
130 East 17 Str.
New York, NY, USA

June 14, 1933

Dear Moshe Starkman,
What's wrong? Even when we don't have pronounced business interests, and the letter does not need to be answered, I am still wondering why you don't write back. Especially after I sent you my picture, a photo of my portrait where I look like a young lady from Tahiti.[42] And I am anxiously waiting to hear what you think! Perhaps you did not receive my letter? Without a doubt, one cannot get letters which were not actually written, but I did write the letter. I have stopped thinking about the trip to America, since you have not answered my query if I can really count on the pay from a talk or a literary reading? As you probably know, I am talking to Teller and Weinstein[43] about a journal. I have some other news. Translations of twelve authors who represent "the newest trends in Yiddish poetry" were published in the last volume of *Journal des Poètes* in Brussels. Among them was my poem "Primitive Life."
    With best wishes,
    Debora Vogel
    Do you know the painter Walkowitz? Is he in New York?

---

42 This is wordplay—an allusion to the motif of women in Paul Gaugin's first Tahitian period (1891–1893).
43 Berish Vaynshteyn (1905–1967) was a Yiddish poet who published his first Expressionist poetry collection *Brukhshtiker* [Trash] in 1936. It featured unconventional syntax and Galician dialect.

To Marcus Ehrenpreis
[Two pages, postcard, original in German]
My dearest Uncle,
Attached is the essay about Lviv Jewry[44] with engravings by Ms. Kratochwila-Widymska. I have indicated the places in the text where it would be best to place the illustrations. The reproductions shouldn't be too small. It would be best if the measurements were exactly like those I am sending to you because they are already miniature.

Please return these pictures and the manuscript to me when you don't need them anymore.

I also ask for three copies of the published article for the artist and for myself.

The title of each engraving and their order in the text are marked on the other side of the photos.

Congratulations on the award and warmest hugs to all of you,
Dosia
September 29, 1935

To Aaron Glantz-Leyeles
[Two pages, original in Yiddish]

October 18, 1935

Dear A. Leyeles,
I could not answer your letter right away because I am not entirely "well." Perhaps my letter today will not be successful for the same reason.

I must admit that each of your letters brings warmth to me in this cold environment where I am forced to live. Even although I am a person who can live alone and had to get used to that.

How should I explain this to you? I don't like sentimental talk, but with your question you provoke me to disclose more details about my life. I have gotten involved with Yiddish literature, but I did not grow up with it. (I wrote in German and Polish before, yet I did not publish much. These poems were very experimental, and I felt that their form is transitory and short-lived.) Yet it could not have been the root cause of my otherness. There was another reason: being in closer contact with Yiddish writers here in Poland, for instance, in Lviv and Warsaw, does not appeal to me, with a few exceptions, of course. These are horrible

---

44 "Judekvarteret i Lemberg" appeared in *Judisk Tidskrift* in September 1935. The same essay appeared in Polish "Lwowska Juderia. (Ekspozycja do monografii żydowskiego Lwowa)," *Almanach i Leksykon żydowstwa Polskiego* [Lviv] 1 (1937): 89–98; the essay included ten illustrations by Józefa Kratochwila-Widymska.

people, trust me; it seems as if they have lived for more than a hundred years, however they don't fully live: they are *"luftmentshn"* in the fullest sense of the word, they do not belong anywhere, nor do they continue anything, not even their own accidental successes, finally, they don't draw any conclusions from life; and how should they if they don't live at all? They don't have an occupation, they don't belong to any social class, or have strong convictions in life from which they would either like to be free or persist in them. They are too arrogant for that, and they don't recognize any authority but themselves. Moreover, they are simply uncultured, ignoramuses who don't read anything and know absolutely nothing about what happens in the literary world. The presence of culture and personal cultivation evoke in them suspicion, displeasure, and othering.

It doesn't mean that I don't have a few supporters among writers or a circle of readers. However, as a rule, I feel a distance between myself and these other writers. However, the best part is that they can't stand each other either. If you meet someone here who says a kind word about someone else, that is the exception. This is the milieu in which I live.

Moreover, I cannot publish anywhere, I am too often forced to approach Polish journals with my art criticism (essays on the visual arts). There I am a welcome and popular contributor, and they also pay me. You often ask about my relationship to *Literarishe bleter*. I ask myself how it is possible in the literary world that such an ignoramus and a fool like Nachman Maysel is the editor of such an important journal like *Literarishe bleter*. I don't know if you know him personally, and if you know that he reads only the first page of any book he gets, he is simply an illiterate person. I will spare you the details of my only conversation with him which ended unpleasantly. But this is not the reason behind the boycott of my work by *Literarishe bleter*. The boycott has been going on for quite some time, and it will remain so on my part. (I know very well that they, the hypocrites, won't publish any reviews of my books especially when the review is positive.)

By the way, I have searched for your book this fall and could not find it anywhere. To whom did you send it? Naturally, *Literarishe bleter* did not give me the book. I put some pressure on them, but the result of this pressure will be surely negative. I would really like to read the text from which I know only a few fragments. (By the way, perhaps you know that the Jewish column in the Polish journal *Sygnały*[45] was relaunched. For its first volume, I have prepared a translation of your poem "In the Subway.")[46]

---

45 *Sygnały* (1933–1939) was an independent Lviv journal of the leftist intelligentsia. A large part of its material consisted of columns about Ukrainian and Jewish artists and cultural events.

46 See Debora Vogel's translation of the poem by A. Leyeles, "W metro" (from the cycle "New York," 1926), *Nasza Opinja* 5, no. 81 (1937): 6.

Let us talk about other topics because I already fear that you will consider me a bitter person who only sees the negative sides of life. I assure you that, objectively speaking, I am in love with life and that life, art, and poetry are valuable to me. I was forced to utter these few bitter words in my letter today because I was made to speak them, I am not guilty of them.

You are inquiring about my new poems. I am not writing any new poetry now, only lyrical prose similar to *Acacias*. I am thinking about works like *The Building of the Train Station*. I would like to send you some fragments of my new montage pieces, yet I believe it's unnecessary as long as the *Acacias* are unknown and unread. Readers should get accustomed to the form first which is offered to them in *Acacias*. Later I will demonstrate the form's next stage. For me, form always develops from other forms, and it is a privilege for me to gradually grasp the wonderful dialectic of forms and life in their development. I wanted to send you the essay about "Reportage and Montage" but it is not ready yet. I would also like to know if you are interested in this essay at all. I don't want to write it and send it to you regardless of whether there is interest. This essay is something which occupies me at present, my current topic. I don't have any inclination to send essays into the unknown since I have already written a couple that I could not publish anywhere.

I need to mention two more points so that my letter will be more or less an answer to your questions about me and my life. But it is enough for today. Obviously, I would be pleased if you published a review of the *Acacias* to help to sell a few copies. I did not get a single penny for all three books. Do you believe me?

With warmest wishes,
Your Debora Vogel

To Marcus Ehrenpreis
Rev. Prof. Dr. M. Ehrenpreis   Vogel
Stockholm   Lviv
6 Grevmagnigatan   18 Leśna
Sweden   Poland

December 7, 1935

Dearest Uncle,

Thank you for the manuscript and for the money. I would have liked to have received more money but even this honorarium I take gladly. I also wanted to use the occasion to ask you, dear Uncle, if you regularly send the *Judisk Tidskrift* to YIVO Institute in Vilnius, Basachkova Str. They have wonderful bio- and bibliographic capacities, and they enter anything ever written by Jews into their database, making the work "last." They are also planning to establish an art museum there.

Mirchen wrote a nice letter, she talks about her boy as "horribly hateful." Congratulations on Dori's promotion which apparently has already happened. Best, Dosia and Shalom

To Melekh Ravitch
[Postcard, original in Yiddish]

Mr. M. Ravitch
c/o Mr. J. Sher
2 Sydney Rd.
Brunswick
Melbourne
Australia

Dr. Debora Vogel
Lviv, 18 Leśna
Poland

December 11, 1935

Dear Melekh Ravitch,

How can I write something to you when you only receive the letter a month later? I cannot talk about what's current, here one can only talk about the eternal. ...

Do you have a similar approach to writing to a foreigner, even an Australian? If not, I don't understand your request for the two books which I am only sending to you today. They will arrive only in a month. I take it from your letter that you are already somewhat "weary" from your travels around the world and would like to be a tree which has its grown roots once again. It seems that a person should not hang in the air for too long. Still, a person is hungry from time to time. Occasionally, I am overcome by a hunger for distance and space, but I should not think about that right now since I don't have any money for travel. And if I want to publish a book every so often, I need to limit myself and be very modest in my human wishes and longings. I am writing a new book in the genre similar to *Flower Shops* and yet different. I am curious about your thoughts on my books, their ridiculously bad quality of print shouldn't deter you from reading them. Alquit has discussed *Acacias* in *In zikh*. I have good friends among the Introspectivists.

In Lviv, we are preparing for the writers' congress, and I have a lot of work in relation to it. Have you already received the *Small Anthology of Galician Writing* by Neugroschel?[47]

Write a little something about the world where you live.

With warmest greetings,

Debora Vogel

---

47 Mendel Neugroschel (1903–1965) was a poet, publisher, and editor of anthologies. He edited *Kleyne antologye fun der yidisher lirik in Galitsye 1897–1935* [Small anthology of Yiddish poetry in Galicia 1897–1935] (Vienna: A. B. Tserąta, 1936).

To Aaron Glantz-Leyeles
Tsushtayer shrift far literatur, kunst un kultur
Pismo literacko-artystyczne "Cusztajer"
[Two pages, original in Yiddish]

Lviv, March 12, 1936

Dear A. Leyeles,
I have finally completed the article I promised, perhaps it is over the word limit. There was continuously a thousand external distractions and internal hindrances, and now is the best time to control the unpredictable events which make our life ever more difficult.

It is good that there is occasionally some certainty that there are people whose names you know, as well as the anonymous and unknown ones who somehow take part in your life, and it is beneficial to think about these people not to reject your very own most difficult thoughts and knowledge while writing.

Back to the essay: it is somewhat long. However, it is organically subdivided into two parts: the general theoretical part, and the practical subjective one which aims to clear any misunderstandings regarding *Acacias*. You could divide it between two issues if you consider it to be too long.

(I have also written another article "Stasis, Dynamism, and Topicality in Art." I think that if you really want the essay, you can wait a little longer. Perhaps you can print it somewhere else and perhaps … I can also get some money for it? The money issue is a long story.)

I am advertising *In zikh* here and I want to send a note about it to *Morgn*. I haven't been able to find any subscribers until now because of assimilation on the one hand, and on the other because of our own local limitation that few reckon with *Morgn*. When a woman asks who a great Yiddish poet today is, a person answers (?!), Manger, adding "there are two more greats, Leyvik,[48] and M[ani] Leyb …" (judging from the portraits on the latest cover of *Oyfgang*).[49]

I am happy about the publication of these couple of new fragments. I am curious if you would like to publish all of them. That would be great because only together do they reflect the totality which consists of two elements, as in the sample I sent you.

PS: Could I ask you to send me the two copies of *In zikh* with my essay?

I am also sending separately a short answer to Mr. Alquit's discussion of my work in issue 20 of *In zikh*. I ask you to publish it since there is no direct answer

---

48   Halper Leyvik (Levi Halpern) (1888–1962) was a Yiddish poet and dramatist. A Bund activist, he fled Siberia for New York, where he became one of the poets of Di Yunge.
49   Mani Leyb (1883–1953) was a Yiddish poet and member of Di Yunge.

in the essay. What else should I tell you? I really enjoyed your latest essay in issue 20; by the way I have already received issue 21. I am in solidarity with *In zikh's* stance on Communism and its relation to the Jewish question. All of you seem to have a general stance towards it, even though it is expressed in various nuances. I might translate a few excerpts for the "Jewish Column" in *Sygnały* just as I am preparing a few fragments from Leyvik's essay[50] for the next issue. I must be very careful here for the issue not to be confiscated.[51] Besides the fragments, two of your poems,[52] and two by Anna Margolin[53] were published in my translation. I hope the editors will not play this trick on me when they make alterations as happened in the last column (you have received it, yes?).

Is there anything else I need to tell you? Oh, one more thing. I recently received a letter from M. Ravitch from faraway Melbourne, and there was this "point" there. Ravitch writes: "'Go,'" everyone should leave Poland especially, take all the nails from their old homes and all the tombstones with them!"

At present, he is in love with travel, and he stirs my deep longing for travel by reminding me of it. No, a person does not need to be traveling all the time. A tragic and real life is only possible when one is bound to a place and grows into the mood of the cities and the streets, their dawns and autumns. Only then does stability yield the fruitful and difficult monotony which gives birth to hard and shiny "life." However, from time to time, a person longs for travel, especially to big cities from cities where there reigns the sweet smell of potato blossoms. I am in love with big cities. However, how does one travel without money?

Warm greetings to you and to everyone,

Your Debora Vogel

Would you agree if I published some fragments from the essay in another journal, *Inzl*, if the journal still exists? I will not send the article to them without your consent because it is very important for me to see the whole thing published in your journal.

---

50   Vogel translated Leyvik's essay about Yiddish literature. See H. Lejwik, "Uwagi o współczesnej literaturze," *Sygnały*, no. 16 (1936): 9. The abridged translation of Leyvik's talk "Literatur in klem," which he read on October 20, 1935, was published in *In zikh*, no. 20 (1936): 48–59.

51   In Poland, de jure there was freedom of speech, but de facto Sanacja (Yu. Pilsudski's government [1926–1939]) imposed censorship. Leftist publications were a special target. *Sygnały* suffered from both censorship and attacks by Polish nationalists.

52   The Polish phrase *z cyklu* means "from the collection" (poetry collection). See A. Glantz-Lejeles, "Most Manhattan" [*New York*, 1926], "Listopad" [*Jesień*, 1926], *Nasza Opinja* 5, no. 77 (1937): 7.

53   Anna Margolin, "W kawiarni," "Dziewczęta w parku," and "Brodway o zmierzchu (z cyklu Słońce asphalt drogi)," *Nasza Opinia*, no. 75 (1937): 10; Anna Margolin, "Piąta Avenue o zmierzchu" and "Portret," *Kontratak* 2, no. 14 (1937): 4.

To Melekh Ravitch
Tsushtayer shrift far literatur, kunst un kultur
Pismo literacko-artystyczne "Cusztajer"
[Two pages, original in Yiddish]

March 20, 1936

Dear Melekh Ravitch,

Thanks for your letter from a distant land. You talk about a wonderful topic: travel. I must say, longing for travel overcomes me every once in a while, yet it is quickly soothed due to the lack of means. But then, the monotony of a place is that which is fruitful in life. In monotony there originates the colorfulness and the shiny outlines of events which changing landscapes of shimmering color cannot provide.

I am pleased that you have decided to "figure me out." You know that I have never wondered or complained why somebody does "not understand" me. I know there are worlds that at first appear foreign to us on the surface. We reject books which represent such worlds to us only to discover the beauty of these worlds later. I had this experience with Joyce's famous *Ulysses*, and also with the prose of the Surrealist Tzara, and only the second reading showed me what they were doing, teaching me to read and understand their work.

And I think that this can also be the fate of my poetry and prose. Perhaps the stillness and solitariness of Australia—an invented image?—is quite appropriate for reading my work. Norwid once said that everything should be read in a setting like the one where it was written.

Perhaps Australian tranquility is similar to the melancholy rhythm of Galicia, to the monotony of my imagined landscape?

And one more thing is important when you approach my poetry—trust that these are no artworks, no surface "experiments," but extracts from life and experiences for which I paid a high price, and which lead only to this form, not to another. Such a serious attitude is the main prerequisite for "deciphering" me. And I hope that it is your attitude.

I receive *In zikh* on a regular basis, so upon reading your poem which I really liked, I decided to translate it for the Jewish column in *Sygnały* which appears every two months. (The second column of which I am the editor will appear on April 1 with my translations of Leyeles, Anna Margolin, and a shortened essay by Leyvik "Literature in Crisis," which I know from *In zikh*.) I would like to ask you to send me your books *Prehistoric Landscapes*[54] and *Naked Poems*.[55] I would

---

54 See Melekh Ravitsh, *Prehistorishe landshaftn* (Varshe: Kultur-lige, 1924).
55 See Melekh Ravitsh, *Nakete lider* (Vin: Kval farlag, 1921).

like to read them again and have them for reference in general, since it is difficult to obtain these books in Lviv.

(In the April issue of *In zikh*, a few fragments from my new prose work were published, and in the later issue—a larger essay "Montage as a Literary Genre," where I analyze this genre and interpret it based on examples of my montage pieces. If you are interested in the topic, please read the essay and let me know what you think!)

How long are you planning on staying in exotic Melbourne? I ask myself often if I would thrive in such a strange land. You are right, a person should flee from here! But how should the Wandering Jew flee?

Warmest greetings,
Debora Vogel

The notes in the margins in my previous postcard were by Mendel Neugroschel who spent a few hours with me on his trip to the Soviet Union.

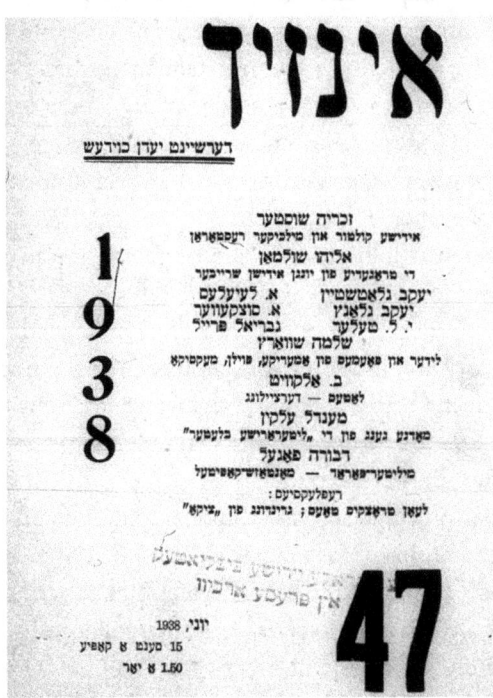

Figure 49. Cover of *In Zikh* journal, 1938.

To Aaron Glantz-Leyeles
Tsushtayer shrift far literatur, kunst un kultur
Pismo literacko-artystyczne "Cusztajer"
[Two pages, original in Yiddish]

April 25, 1936

Dear A. Leyeles,

It so happens that a person writes a letter in a moment of great sorrow, and then one must be very careful. What a burden of sadness may gather in a person, what a comical fate can descend upon her! Nevertheless, one shouldn't say or speak too much—it is somehow harmful for the soul when it is too light and cheerful!

As you see, I write to you occasionally even though you don't respond. I have developed a phobia for writing letters and yet I write. Wouldn't you feel the need to answer at least once, for instance, this letter of mine?!

I am a little afraid to send you fresh manuscripts, since you haven't published the previous ones, but what should I do with myself, judge for yourself. It is a good time for me in terms of writing. I write a lot, but I don't see any possibilities to get published. Whether it is because of the type of things I write that, for instance, don't fit the format of the newspapers, or whether it is because of my pride—very dangerous in literary matters—and the emptiness which overcomes me when I begin to think where I could publish. It is easier for me to help others than to be an ambassador for myself. To summarize, I will send you a poem and an essay "Stasis and Dynamism," which I significantly shortened. The essay obviously has "priority;" it is more important for me than the poem. I will not "terrorize" you anymore with the publication of the other essay in *In zikh*. Could you at least give me a sign where else can I publish it?

I have changed the montage entitled "The Building of the Bridge Pillars," and I am very satisfied with the changes. Its scope is somewhat larger than that of *The Building of the Train Station*. I am sending you the manuscript for the second time; "I am ashamed" to do that. I am curious to hear your feedback. Besides, I am giving you the authority to publish it somewhere and thank you in advance. (At times you publish collected volumes, perhaps an occasion would present itself then. ...)

I have attached two notes about *In zikh* which I published in the Lviv newspapers, as well as my shortened version of Leyvik's essay "Literature in Crisis," published in the Polish journal *Sygnały*. One more thing about the notes and the essay (I hope that Leyvik will not hold a grudge against me that I have not asked for his permission first): the shortened version was successful, the whole argument was preserved, and at the same time all the words like "Communist Revolution" were cut because of censorship. One shouldn't use these dangerous notions here, even if you criticize the Russian Revolution and the Communist writer. In my shortened version, I emphasized the literary material. However, the censor did have a problem with a few expressions, and they have cut out the most important connecting sentences. Yet, I have managed to smuggle in the essay, which, for instance, *Literarishe bleter* couldn't do. Translations of your and Anna Margolin's poetry will be published in the next issue.

I have started my letter with "sorrow." And I did not give examples or reasons for it. I was told: whenever possible, don't read life from an extract of life experiences, don't be superficial and impatient and don't burden yourself with getting to know a world which costs much—all of life. Or should one treat life only as a formal experiment?

It seems that people like an easy and irresponsible life, and their own fate, which is difficult and complicated, scares them.

Greetings to you and others,
Debora Vogel

PS: A request: if my essay on montage is not being currently printed, I ask you to change the previous beginning until the words "yet the connection happens," and replace it with the attached fragment entitled "1. The Notion of Montage"; from the "need ... until one needs to find it" the second footnote should be inserted in the place of the previous one.

To Marcus Ehrenpreis
Inż. S. Barenblüth
Uprawniony inż. bud.,
Lviv, 18 Leśna
[Two pages, original in German]

Lviv, May 18, 1936

My dearest Uncle,

My writing to you is accompanied by my son's crying. He is usually well behaved but sometimes he lets us hear him; it happens when he needs our company, to feel that someone is close by, only then does he calm down. This Adlerian need for recognition[56] is displayed in such a little munchkin! Besides, I have found in

---

56   See Vogel's "Choroba nerwowa i psychiczna w swietle teorji Adlera," *Przegląd Społeczny* 3, no. 9 (1929): 332–340.

his very mobile facial expressions one expression which is very similar to yours, dear Uncle.

As you can see, I am just as crazy as all the other mothers. But he is so terribly sweet, this son of mine! The grandma feels the same love for her grandson; she does not want to go on her summer vacation without him now.

On the eighth day after his birth, on May 10, Asher Joseph was initiated into Jewishness. He courageously endured the ceremony in the *shul* and was tranquil shortly afterwards. But the whole thing was stressful for us. Because I stayed at home, Mom worked herself to exhaustion; we had a lot of guests, and Mom made all the arrangements wonderfully. She will now rest a little, even though we have more guests. I got out of bed, having been in it since Tuesday of the previous week, and I feel that my health is restored. Now it is difficult to find time for everything because I nurse the child (a new form of literary work!), and I am busy for almost an hour every three hours. I want to take care of the child on my own, I just need to get used to the fact that he is not made of porcelain or some other fragile material; I'll get used to it eventually.

Warmest thanks for your well wishes and kisses to all
Dosia

To Shloyme Bikl[57]
Shoybn editorial office[58]
Bucharest
3 Doamnei str.
Romania

June 5, 1936

Dear Dr. Shloyme Bikl,

I am thankful for your invitation to contribute to the issue on Sternberg.[59] He is a true poet and one should write about him. I now encounter great difficulties to find a little bit of time, which is necessary for this work, but I will go to the trouble, and you will receive the manuscript in July at the latest.

As for your shipments, I don't understand why I haven't received a single issue of *Shoybn* until now. For this reason, I have not written to you about my

---

57 Shloyme Bikl (1896–1969) was a poet and editor who published journals mostly in Czernowitz, which was in Romania at the time.
58 *Shoybn* [Windowpanes] was a journal in Bukovina which was published from 1924 to 1936. Such important authors as Itsik Manger and Eliezer Shteynbarg published there.
59 Jacob Sternberg (1890–1973) was a Romanian dramatist and avant-garde poet, director of Yiddish theater, and one of the publishers of *Shoybn*.

thoughts on the journal. I learned about the journal from a note in *Literarishe bleter*, and I would be very grateful if you could regularly send me the issues.

Thank you for your compliments regarding my expertise in art. It is always a delight to find fellow colleagues who understand my art criticism and my own philosophical pursuits.

I will write to you about *Shoybn* when I become familiar with it.

With friendly greetings,
Debora Vogel

To Aaron Glantz-Leyeles
Mr. A. Glantz-Leyeles
c/o "The Day"
183 East Broadway
New York, USA
[Postcard, original in Yiddish]

Dr. Debora Vogel
apt. 1 bld. 18 Leśna
Poland

Brzuchowice, July 23, 1936

Dear Glantz-Leyeles,

In what is my almost exclusive monologue, dear Leyeles, there has again been a long pause. ("My almost exclusive monologue" means that sometimes there has been an answer from you when some of the things I have sent you were published.)

Besides some other things, the main reason for this pause is my son who was born two months ago and who now requires a lot of time from me.

The "fragments of montage" in the most recent issue of *In zikh* put me in a very unpleasant mood. I sent the three fragments together with a note that they constitute a whole because of the two sorts of facts which they represent and from which the montage is pieced together. The publication of only two fragments, and, moreover, the second one cut off in the middle does not do justice to this piece and to me. I hoped that *In zikh* would be a venue where I am trusted and where my manuscripts are not changed (besides the acceptable linguistic changes). Do you think that *In zikh* is such a venue?

In any case please ask for my consent when you introduce changes. I am saying this officially, and that concerns especially the essay on montage. When will it get published? If you don't want to publish it as is, I could shorten it to the parts which are important to me.

Greetings to you and others
Debora Vogel

To Melekh Ravitch
c/o Mr. J. Sher
52 Bouverie Str.
Carlton-Melbourne
Australia

September 10, 1936

Dear Melekh Ravitch,
A few weeks before I received your letter, the review of *Mannequins* appeared in *Folks-Tsaytung*.[60] From what I gather, the review was negative, even while the author (I) was taken seriously. Therefore, your letter to me was a surprise. Perhaps you would like to separate me as a person and as a writer, and to treat the person warmly, and the author with antipathy? However, it is difficult to perform such a vivisection on me because behind my poems is my difficult life. These poems took a long time to be born out of the experiences which preceded them. Thus, I write very little and my poems are dense; this denseness of experiences is perhaps the main reason for the "incomprehensibility" of my poetry. You don't say anything (perhaps only for the time being?) about *Acacias*. I am already curious as to what you would say about my prose which goes a step further than realism and reportage, insofar as realism can grow out of Cubism. I have not translated your poem yet. *Sygnały* became Marxist and the first consequence of that was that they discontinued the column on Jewish affairs, since Marxism does not want "any nationalism." This tells you something about the times! I read your poems, and your reportages to a lesser extent. I like them; it's a pity that it's only a one-sided sympathy. However, I am a generous person, and I don't let myself be influenced by a negative judgement into having a similar attitude. Thank you for your well wishes. I gave birth to a son, I did not know that the news has reached even distant Melbourne!!! That is the reason that I am only writing a postcard to you, I am afraid to begin a letter which I will not be able to finish. Lots of greetings,
    Your Debora Vogel

---

60 See Melekh Ravitch, "Vegn bikher un shrayber," *Nayer folkstsaytung*, no. 196 (March 7, 1936): 7.

To Aaron Glantz-Leyeles
[Two pages, original in Yiddish]

Lviv, October 30, 1936

Dear Leyeles,

I am sending my greetings to New York—the essence of all cities. How I regret that during my longing for urbanism I did not live in New York. Will I feel the wonder of the mobile city which never grows tired when I come for a visit? The wonder of a grandiose machine soul, the soul of the city? I think that I have still retained some reserves of urban longings which await realization, although in dialectical terms they do not officially count anymore, so to speak. Yet they do count when sometimes it is hard to live in gray and gloomy Lviv. When a person must distill the last colorfulness from gray to be able to live in grayness.

A long and sentimental preface to my letter. Now more to the point. First, I did not receive the letter you mentioned. The last letter from you arrived over a year ago. Perhaps it is possible that the letter was lost when I was away from Lviv during the summer vacation. What a pity. The question is what did you write in the letter?

À propos the translations, reviews, and everything else, I am finally slowly returning to work after the long pause because of the "event." I owe so many things: I really don't know how and when I will be able to finish these few projects I started, but it will happen eventually. Writing letters also takes quite some time. And there are new viewpoints on things, so I need to write. I published translations of two of your poems in the Polish journal *Sygnały*. However, imagine the unfortunate and hopeless situation of the journal ... it is leftist and it did away with the column on the Jewish affairs, for which it provided a scientific argumentation. However, with these translations, I would like to start a translation series in a Jewish-Polish weekly. I am looking forward to your new poetry collection; I kindly ask you to send it to my private address to avoid the trouble with the previous collection which I can't find, and which I'll now have to borrow from someone when I need it. And before I forget, please thank Glatstein[61] for his interesting poetry collection which he sent me. Please do that before I write to him myself.

I am truly happy to receive greetings from New York from those who like my work. Nevertheless, the fragmentation of my montage pieces in the publication

---

61 Jacob Glatstein (Yankev Glatshteyn) (1896–1971) was one of the most well-known Yiddish poets after the Holocaust. His style was marked by erudition, irony, and wit. He was one of the founders of the Introspectivist group.

is unpleasant for me. But it has already happened. I am delighted with the good reception of my essay on stasis and dynamism. Whatever happened to my essay on montage? I hope you have received it? Is it too long? Perhaps you would like to publish the theory part without the prospectus for the time being, of perhaps you don't have the space? Or perhaps the prospectus without the theory?

I am sending you some pieces of a shorter montage and I will also send you a poem once I write it. Apparently, I am not pensive lately, thus I don't write any poems. It is interesting to see how much contemplation is necessary for a poem. We don't value the mood of reflection when we find ourselves in an "enthusiastic" state.

Warm greetings to everyone at *In zikh* and everyone else.

Debora Vogel

Melekh Ravitch wrote a review of *Mannequins* in *Folkstsaytung* in Warsaw a few months ago, and I need to write a commentary to my texts. The essay and the prospectus are precisely such a commentary!

To Shloyme Bikl
[Two pages, handwritten, original in Yiddish]

November 5, 1936

Dear Dr. Bikl,

The colleagues from *Shoybn* and you have every right to feel offended. It is unlike me to stay silent for no apparent reason. However, it was not possible for me, and even today I don't feel good about sending this letter without the article "The City in Profile"[62] which I promised. However, I console myself with the fact that there is still time and that I will manage to write the essay after I take care of the most important things in my work.

I owe you an answer about *Shoybn* and your assessment of my books.

I read your journal with great interest: there I found European culture adapted for our cultural life. The poetry column featuring Shternberg, Rivkin,[63] Saktsir,[64] the translations by Shvarts,[65] and the critical-polemical part with your and Gininger's[66] names evoke a satisfaction and trust which is rare in my experience with Yiddish critics and polemicists.

---

62 See Jacob Shternberg, *Shtot in profil. Lid un grotesk* (Bucharest: Farlag Di Vokh, 1935).
63 Borukh Rivkin (1883–1945) was a Yiddish literary critic and essayist; he lived in New York since 1911.
64 Motl Saktsir (1907–1980) was a Yiddish author.
65 Shlomo Shvarts (1907–1988) was a Yiddish author from Belarus who lived in Chicago.
66 Chaim Gininger (1905–1994) was a Yiddish philologist.

Most important of all is the liveliness of the journal, its relevance! What I mean under the oft-abused notion of "relevance" is the consideration of diverse influences from various distant centers like New York and debate with them—building a spiritual center in the absence of the territorial one. Optimism and freshness are in order here. You know, sometimes I am afraid of the great number of Yiddish cultural centers, which is apparent in the great number of journals, newspapers, and publications. Such a wealth of work: if we were to gather it in one place, what a colorful diversity it would be. However, it is what it is—the sadness of disunity, the horrible loneliness among one's own. Who among our intelligentsia knows about us, is influenced by us, or discusses our work? A confused fear sometimes grips me when I think about the multiplicity in the larger world. A paradox, a logical paradox with which, however, our sensibility does not reckon. A person, just like all others, would grow if she had an environment visible to the people who read what we write, an environment which would cultivate the mutual exchange of ideas and experience.

(I have just received your book *In zikh un arum zikh*[67]—thank you. I will write to you about the overall impression from the book and your essay with the same title.)

Concerning your reaction to my book, or rather, to the two of my books, I agree with your approach to the substantial question which you answer yourself, "a tree with many leaves stands in front of my window. In its silent loneliness, it makes fun of both definitions."

The tree clearly makes fun of definitions. And it has the right to do so. We cannot "define life" because the definition is always one-sided. We can only reproduce what we see from life, or, better, "in" life. Our construction is always only connected with the one side in life—with the colors and the spirit of the side to which we adhere.

(You will find an indirect and systematic answer in my essay "Stasis, Dynamism, and Topicality in Art" in *In zikh* volume 27.) In reference to the tree, it carries all of life in its leaves, its wonderful growth.

Should I send my books to *Shoybn* separately in case someone needs them or would like to discuss them eventually, or could you consider the books I sent to you personally as if they were sent to the editorial office? Perhaps you and *Shoybn*

---

67 See Shlomo Bikl, *In zikh un arum zikh:notitsn fun a polemistn un kritishe bamerkungen*. (Bucharest: Farlag Sholem Aleykhem, 1936).

would be interested in a discussion of *Acacias* by Mendel Neugroschel?[68] (Vienna, 11/12 Sterngasse). He wrote some interesting remarks about the book for me.

I have only received three isssues of *Shoybn* to date and M. Saktsir's poems. Please continue sending me the journal and thank Saktsir for his poems before I write to him.

Regarding the essay "The City in Profile"—Rivkin's poem dedicated to the book is wonderful, I will send it for sure, but I cannot commit to saying when, not to be late. I am sending you two fragments of a montage and ask you to publish them in *Shoybn*.

Best greetings to you and others,
Your Debora Vogel

To Melekh Ravitch
[Two pages, original in Yiddish]
Dr. Debora Vogel
Lviv, 18 Leśna

Lviv, December 1, 1936

Dear Melekh Ravitch,
The works I began, the unanswered letters, and the unread books pile up on my table. And I push all this away to answer your letter. Such a letter demands an answer, calls for a response. I shouldn't think that you will read these words in about six weeks, and the spirit of these words will have cooled down and turned old. Or perhaps such reactions do not get old?

The first impression from your letter is a recollection of something lost. Could this association be interpreted as healthy and normal? And yet you write about being close to me, about friendship—who among us, the people and the Yiddish poets, the lonely poets without readers who hold onto every invitation of friendship, who does not feel the loss when they are brutally rejected? This is the reason for my association. For a moment I thought that perhaps I wrote the postcard in an offensive way—did something unlike me? You may not believe me, but I was not angry or bitter in the very least on account of your bad review. You liked the line from a poem "The Inscription on the Matzevah," "what is life …"; this line—a question and simultaneously an answer—is a set expression I use. This is how I feel about all confusions,

---

68 Compare Mendel Neugroschel, "Der letste dor yidishe poetn in Galitsye.1. Dvoyre Fogel (1902–1942)," *Di tsukunft* 61, no. 1 (1951): 25.

colors, and needless fates—what is life. ... Somebody who is permeated with this bittersweet understanding: he who is perpetually lonely, sad, and hopeless is close to life itself, cannot take someone else's opinion tragically to such an extent as to become angry or mad. I am well aware why people misunderstand me in the same way as I can clearly see the good and warm comprehension which comes from absolute strangers who send me letters with a couple intelligent of words from a faraway place. However, it is beyond me how you can like a person without understanding her. What do you like in that person? You probably need to ignore the person's books if that person happens to be an author and think of her as an exclusively private person. I am certain that you think of me that way.

What are you doing in the desert, how do you write? Is the life there similar to our life here? Do you feel the pulse of life better there? I am now occupied with the sweet being of my son, my life is quick and intensive, I couldn't live faster in a big city.

When will your poetry collection be published? Or perhaps it was published, and I did not notice the announcement? I only read a few poems published in *Literarishe bleter*.

Best greetings. Please write!
Your Debora Vogel

To Aaron Glantz-Leyeles

Dr. Debora Vogel, apt. 1 bld. 18 Leśna
[Postcard, original in Yiddish]
Mr. A. Glantz-Leyeles
c/o "The Day"
183 East Broadway
New York, N.Y.
USA

December 14, 1936

Dear and esteemed Leyeles,

I received the last issue of *In zikh*; it is interesting as always. And it is truly alarming that there is not a single *In zikh* subscriber in Lviv. I have published notes about the journal in the Jewish and Polish-Jewish newspapers. Perhaps it's not enough but I am the last person to advertise because I cannot do that even for my books. We have no mediators between authors and readers, and this lack is felt significantly. I read the pre-announcement of the publication of "Montages" in the next issue of *In zikh*. I take it that this concerns a couple fragments from "The Building of the Bridge." You don't like the essay about montage and will not publish it? It's important for me that at least the theoretical part is published, hopefully it is not too long. I am working on a new article.

Greetings,
D. Vogel

To Aaron Glantz-Leyeles
[Postcard, original in Yiddish]

January 4, 1937

Dear esteemed Leyeles,
Warm greetings to you from afar. I feel the need to send you a sign of life from time to time.

Today I am sending two montage pieces which I ask you to publish together. I have asked you for a response regarding my theory of montage, and you still owe it me. These are all my editorial queries.

Now some personal updates. I write a little and I am working on a longer montage and an essay entitled "The Social Order in Art" where I write about some current issues.

I am impatiently looking forward to your new poetry collection. Please forgive me that I have not voiced my opinion either on your collection or on Glatstein's for the time being (I haven't yet written to Glatstein). This is due to lack of time on the one hand, and on the other—due to waiting to find an appropriate reaction within me. I don't want to promise or set a deadline for it, and yet it will happen, just as everything happens someday. Understandably, with such a fatalistic attitude it may happen too late, when it is no longer helpful and necessary, but I have only this fatalistic consolation.

What do you think about meeting in Paris this summer? I have already seriously considered this refreshing trip. When I will be able to part from my son for a few weeks, I would like to use the time for Paris. It would be great if we could meet there!

Lots of greetings to you and all the Introspectivists
Debora Vogel

To Aaron Glantz-Leyeles
[Postcard with business address, handwritten, original in Yiddish]
Tsushtayer shrift far literatur, kunst un kultur
Pismo literacko-artystyczne "Cusztajer"
Lviv, 26 St. Marcin Street
PO Box 154.472.

Mr. A. Glantz-Leyeles	Dr. Debora Vogel
c/o *The Day*	Lviv, apt. 1 bld. 18 Leśna
183 East Broadway	Poland
New York	
USA	

January 21, 1937

Dear Leyeles,

When I wanted to complain that I did not receive the December issue of *In zikh*, it arrived. And I must already seem like a "madwoman in the attic" with "demands." And yet, I need to insist, the pieces are not at all a part of a novel, they are not fragments from an exemplary montage.

What is worse are the three horrible mistakes that I would like to correct if possible:

a. In line 6 in (1) *pasazh* should be *peyzazh*.
b. In line 13 in (1) *bashtrofte* should be *bashtrokhene*.
Line 8 in (2) *blend* should be *plen* (you write *pleyn*).

I would like to ask you for some other information. I made an agreement with a Polish-Jewish weekly to publish the translations of the Yiddish poetry. Margolin was published first (in "Women's Front"). This week it's your turn, and then Glatstein's in two weeks. I need the bio and bibliographical notes about Glatstein, Alquit, Weisman,[69] S. Shvarts, the current Introspectivists, please obtain this information for me (it must be short and on paper). I am providing short notes on the translations. There are probably some inaccuracies, so I ask for your help and leniency.

With warmest greetings,
Your Debora Vogel

---

69 Ye. Weisman was the author of the poetry collection *Yung groz*, published in New York.

To Shloyme Bikl
Tsushtayer shrift far literatur, kunst un kultur
Pismo literacko-artystyczne "Cusztajer"
Lviv, 26 St. Marcin Street
P.O box 154.472.
[Postcard, original in Yiddish]

January 23, 1937

My dear Dr. Bikl,

I treat you as a representative of *Shoybn*; therefore, I am turning to you with editorial queries. First, thank you for the fourth issue of *Shoybn*. It is lively and very well edited. One more thing: some time ago I wrote a "prospectus," and now the review by J[oshue] Rapoport urges me to publish it. I have only revised the ending and I would like to ask you to publish it, perhaps even in the next issue instead of the promised montage. I believe that the essay is more relevant. And please don't be offended that I did not reply to your and Sternberg's letters, as well as to any recent poetry collections which I received from Romania. I am behind … in my work for all parts of the world. (Please don't think it arrogance, it's simply a fact.) I am very slowly dealing with things.

    Best regards,
    Your Debora Vogel

To Aaron Glantz-Leyeles
Tsushtayer shrift far literatur, kunst un kultur
Pismo literacko-artystyczne "Cusztajer"
Lviv, 26 St. Marcin Street
P.O box 154.472.
[Original in Yiddish]

Mr. A. Glantz-Leyeles	Dr. Debora Vogel
c/o *The Day*	Poland
183 East Broadway	apt. 1 bld. 18 Leśna Lviv
New York	
USA	

January 27, 1937

Dear Leyeles,

I am taking back the pressure I put on you regarding the fate of my essay on montage. I became irritated with revisions, and because of this "activity," another stylization of the text came into being—a division of the material into a few (3) essays and questions and a shortening of the essay in question. Therefore, I am asking you not to publish the essay I sent you, in case it was planned for publication. I am awaiting the bio-bibliographic notes from you and J. Glatstein and sending you warm wishes,

    Your Debora Vogel

    When will your book be published?

To Shloyme Bikl

Dr. Sz. Bikl	Dr. D. Vogel
c/o *Shoybn*	Lviv
București IV	apt. 1 bld. 18 Leśna
26 A Stefan Mihaileanu str.	Poland

February 10, 1937

Dear Dr. Bikl,

I received your postcard a few weeks ago. Thank you for your taking care of my literary affairs.

    We subscribe to *Chwila* at home.[70] I would have noticed a review about Sternberg, especially if it had appeared in this assimilated publication with Zionist leanings. Discussions of Yiddish books are few—who could have written it? The editorial office does not consider our requests. If you know approximately when the article appeared, I could obtain it from the complete archive of the period and look at its contents again. If you give me permission, I will do it immediately. I am glad to have met you. As you see, I take your "perhaps" for "sure." I need to clarify a few things regarding my trip to Paris in the summer, and I don't know yet if I'll manage to go, for many reasons. My best wishes, Debora Vogel

To Aaron Glantz-Leyeles

[Two pages, original in Yiddish]

April 10, 1937

Dear A. Leyeles,

I have been trying to write a letter to you for a long time. (Obviously your anonymous response encourages this!)

    Your essay about the fate of Modernism in Yiddish literature[71] is worthy of discussion, even in a time like ours, which seems to have no time for questions

---

70 *Chwila. Dziennik poświęcony sprawom politycznym, społecznym i kulturalnym* was a Jewish Lviv daily with Zionist leanings published in Polish from 1919 until 1939. From September 1934 it was published twice a day. Vogel contributed to the publication.

71 See Aaron Glantz-Leyeles, "Vegn eynem a durkhfall," *In zikh* 18, no. 31 (1937): 27–31.

of form and art. I fear that this essay did not find the resonance it deserved. I really liked the marker of "intellectualism" as the characteristic feature of Modernism setting it against rationalism and emotionalism. The "failure" of Yiddish Modernism as you call it is very important; the same phenomenon is noticeable in all literatures which develop at a slower pace; for instance, in Polish literature. Only at a high level of the literary development will the avant-garde be accepted as an element of culture and defined as such. Yiddish literature which, in fact, does not have control over itself and which has no foundation to its own specific life, continuously limits itself—we can't, God forbid, go too far; the stages of development shouldn't be skipped; and at times a contemporary person has no place here and nothing to do! Every issue of *In zikh* is, thus, a greeting and a confirmation that there are other people in Yiddish literature as well.

Now—after a certain time yearning for balance and a wish to bring everything under one denominator—I am currently extremely unwilling to abolish limits. There are situations where equalization, compromise is impossible. You need to establish and sustain contrasts and combat hostility. At times, equalization is no longer possible, and a common ideological front is impossible. How can you reach an understanding with someone who has developed so much animosity that they harbor an instinctive reluctance against the "Modernist" and negate the social value of his work in advance, since they no longer believe that it's possible that he could work with a relevant social theme. One example is to be found in Polish literature where certain leftist elements are not ready to consider the work of T. Peiper,[72] the founder of Polish Modernism. Peiper introduces into poetry distinctly relevant but not propagandistic themes; he uses elements of Constructivism, and apparently it is enough to be distrustful to him. Sometimes it seems that the artistic element hurts art!

(In this respect, I would like to mention the fate of my translation—the work I wished to conduct programmatically and systematically. I suspect that one poet from Lviv has informed the editors that I give preferential treatment to "Modernists," who have absolutely no significance for Yiddish literature. Otherwise, there is no reason that the agreement that I signed was terminated after the translations of Glatstein and Minkoff[73] were in the editorial

---

72 Tadeusz Peiper (1891–1969) was a Polish avant-garde poet, critic, and art historian. In 1922 he published an Urbanist manifesto *Miasto Masa Maszyna* [City mass machine].
73 Vogel published poems by Minkoff—"Meg Boyrnet," *Nasza Opinja* 6, no. 144 (1938): 1 and and "Ya-Kid Karter," *Kontratak* 2, no. 15 (1937): 6.

office for more than two months. I would like to submit this work to a journal which is less read and of a lower quality, but still with an adequate number of readers.)

PS: The journal changed its mind and will publish the translations after all.

The essays of Z. Shuster,[74] especially his essay about points of contact between various Jewish cultures are of a high caliber and worthy of discussion. I agree with Shuster, especially on relations with Hebrew literature.

Why haven't I received your book yet? I am waiting for it impatiently. I have a request to make. H. Segal,[75] a professor of mathematics at a technical university, an art connoisseur, and a warm-hearted person lives in Czernowitz. He leads a "Seminar on Yiddish Literature," with lectures and publications together with a lecturer and critic, I. Shvarts. Thanks to a coincidence, I have been in contact with him for some time, if the review about my work that both of them published in the Romanian press could be called a coincidence. I would like to introduce you to each other. Could I ask you to send him *In zikh*, perhaps along with the ten to fifteen previous issues if it is too difficult for you to send him all the issues. You will not regret it! The address is Prof. H. Segal, Czernowitz, 17 Delavrancea, Romania.

I am sending you some new things for *In zikh*. Warmest greetings to you and other Introspectivists.

Yours,

Debora Vogel

PS: I am sending two parts which only make sense as a whole if they are published together: a depiction of important, relevant main events in the foreground and insignificant marginal occurrences which could be generalized under the notion of banal events. It would be best to publish the two fragments together.

---

74 Zechariah Shuster (1902–1986) was a Polish Jewish journalist; since 1927 he lived in New York.

75 Hirsh Segal (1905–1982) was a professor of mathematics and a Yiddish journalist. Together with Itsik Shvarts he founded a seminar on Yiddish language and literature in 1932. He worked with Chaim Gininger to publish a 1924 anthology *Naye yidishe dikhtung*. See Itsik Shvarts, "Modernistishe dikhtung (vegn Debora Vogel 'tog figurn.' Lider farlag tsushtayer lemberg 1930)," *Tshernovitser bleter*, no. 190 (1934): 3; see also H. Segal, "Dvoyre Fogels naye lider bukh 'Manekinen,'" *Tshernovitser bleter*, no. 210 (1934): 2. Itsik Shvarts's and Hirsh Segal's reviews of Vogel's work can be found in English translation in this volume.

To Marcus Ehrenpreis
Inż. S. Barenblüth
Uprawniony inż. bud.,
Lviv, 18 Leśna,
Tel. 271–38
[One page, original in German]

April 13, 1937

My dearest Uncle,
Our whole family would like to see you this summer in a somewhat dirty and neglected town in Poland. Mom wanted to travel to visit you, but she doesn't look good right now; you are much more mobile and used to travelling and you could spend two very pleasant weeks here.

In our household we have tidied things up a bit. I employed a nanny after the first year of taking care of the boy. He is grown now and can get used to a stranger. I need to get back to reading and writing.

We are happy that the boy has the calm and optimistic temperament of the Vogel family. Shalom has work and feels much better. What are you currently working on, dear Uncle? How are Dori's work and studies? Please send us a picture of the Nathanson family! We are sending you an amateur picture of Edzio which we took in December. The boy has grown up now.

Many kisses to all of you
From Dosia and Shalom

To Shloyme Bikl
[Postcard, handwritten, original in Yiddish]
Dr. M. Bikl, c/o *Shoybn*
București, 3 Daamnzi Street.   Lviv, 18 Leśna
Romania   Poland

June 27, 1937

Dear Dr. Bikl,
I regret that I could not keep in touch with you. It was one of the best contacts I have ever had in the Yiddish literary world. A fatal year without excitement and color—regardless, or perhaps because of, the fact that I was continually "busy"—is behind me. My professional activity and household work, and perhaps also a certain fatigue caused a decline in work and interactions with people.

I have not yet thanked you for the last issue of *Shoybn*. I am thanking you now, even though I still haven't read it. Imagine this: I let an acquaintance borrow the copy without reading it myself first, and he lost it. I would like to ask you to send me another copy if possible. Thank you in advance. I only read my essay from this issue. I am satisfied that it appeared in your publication in good society. Reading the text again after a long pause as if I were an ordinary reader, the essay seemed to me to be very straightforward and comprehensible. You once wrote to me that it would be too difficult for readers.

My longer study "Montage as a Literary Genre"[76] was published in the last issue of *Bodn*. If you haven't received it, I will send you the issue.

Warmest greetings to you and others. What is the news about your trip to Poland?

I have been awaiting you. XXXX[77] I am traveling for two months, I will be spending them in the mountains.

To Aaron Glantz-Leyeles
Dr. Debora Vogel
Inż. S. Barenblüth
Lviv, 18 Leśna
[Two pages, original in Yiddish]

Lviv, July 16, 1937

Dear A. Leyeles,

An oppressive and painful mood which has taken a grip over me lately is the main reason for my silence. I haven't thanked you for the book which I received two days ago after I sent my letter with greatest urgency. If only I had read it sooner.

You ask for my opinion about the book. I will not be able to provide an objective evaluation. I need to write an official review to get some distance from the text itself and from you. As I am now writing my letter to you, I can only give you an unmediated impression. These texts are close to me in terms of prose and in their ethical pathos. When I speak about "prose," I don't mean banality but rather the contact with everyday and topical life which is characteristic of Modernism, although a different opinion on the subject dominates. We are very close to life while the "Naturalists" only move at the surface level, the outer layer of things. It seems that our perspective on things is too close to become too foreign or improbable like a perspective which is too distant. I am used to the attitude of the "public," which perhaps has to do with my overly passive stance lately. The emphasis of your "old" answer in the book refers to something else—it shows your militant

---

76 See Debora Vogel, "Di literarishe gatung montazh," *Bodn* 4, nos. 3–4 (1937): 99–105.
77 This is where the postcard is damaged.

stance which has not lost its power. It is good that there are people like you who are the conscience and external control of the events. And something else in this regard: is "Modernism" an immobile and petrified movement? Do we not notice how it transforms before our very eyes, in our work, how it achieves social elements and relevance? We are all consciously and unconsciously the agents of the Hegelian dialectic—we develop and change, only they, the opponents, are stuck in their definition, in their attitude towards the movement.

But I would like to speak about your poems ... the ethical pathos: I believe it is characteristic for Yiddish Modernism in general. It is a comical paradox: we are barely connected to social and political life and mean nothing for active world history. We are, or must be politically passive, and yet we cling to life asking ourselves, "how should we live." Our Modernism is constantly a clear answer to this question, while European Modernism is already so far removed from its origin—I mean the current question of the source of every creation—that it is almost unrecognizable.

You are an unmistakably ethical writer. Your wonderful poems from *Fabius Lind*[78] or from *Tsu dir-tsu mir*[79] attest to that. I wanted to become aware of where there is a bit of irrationality in your poetry. Without it, no poetry exists. And it seems to me that the irrational is excluded from the logical and rational sentence, as well as from measured and almost regular rhythm—even though it often changes within a poem; the irrational took refuge in image and metaphor. In your work image and the metaphor are poetically irrational. Whoever searches for the essence of poetry or form—colorfulness—may find it in your strong metaphors. There are certain poems like "Shtimen in der nakht," "An akord," "Zumer," "Beymer," the cycle *Sin in farb*, "Shvartse murmeln," and others, where rationality is propitiously linked with the irrational, which yields—let us not shy away from the expression—"lasting poetry." Perhaps during my vacation, I will manage to write a couple of articles about the poets in our literature who might have participated in mainstream cultural production if they didn't write in Yiddish.

In this regard, my translations come to mind. I had the best intentions. Besides the already published texts by Leyeles, Glatstein, Anna Margolin, Minkoff, Teller, Tabachnik, and others, as well as Leyvik from *In zikh*, I have made some new translations which I cannot publish anywhere. I might have more luck in the fall when signing a contract with a Polish literary journal which might be more interested than the Polish-Jewish press. I have been tired lately

---

78 See Aaron Glantz-Leyeles, *Fabius Lind* (New York: Farlag Inzikh, 1937).
79 See Aaron Glantz-Leyeles, *Tsu dir-tsu mir. Poeme* (New York: Friling, 1933). Self-published.

and have had no strength to fight and demand. I am going to the mountains for a few weeks in the hope of recovering my energy.

I want to ask you about a part of your letter which is unclear to me. There you remind me of my dissatisfaction that *In zikh* affords too little space to my texts. When did I say that?! I know very well what I owe you personally as well as *In zikh*, and I don't think the journal needs to be inundated with works by one poet. Besides, I don't write as much, and I am simply asking you to publish the two fragments I sent to you together because they represent two types of elements introduced in the montage. I said this and nothing else. I need to add one more thing: please respond to my questions. For instance, when I ask you if you are interested in my essay "The Problem of the End of Art" (or other essays, I haven't sent you that one), please reply, so that these essays don't share the fate of my essay about montage. The latter was in your office for more than a year. After asking you about it a few times, I sent it to *Bodn* at Minkoff's request.

I am sending you two additional pieces. I did not receive the latest issue of *In zikh*. With the warmest greetings to you and others,

Your Debora Vogel

PS: I got *In zikh*. According to my estimations, you still need to pass a verdict on two pieces—"The Military" and "From Banal Events." Should you decide to publish them, please include the headings in bold not as regular text. Every part builds a whole with its title.

Have you sent *In zikh* (all issues) to Dr. Segal's "Yiddish Seminar" in Czernowitz, 15a George Lazar str.?

To Marcus Ehrenpreis
Inż. S. Barenblüth
uprawniony inż. bud.
Lviv, 18 Leśna
[Two pages, original in German]

Lviv, September 9, 1937

My dearest,

We hope that you, dear Uncle, feel better. I am taking it upon myself to mediate between you and the translator of your book about Spain whom I don't know. His name is M. Forlerer. Some time ago, I received a letter with a note from my friend, the poet Dr. Neugroschel. I attach it here. I would like to use my authority—if I have any—in this matter. Initially, I just wanted to forward the letter to you but now I am asking you to read it yourself. The matter is somewhat complicated: in short, Forlerer thinks that he incurred moral and material damages because you did not reply to his letter which was a simple request to send him a document that he had your authorization for translation. Having not received the document, he didn't have any proof when the Warsaw Jewish newspaper published a translation by someone else and rejected his even though he was the first to submit. Another newspaper does not wish to publish the few fragments as a sequel, since another newspaper has already published something. It is also a mystification that the newspaper published another translation as if it depicted contemporary Spain. As I understand it, he asks you for a small material compensation, since he is in despair. Please read his letter to you and the letter he plans to send to the editors of *Ekspres*. If possible, do something for the translator. I will reply to him that I spoke to you. His address is Mordko Forlerer, Warsaw, 24/89 Zamenhof str.

I returned to Lviv from Brzuchowice [today, Bryukhovychi in Ukraine] a few days ago. We made use of the wonderful weather and compensated for the failed summer vacation. My Parisian vacation was postponed until the 20th of this month. I will return to Brzuchowice and will come to school to teach a few classes. Mom is there with Gusta and Asher. It is amazingly beautiful there. Gusta slowly recuperates, and the child literally thrives. I should have brought the letter to Mom so that she could write to you as well but I don't want to waste time with the "Forlerer matter," and I am expediting my writing with the best wishes for the New Year from Mom, Shalom, and I.

Once again, I ask you, dear Uncle, to consider Forlerer's request, and, if possible, to settle the issue.

With the warmest greetings to all of you,
Dosia

To Marcus Ehrenpreis
[Two pages, original in German]

January 23, 1938

My dearest,
We haven't responded to each other's letters for so long, as if we have been waiting for something out of the ordinary to happen. Something extraordinary happens every day and one needs to have enough joy inside and also enough of the costly "time," which Thomas Mann analyzes so brilliantly, to have a lot of material, perhaps even too much material for a letter.

Now that, for instance, Asher has gone for a walk, I need to use the time quickly. When he comes back soon, he will realize, "Mom is writing." He will then sit in my lap and order me around, "Mom, write!" He is terribly sweet and excessively smart—as a well-known pediatrician Prof. Groer says about him. He is "excitable," his body is too small, yet he is strong. He talks a lot, is domineering, and he is also a bit of a comedian and a dreamer. When somebody asks him what a thing is which he doesn't know the name for yet, he answers with a new fantastical syllable combination. He is the colorful, optimistic mood of our home.

Does he enrich my poetry? I have no control: he hasn't been a theme until now, and he hasn't influenced the form either. I also need to be a bit "emancipated" from him when I wish to work, otherwise he will take all of me.

I have not written anything for *Judisk Tidskrift* for a long time. I wanted to write something about an excellent painter,[80] a former yeshiva student.

Best,
Dosia

To Aaron Glantz-Leyeles
[One page, original in Yiddish]

January 28, 1938

Dear A. Leyeles,

I am sending you a poem from the series *Legend of the Twentieth Century*. I am also using this opportunity to remind you that you currently have two of my other montage pieces under review.

I would very much like to publish more in *In zikh*, including theory. Unfortunately, I see that I have failed.

Lately, the Jewish world has become active here in Lviv. For February and March, the Jewish People's University has organized four talks[81] around the theme "The Centennial of Yiddish poetry" from Ettinger[82] to the Modernists. I will present the fourth lecture entitled "Urbanism in Yiddish Poetry." I do not only consider city themes as urbanist. I would like to attempt to return a more general and at the same time less blurry or fragmented meaning to the notion of urbanism.

I don't have a lot of time now and I am working a bit intensely.

Has Shvarts's poetry collection already been published?

Best greetings to you and others,
Debora Vogel

---

80 Nathan Shpigel (1886–1942) was a Polish Jewish artist and a member of the Expressionist group *Yung Yidish*. See Vogel, " Di bilder-oysshtelung fun natan spigel," *Der nayer morgn* 21, no. 12 (1938): 3.
81 The lectures took place on April 14, 1938.
82 Shlomo Ettinger (1803–1856) was a Yiddish author who mostly wrote fables. He is considered the "grandfather" of Yiddish literature.

To Shloyme Bikl

Dr. Sh. Bikl
c/o editorial office of *Shoybn*
București
2 Criștnlui Str.
Romania

Poland
Dr. Debora Vogel
Lviv
apt. 1 bld. 18 Leśna

February 28, 1938

Dear Dr. Bikl,

I would like to thank you for all the *Shoybn* issues which you have sent me up to now. The seemingly insignificant and secondary action of sending the newspaper may become a symbol—a sign of an existing relationship even though we don't write to one another. I consider *Shoybn* in this light. Please continue sending me the journal. These few issues which I have received are animated and relevant. However, at the same time *Shoybn* has a somewhat static character which aligns well with my way of writing. Therefore, I won't remind you to publish these few fragments which I sent some time ago for the "previous" *Shoybn*. Or perhaps the materials are still relevant for you? Maybe you have space and would be interested in a poem? I stayed in Paris for a few weeks this fall at a later time than everyone and the Congress.[83] It's a pity I also didn't have a chance to meet you. Perhaps this summer I will use up my vacation time to come to Romania and meet all of you.

Warmest greeting to you, Yankl Yakir,[84] Motl Saktsir, and others.

Your Debora Vogel

---

83 The International Congress of Yiddish Literature took place from September 17 until September 20, 1937 in Paris. See "From Czernowitz to Paris. The International Yiddish Culture Congress of 1937" in *Czernowitz at 100. The First Yiddish Language Conference in Historical Perspective*, ed. Kalman Weiser and Joshua A. Fogel (Lanham: Lexington Books, 2010), 152–154.

84 Yankl Yakir (1908–1980) was a Romanian Yiddish author.

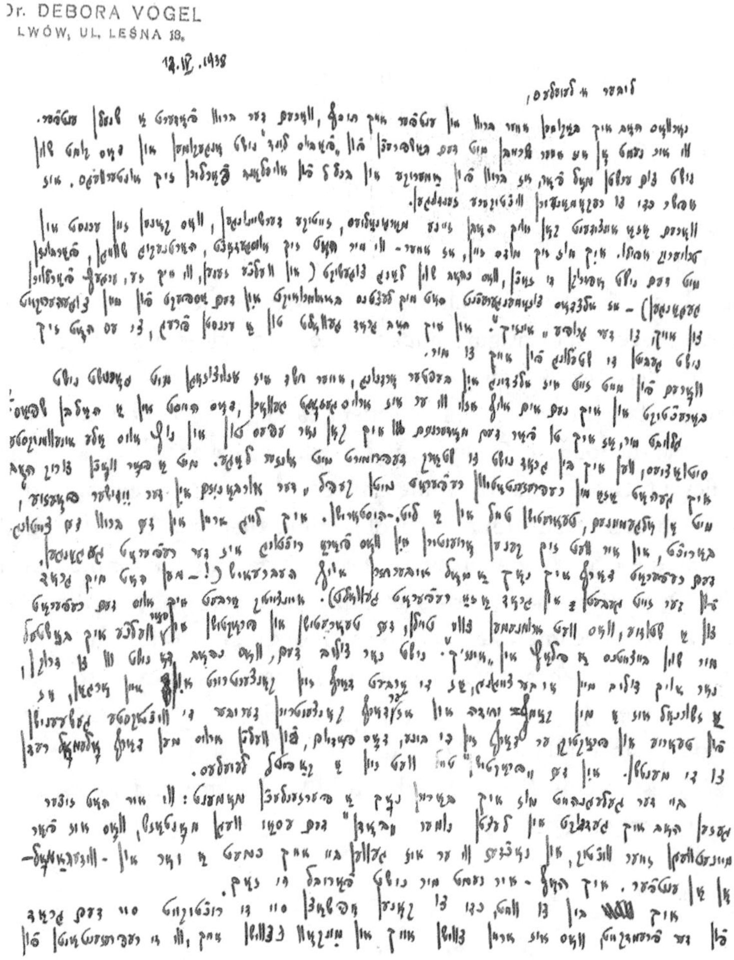

Figure 50. Letter to A. Leyeles, April 12, 1938.

To Aaron Glantz-Leyeles
Dr. Debora Vogel
Lviv, 18 Leśna
[Two pages, original in Yiddish]

April 12, 1938

Dear A. Leyeles,
I am responding the minute I received your letter because it calls for an immediate reply. As you might expect, the letter where you discuss *Fabius Lind* did

not reach me. It seems that it is not the first time that letters from America and abroad in general have got lost somewhere on the way. Perhaps one should send the more important messages as registered letters.

This incident could have its own marginal, insignificant events which might have serious and even tragic consequences. I must admit that I thought your stubborn silence is connected to the fact that my texts which I sent you some time ago were not published (and as I see now, they must have gotten lost somewhere). Due to that, I was concerned about my affiliation with you, the *In zikh* group, lately. And I wanted to ask you in earnest if you have changed your mind about me.

Everything is improving in my life, and your praise is unjustified. I perceive it in the same way it was probably uttered—half seriously? Trust me, I am working for Modernism where I can do something, using all opportunities when I am not too pessimistic about the state in which we find ourselves. A few weeks ago, I gave a talk under the title "Urbanism in Yiddish Poetry" with a general theoretical and a literary-historical part. Attached is the newspaper report[85]—you may learn about the course I charted in my talk. I need to translate the talk once again into Hebrew (I was asked to do that a few times because there was a need for a talk like that!). Currently, I am reworking the talk into a study comprised of two parts—theoretical and practical. I am already asking for it to be placed in *In zikh* not because I cannot publish anywhere in Poland but, first and foremost, because of my conviction that work in the publication venue should intensify, that the journal is a solitary fight. Therefore, it should offer a concentration of the most important things from theory and praxis; it must be a podium, a stage from which one can always talk to people. In the "practical" part there will be a subsection on Leyeles.

I would like to mention something personal using the occasion. Surely you have seen that in the last issue of *Bodn* I published the essay about montage, which is very important to me. I did it after the essay was on your desk without an answer for over a year. Please don't take what I did the wrong way.

I am too far away to judge the orientation, or the degree of tension, between you and Minkoff to evaluate you, as well as the representatives of the two groups which spread and gather around you both. From afar—this fortunate position at a "distance," which from the other points of view I find unfortunate, I can surely see the proximity, and I would like to see that which is common and

---

85 See Vogel. "Okres modernizmu w literaturze żydowskiej," *Chwila* 20, no. 6796 (1938): 13. This is a summary of the first talk from the series of talks dedicated to the Centennial of Yiddish Poetry at Towarzystwo żydowskiego Uniwersytetu Ludowego im A. Einsteina, "100 lat poezji żydowskiej".

connecting between you, rather than that which divides. If it were up to me, I would suggest and even insist that the two camps unite.

Both are close to me. I see what unites them—genuine Modernism, culture, and the heroic. I belong to both as it were. Perhaps it seems different from the viewpoint of the immediate proximity. Yet at a distance, my attitude to both groups is consequential. I hope that you understand my inner situation in this regard.

What concerns the poem I sent you: whenever possible I simply added the right intonation to irony, I attempted to change the lines somehow, and the result seems to me awkward. An artificial change is impossible, it is successful only when it is natural. Overall, the poem is no different than, for instance, "The Legend of Oil." I would like to ask you to print it as is. Is it even possible that the poem be considered an apotheosis of fascism? Meanwhile, I am sending you two other poems and another piece which you either did not receive, or which was lost somewhere in the editorial office. This is understandable. However, I cannot forgive you when you don't answer questions at all (for example, when I ask you if I should send this or that essay), and when you don't acknowledge the receipt of texts. A postcard with a few sentences would be enough. Sometimes I don't know why certain things which I considered promised are not being done.

How are things in general in my life? I am often overcome with a fear of wasted time. The tragedy of freedom! Time has become a problem; professional and motherly duties frequently leave me with little time which I then use for writing poems and montage pieces I would like to publish in the fall, as well as essays and talks—I am sending you the issue of *Inzl* where I published an essay. I am now writing an article about urban art in its dialectical development. But, as I said, it is very little. And even an "abstractionist" like myself cannot renounce "life."

I have recently completed my library of Yiddish poetry. I am only missing the book by Shvarts. Could you please ask him for a copy on my behalf? Does Alquit have a poetry collection published?

Thank you for your letter and warm greetings to you and others

Debora Vogel

PS: Another request: Merkel,[86] a well-known Jewish painter who lives in Vienna, wrote a desperate letter to me.[87] He cannot stay in Vienna much longer

---

86 Jerzy Merkel (1881–1976) was a Lviv artist who studied in Cracow and Paris and lived in Vienna. Compare Vogel. "Jerzy Merkel (Z okazji retrospektywnej wystawy w Tow. Sztuk Pięknych we Lwowie)," *Nasza Opinja* 3, no. 7 (1935): 12.

87 After the Anschluss, the the Nazis intensified their attacks on Jews. Many Jewish artists and intellectuals committed suicide under these conditions.

and has no place to go. Perhaps you could think of something in New York? Would he have opportunities there, is there a union of artists willing to take care of poor Merkel? This is an important matter, please send me a couple words.

To Aaron Glantz-Leyeles
[Postcard, original in Yiddish]

June 8, 1938

Dear A. Leyeles,
After two months of wandering, the letter to Glatstein where I thank him for the books he had sent me and for the latest prose volume returned to my address. I rewrote his address from the parcels I had received from him. I am sending the letter once again to your address with a request to give it to the addressee. I am very grateful to you.

My update is that I am awaiting a vacation with the hope that I can finish my book of prose and perhaps also a collection of critical essays. In addition to the already written essays, I have drafted two new studies and an essay on Yiddish Modernism.

Is there any news about the poems and prose that I submitted?
Best wishes,
Debora Vogel

To Aaron Glantz-Leyeles
[Four pages, original in Yiddish]

Skole, September 2, 1938

Dear Glantz-Leyeles,
Now I owe you a reply. I hope for your discernment in matters which distance us from people, even those close to us whom we need. It always happens at the end of the year with its fatigue and depression, on a sweet gray morning, or on a solitary night, when a person understands that she is lonely. It makes no difference that this is an illusion: people are always there with their judgments and feelings about us, yet we sense once again a bitter scent of loneliness. People start feverishly reminding us of their existence—the great season of letters begins. My letter today is also under the sign of the great solitariness of summer.

You especially remind me about the inner solitude in each of us. Evaluating our situation in a cold and clear manner will result in striving or perhaps ceasing to write. We cannot deny this: nobody needs Yiddish literature. The intelligentsia, the only consumer of culture, is too far away from us, and the masses follow it, tread in its footsteps with their own argument of the "anti-rational." There is no hope that things will change, and here lie the difficulties, perhaps even the tragedy of the absolute absence of critics. If there were readers, critics would follow. (In contrast, our few exquisite readers are other poets.)

And yet we are the "agents"[88] of the law or idea, even though we don't have the necessary heroism—and nobody can demand it from us—to say, "It is bad for reality" when it doesn't agree with the idea.

Here it's a matter of life—singular and exemplary at the same time—which is squandered in the process. Let's not deny it, squandered.

And yet we must live. Only stoicism—a state of resignation which allows us to reach the specific balance and fatigue necessary for living a controlled, historically and dialectically justified life, even though a person lives anonymously before history as it were—may help us. In this responsible life, no moments and gestures will be lost without a reason. Even though there is no control through society and nobody expects anything from us, even though we live anonymously and full of sorrow.

Back to my case and our case—the case of the Modernists—of mutual escapes and fleeing from work: you reproach me for passivity. If I am to be honest with you, severe depression, with somatic causes perhaps, and a purely technical lack of time has not let me work of late. But there is something else: I publish also in the journals of half-scribblers, sometimes I even don't know where to publish at all. My place is defined, or, according to alternative opinions, lost (even if the "others" wanted to have me among themselves); my world loses its potentialities. And I am critical enough to be able see that, and sensible enough to be colder or broken.

Nevertheless, I am not silent. I gave a few talks on Modernism and other topics (even here in Skole where I spent the summer at a workers' organization). Now I would like to put it in writing. It will be a longer study, with systematic theoretical and literary historical parts.

I need to make one more thing clear: I don't systematize, I am not a historian either. Historical material, as I see it, is rather an example and proof for theoretical formulations—a thing itself to be analyzed. I would like to be the analytic.

What concerns the diversity of names I used, with which you have reproached me: many names are mentioned in general *ex negativo* (for instance,

---

88 See Karolina Szymaniak's monograph *Być agentem wiecznej idei. Przemiany poglądów estetycznych Debory* Vogel [To be an agent of an eternal idea: Modifications of Debora Vogel's aesthetic views] (Kraków: Universitas, 2006).

Feinberg,[89] Weinper), and a part *ex negativo* along with the theme of "urbanism"— where the name emerges simultaneously with the development of Modernism and, where, from a purely thematic viewpoint, one should consider all the poets who treated the city as a theme. Here rightfully belong not only contemporary poets, but also the Impressionists with Reuben Iceland's, Neugroschel's, and Shternberg's ("The City in Profile") discussion of city themes. I defined the group as pioneers and predecessors—unconscious and not programmatic, perhaps even against their own program—of urbanist expression. If one wants to be a literary historian, one must be objective and distance oneself from likes and dislikes. I allocated the most space to the programmatic Modernists, citing their theoretical views and poems (yours, Minkoff's,[90] Likht's), I also quoted a lot of poems. If you look at it more closely, perhaps you will change your verdict to a lighter one.

Until today I have not received the issue 54 of *In zikh* with my published poems. It is an unpleasant thing when relevant "documentary" poems need to wait for so long until they receive a little bit of publicity.

I want to send you the new texts soon. I would like to finish my book of prose and perhaps publish it this winter.

I spent two months in the mountains and I feel stronger, strong enough to combat myself.

I would like to use the occasion and thank Glatstein for his wonderful letter, which I received as a reply to my letter travelling over the oceans and back for two months. I would like to write to him at the earliest opportunity.

Best greetings to you and all the Introspectivists: Debora Vogel

PS: Do you know the fate of the poet Neugroschel who is interned in Dachau (or was interned there)? After the *Anschluss*? Can the American-Yiddish PEN club do something? I am powerless, and I don't know if somebody here has done anything. It's critical to take action; he is a person with very fragile health and extremely psychologically sensitive.

D.V.

---

89 Leonid Feinberg (1897–1969) was a Russian Jewish poet born in Odessa. Since 1922 he lived in New York.
90 Mikhl Likht (1893–1953) was a Yiddish poet and essayist. He lived in New York since 1913. He started out writing and publishing in English. He published three collections in Yiddish: *Egoemen un andere lider* [Egoemen and other poems] (New York: Gelye, 1922); *Vazon* [Vessel] (New York: Gelye, 1928); and *Protsesyes un andere lider* [Processions and other poems] (New York: Gelye, 1932). He was a prolific translator of the work of Anglo-American Modernists into Yiddish.

To Aaron Glantz-Leyeles
[Two pages, handwritten, original in Yiddish]

May 23, 1939

Dear A. Leyeles,

I have not responded. Please forgive me. I haven't thanked you for the 50th issue of *In zikh*, even though I received it twice. I have also not sent my greetings for your 50th birthday, which I am doing only now. Yiddish literature has a great need for people like you. I am amazed by your constant readiness and responsible conscientiousness. This observation arises in part because I also have this quality, yet I cannot express it as fully as you do because—I say this carefully—I have had the unhappy fortune of being a woman. "The metaphysical" role of a woman is blurred in the flow of stressful details. The female professional occupation which is rewarded with ludicrous compensation—a sum which could be earned for two essays a month—is exhausting. Male competition does not allow a woman to earn a living by writing for a newspaper (in some newspapers, even dull scribblers are compensated, while women's labor is unpaid and only acknowledged with honors). But let us talk about things which are more interesting.

Upon reading the advertisement for the next issue of *In zikh* devoted to your work, it became clear to me that it is a good opportunity to publish something about you. And if the issue is not to be published too quickly, I would like to submit the essay "The Metaphor of A. Glantz-Leyeles"—a fragment of a larger and not yet finished work. I am also sending you a poem, one of many which editors are afraid to publish here in Poland because of its "pacifist tendency." In fact, I worry about the fate of my planned poetry collection which resolutely moves in this "dangerous" direction.

I am happy about *In zikh*'s publication. (I have already received issue 51). At the same time, I am a little saddened by its somewhat eclectic character. Perhaps I am not correct and now is not the time to make demands, yet my strong yearning for uniformity and style suggests that only stylistically exquisite works should qualify even if the journal loses popularity. What is popularity, fame, and being known in wider circles compared to the proud and sweet feeling that you are right and thanks to wonderful luck you have found life's golden mean? Please don't misunderstand me: I am far from advocating a hermetic closing off from wider circles of readers—however, not at the cost of the stylistic excess.

In the last issue, *In zikh* comes close to a literary magazine where everything may find a home at the expense of quality. I must confess that to find myself in the same issue with my opponents aroused a strong mood of sorrow in me. As the one who joined later, I would be much happier to see my name added to the initial circle of the Introspectivists with Glatstein, Minkoff, Likht, Kuperman,[91] and others, among the true spiritual elite of Yiddish poetry. I am also certain that after some time you will return to proven people, and in attracting groups of younger poets, you will become stricter. Please forgive me: I offer unsolicited criticism here. I consider myself "an ambassador" of Modernism in Poland, and too closely tied with the journal not to feel responsible for its profile.

I have been writing a little lately. I would like to publish a poetry collection and a book of montages this fall. This fall … if something else doesn't happen. …

Warmest greetings to you and all the acquaintances.

Special greetings to S. Bikl with whom I have corresponded for a short time.

Your Debora Vogel

To Aaron Glantz-Leyeles
[Postcard, handwritten, original in Yiddish]

Mr. A. Glantz-Leyeles	Poland
c/o "The Day"	Dr. Debora Vogel
183 East Broadway	Lviv
New York	apt. 1 bld. 18 Leśna
USA	

Skole, July 23, 1939

Dear A. Leyeles,

Again long weeks have passed by since I last wrote to you. It was a long letter and XXXX[92] a poem, which was very close to me, and which I really wanted to publish. For certain reasons, it cannot be published in our country now. It was to be published in *Morgn* in Lviv, where I publish from time to time at moments of sharp loneliness, when "it doesn't matter anymore"—moments which cannot withstand the criticism of a venue like today's *Morgn*.

Here, among the light-blue mountains where I am staying with my son for two weeks (by the way, he is three and already wants to rhyme), I have tragic pacifist poems with strange and somewhat cheerful titles like "Potato Blossoms in 1939" and "Mountains in 1939."[93] I don't know how to put aside my protest, which stifles my activity. We must ask together with Kulbak:

---

91 Eliezer Pinkhas Kuperman (1883?–1949) was a Romanian Yiddish author.
92 The postcard is damaged here.
93 Manuscripts of these poems were not found.

"What can I do with my hand, the unnecessary one, or with my superfluous heart?"[94]

Until now I couldn't make myself do critical work. Now, already a bit saturated with colors and smells, I would like to try. I promised *Literarishe bleter* a few essays about Modernism. Please write something about *In zikh*.

Greetings to friends and to enemies
Warmest,
Your Debora Vogel

To Marcus Ehrenpreis
[Postcard, handwritten, original in German]
Prof. Marcus Ehrenpreis
Stockholm
6 Grevmagnigatan
Sweden, Sverige
Via Moscow

Lviv, August 3, 1940

My dearest,
We are always happy to receive a sign of life from you. You are an island of normal life which Europe no longer knows. I am on vacation right now. I am spending time in the Kaiserwald[95] which has lost the last traces of the forest this winter, and at work. This year I already need to teach in Ukrainian in my school. I am learning a little. Shalom never comes home in the afternoon, he eats only at 9:00 p.m. Mom keeps calm.

Greetings to all of you. Dosia

---

94 Compare with "White Words in Poetry."
95 The park in Vogel's hometown. Vogel lived near the entrance to the park.

Part Five

"Distilling the Figure of Thought": Reviews and Polemics around Vogel's Work

Reviews of *Day Figures* (1930) and *Mannequins* (1934)

29

Ber Shnaper,[1] "Cards on the Table: On Poetry, the Market, and Stereotypes (A Few Remarks on the New Poetry Collection)" (1930)[2]

Debora Vogel's poetry collection *Day Figures* was published a few months ago in Lviv. Besides a couple of reviews in the local press, the book went fully unnoticed (at least until now). Yet, the book was discussed backstage. Two camps formed there—a small group of supporters and a crowd of bitter "detractors"—the usual fate of a book born in unfortunate times (according to our criteria, "fortune" also means the condition for success). However, this case is also interesting in a different regard.

Day Figures is an experiment, the poetic equivalent to the new forms in contemporary painting, a daring and successful attempt at a new kind of poetry. Notably, the book is ignored or angrily rejected precisely as such an attempt.

There were times when every successful and even unsuccessful piece of work was received with enthusiasm, every new "-ism" was celebrated with drums and trumpets. Now, the response to the book was very limited and quiet, so quiet that one could even hear the grass grow. And grass grows without any obstacles until now. Our entire young poetry is overgrown with grass right now … there is no new expression … or new color, everything is established and solidified into one clichéd pattern.

Cliché instead of form. Marketability instead of personal expression. And when a great talent strives for something new, powerful, and singular (for

---

1 Ber Shnaper was a Yiddish Galician poet. He was one of the poets affiliated with *Tsushtayer*.
2 See B. Sh. [Ber Shnaper], "In ofene kortn. Vegn dikhtung, koniunktur un shablon (oyfn rand fun a nay bikhl poezie)," *Der Morgn* 4, no. 1121 (1930): 11.

example, Rokhl Korn, or Manger),[3] their environment influences them more strongly than they act upon it. And we simply become "enriched" by one more model to be copied not only by imitators but also by creative minds. In such an environment, they imitate and simply repeat that which has already been said and given.

The result of this or perhaps even a cause for it is the unification of personal style among our younger poets. If you gathered twenty-some young Yiddish poets from Poland and published them under one name, you can bet that even a great connoisseur would not notice that the poems have different authors. So little do the authors differ from one another, so minimal are the differences in subject matter, form, and style. This new poetry industry does not work in a vacuum. A person knows what the market requires, and he supplies that. If what "fits" needs to be "descriptive," then everyone becomes "descriptive," if to be "proletarian" is in vogue, then everyone today is "proletarian" tomorrow. Long live the market? Long live the white terror of universal dogmas!

One measure for all, one recipe for all!

So it is no wonder that every deviation from this wide, comfortable, beaten path, every single detour is scorned, mocked, and disdained, either by poets or "critics," and by our few readers. And Debora Vogel's poems have the courage not to follow the wide road of the market, or as others may think, they learn to go their own separate way. They go alone, using their own power, carrying their own responsibility. And we have already unlearned that. We have become too lazy to think, too passive to experiment and to ask ourselves maybe we should try?

It is called shrinking back from discomfort and from creating a new way in. It is the fear of life.

---

3   Itsik Manger (1901–1969) was one of the most famous Yiddish poets. He was born in Czernowitz and died in Israel. He combined European and Jewish motifs in his work, especially when writing ballads. He is best known for his collections *Itsik's Midrash* and *Songs of the Megillah*.

30

Itsik Shvarts,[1] "Modernist Poetry (On Debora Vogel's *Day Figures: Poems*. Lviv: Tsushtayer, 1930)"[2]

1

The artist of the twentieth century "feels bad." Troubled by the passage of social conflicts, nervous because of the tumultuous chaos of large cities, bewildered by highly-developed mechanization and the Americanization of life, immersed in herself due to a lack of contact with the masses whose feedback she needs, disappointed by the belittling of art by the social classes in whose hands—she believes—culture finds itself, she stands helpless and confused. To find her place, she seeks new roads and ways towards clarity in the world, in the world's reflection within, and in expression.

Dramatic Futurism—from Marinetti to ... Mayakovsky—anti-logical stammering Dadaism (T. Tzara)—intuitive Expressionism, Imagism, integrating Constructivism, inquiring Surrealism (Louis Aragon and others), whose followers have lately transitioned to proletarian literature and its earnest endeavors to feel the pulse of life and be united with mass readers with their most urgent interests and strivings, and to become an expression of search and experimentation, of ways and detours by artists in our times.

---

1   Itsik Shvarts (1906–2001) was a Romanian Yiddish writer, folklorist, and the director of the Iassy Yiddish theater. He studied in Czernowitz during the 1920s and launched his literary career in the same period. He was a close friend of Itsik Manger. Together with Hirsh Segal, a professor of mathematics in Czernowitz, I. Shvarts lead a seminar on the Yiddish literature which Vogel mentions in her letters.
2   See Itsik Shvarts, "Modernistishe dikhtung (vegn Debora Vogel 'tog figurn.' Lider farlag tsushtayer lemberg 1930)," *Tshernovitser bleter*, no. 190 (1934): 3.

One of the roads of the new Yiddish poetry is Modernism—Yehoash,[3] with Symbolist influences in his latest works, Di Yunge[4] (Leyvik, M. L. Halpern, and others), Glatstein's matter-of-fact Modernist lyric. "Modern" here means topical, renewed, while "Modernist" means "defiant"—to be completely different from what one has been until now—at any price—even if the results are absurd. In part, it means to outshout and contradict oneself. Within Modernist movements there is Futurism—from Broderzon[5] to Lutski,[6] Di Khalyastre,[7] and the proletarian poster-worthy poetry of part of the Frayhayt-Hamer group[8] (for instance, A. Kurtz).[9]

Dadaism, Constructivism, and the like were rare guests in our literature, and Cubism likewise. Hence our interest in Debora Vogel's poetic experiment to create a Yiddish Cubist lyric. A singular and to a large extent a successful experiment. "Lyric is nourished by the most concealed experiences of the soul. ... The effect is created through rhythmic-musical form. ... With poetry's idea

---

3   Yehoash (pseudonym of Solomon Blumgarten; 1872–1927) was a Yiddish poet and translator who is best known for undertaking a monumental translation of the Bible into modern and idiomatic Yiddish.
4   Di Yunge was a group of American-Yiddish poets founded in 1907. These writers advocated for art for art's sake and pursuit of the mood ("*shtimung*") while rejecting the poetry of the Sweatshop poet generation that preceded them.
5   Moyshe Broderzon (1890–1956) was a Yiddish writer and playwright who lived in Moscow and Łódź. He was one of the founders of the group Yung-Yidish in Łódź.
6   A. Lutski (pseudonym of Aaron Zucker; 1894–1957) was a Yiddish writer from Volhynia in Ukraine who later lived in New York. He published his poetry in *Forverts, Fraye Arbeter Shtime, In Zikh, Tsukunft,* and *Di goldene keyt*. His most well-known poetry collection is *Bereyshis-Inmitn* (*Mid-Genesis*, 1932). Known for his unique style, he often animated the inanimate things in his poems.
7   Di Khalyastre [The gang] was a Yiddish Expressionist group in Poland between 1919 and 1924. Moyshe Broderzon's poem which starts with the line, "Mir yungen, mir a freylekhe tsezungene khalyastre" [We, the young, a happy, boisterous gang] became a motto for the group that used provocative recitals, journals and graphic work to advance their Expressionist aesthetic.
8   "Frayhayt-Hamer": Proletpen group of Yiddish writers active in the 1920s published in venues with a Communist bent like *Frayhayt* and *Der hamer*. Proletpen writers wrote about social problems of their time like poverty and racism. Debora Vogel mentioned Proletpen writers Zishe Weinper and Moyshe Nadir in her essay "First Yiddish Poets." For more on Proletpen writers, see Amelia Glaser, David Weintraub, Yankl Salant, Dana Craft, and Dovid Katz, *Proletpen: America's Rebel Yiddish Poets* (Madison: University of Wisconsin Press, 2005).
9   Aaron Kurtz (1891–1964) was a Yiddish poet. Originally from Belarus, he emigrated to the US and lived in Philadelphia and New York among other places. He rejected the Introspectivist poetry as well as Socialist Realism. He became a member of the Communist party and wrote in leftist organs like *Der hamer* [The hammer].

content, form-building rhythm completely changed," writes M. Shats-Ansky[10] in his greatly intriguing work "*From Space to Time.*" The complete course of modern poetry exemplifies this well.

2

And the helpless tin figures are sketched
on the flat sign of the world.[11]

"Cubism analyzes and synthesizes all phenomena in the scientific-geometrical forms of pyramids and cubes." In Cubist painting (Piccaso), the literary idea plays a great role. In literature, especially in Yiddish literature, Cubism rarely makes an appearance. In the preface the poet formulates her view on art, "Simplifying the seeming multiplicity of events and reducing them to a few simple, angular and repetitive gestures—to monotony and cool stasis—is a tendency in Cubism in general."[12]

"Such simplification originates in the realization that complexity and multiplicity are simply an addition and a superstructure. However, a schematic figure contains the unchangeable."[13] The poet is true to her vision in the whole book. This geometrical schematization, stylization, the charm in the plots of poems—descriptive, two-dimensional sketches—where the mood is created completely indirectly—through the eye, through (or in spite of) evocations of stylization. The themes and the titles of the poems already demonstrate this—"Cross Section," "Still Life in Glass," "Autumn Sketch," "A Poem about Colors," and so on.

Geometrical stylizations (not only the surfaces but also volumes) appear also in Constructivism. But it is dynamic, explosive, full of zest for life, unrest, and drive. Debora Vogel's Cubism, however, is "a lyric of cool stasis and geometrical ornamentality with its monotony and rhythm of return. This lyric may replace dynamism, or melodiousness, which until recently has been regarded as the single principle in poetry."[14] In a purely geometrical-schematic and coagulated sense, we see the world purely externally, purely ornamental—where a person and every living being is made "thing-like," where events are "cooled

---

10 The name should be M. Shats-Anin (1885–1975). The reference here is to his book, *Fun Roym tsu tsayt: gedanken tsu a kulturfilozofye* (Rige: Arbeterheym, 1922).
11 See Debora Vogel's poem "Signs with Kerosene Bottles," p. 170.
12 See Debora Vogel's preface to the *Day Figures* collection, p. 123.
13 Ibidem.
14 See Debora Vogel's preface to the *Day Figures* collection, p. 124.

like glass," a clear approach to life is apparent—passive contemplation and distancing from the boiling pot of socio-individual struggles, a withdrawal into what Alfred de Vigny called the "ivory tower." Her Cubism exhibits pure play, even though the poet assures us that the poems are not an artificial experiment: "Such a formal attempt is a necessity, attained and purchased by the trials of life."[15] Is it still a formal experiment?

Debora Vogel deals with a limited number of figures and colors—gray rectangles, glass spheres, yellow triangles, angles, and that's all. Surfaces and colors each have their own meaning like in Mallarme's work ("the sounds, the colors, the smells mix"), "The cherry red is long. It carries the history of waiting" (waiting is a restricted feeling which often appears in the author's poetry). "The orange red is round and deep" ... "The citrus yellow is the color of flat coolness. / It extinguishes stuffy elliptical lamps of waiting / and round lamps of murky abandonment. / With a rectangular glass pane of gray days." "A Poem of Colors" [p. 56 in the original] is almost an explanation of a deeper sense of colors. In this regard, "A Colors-Poem in Summer" is characteristic.

The poet uses the materials of a bookbinder or a magician: paper, cardboard, wood, clay, tin, glue. And every material bears a particular smile. Materials carry their singular life while living things become "material-like." "The paper is flat and light."[16] "The faces of the shoemaker and barber mannequins"[17] are made from paper, "and the figures of retired officers"[18] ... "The milk is stiff, watery and sweet, like paper."[19] The poet likes those "materials" (the title of one of the poems) whose life she has discovered. "You can live like porcelain and like wood, like flat paper and old wily tin."[20] She dedicates a lot of poems to tin—and to materials in general ("Metal," "Tinsmith," "A Sign with Oranges," and the like). To represent monotony and ornamental, monotonous rhythm, the author uses the juxtaposition of numbers and of repetition: "One gray house. / The second gray house. / A third and fourth gray house. / Go together / one day. A second day. / 7 weekdays long" ("Gray Houses").

The moods are: waiting, hopeless waiting, resignation: "Every evening my body becomes / a porcelain vase wanting to spill the fragrant oil / of its longing. / And when no one comes / the waiting slowly trickles out, / until the very last

---

15 Ibidem, p. 124.
16 See Debora Vogel's poem "A Panorama of Paper Figures," p. 165.
17 Ibidem.
18 Ibid., p. 166.
19 See Debora Vogel's "A Poem about Milk," p. 167.
20 See Debora Vogel's poem "Materials," p. 173.

drop" [p. 48 in the original]. When the poem comes close to the purely urban lyric of "matter-of-factness" with its sparse Cubist stylization, like, for instance, her very successful poem "Suburban houses" [p. 16 in the original].

Of course, there is a lot of density, intellect, intellectual work in this type of poetry (also typographical techniques, among others). However, lyric is a "stylized emotion" and who has the right to say how far stylization can go and how far it may reach? In its impulse to depart from the banal, the worn-out which awakens few associations in us, is the poet not allowed to look for new ways, to experiment? The main thing is the earnestness of the artist regarding herself, her talent, and life.

This way of constructing a contrived world for oneself, without any ordinary life, without the slightest echo of the breath of our restless era, hollowed-out from any societal content, is not so close to us. This points to the intentionally removed sense of our reality—because Debora Vogel's Cubism is not only a formal experiment, but a whole take on the sense, value, and task of poetry.

This simple melancholy view of reality under the angle of geometrical ornamentality can serve as a breather between freeing oneself from old, worn-out art forms and conventional, false content, and accepting the new, integral outlook of art, and of art in the world, as well as their mutual effects, both artistic and societal.

Underway, there are more or less successful searches for form, justified and desirable for the new unstable life states, corresponding forms, new expressions, new realities.

31

Ber Shnaper, "The Lyric of Cool Stasis" (1935)[1]

There is no other poet like Debora Vogel, whose poetry needs an explanation I wish to provide here. Not just any commentary, in which anyone can find something they want to emphasize, but an unequivocal, clear, and comprehensible interpretation is necessary, or better put, a criterion without which the poems sound like a "world of barricades," a web of words, without any sense or narrative, a hieroglyphic writing of sorts which at best only the experts—poetic "Egyptologists"—can decipher.

Vogel's poems are pure experiments and you should view them as such when you approach them to examine their spiritual and emotional content. In the preface to the poetry collection, the poet herself admits, "I consider my poetry to be an attempt at a new style. I find analogies to modern painting in these poems."[2] These poems are a certain poetic counterpart to the new forms in modern visual arts. One must admit, it is a daring, and a very thorough attempt at a new form of poetry, a poetry of "cool stasis."[3]

In a range of constructions made from ordinary words—"white words" as the poet describes them—Vogel attempts to hold on to her worldview, in which everything is about number, measure, and calculation. The multiplicity and colorfulness of what we call "our life" is reduced to the utmost facticity; it is only an addition, a "superstructure" to the single existing life scheme of monotony! Monotony, as it were, is the immutable and immobile, the stable and static in life. It only simulates the multiplicity and fullness of things and events, facts and occurrences, which take place on the static stage of life. In reality, they are strongly reduced, stable, and constantly repeated; their eternal resonance supplies us with an illusion of multiplicity and colorfulness, movement and occurrences—an illusion of dynamism!

---

1 See Ber Shnaper, "Di lirik fun kile statik," *Literarishe bleter* 12, no. 40 (1935): 642.
2 See Debora Vogel's preface to *Day Figures* collection, p. 123.
3 Ibidem.

And when that which is dynamic—the active and the lively aspect of our lives—is no more than an illusion, a "world as will and representation," art which depicts such a life, the illusory and false, does away with dynamism and turns back to the immobile and the unchangeable, that which is passive and dead at a first glance, and yet, in fact, is all that lives and moves—to the principle of stasis!

Together with Debora Vogel, we ask ourselves and answer in the following way, What is "life," our life? It is a distant, empty, monotonous surface, a tabula rasa, where something "happens"; changing multiplicity, colorfulness, and fantasticality are nothing more than repetitions of the same limited events or encounters in their different constellations. The chaotic multiplicity and fantasticality of our life today is nothing but a piece of ornament, an arabesque, a kind of baroque addition; flesh on the skeleton of life reduced to the minimum, the utmost layer of life material—revealed as an ordinary geometrical, or stereometrical figure: a line, square, rectangle, circle, ellipse, etc.

This is the philosophical background on which Debora Vogel builds her aesthetic program. The method which she utilizes in her poetic constructions (not poems) obviously coincides with her artistic demands—they are analogous to the contemporary poetry which depicts not things but rather a principle, the law, according to which things exist, reduced to painterly matter. Debora Vogel wishes to free poetry from literariness and perhaps also from themes, treating it only as a construction from word material.

Modernist poetry has not been the only attempt to free itself fully from literary content, from concrete materiality, and consider itself exclusively as construction from word material. And, as we see, it has been to no avail. Dadaism, Formism,[4] Constructivism, and—to a certain extent in our literature—Introspectivism did not understand that to become more deeply rooted in poetry all attempts to treat words or word complexes in a sentence as only material and not as expression, only as the shell of thoughts, feelings, views, or representations, often led to unsuccessful, often intellectually prepared mechanisms of poetry, to a type of a poetic homunculus which lacked only one small detail: life!

Will Debora Vogel animate that which is dead? Her two poetry collections have needed to show that this kind of lyric is possible. Indeed, a person must be aesthetically overly refined and "have had enough" of all these old-new styles

---

[4] Formism (previously known as Polish Expressionism) was an avant-garde movement which lasted from 1917 until 1922. Formism valued form over content. It moved away from realist tendencies in art.

in art, which barely function even to today, to be awakened by the freshness of such constructions and to wonder with the poet: "And the wonder is that space could be fit into the boundaries of construction with very little—a couple of simple elements."⁵ And further, "since the number of stable things is limited, and their structure is very simple, the poetry which utilizes them can appear 'impoverished and cold.'"⁶ Debora Vogel acknowledges, the "new elements in art are not yet overgrown with associations, however, they almost always possess naturalistic elements. Perhaps the impression of the impoverishment and dryness of simple constructions stems from this. And yet, the frequent use of geometrical elements in art also enriches them with necessary associations, and these elements will also one day become 'colorful' and 'melodious.'"⁷

Therefore, what is lacking in her poems—the poet herself confirms it as you can see—are "necessary associations."⁸ Once they appear, her poems are no longer "impoverished" and "cold," but "colorful" and "melodious"—the question is whether they still remain "static."

Perhaps Debora Vogel makes a fundamental mistake here. Every artistic sphere is a territory with laws and solid boundaries. And the smuggling of painterly categories into poetry is strictly punishable. In fact, perhaps a person can paint this way: "a vertical line between two objects expresses the same thing as the tree with two bodies on two sides did before."⁹ The word, however, is no line, or rather the word itself is already an addition, it is a designation for something which exists from before, vibrates, and is full of movement—dynamism. And expressing stasis through dynamism is already out of the question.

Therefore the "static word" cannot be truly painted, since the combination of these two notions is already a paradox. Even though the New Testament begins with the following words, "In the beginning was the Word" (John 1:1), it is nevertheless a secondary phenomenon and, thus, belongs to the "superstructure" of our life. Since we can only enjoy life, whether in art or in reality, as a prepared raw material, not as a surrogate, not in its simple, or simplified, limited elements; and not in its schematism and its static durability, only as colorful and melodious, and only in its multiplicity of the difficult and fantastic and—dynamic!

---

5   This quote is from the preface to *Day Figures*, p. 10.
6   See Debora Vogel's essay "White Words in Poetry," p. 7.
7   See Debora Vogel's essay "White Words in Poetry," p. 11.
8   Ibidem, p. 11.
9   Ibidem, p. 3.

32

Joshue Rapoport, "The Apotheosis of Monotony" (1935)[1]

Debora Vogel would like to be a trailblazer. She is one, regardless of how negatively her attempt to create a new style in poetry—to transplant the Cubist-Futurist formal experiments into Yiddish—is perceived. It should be noted that we have a serious attempt here, undertaken by a person who knows what she wants, can defend her artistic ideas, and attempts to dress them in tidy clothes fitting for her art theory. One should fight against Debora Vogel's attempt, yet one shouldn't discard the author's explanation: "I consider my poetry to be an attempt at a new style. I find analogies to modern painting in these poems."[2]

Yet this explanation requires a small correction. … Debora Vogel did not accidentally find analogies to modern painting in her poems. Rather, she consciously created her new poetic style as equivalent to modern painting. Her poems are attempts to solve painterly tasks in words. Debora Vogel would like to reduce the word to the level of colors and lines—to the level of bare material. She complains that the word is "too strongly bound to rationalized life; it is too much of a carrier and mediator of needs and orientations in life."[3] It is undoubtedly unnatural when Debora Vogel would like the word to take on "the role of line and color."[4] However, Debora Vogel tears herself apart and invests lots of intelligence, ability, and even talent in this hopeless struggle.

The essays by Debora Vogel in the Lviv quarterly *Tsushtayer*, the author's preface to her poetry collection and, above all, her poetry shows that we are dealing not only with a connoisseur of modern painting but with someone who

---

1   See Rapoport, "Apoteoz fun monotonye": 4–5. Also in Joshue Rapoport, *Tropns gloybn (mayn antologye)* (Melbourne: Byalistoker tsentr, 1948), 36–43.
2   See the preface to *Day Figures* in this volume, p. 123.
3   Ibidem, 123.
4   Ibidem, 123.

thinks and perceives life in painterly categories. Most of her poems leave the impression that Debora Vogel thinks in lines and colors. Her thoughts concretize in linear figures and colorful surfaces. Since the arsenal of the purely painterly element is very limited, Debora Vogel attempts to limit the multiplicity of life—the object of her poetry: "this simplification originates in the realization that complexity and multiplicity are simply an addition and a superstructure. However, the schematic geometrical figure contains that which is unchangeable. … The geometrical figure is the principle of monotony with its repetition of one contour. A new type of lyric can arise in this way—a lyric of cool stasis and geometrical ornamentality, with its monotony and rhythm of return. This lyric may replace the dynamism, or the melodiousness, which until recently has been regarded as the single principle in poetry."[5]

The preface—so necessary to understand the book—is the preface written in Debora Vogel's style. This short preface includes only algebraic formulae and exercises which the poems try to solve. Remarkably, the solutions to the proposed problems are very successful—as logical absurdities of sorts.

Debora Vogel would like to justify her attempt to create a new style in poetry, or rather—to theorize it. She says, "Gradually, boredom can be a style. This means that form combinations of a certain kind become exhausted. … Thus, they say, that a worldview has become exhausted—it has reached its end. Boredom comes in this way: the fact of life and the combination of forms do not possess the rhythm and the excitement of experiences anymore. Without boredom, any attempt at a new style is incomprehensible. Here lies the origin of my poems."[6]

Evidently, Debora Vogel connects the exhaustion of form combinations with the erosion and transformation of the worldview. However, it is not clear what is the cause and what the result, the essence and the byproduct for Debora Vogel, that is why there is talk of boredom.

Every change in the world or the feeling of life in a person calls for a transformation in the forms of expression. Whoever feels the burden of the old contents and replaces them with the novel ones is the only one who could make the urge for form fruitful. Only under the pressure of the new content, the new form can arise. However, when one does not sense the burden of the old content but only the boredom of worn forms, then search for form is doomed to yield no results. The new fruitful style does not originate in the boredom but

---

5   Ibidem, pp. 123–124.
6   Ibidem, p. 123.

in the new content, the new rising abundance. Searching for form for its own sake may be even more boring than the dull—old and exhausted—forms. All the Cubist and Futurist formal searches in painting and in poetry demonstrated this point. Rabindranath Tagore writes in a poem: "No, it is not for you to open up the buds as flowers. / The bud trembles, beats, it is not in your power to make it bloom ... The one who can open the bud, does it easily. / He sends it his glance, and the juice of life flows through its veins. ..."

To carry out her experiment of artificially creating a new style in poetry—the lyric of stasis instead of dynamism—Debora Vogel executes an operation of the simplification on life. She reduces the diversity of life to the geometrical figures or negates the dynamic abundance in favor of the static monotony. However, life is only viable in its dynamism, the same goes for poetry—the most intimate expression of life is purely dynamic.

In abstract terms, Debora Vogel is correct. The multiplicity of life is only an "addition and a superstructure," while a couple of "lasting elements," "a couple of angular, unhewn blocks of situations"[7] form the foundation for all of life. Yet between this theoretical truth and the truth of the real life there is the same boundary as between the Schopenhauer's metaphysics of love and love in reality.

Schopenhauer is right in his metaphysics of love—love is simply a means to an end to fertilize nature.[8] However, on the journey from the means to the end there blooms one of the most beautiful blossoms in human life, love, crowned by both the means and the end, and autonomous in its abstractly correct relation. What is the painting of a great artist? It is merely the canvas and the dashes of color. However, the superstructure of these two principal elements is more than the abstractly right truth. In fact, the painting is nothing more than the canvas and the paints, however, art is added to the mix; it changes these limited and always similar elements into a multiplicity which neither the canvass nor the colors abolish. The superstructure becomes the essential thing. Who is our neighbor? He consists of the materials in certain quantities. That may well be true. However, the person in general, especially our neighbor, is worth a million times more than the limited components which comprise his body, he

---

7   Ibidem, p. 124.
8   Compare "Metaphysik der Geschlechtsliebe," in Schopenhauer, "Metaphysik der Geschlechtsliebe," in *Die Welt als Wille. Zürcher Ausgabe. Werke in zehn Bänden*, vol. 4 (Zürich: Diogenes, 1977), 621–665.

is completely different. The same goes for life and poetry. Statistically, Debora Vogel is right that life and poetry become life and poetry proper only when the static becomes dynamic, and a limited number of the monotonous arch-elements become colorful, exciting, mobile, and rich.

Debora Vogel's poem "Weariness" is not only typical for the poet's principal perception towards life—everything is monotonous, boring, hopeless—but also for her poetry, which must be monotonous, boring, hopeless because it turns around particular geometrical figures like a horse on the racing track. Debora Vogel's writes,

> Years do not count.
> Only days are there:
> a single day that returns a thousand times.[9]

The same is true of her poems. We may write:

> Poems do not count.
> Only the motif of boredom is there:
> a single motif that returns a thousand times.

The geometrical figures of various colors on the palette are truly the main affinity in Debora Vogel's poems. Only on the first seven pages of the book, I counted that the word "rectangle" appears eleven times. I didn't have more patience to count further: it was boring. The pages also teem with triangles, quadrangles, ellipses, cubes, circles. A square is also a frequent guest. All this is combined in various hues of color. The interpretation of the geometrical figures and colors is often very successful and vivid (Debora Vogel does not do away with her opponent—the metaphorical style which infuses her constructions with life): days are as "fantastical as ellipses,"[10] "streets are as dull as circles,"[11] and similar sentences are fine and quite pictorial. The same should be noted about Debora Vogel's perception of the essence of color nuances. However, when she fits the whole multiplicity of the world and life—days, nights, space, houses, streets, people, love, yearning—into these colorful geometrical figures, when she would like to convince us for the thousandth time that "a square

---

9   The quotation is from the poem "Weariness," p. 148.
10   The quotation is from the poem "Spheres of Glass," p. 172.
11   Ibidem.

surface of sweet monotony is life, is the world,"[12] then we find that it is narrow, boring, and tiring within the frame of this volume.

Most titles of these poems refer to their painterly-theoretical sources: "Still Life in Cold," "White Squares," "Still Life in Glass," "Flat Afternoon Décor with People," etc. We have a feeling that we find ourselves in front of the props for the puppet show:

> ... the same color as the streets
> where everything is always the same.
> ... The color of aimless strolls
> with multiple returns.[13]
>
> And nothing comes.
> How many times have the sprouts sprung up
> how many times the white paper days arrived.[14]
>
> Seven times the four-sided figure comes.
> You ask again ...
> why lift your feet, why lift hands.[15]

And this feeling is very accurate. In an artificial world without fresh air, you don't want to lift hands or feet: they wither.

In the book's seventy pages, one can find hundreds of quotes like the ones above because most of the poems consist of such lines. The number of words, colors, comparisons, feelings is limited. They are repeated. The poems are monotonous like the monotony they depict, which they would like to impose on us. They reach this aim. The harmony between Debora Vogel's view of art and the effect of her poems is surely an expression of poetic talent—also apparent in the beautiful and impressive lines and stanzas—used in a losing battle against the arch-sense of the human word and poetry. The poet wants to petrify the colorful dynamism of life and compress the free air of the world of feelings into certain prepared formulas and static notions, which is reflected in her poems. They are so cold, strange, and unnatural like their mother—an artificial

---

12 The quotation is from the first poem in *Day Figures*, in the *Mannequins* collection, p. 177.
13 The quotation is from the poem "Autumn Décor with People," p. 132. The order of the stanzas is different from the original.
14 This is a quote from the poem "Cross-Section," p. 127.
15 The quote is from the poem "White Squares," p. 128.

attempt to create a new lyric. When Debora Vogel writes the following—these lines are chosen accidentally—it is pure rhetoric which may be true or not true of a thousand other things at the same time:

> Yellow spheres of voluminous lamps which between bronze-red leaves
> are like long sighs, a remainder of days
> fantastical as ellipses.[16]

We hope that Debora Vogel will be content with her brave poetic-non-poetic caprice, and if she should stubbornly remain in her monotonous worldview, she could at least express this worldview in a poetic form which would make us empathize for her painful world, rather than become victims of the monotony.

---

16 The quote is from the "Spheres of Glass," p. 172.

33

J. A. Weisman,[1] "Debora Vogel and Her Monotony" (1935)[2]

If one should put together a lexicon of Debora Vogel's language, I am not sure that one would be able to fill out a page in the usual format. Besides, there would be a need for an appendix for the foreign words. Between Debora Vogel and contemporary poetry is an abyss which she cannot yet cross.

It is a pity that the mission of contemporary Yiddish poetry in this country, and of prose to a certain extent, is to shake up the baggage of linguistic clichés with new word associations and experiments. While Yiddish has been living for so many centuries, its linguistic and poetic achievements are vague and raw. When a poet with a fresh approach to image and form appears on the scene, he doesn't have anyone from whom to "inherit" in his own tradition.

And tradition is greatly important. The artist creates the best poem not on his own, but on the soil of his poetic or artistic era. The poet is only the one who executes: he plucks the poem from non-artistic chaos and serves it to literature on the tablet of gopher wood. The tablet is heritage, and, naturally, also the milieu. We learn that poems by Debora Vogel published in this issue of *In zikh*, like "the Legend of Silver,"[3] are expressions of a new "legend" which has crept in under the provincial caftans of Yiddish poets in Europe. The poet—if she were not from a big city or not well travelled—could look through the window of such poem and catch sight of fresh horizons with new outlines. Debora Vogel carves a window to these wider possibilities in European Yiddish poetry. She does this with wonderful agility.

Vogel's "monotony" is external, it gives off a breath of static coolness. Her poems hold up a sign towards the outside world: here lives monotony.

---
1   Jehoshua Weisman was a Yiddish poet and author of *Yung groz* (New York: Oyfgang, 1928).
2   See i. a. v. n. [J. Weisman], "Debora Vogel un ir 'monotonie,'" *In zikh* 16, no. 11 (1935): 206.
3   See Debora Vogel, "Legende fun zilber," *In zikh* 11 (1935): 196–197.

Here poems are also "monotonous" because the poet forgot to take the most important weapon for her hunt—language (the poverty of language causes monotony).

Monotony—poetic means—is not the aim and the purpose, but rather the poem. When the poem becomes a monument to monotony through the artistic preparation, the gesture is inappropriate. I hope that Debora Vogel, who conducts such an energetic experiment in order to take her place in Yiddish poetry, moves away from monotony as soon as possible, and begins to befriend the Yiddish language.

34

Hirsh Segal, "Debora Vogel's New Poetry Collection *Mannequins*" (Warsaw-Lviv: Tsushtayer, 1934)[1]

> You are limited in expecting a new word,
> do you wish to hear that what you have already heard?
>
> —Goethe

"Gradually, boredom can be a style. This means that the form combinations of a certain kind are exhausted. The forms may become exhausted like things and events,"[2] writes Debora Vogel in the preface to her first poetry collection *Day Figures* (Lviv, 1930). This collection of poems is an example of the new form of lyrical poetry. The poems in the first collection left an impression of an experiment on many of us readers. With a lack of understanding and without context, we approached the metaphors of geometrical figures. They did not reveal much to us. Too many constructions, too much borrowing from modern painting and the visual arts. We agreed to the new form in the lyric, but we did not believe in the vitality of the geometrical symbols. And the line "seven times the tin rectangle opens"[3] seemed to us an artificial experiment, even though Debora Vogel warned us, "It would be a misreading if you were to believe the poems to be an artificial experiment. Such a formal attempt is a necessity, attained and purchased by the trials of life."[4]

The new poetry collection *Mannequins* is partially a continuation of *Day Figures*. Only partially. Mostly, in the cycle "Mannequins" we find the following

---

1   See Hirsh Segal, "Dvoyre Fogels naye lider bukh 'Manekinen.'" *Tshernovitser bleter*, no. 210 (1934): 2.
2   See Debora Vogel's preface to the *Day Figures* collection, p. 123.
3   See Debora Vogel's poem, "Day Figure," p. 125.
4   See Debora Vogel's preface to the *Day Figures* collection, p. 124.

lines: "a square surface of sweet monotony / is life, is the world";[5] "the circle is a tired body";[6] "the ellipse is the yearning of space."[7] The deeper we move within the poetry collection, the less we see the geometrical symbols. The poems become clearer and simpler. Slowly, we begin to grasp the new form and the essence of the thought process in Debora Vogel's poetry.

THE FOREGROUND

Strange themes: things from our daily lives like houses and streets, furniture and water, kitchen pots and herring barrels—all the things grasped in a matter-of-fact way, contoured in their bareness, not symbolic at a first glance:

> In many houses servant girls scrub large floors
> and soldiers in blue march on the streets
> and on soldiers' stiff uniforms
> on soldiers' blue uniforms
> there are four shiny round buttons.[8]

Here everything is so true, treated in a matter-of-fact way, only that which you see to the point where you forget the associations and the intimate relationships between the maids and the blue soldiers whom they like for their shiny, polished round buttons. Here the visual element predominates, before it appear purely mechanic movements without any melancholy. The chant of things is around and beyond things and awakens the contours of things in relation to aural sensations, which are more subjective compared to seeing. However, here, in Debora Vogel's poetry everything wishes to be objective—nothing more than what is seen. For instance, there is no tangible yearning in the soldiers' uniforms or in the servants' floor scrubbing.

However, this "pure matter-of-factness" becomes in part symbolic. The contoured visual becomes marionette-like—the streets are static and lifeless, the people are dolls. The difference between the dolls—the mannequins in the vitrines and the dolls—is effaced.

---

5   See Debora Vogel's poem, "Figure Poem II," p. 177.
6   See Debora Vogel's poem, "Figure Poem III," p. 177.
7   See Debora Vogel's poem, "Figure Poem V," p. 179.
8   See Debora Vogel's poem, "Figure Poem IV," p. 178.

> With half-open eyes
> the porcelain smiled
> smooth and watery, as if enchanted
> by everything which happens in the world
> on the second, the other side of the window.
>
> And on the other side of shop window
> elastic dolls stroll
> with sweet long almonds of eyes
> and agile hands and feet.[9]

People are not exclusively mechanical-marionette-like in this poetry. The sky is "linen" from "elastic gold tin,"[10] the sun is "paper."[11] The lines are like the things—sparse and resigned. Resigned to not express many feelings, which should remain hidden. Only the complete and pure truth of the mechanical happening is shaped without a Romantic or subjective-lyrical echo. It is a turning away from the older Romantic poetry, which always kept in mind the poet's suffering or joy. In poetry, there are no more esteemed objects like "spring," "love," "evening," and others, as in previous poetic traditions. Here the objectivity of a phenomenon which only later completely becomes a symbol is of interest.

> Water flows over thousand-year-old stones
> water stands in wells three hundred feet deep
> and in large banal kitchen pots.
>
> And in round tin kitchen pots
> lye water lives, fatty like boredom.[12]

THE BACKGROUND

This world of chiseled things and of marionette-like people is enclosed by a strange melancholy and gray monotony. The rooms are abandoned like the people

---

9   See Debora Vogel's poem, "Dolls," p. 182.
10 See Debora Vogel's poem, "Mannequins," p. 184.
11 Ibidem.
12 See Debora Vogel's poem, "Water," p. 185.

> between quiet tables and china cabinets
> melancholy ensnared fates once took place.[13]
>
> Yet under the bed two black shoes
> stand, still going someplace
> shoes with a thousand wrinkles.
>
> two worn-out black leather shoes
> that know the pavement of Zhulkevska.[14]
>
> In all rooms
> behind all lit window panes
> people sit at tables and against walls
> and nothing happens in the rooms
> and it's all that could ever happen.[15]

The melancholy of monotony encloses all things in this poetic world of Debora Vogel. And the melancholy is understandable in reference to things, things simplified as geometrical figures which "reveal the arch-scheme of monotony."[16] Suddenly, we understand that the symbol of the geometrical figure which the poet borrowed from painting (Cubism) goes well with this world.

The foreground and the background build a unified content, the whole world. In the background is a predominant mood of sadness which always revolves around the monotony of things. This is the true and underlying tonality.

Everything which was so strange to us in the world suddenly becomes very close. "The leaves are a … coat of rust on the sidewalks"; the Parisian "bridge with the tragic gesture of an arc" and the ballad "of a street walker with the brass name Maia,"[17] and we are trembling while reading *Drinking Songs*:

> Today the time has come
> the time of drinking songs has come
> for we are sad unto death.

---

13 See Debora Vogel's poem, "A Poem About Furniture," p. 185.
14 See Debora Vogel's poem, "Shoes," p. 199.
15 See Debora Vogel's poem, "Drinking Poem II," p. 191.
16 See Debora Vogel's afterword to *Mannequins collection*, p. 216.
17 See Debora Vogel's poem, "Ballad of a Streetwalker II," p. 210.

What then can you do
when sadness takes hold of you
like a coral reef with a thousand hands
on this side and on the second side
what can you do then …

When you cannot live without people
yet you cannot live with them!

Then you should sit around the table
women should dress in soft velvet
men should bring hot lips
and caressing hands sad hands.

And you should set crystal glasses
glasses from cool amber, from red beads—
and drown in the sticky drink
in the drink from grapes and kisses.

And nothing more
and do nothing more
well, what else is there to do … [18]

---

18 See Debora Vogel's poem, "Drinking Song I," p. 190.

Reviews of *Acacias Bloom*

Discussions of the Yiddish Edition of *Akatsyes blien* (1935)

35

B. Alquit,[1] "Modern Prose" (1935)[2]

All is quiet on our prose front. There is nothing new—absolutely nothing. From time to time, some new names appear, yet it is truly unbelievable how young novelists and short story writers are led by their talent like the biblical child of peace on the same path, treading in the footsteps of their predecessors.

It is no coincidence that in our literature almost all literary journals are published by poets. In poetry there is a search, a rebellion. The fact that the new prose writers are not drawn into our "war against the world" shows, firstly, that they are pragmatic readers as well as realistic writers of a particular kind, and that their interest in what is happening in other forms of art like painting, for example, is very low. Secondly, it seems that realistic prose writers are also pragmatic people and they write in such a way that their talent sways in the direction of superficiality, so that even a blind person or newspaper editor can sense it with the palm of their hand, and the question of acknowledgement is often the most obvious for them.

Ten years ago, a well-known prose writer was asked why there are no experiments in prose. "Because prose is prose," the esteemed trailblazer answered.

Meanwhile significant experiments in modern prose were nevertheless undertaken merely by poets. Debora Vogel, a poet, wrote *Akatsyes blien*, the book which is now in front of me.

This book of prose was written by a person full of ideas which are reflected in a particular view of life. Vogel sees people as anonymous, as elements or things marked by fate which can also forget about them. Here the method leading to the artistic solution is important; it is somewhere on the border between the unconscious and the consciousness of a "higher reality."

---

1 The pseudonym of Eliezer Blum (1896–1963) who was a Yiddish poet. He belonged to the younger generation of the Modernist group In zikh in New York. He published one collection of poems in 1964.
2 See B. Alkvit [Eliezer Blum], "Moderne proze," *In zikh* 16, no. 17 (1935): 132–135.

This principal view is typical of those postwar poetic circles who searched for freedom in art—and escape from life—through eliminating the "censorship" of pure reason. Vogel's method is quasi-Surrealism.

Vogel stands a bit on the other side of Surrealism as formulated by A. Breton in 1924, since she directly unravels the secrets of the geometry of the life of forms—thus, Vogel's work is closer to painting in this movement.

In *Day Figures*, her first poetry collection published five years ago, Vogel attempted to create a style in unison with Cubism which she discussed in the preface, "the surface, line, and color are simply the elements of a distinct reality constructed in a composition."[3] The author calls the texts in her current book "montages." In these montages—a term from painting—Vogel goes a step further and comes close to Surrealism. Vogel could be considered one of the innovators of modern Yiddish literature if only this innovation were not belated.

Some Surrealists recognized that this movement leads astray. Their hope of finding artistic individuality in "psychological automatism" through a revolt against the "control of reason" over the "real course of thought," "beyond every aesthetic or ethical view,"[4] lead to the expression of the collective turmoil. It is inescapable when super- or un-consciousness gets the upper hand, and the personality with its "pedantic intelligence" recedes into the background as an anonymous pole.

Some poets turned to urgent issues—economic and social transformation—which another war brought into literature. One shakes oneself off from the Surrealist horror. Others, like, for instance, Louis Aragon, became so far removed from Surrealism that there looms another danger, of artistic collectivization—the proletarian literature of utilitarianism.

Even the highly esteemed A. Breton is already a proletarian writer.

Vogel's innovation is late in terms of the idea. Yet one cannot say that Surrealism is "lost without a trace." Surrealism enriched literature with countless metaphors and possibilities of expression. Language as an instrument became more refined thanks to it (the abovementioned young realists should know that every search, every experiment, every new direction enriches literature). I found elements of this inventory in Debora Vogel's work. In the background, I see her affinity with the Introspectivists—all the new literary movements are based on the wonderful inventions of modern psychology.

---

3   From the preface to *Day Figures*, p. 123.
4   The citations are from Breton's definition, translated into English by Peter Neagoe in *What is Surrealism?* (Paris: New Review Publications, 1932).

There is an important element in Vogel's style which makes her distant from the Introspectivists—an unfriendly stance towards life. Hence, the anonymity (and anemia) of people which the author describes with such lyrical precision. Therefore, she can see people as mannequins and dolls or even as "heavy torsos on a stroll."[5]

There are three parts in Vogel's book. The first part *The Building of the Train Station* contains painterly and metaphorical reflections on space and all the principal materials necessary for building the train station. The theme of the second part is the transformation of life when the mannequins are "unmasked"[6] and one discovers "the soul of materials"[7] in people. The third part is a chronicle (almost a social one) which is interspersed with parodies of events from a pulp novel. You will not find a single name of a person in the whole book, no one who would need a name. Only once did Vogel almost gave us a name, an initial "L.," as if in jest.[8] On page 61 my eyes caught the proper name "Bursztyn"![9] And I immediately felt comfortable. I quickly skimmed the text before that line—everything turned out to be a mirage. The author only writes about strolling in the "amber dusk of October."[10] The names of famous painters which are mentioned in the text are almost all the names of Surrealists or artists close to this movement; one obvious exception is Renoir whose art has been admired by representatives of all artistic movements.

Vogel's chief achievement is that her representation is, in fact, very close to modern painting. It is not pictorial; rather, it is real painting. The author sees words before she hears them. Words create surfaces, contours, symmetry which the boredom, sadness, and yearning deepen, and lines live under the sign of a forced or accidental relationship. Yet the word—the mediator of human will and understanding—is emptied of its actual sense when a person is presented on the same surface with lines and contours. This results in Vogel's most peculiar helplessness. Even though the author's Yiddish is very rich, flexible, and authentic, she insists on using the word "like" to the point that it becomes

---

5 See "From the Second Chapter of the Treatise." The full quote is the following: "In the city park alleys, heavy torsos with round breasts stroll," p. 241.
6 See "The Mannequins are Unmasked," p. 251.
7 See "The New Mannequins Walk," p. 253.
8 The full quote: "Surely, the novel had to open with the following sentences: 'That day …' and 'In the gray clarity of a day with streets like gray seas, [the calendar date comes here], a man in a gray coat and a black bowler hat strolled along L. Street, reflecting on his life up to that point …'" ("Streets and Sky"), p. 223.
9 *Bursztyn*—"amber."
10 From "The Third Sentence of Treatise," p. 239.

irritating, "spaces, boring like,"[11] "like the circular landscape of a calendar Sunday that features people who have misplaced their fates, even if only for a few hours,"[12] "gray walls, hard like tragic decisions,"[13] "like the grotesque tagline of a pulp novel, the following sentences form,"[14] "when the sky is gray, the streets are matte and sweet, like a warm gray sea."[15] These short accidental quotes show, to put it casually, that in Vogel's text there is more lyrical than artificial, doll-like, creation.

Hers is prose for poets—yet not for all, and certainly not for our critics. Vogel might possibly return to poetry with the newly discovered possibilities. Due to the realities of Jewish life, a Jewish artist is too realist—and he was that way even in 1924 in Europe, which made adopting Surrealism or its quasi-form impossible. Only perhaps when he had an opportunity and did not want to fight with its influence. However, a Jewish artist cannot escape the influences of a specifically Jewish reality which demands a certain dose of rationalism. To shake it off means to lose one's particularity.

---

11 The full quotation is "And the space is dull like people with their squandered lives"—"The Building of the Train Station 1," p. 271.
12 See ibid.
13 See ibid., p. 274.
14 See "Flower Shops with Azaleas," p. 231.
15 See "Streets and Sky," in *Flower Shops with Azaleas*, p. 223.

36

Debora Vogel, "A Response to B. Alquit's review of *Acacias*" (1936)[1]

When I read each new issue of *In zikh*, I feel the refreshing breath of a quality intellectual and artistic-cultural level which I can trust. In our conditions, to have someone you "can trust" is to be truly fortunate.

I wish to make a few remarks on Mr. Alquit's impressive and incisive review of my book *Acacias*. I would like to extend my sincere thanks to Mr. Alquit for the review. I would also like to share some reflections with him.

My remarks are the following: I have always feared that my book could be misunderstood as the Surrealist. True, the method of combining different and foreign (seemingly foreign) things and situations into totality is very close to Surrealism. However, it is quite different—at least I consider it to be different—I did not want to subject my writing to the free flow of associations, as is Surrealist practice—I did not search for the logic of feelings or subjective reactions to things. I wanted the objective logic of things, their reciprocal belonging, the symptomatic in them, through which seemingly different and strange situations and events become symptoms of a principle. Thus, a certain type of Surrealism came out of this—since it is a combination of various life elements. Thus, I am asking you to listen once again to the inner pulse and the train of thought in the montages, and you will notice the difference between my montage and the Surrealist one. The method of montage is what they share. And yet, like there is difference between Cubist and Surrealist montage, there is also a difference—perhaps a less clear one, but a difference nevertheless—between Surrealist and post-Surrealist montage—which is what I would like to call my montage. I consider my attempts a transitory form on the journey to realist montage.

---

1 See Debora Vogel, "Vegn B. Alkvit's opruf oyf mayn bukh Akatsyes in num. 17, *In zikh*," *In zikh* 17, no. 20 (1936): 62.

Besides, the concept of certain passages was a response to the poetry of agitation which currently takes up so much space in young poetry. New life with its calm—rather than formal preparation for this life—will be fitted into a framework of a productive construction, in its understanding of the processing of raw materials. I don't need to suggest any interpretations, and if you don't see it in the text, then it is surely in part also my shortcoming. I presently feel the need to formulate an essay on montage the contents of which I will not disclose here. I will send another article in the hope that it might be interesting to *In zikh*.

One more remark: how is using the word "life" a sign of "hopelessness," as you say? For my purposes, simile is more fitting than metaphor. I like comparisons better because of their specific role. While metaphor tends to cancel the two things, make them one, simile holds them separate, yet close. Thus, I prefer simile to baroque metaphor.

37

B. Alquit, "A Response to Debora Vogel's Letter" (1936)[1]

Debora Vogel writes, "I have always feared that my book could be misunderstood as Surrealist." I was prepared to say: "I apologize; I made a mistake." However, she adds in her short analysis that "a certain type of Surrealism came out of this." In my review, I wrote, "Vogel's method is quasi-Surrealism." Since the poet said that she will write an essay on montage and her own method—perhaps she might consider also the fine difference between "quasi-" and "type of." The prefaces to the author's poetry collections make me certain that Vogel's essay will be a good contribution to *In zikh*. Perhaps it might be even more necessary to answer further the artistic questions which the poet touched upon in her letter. The letter was published because it has the aroma of Vogel's prose and her epistolary clarity.

---

1 See B. Alkvit [Eliezer Blum], "Vegn di tsvey briv," ibidem, 79.

38

Joshue Rapoport, "Like a Squirrel on a Wheel" (1936)[1]

Debora Vogel's second poetry collection *Mannequins* is very similar to *Day Figures*, the author's first poetry collection. Often, it is identical with it. And the third book, which is her first prose collection, *Acacias Bloom*, is very much like her two poetry collections—frequently identical with them. If Debora Vogel stubbornly stays with her painterly word experiments—Vogel would like to transplant Cubist painterly experiments into writing—and with her simplified worldview reduced to the minimum (life only consists of a few geometrical figures, depicted in a few colors which are often repeated), then her fourth book will surely be like the previous ones. One may bet one to ten. However clever or quick, the squirrel is locked up and must turn the wheel absolutely in vain. Debora Vogel locked herself into the narrow wheel of a worldview reduced to the three-dimensional existence of matter, with a bit of color and sound for dessert.

The montage book consists of three parts: 1. *The Building of the Train Station*; 2. *Acacias Bloom*; and 3. *Flower Shops with Azaleas*. Among these titles, *The Building of the Train Station* is a constructed whole. The other two parts are collections of prose poems. In *Acacias Bloom*, we often encounter the same expressions and sentences as in Vogel's *Mannequins* and *Day Figures*. We may find there a lot of boredom, a vast amount of geometry, lots of gray melancholy and gray walls, "like hard decisions."[2] There is enough to see well-known metaphors and images on every page—the "citrus-yellow is the color of cold resignation"[3]—to understand how real life is emptied out from Vogel's world; it is an endless paraphrase of the same concepts and words.

The Building of the Train Station depicts—by geometrical-painterly means—the body and soul of raw materials. Vogel describes—often in a very

---

1 See Joshue Rapoport, "Vi a veverke in a rod," *Shoybn*, no. 4 (1936): 37.
2 See Debora Vogel's montage, "Building of the Train Station 4," p. 274.
3 See Debora Vogel's montage, "Building of the Train Station 7," p. 277.

original manner—how the body of material becomes a material thing with a soul, how "boredom, the hopeless and monotonous body of materials"[4] is processed into a higher spiritual level of boredom and monotony. Besides her outstanding signs of talent and a few successful images, Debora Vogel does not process her own boredom (actual or theoretical, or both)—the helpless and monotonous body of the material of her poetry—into something spiritual. Her poetry remains raw material in the state of a body lacking a soul.

It is not possible for me to analyze Vogel's prose work in detail: I have already analyzed her *Day Figures* and *Mannequins*, and I will be only repeating myself.

Not only the negative but also the positive sides of her previous works are strengthened in Debora Vogel's prose.

We have already established in *Day Figures* that we are dealing with a cultured person full of ideas; that Vogel not only works with the categories and notions of modern painting, but also lives according to them—she perceives the world in a painterly way. The previous impression is also strengthened by *Acacias Bloom*. Debora Vogel has a strong sensibility for colors and the sound of colors.

"[C]opper brass, sad and fantastical"[5] is not a meaningless expression; it is laden with concrete contents, with psychological physical experience. And such expressions are not the only ones; this sentence is by far not the most successful of them.

Notably, *Flower Shops with Azaleas*, occasionally interspersed with wonderful Impressionistic descriptions and light moments, contains very fine psychologism. At times, one may even be inclined to think that *Flower Shops with Azaleas* could be considered some of the most interesting prose in our literature.

It is full of risk and a wild, breakneck talent. The impression of purposefulness and determination created by *Day Figures* is amplified three times in Vogel's prose: even the *curves* of her montages testify to much greater constructive and stylistic tensions (and fewer wins) than a dozen smooth novels of our sterile prose literature.

It is a shame that Debora Vogel has imprisoned her talent in a narrow circle of defined artistic ideas and stubbornly serves them, when her talent

---

4   See Debora Vogel's montage, "Building of the Train Station 10," p. 281.
5   See Debora Vogel's montage, "21. Second Commentary," p. 249.

should be engaged in other, more fruitful work. To force the human word to behave in a geometrical-painterly way and to reduce life to raw materials and primitive lines is Sisyphean work. Her ideas about art and fixed outlook on life has left Debora Vogel with a lot of scars; she could graciously leave the battlefield—it's time, since she is not going to get anymore trophies. Perhaps the experience of her experiments will turn out to be more productive and feasible in the area of "normal" word creation, where life is multifaceted and rich in its versions, and geometry stays geometry and not the principal law of life. After all, laboratory experiments are conducted to achieve fruitful results in life. If the experiments don't turn out to be feasible, then it is best to finish with them.

39

Debora Vogel, "A Couple of Remarks on My Book *Akatsyes Blien*" (1937)[1]

The three parts of montage in *Acacias Bloom* are built according to two principles—the principle of chronology (a sequence of facts) and of simultaneity (concurrence).

The first principle results in the form of chronicle, the second creates an impression of the arbitrary combination of gestures and situations.

The construction of montage is strict and deliberate. This kind of restraint is difficult to a certain extent, since the idea is always one-sided, and there is a diversity of beautiful colorful elements which "have nothing to do with the matter," but beg to be included in a composition nevertheless. However, one should resist the enticement and select only the facts which fit the construction—the principal idea. In the artwork, construction is another term for "worldview." Thus, only "exemplary" facts make their way into montage.

Montage—the relationship between chronology and simultaneity—is represented by the part *Flower Shops with Azaleas*.

Why shouldn't the book's three parts be similar—written by one author, they are part of a personal, and, perhaps, even a universal history? Together with the sequence of poems *Shoddy Ballads* from the *Mannequins* collection, the *Acacias Bloom* and *Flower Shops* montage parts overcome the "Cubist" worldview.

This is what I aimed to demonstrate by depicting the "contents."

Acacias Bloom is a chronicle from the "era of geometry." When I speak about this era as if it was universally recognized, it comes from a conviction that it was a dialectical stage in the history of values in life—even though it remained at the stage of a legend which did not fully permeate life with its philosophy.

---

1 See Debora Vogel, "A por bemerkungen vegn mayn bikhl 'Akatsyes blien,'" *Shoybn*, no. 5 (1937): 38.

Or rather, we have not yet codified the features of the Cubist worldview in all aspects of life.[2]

For me, this Cubist orientation was an experience which called for reworking and rationalization. It was connected to the experience of the sense, rhythm, feeling, and color of the figure of the rectangle and gray. These two elements became meaningful means of describing particular life moods—not through in their visual-painterly aspects, but in the content of feeling and life values. Additionally, these opened a fruitful insight into the "soul" of the geometrical figures and colors.

In the dimension of feelings appeared a longing for constructivism and stasis; a critique of the stance of waiting for unexpected events, and of wanton corporeality; a yearning for static constructive monotony—as the last value in life.

I described this Cubist world in the first part of *Acacias*; in the second part, the decay of this world; and in the third gestured to the new value which remains after the exhaustion of the previous possibilities.

It is no accident that one of the parts and the whole book received the title of this short third part.

The new value is called banality—the rehabilitated banality of life—those events which remain unnoticed, either due to a perspective which is too close, or perhaps due to their alleged triviality. This type of events is shown in the book through shoddy calico flowers, acacia blossoms, and conversations which revolve around the subject of yellowing autumn leaves.

The return to these kinds of events means the overcoming of Cubist time, the "meaningfulness of categories of thinking," in the view of the theoretician Franz Roh.

Flower Shops with Azaleas takes up banality as its plot—the development of the content of the legend of banality.

Kitsch in life is stylized for this purpose. Stylization uses the following means—vulgarity, the theorizing of banality, bringing the latter in relation to that which is the "abstract" and the "incomprehensible" in the Hegelian system, making it analogous (the structure of the three sentences of banal life philosophy); the citation in quotation marks of the shoddy street and dancing songs.

One more thing is important: banality here is introduced together with the relevant social element and rehabilitated through the confrontation with the latter.

---

2 The expression here is "*bavegung flakhn*" (the surfaces of movement).

The principle of simultaneity is to be understood as a result of a worldview which attempts to negate the hierarchy of events—to abolish the difference we are used to making between "great" and "small" events, "relevant" and "secondary" happenings.

This rationale suggests that everything belongs to life. As a result, heterogenous things and situations are combined into a whole—scenes with the unemployed, spring scenes with women's hats, and blooming chestnut trees.

Montage composition comes into existence in this way. (Notably, the relevant social element is not degraded. Rather, the banal is elevated in the hierarchy.)

In the contemporary constellation, the world should reckon with the banal events which save life in a disguised and an evasive way. Perhaps kitsch belongs to life as its "lasting" element?

In any case, the worldview which finds its expression in the method of simultaneity greatly differs from the Cubist worldview, which strictly adheres to a hierarchy of values and places a higher value on stasis, stability, and the ascetic monotony of repetition.

The ideal montage would be able to embrace all of life's colorfulness. This is the reason that it has been little developed as a method.

Yet even today one should be able to demand that a critic of Rapoport's caliber see the evolution from *Day Figures* to *Flower Shops with Azaleas* rather than simply note the repetition of metaphors and images.

Reviews of the Polish Edition of *Akacje kwitną*

40

Zofia Nalkowska,[1] "Acacias Bloom" (1936)[2]

There exists a curious literary position which seems almost improbable. There is some speculation: is this Cocteau? Or Schulz (there are, after all, *Mannequins*)? After careful consideration, the book is entitled to full autonomy. Even though the author creates reality from every possible reagent in intellectual chemistry, this reality glows with meaning; it is dense, plastic, and vivid. Mobile, shimmering, and colorful matter fills space. Physical and metaphysical notions direct the narration, its lyrical melody determined by the philosophical version of the poem of a broken heart.

---

1 Zofia Nalkowska (1884–1954) was a Polish writer and journalist. She presided over an important literary salon in Warsaw.
2 See Zofia Nalkowska, "Debory Vogel Akacje kwitną. Rój. 1936. Stron 170," *Studio*, no. 2 (1936): 62.

41

Marian Promiński,[1] "Acacias Bloom" (1936)[2]

Ms. Vogel's book should be considered one of a series of experiments on the fringes of mainstream contemporary prose. The basis of the experiment is the following: we are handed condensed formal elements which rarely appear in the prose by other authors. These elements attempt to transpose certain feelings, sensations, and abstractions in concrete sensuous forms, whether through ordinary metaphor, large-scale paraphrase, or analogy. The secret of this alchemist's crucible lies, among other things, in an individualized perception of the world independent of individuals and their singular sensations, which brings out the synthetic nature of events. For instance, for Ms. Vogel, the sight of shop windows in a spring dusk will always have an equivalent in a complex multilayered sensation, in which it is difficult to distill certain states from singular causes. An arithmetical means of life experiences is easily discernible here. This is the author's method, yet whether it leads to super-individual truths is an altogether different question. The counterpoint of representations under the author's pen is as ambitious as it is gloomy, at times it appears tiresome due to its one-sidedness. Obviously, life and its justification in art is not fully represented only through colors, geometrical forms, labels for feelings, cardboard, glue, and makeup; it always remains marionette-like. At the same time, the author should be given her due—she is an outstanding expert on the phenomena she describes. She utilizes some of them like the perfect number of objects in a restructuring of inner space, or indisputable knowledge of the laws which dominate the visual arts. No wonder that these montages are to a certain extent "stillborn" in prose. However, "dead" does not mean uninteresting. One should not search for any sort of emotion, there is only the cold play of imagination. Among the three parts, *Flower Shops with Azaleas, Acacias Bloom*,

---

1 Marian Promiński (1908–1971) was a Polish author, translator, film critic, one of the founders of the journal *Sygnały*, in which Vogel published.
2 See Marian Promiński, "Akacje kwitną," *Sygnały* 4, no. 15 (1936): 8.

and *The Building of the Train Station*, the third part makes the fewest mistakes of the other montages: it positively stands out through the nuances of the word material in relation to the depicted reality. The execution is even, goal oriented, and developed to the smallest details—in the building of the train station, as well as in the construction of the work.

42

Emil Breiter,[1] "Debora Vogel—*Acacias Bloom: Montages*" (1936)[2]

The first book[3] by Ms. Vogel can be passed over in silence. That would be in the best interests of the author, as well as the reader. However, the silence could be considered "withholding." Thus, we should make a few remarks regarding Ms. Vogel's prose.

The author cultivates an unbearable style of writing. It is serious trivial literature, which is different from ordinary trivial literature because it works out of its own theory, so that it can be mistakenly perceived as intellectual. Writing ability distinguishes the art of writing from serious trivial literature.

Ms. Vogel, undoubtedly, has a lot to say in private and "important" conversations on the subjects of life, art, forms, colors, etc., yet she cannot write about them. Clearly, that absence of orthography is the cause. The first dangerous and dismal mistake which downgrades the writing is the author's obsession with certain words and terms. Vogel has favorite words which usually happen to be adjectives. The adjective "sticky" appears at least twice on every page. The repeated insertion of the same adjectives into unexpected combinations with nouns (boredom, number, leaves, heat, etc.) initiates a deadly "rhythm of monotony" which hinders the reading of "montages" on a train. There is nothing to replace the absent plot. The incomprehensibility of this montage borders on muddled vision.

---

1 Emil Breiter (1886–1943) was a polemicist and literary critic who published a review of Vogel's book together with a review about a book by Gustawa Jarecka, grouping the two authors under the title "Two Women's Novels." This illustrates the attitude of male critics to the work of female authors at the time. Women's writing was considered a group phenomenon and not the production of individuals.
2 See Emil Breiter, "Debora Vogel. Akacje kwitną. Montaże. Warszawa. Rój, 1936; str. 170 i 6nl," *Wiadomości Literackie*, no. 11 (1936): 4.
3 The first in Polish literature.

Another deficiency is the impersonality manifest in impersonal verb forms. For instance, the author writes a whole series of incomprehensible maxims, and suddenly switches to an impersonal tone: "it was noted," "it was decided," "it was done." It is unclear whom Ms. Vogel has in mind here: her acquaintances, unidentified general populace, or a narrow circle of elite insiders? After the attempts to define these "events" more precisely, we reach the conclusion that the author means herself exclusively.

The third natural deficiency is Ms. Vogel's color blindness in relation to the outside world. The author's absolute blindness conceals the richness of colors and geometrical figures (she paints like a visually impaired person). For her, everything becomes figures in space: life has the form of a rectangle; yearning becomes an ellipse; weariness, a circle; and resignation, a square. These "inventions" swarm over all three Cubist montages, which mean nothing, express nothing, and attest to nothing. This is a romance of geometrical figures borrowed and adopted literally from French Cubism and Picasso's technique. While the question of the primacy of form over content has become the focus of discussion in painting the visual arts, implementation of this technique and manner of asking questions in the art of writing only results in absurd and hieroglyphic prose.

Occasionally the author becomes aware of the absurdity of her theory. Thus, she finishes one of the parts with a sentence which is seemingly not so meaningless, as if making a gesture in the direction of "old-fashioned" technique.

All the montages are fantasies on incomprehensible themes with the use of intelligible words. One thing is clear: from the author's point of view, all people are dolls and mannequins (literally), cities are the beautiful "trees of horizontals and verticals," and all other things are spherical and angular forms.

Longing for "full roundness"[4] could even incite to revolution. The "ambiance" of these montages is on the level of a very selective understanding of things. Even simplicity cannot save Ms. Vogel.

---

[4] From the poem "Ships Carry Gold," p. 235.

43

Bruno Schulz, "Acacias Bloom" (1936)[1]

People often say that an author reconstructs in a novel "the whole of life," or its "part," the totality of a "human fate from birth until death." In fact, the novel contains only some or a dozen exemplary episodes, a certain number of abridged versions of reality. These are connected through the lines of what we call content, idea, witticism, collected and grouped in such a way as to form a particular figure of thought. Clearly, we may arrive at this "figure" only through a kind of reduction of life material; it is invented by means of arbitrarily selected elements of a life; thus, in this sense, we may talk about "all of life." Some writers distill this higher sense on its own, as it were—from the pulp of reality; in other novels, the author himself is involved in the process through a sort of "midwifery"—reason. In both cases, distilling the "figure of thought" from the narrative content is one of the main charms of the novel. The traditional novel always retains the division of a double logic—the autonomous logic of the realistic material and the logic of deeper sense, the intrusive narrator's superstructure. In the few overlapping moments, in which they harmonize, integrate, and diverge yet again, there is an intellectual play that constitutes the charm of this kind of work.

The singular originality of Debora Vogel's book, which disorients the reader—cuts the ground from under his feet—is an absolute break with conventional form, the principle of the traditional novel. The author does not draw attention to single events—the individual fates of people and characters. She does not need realistic material to exemplify the sense discovered in life. The author does not show state of affairs in life as direct personal experiences in their completely individual essence. She only allows these to be expressed once they pass through thousands of hearts, when they become colorless, impersonal, and representative—coins for exchange, anonymous, worn-out, and banal formulae. The author acknowledges these expressions and engages them

---

1 See Bruno Schulz, "Akacje kwitną," *Nasza Opinja* 4, no. 72 (1936): 9.

only on the level where they are the common property of a passerby on the street, a female shop assistant, and a bartender. They pass the test of their capability for reality when these expressions can function as texts for a street song.

There is no individual protagonist in the book, only an anonymous mass of dolls and mannequins from barbershop windows, passersby in stiff hats, manicurists, and waiters, involved into the mechanism of the city—*flânerie*. These are faceless figures without individuality.

The author takes this reduction of a person degraded to a pawn, a mechanical figure, a hook for hanging a hat, from the Constructivist worldview in contemporary art. It seems to be the latest consequence of urbanism, the transposition of statistics—the principles of enormous numbers and the new atomism—onto the life and biology of great masses of people.

In such a degradation and rejection of individuality there is an altogether Spinozist pathos, a monumentally melancholy agreement with mechanism, a union with determinism, which almost leads to conscious effort. In this world of human atoms which circulate according to preordained rules, there is no space for individual destinies. There are only common fates, movements fixed forever, cyclical and repetitive stages. A world full of the pathos of geometry, masses, and weights originates around the mannequins wandering through the desert of streets. "The appearance of the dense canvases of white space is treated like an event. Walls occur in this novel, thick like longing and sweltering heat. Walls: whiter than in reality, melancholy white or hard white. …"[2] It is as if we have found ourselves in a Surrealist landscape restricted to flat houses without windows, figures of advertisements and signs, under a lacquered cardboard sky, in late and resolute light. This world of colors, materials, kitschy labels and signs, metals, and geometrical masses proceeds according to its own calendar and produces the animated decoration of life. The sense of life—those fluctuations and constant recurrences of the eternal matters of human hearts—is expressed in the transformations of successive stages. From the faceless mannequins which circulate in the cardboard cosmos of the book, the author creates the banal history of women's hearts. This combination includes both general and well-known things, as well as refrains of popular songs in quotation marks—stories of "hearts forever broken,"[3] the story of a "squandered happiness"[4] which would be better completely forgotten, but without memory of

---

2   This quote is from "Streets and Sky," p. 224.
3   The quote is from "The Mannequins are Unmasked," p. 251.
4   The quotation is from "Street Dust," p. 225.

which one cannot survive, "squandered fates,"⁵ "unhappy loves,"⁶ waiting for a life "when something can still happen,"⁷ and a resigned acceptance of "that which has to come."⁸ And everything is dominated by the tragic monotony of a world which is finished and immobile in its essence.

The experiences of the author have reached this depersonalized anonymous form distilled into the melody of common sense, sad and banal cliché. The author prefers the sound and sweetness of banality as a withered and sickening aftertaste of the last stage of ripeness.

This is not a book with which one may become too intimate. And it is feminine through and through—in sensations and psychological substance, in its vegetative rhythm, cosmic extraction of pulsations, periods, and fluctuations of sense connected to the rhythm of everything.

Some readers and even reviewers noted an analogy to *Cinnamon Shops*⁹ in this book. This observation does not demonstrate a great perceptiveness. In its essence, the book originates from a thoroughly different and original worldview.

A singular worldview—not rationalized, but intrinsic and originary, already inherent in every sensation—is, according to St. I. Witkiewicz, the dowry with which a true poet comes into this world. This absolutely organic worldview permeates and constructs this book. We might say that it is a textbook example of a poetic worldview realized with the help of minimal external material. The author does not have a talent for realism. To obtain the material to demonstrate her arguments, she runs into difficulties which are almost too difficult to overcome, and yet the difficulty itself, this resistance, as well as the elegance of withholding and an inability to assimilate external content, guarantee the purity of her vision. It seems that the author possesses a few secondary features, like agility, cleverness, and the ability to arrange—the characteristics of

---

5   This quote is from "Flower Shops with Azaleas," p. 231.
6   The quote is from "Acacias Bloom," p. 267.
7   The quotation is from "The Next Chapter of Decay: One Seeks Adventures," p. 265.
8   The quote is from "Life," p. 239.
9   Jerzy Ficowski, the Schulz scholar, mentions the author's relationship to Vogel in his biography *The Regions of the Great Heresy: Bruno Shulz, a Biographical Portrait*, trans. Theodosia Robertson (New York: W. W. Norton, 2003). The problematic perception of Vogel as Schulz's muse is discussed by Annette Werberger, the German scholar of the author, in her essay, "Nur eine Muse? Die jiddische Schriftstellerin Debora Vogel und Bruno Schulz" [Only a muse? Yiddish writer Debora Vogel and Bruno Schulz], in *Ins Wort gesetzt, ins Bild gesetzt. Gender in Wissenschaft, Kunst und Literatur*, ed. Ingrid Hotz-Davies and Schamma Schahadat (Bielefeld: Transcript Verlag, 2007), 257–286.

light talents. She possibly does not win her reader over directly but marginally, as if by chance, the result is accidental and unplanned. Perhaps she is not fully convincing when the sentimental formulae of women's hearts serve as captions for cosmic processes and the mechanics of the represented world. The dynamics of feelings may not be particularly moving when expressed in this abstract and anonymous form. Yet around this perhaps unreachable goal, the author has accumulated so much new and unexpected content, so many accidental discoveries of her singular vision, that she has won her case by means of a detour.

Acacias Bloom is an extremely interesting, original, and unusual achievement, even if these montages were not experiments for the author but rather a necessity imposed through her whole creative program. The novelty of this book does not lie in its particular details, or new variations on old means, but in the substance of the prose itself, the style of narration itself. We can say that conventional novelistic prose is based on the fundamental view that the world transpires, becomes, flows, and strives for some result. Debora Vogel's prose is the equivalent of a world which is always realized, immobile, and mechanized.

Here movement is only an illusion, a fantasy of human knobs and cones; narrative is only an appearance, a trick; it is parallel and loosely woven to the rigid, tragic world contained within its vision.

Beautiful and virtuoso Surrealist illustrations by Henryk Streng, whose rich and original artistry is not yet well known to the public, accompany the text.

Index

Adler, Alfred, 308
Alquit, B., xxxi, 302–303, 318, 332, 366–372, *see also* Blum, Eliezer and B. Alkvit
Annenkov, Yury (George), 208–209
Apollinaire, Guillaume, xxvi, 33
Aragon, Louis, 33, 116, 343, 367
  Bells of Basel, 116
Argentina, 264
Aronson, Chil Aaron, xviii, 293
Artes group, ix, xix, xxvii, 3, 70n2
Ashendorf, Sh., xxxi
Auerbach, Rachel, xvi, xx–xxi, *see also* Oyerbakh, Rokhl
  Nisht oysgeshpunene feder (Unspun Threads), xx

Balázs, Béla, 116
  Impossible People, The, 116
Baltic Sea, 208, 228
Balzac, Honore de, 19
Banach, Stefan, 226n10
Barenblüth, Shalom, xxiv, 291n25, 308, 323–326
Baroque, 5, 63, 75–76, 101, 247, 260, 349, 371
Barr, Alfred, 53n12
Beilis case, xvi, 108
Benjamin, Walter, xxvi, 22n2, 30n3, 30n5
Berlin, xvii–xix, 16n4, 22n2, 48n10, 106, 188, 189n14, 207, 230n21, 292

Bikl, Shloyme (Shlomo), xxvii, 309, 313–314, 319–320, 323, 329, 337
  In zikh un arum zikh, 314
Blok (group), 18n7
Blok (publication), 54, 57
Blonder, Sasha, 66n2, 67–68
Blum, Eliezer, 366n1–2, 372n1, *see also* Alquit (Alkvit), B.
Blumgarten, Solomon, 344n3, *see also* Yehoash
Bodn, 324, 326, 331
Bomse, Nahum, xxxi, *see also* Bomze, N., xxxin31
Brandes, Georg, xxi
Braques, Georges, xix, 55
Brazil, xxv, 264
Brecht, Bertold, 209n31
  Three Penny Opera, 209n31
Breiter, Emil, 383
Brentano, Franz, xvii
Breton, André, xxvi, 33, 55n11, 56, 71, 367
  Manifeste du surrealism, 55n11
  "Second Manifesto of Surrealism," 56
Broderzon, Moyshe, 344
Brownstone, Ezekiel, xxvii, xxx, 297
Brunngraber, Rudolf, xxvi, 22n2, 23–26, 30n4
  Karl and Twentieth Century, xxvi, 23–26, 30n4
Brussels, 298

Brzozowski, Stanisław Leopold, 124n2
Bucharest, 309, *see also* Bucureşti, 320, 323, 329
Burshtyn (Bursztyn), xv–xvi
Bursztyn, 198n24, 368, *see also* Burshtyn

California, xxv, 264n147, 266
Canada, 6n10, 258, 264
Carlyle, Thomas, 22
   On Hero Worship, 22
Chicago, ix, 213, 296, 313n65
Chwila, xxxi, 320
Céline, Louis Ferdinand, 19, 91–92
   Journey to the End of the Night, 91
Cézanne, Paul, 55, 154
Citroen, Roelof Paul, 54–55
Chagall, Marc, xviii, xx, xxv, 40, 42–53, 111, 286, 293
   Cattle Dealer, 42–43
   Small Birth, 44, 47, *see also* The Birth, 44
   In Vitebsk, 43
Chirico, Giorgio de, xxii, 183
Chopin, Frederic, 8n13
Cocteau, Jean, 380
Communist (Communism), 116, 304, 308, 344n8–9
Constructivist (Constructivism), xix, xxii, xxviii, 3n2, 18n7, 54n4, 55, 60–61, 63–64, 66, 70–72, 113, 216–217, 321, 343–345, 349, 377, 386
Cracow, xvi, 66–67, 68n13, 221n1, 332n86,
Cracow Group, 66–67, 68n13
Cubist (Cubism), xxii, xxvii–xxviii, 3, 33n8, 55, 62, 65, 66n4, 70n2, 123, 217, 311, 344–347, 351, 353, 362, 367, 370, 373, 376–378, 384
Chwila, xxxi, 320
Czernowitz, xxvii, 309n57, 322, 326, 329n83, 342n3

Dadaist (Dadaism), xvii, xxvii, 4, 33n10, 343–344, 349
Day, The, 310, 316, 318–319, 337
Delacroix, Eugène, 19
Delaunay, Robert, 33, 55
Deleuze, Gilles, xxxiv
Detroit, 213
Dietrich, Marlene, xvii, 188n12
Dos Passos, John, xiv, xxvi, 33
   Manhattan Transfer, xiv, 33
   42nd Parallel, 33
Dreyfus affair, xvi, 108Eastman, Max, 53n12

Ehrenburg, Ilya, 291
   The Life of Cars, 291
Ehrenpreis, Jacob, xv, 108
Ehrenpreis, Lea, 198n24, *see also* Vogel, Lea
Ehrenpreis, Marcus, xvi, xviii, xxi, 285–287, 296n37, 299, 301, 308, 323, 326–327, 338
Ehrenpreis, Miriam (Mirchen, Miri, daughter of Marcus Ehrenpreis), 198n23, 287n8
Ehrenpreis, Theodor Saul (Dori), 287n9
Eichberg, Richard, 189n14
   The Chaste Susanna, 189n14
Einhorn, David, 293
   Violet, 293
Ekspres, 327
Empirio-critics (empirio-criticism), xvi, 17
Ephros, Abraham, 45, 45n5, 46n5, 53
Ernst, Max, 32–33, 58, 71, 257
   Les malheures des immortels, 32, 58
Ettinger, Shloyme, 328
Expressionism, 4n4, 22n2, 36, 38, 47n6, 53, 298n43, 328n80, 343
   German, 48n9–10
   Polish (Formism), 349n4

Russian, 208n30
Yiddish, 344n7

Feinberg, Leonid, 335
Feuerring, Maksymilian, 289–290, *see also* Feyering, Maks
Flammarion, 84–85
Folkstsaytung, 311n60, 313
Forlerer, Mordko, 326–327
Formism, 349, *see also* Expressionism, Polish
Forverts, 344n6
Frank, Willy, 77
Frayhayt-Hamer group, 344, *see also* Proletpen
Fröding, Gustaf, xviii
Fraye Arbeter Shtime, 344n6
Futurism (Futurist), 343–344, 351, 353
Fülöp-Miller, René, 53n12

Galicia, xv, xviii, xx–xxi, xxvi, 6n10, 12–13, 102n3, 109, 188n13, 289n14, 292n26, 294, 298n43, 302, 305, 341n1
Germany, ix, xvii, xix, 188n12, 285
Gininger, Chaim, 313, 322n75
Giżycki, Kamil, 91–92
  Whites and the Blacks, The, 91–92
Glantz-Leyeles, Aaron (A. Leyeles), xviii, xixn9, xxvii–xix, xxxi, 284, 295, 299, 303, 307, 310, 312, 316–320, 324, 328, 330, 333, 336–337
  "In the Subway", xxxi, 300
  Fabius Lind, 325, 330
  "Manhattan Bridge", xxxi
  "November", xxxi, 264n145
  Tsu Dir-Tsu Mir, 325
Glatshteyn, Yankev (Glatstein, J.), xxxi–xxxii, 4n5, 295n34, 312, 317–318, 320–321, 325, 333, 335, 337, 344

"Boy and a Roll, A," xxxii
Exegyddish (Yidishtaytshn), xxxii
Goethe, Johann Wolfgang von, 79, 359
  Theory of Colors, 79
Gothic, 76
Grabowski, Zbigniew, 91
Gonsiorowski, Zygmunt, 66n2
Goya, Francisco, 71, 210n33
Greding, 292
Gronowicz, Antoni, 72
Group of the Living, 66
Grunberg, Berta, 66n2
Guattari, Pierre-Félix, xxxiv

Hahn, Otto, 62
Halpern, Levi, 303n48, *see also* H. Leyvik
Halpern, Moyshe Leyb, 13, 344
Halpern, Romana, xxiii
Hartleben, Conrad Adolf, 108
Hashomer Hatsair (The Young Guard), xvi, 198n23
Hegel, Georg Wilhelm Friedrich, xvi, 23, 56, 232n23, 289n16, 325, 377
Heraclitus, 17
Hugo, Victor, 19
Husserl, Edmund, xvii

Iceland, Reuben, 13, 102, 335
Imagism, 343
Imber, Shmuel, 13–14
Impressionism, 13–14, 36, 38, 55
Innen Dekoration, 75
Introspectivism (Introspectivist) xxvii–xxviii, 4, 349, *see also* In Zikh
Inzl, Der, 13n8, 304, 332
Irzykowski, Karol, xxxvii, 7, 90, 124
  Hag, The, 124n2
In Zikh, xxviii–xxix, xxxii, 4n5, 33n11, 295n34, 302–307, 310, 313–314, 316–318, 321–322, 325–326, 328,

331, 335–336, 338, 344n6, 357, 370–372

Janisch, Jerzy, 60
Jarema, Maria, 66n2, 68
Java, 264
Jazwecky, Franciszek, 66n2
Jeanneret, Charles-Édouard, 66
Jewish Literature and Arts Society, xix
Journal des Poètes, 298
Joyce, James, xiv, 305
    Ulysses, xiv, 305
Judisk Tidskrift, xviii, xxi, 101n1, 285n1, 287n12, 299n44, 301, 328

Kafka, Franz, xxxiv
Kandinsky, Wassily, xxv, 48n9, 79
Karpfen, Fritz, 53
Kenigsberg, Dovid, 13–14
Khalyastre, Di (The gang), 13n6, 344
Kimberley, 258
Kishau, 290
Klages, Ludwig, 17
Kletskin, Boris, 297
Kobro, Katarzyna, 18n7, 67
Kopychinec, 292
Korn, Rokhl, xx–xxi, xxvii, 6, 342
Krasiński, Zygmunt, 113
    Ungodly Comedy, 113
Kratochwila-Widymska, Józefa, 111, 299
Kremer, Józef, xvi, 289n16
Kreuger, Nils Edvard, xviii
Krzywoblocki, Aleksander, 59
Kulbak, Moyshe, xxvii, 9, 337
Kumove, Shirley, xxxiin34
Kuperman, Eliezer Pinkhas, 337
Kurtz, Aaron, 344

La Fontaine, Jean de, 46
Lang, Fritz, xvii, 54n3, 188n13
    Metropolis, xvii, 54n3, 188n13

Laocoön, 38
Larsson, Carl, xviii
Lasker-Schüler, Else, 286
Leda, 257, 257n102
Léger, Fernand, xix, 3n2, 66, 70
    Légerism, 3, 70n2
Lemberg, xviii, 12, 105n8, *see also* Lviv
Leonov, Leonid, 114
Leyvik, H., xxxi–xxxii, 303–305, 307, 325, 344, *see also* Halpern, Levi
Lewicki, Leopold, 66, 68
Leyb, Mani, 303
Lid, xxx, 204n27, 297
Likht, Mikhl, 4n5, 335, 337
Liljefors, Bruno Andreas, xviii
Linfert, Carl, 76
Lingner, Karl August, 226n10
Literarishe Bleter, xxxi, 16, 118n12, 290n19, 294, 300, 308, 310, 316, 338
Lodz, ix–x, 7n11, 245
Los Angeles, xxvii, xxx, 297n38
Lozowick, Louis, 53n12
Lukács, Georg (György), xxvi, 33n11
Lutski, A., 344
Lviv (Lemberg, Lemberik, Lvov, Lwów), ix, xvi, xix–xx, xxviii, xxx–xxxi, xxxvi, 59–61, 66n2, 101–111, 118n10, 198n24, 266n10, 242, 245n60, 283, 285–289, 291–292, 294–303, 306–308, 312, 315–324, 326–330, 332n86, 337–338, 341, 351, 359
Lwów, 343, 359, also see Lviv

Magical Realism, xvii, 4n4, 37, *see also* New Objectivity and New Sobriety
Mallarme, Stéphane, 346
Maltz, Judith, 198
Manger, Itsik, 209n31, 303, 309n58, 342, 343n1

Mann, Thomas, 24, 327
  Magic Mountain, 24
Marcussi, Louis, xix, 55
Margolin, Anna, x, xxxi, xxxiin34,
  304–305, 308, 318, 325
  "At the Café," xxxi, 304n53
  "Broadway Evening," xxxi, 304n53
  "Evening on Fifth Avenue," xxxii,
    304n53
  "Girls in Crotona Park," xxxi,
    304n53
  Sun, Asphalt, Roads, xxxi
Marinetti, Filippo Tommaso, 343
Mark, Franz, xxvi, 48
Marseille, 210
Marxism, Marxist, 311
Maszynski, Adam, 66n2
Mayakovsky, Vladimir, 343
Maysel, Nachman, 300
Melbourne, 13n6, 16n4, 302, 304, 306,
  311
Melcer, Wanda, 93
Merkel, Jerzy, 332–333
Mickiewicz, Adam, 8n13
Minkoff, Nokhem Barukh, xxxi–xxxii,
  295n34, 321, 325–326, 331, 335, 337
  Undzer Pyero (Our Pierrot), xxxii
Misiak, Anna Maja, ix, xxxv, 230n21
Modernism (Modernist), xiv, xxii,
  xxvi–xxix, xxxiii–xxxiv, 4n5,
  13n7, 33, 35, 37, 66n5, 78, 102n3,
  320–321, 324–325, 328, 331–335,
  337–338, 343–344, 349, 366n1
  Anglo-American, xxviii, 293n28, 335
  European, xxi, 325
  Polish, 7n12
  Yiddish, xiv, xviii, xxviii–xxix, xxxi,
    320, 325, 333, 344
Molodowsky, Kadya, xxvii, xxxi, 6, 118,
  118n11, 118n12
  Dzhike gas, 118

Morgn, Der, Nayer Morgn, Der, 286,
  290n19, 294, 297, 303, 337
Moscow Jewish Theater, 51
Munch, Edvard, 47

Nadir, Moyshe, 13, 344n8
Nałkowska, Zofia, 380
Nasza Opinia, xxxi
Naturalism, 7, 33n11, 57, 324
Nayer Morgn, see Morgn
Neo-Romanticism, 13–14
Neugroschel, Mendel, 302, 306, 315,
  326, 335
  Small Anthology of Galician Writing,
    302
Neundörfer, Ludwig, 78n11, 79
New Objectivity, xvii, xix, 4n4, 32n6,
  37–38, *See also* Magical Realism and
  New Sobriety
New Sobriety, 32n6, *see also* New
  Objectivity and Magical Realism
New York, xiv, xviii–xix, xxviii, xxxvii,
  9n9, 7n11, 13n7, 102n3, 212–213,
  283, 289n14, 290, 293–294, 296,
  298, 300n46, 303n48, 310,
  312–314, 316, 318–319, 322n74,
  333, 335n89–90, 337, 344n6, 366n1
Nietzsche, Friedrich, xxi, 17n6
Niger, Shmuel, xxi
Norwid, Kamil Cyprian, 8–9, 80, 305
  Czarne Kwiaty. Biale Kwiaty [Black
    flowers. White flowers], 8n13

Objectivist, xxxii
Osostowicz, Stanisław, 66n2, 68
Oyerbakh, Rochl, xxn11, xxin12, *see also*
  Auerbach, Rachel
Oyfgang, 182n6, 186n10, 195n21,
  200n25, 303
Oyfkum, Der, 195n20, 290, 292
Ozenfant, Amédée, 66, 80

Palestine, xxxvii, 198n23, 286
Parain, Nathalie, 84n5, 85
Paris, xvii–xix, xxxvii, 3n2, 58, 92, 106, 204–210, 230, 234, 292–293, 317, 320, 327, 329, 332n86, 362
Pascin, Jules, 254
Peiper, Tadeusz, 321
Picasso, Pablo, xix, 55, 254, 384
Photomontage, xvii, xxvii, xxxvi, 32, 33n9, 54–63, 66n7
Plato, 17
Poelzig, Hans, 75, 77
Pointillism, 55
Postmodernist, xxxiii
Proletarian, 56–57, 115–117, 342
    Art, 20, 114, 296
    Literature, 31, 343–344, 367
    Writers, xxvii, 118, 367
Proletpen, 344n8, *see also* Frayhayt-Hamer
Promiński, Marian, 381–382
Purism, 65–66, 80

Rapoport, Joshue, 16–17, 319, 351–355, 373–375, 378
Ravitch, Melekh, xxv, xxvii, 13, 302, 304–305, 311, 313–315
    Prehistoric Landscapes, 305
    Naked Poems, 305
Realism, 35, 37, 56, 59, 63, 71, 311, 387
    Constructive, 31, 72
    Naïve, xxvi, 30–31, 34
    Romantic, 31, 114
    Socialist, 31, 114n3, 344n9
Refleksn, 294
Renoir, Pierre Auguste, 258, 368
Ressler, Benjamin, 290, 292–294
Ribot, Theodule, 96–98
Rilke, Rainer Maria, 88
Rivkin, Borukh, 313, 315
Rivoire, Andre, 33

Rococo, 76
Roeder, Emi, xxvi, 48
Roh, Franz, xvii, xxvii, 4, 32n6, 37, 377
Romain, Jules, 33
    Men of Goodwill, 33
Romanticism, 14, 19, 22, 27, 118
    Neo-, 13–14
Rome, 286
Rozanoff, Vasily, 53
Ruttmann, Walter, xvii
    Berlin: Symphony of a Great City, xvii, 188n11

Sager-Nelson, Olof, xviii
Saktsir, Motl, 313, 315, 329
Sanacja, xxxiii, 304n51
Scandinavia, 53n12, 266
Schopenhauer, Arthur, 353
Schulz, Bruno, xxin12, xxii–xxiv, xxxvii, 287, 380, 385–387
    Cinnamon Shops (Sklepy cynamonowe), *Street of Crocodiles*, xxin12, xxiii, 387
Segal, Hirsch, xxvii, 322, 326, 343n1, 359
Seurat, George-Pierre, 55, 55n6
Sielska, Margit, 61
Shats-Anin, M., 345, 345n10
Shmeruk, Chone, xix
Shnaper (Sznaper), Ber, xxxi, 16, 341–342, 348–349
Shoybn, 309–310, 313–315, 319–320, 323, 329
Shuster, Zachariah, 322
Shternberg, Jacob (Sternberg), 309, 313–314, 319–320, 335
    City in Profile, 313, 315, 335
Shvarts, Shlomo, xxxi, 313, 313n65, 314n65, 318, 328, 332
Shvarts, Itsik, 322, 343–347
Shwartz, K., 53
Smyrna, 185

Soutine, Chaim, 293
Soviet
  Culture, 53n12
  Literature, writer, xxxii, 114
Soviet Union, 115, 118, 306
  Russia, 53n12
Spinoza, Baruch de, 17
Spire, André, xxx–xxxi, 296
Starkman, Moshe, xviii, xxvii, 158n10, 288–292, 294–295, 298
Stawinski, Bolesław, 66n2
Stażewski, Henryk, 66
Steinfels, Wilhelm, 79
  Farbe und Dasein, 79
Stern, Anatol, 56
  "Europe," 56
Stern, Jonasz, 66–68
Stiller, Mauritz, xvii, 188n13
  Hotel Imperial (*Hotel Stadt Lemberg*), xvii, 188n13
Stockholm, xvi–xviii, xxi, 108, 207, 285n1, 286–287, 292, 301, 388
Stoicism, 37, 334
Streng, Henryk (Marek Włodarski), ix, xix, xxxvii, 3n2, 63–64, 70–72, 126, 135, 147, 163, 221n1, 222, 227, 229, 232, 237, 239–241, 250, 252, 254–256, 263, 268, 270, 273, 277, 388
Strzemiński, Władysław, 18, 32, 66–67
Sumatra, 264n143, *see also* Java
Surrealism, xix, 35, 37, 55–56, 70n2, 71, 343, 367, 369–370, 372
Süss, Avrom Nissen, 105, 108
Sygnały, xxvi–xxvii, xxxi, xxxiii, 300, 304–305, 307, 311–312, 381n1
Symbolism (Symbolist), 51, 77n8, 118, 344
Szczuka, Mieczysław, 54
Szelburg-Zarembina, Ewa, 84–86
  Travel in the City, 85
Szemplińska-Sobolewska, Elżbieta, 118

Szymaniak, Karolina, ix, xxxv, 221n1, 334n88

Tabachnik, Avrom, xxxi–xxxii, 325
  Van Gogh Bilder, xxxii
Tagore, Rabindranath, 353
Tahiti, 298
Talmud, 12, 93, 291n24
Tarde, Gabriel de, 98
Taylorism (Taylorist), xxvi, 23n4
Tériade, 46
Teller, Y. L., xxxi–xxxii, 294, 298, 325
  Miniatures, xxxii
Themerson, Franciska, 83–84, 86
  Birth of Letters, The, 83
  Our Fathers Work, 83
  Post, The, 83
Themerson, Stefan, 56n12, 83, 86
  Birth of Letters, The, 83
  Our Fathers Work, 83
  Post, The, 83
Toulouse-Lautrec, Henri de, 254
Trecento, 43
Triangl, xxxvii, 293
Tugenhold, Yakov, 45, 49, 53
Tsukunft, Di, 290–291, 293, 344n6
Tsushtayer, xx–xxi, xxx–xxxi, 13n6, 41, 84n3, 287, 289, 291–293, 297–298, 303, 305, 307, 318–319, 341n1, 343, 351, 359
Twardowski, Kasimierz, xvi
Tzara, Tristan, 33, 305, 343

UFA, xvii, 188–189
Unism, 18, 66–68
Urals, 266
Utrillo, Maurice, 47, 137, 236

Vaynshteyn, Berish, 298, 298n43
  Brukhshtiker (Trash), 298n43
Venus de Milo, 61

Vienna, xvi, 12, 16n2, 111n13, 230n21, 285, 315, 322
Vigny, Alfred de, 346
Villiers de l'Isle-Adam, Auguste, 77
Vilnius, 301
Vitebsk, 43, 111
Vlaminck, Maurice de, 47
Vogel, Anselm, xv–xvi, xxii, 198, 198n24
Vogel, Asher Joseph, xxiv, xxxvii, 309, 327
Vogel (Ehrenpreis), Lea, xv–xvi, xxiv, xxxvii, 198n24, 285–286, *see also* Ehrenpreis, Lea

Wajwoda, Antony, 85
Walkowitz, Abraham, 293, 298
Warsaw, xvi, xxiii, 6n9, 13n6,9, 16n2, 91n3, 93, 118n12, 221n1, 299, 313, 327, 380n1
Weinper, Zisha, 13, 335, 344n8
Weisman, J. A., xxxi, xxxivn42, 318, 357
  Yung groz, 318n69, 357n1
Werberger, Annette, xxivn18, 387n9

Wiadomości Literackie, 91
Wiciński, Henryk, 66n2, 68
Wilhelmson, Carl, xviii
Winnicki, Alexander, 66n2, 67–68
Wirta, Mikhl, 12, 13n3
Wit, Juliusz, 52
Witkiewicz, Stanisław Ignacy, xxiii–xxiv, 4n3, 295, 387
Włodarski, Marek, 63, 70n2, 222, 250, 270, *see also* Streng, Henryk

Yakir, Yankl, 329
Yehoash, 344, *see also* Blumgarten, Solomon
Yidish, 180n5, 294–295
Yung Yidish, 328n80, 344n5
Yunge, Di 13n7, 102n3, 303n48–49, 344
YIVO Institute, x, xxvii, 301

Zakopane, 289
Zionist (Zionism), xv–xvi, xxx–xxxi, 198n23, 285n1, 296n37, 320
Zucker, Aaron, 344n6, *see also* Lutski, A.

www.ingramcontent.com/pod-product-compliance
Lightning Source LLC
Chambersburg PA
CBHW051107230426
43667CB00014B/2476